Library and Information Science Research: Perspectives and Strategies for Improvement

INFORMATION MANAGEMENT, POLICY, AND SERVICES
Charles R. McClure and Peter Hernon, Editors

Library Performance Accountability and Responsiveness: Essays in Honor of Ernest R. DeProspo
    Charles C. Curran and F. William Summers
Curriculum Initiative: An Agenda and Strategy for Library Media Programs
    Michael B. Eisenberg and Robert E. Berkowitz
Resource Companion to Curriculum Initiative: An Agenda and Strategy for Library Media Programs
    Michael B. Eisenberg and Robert E. Berkowitz
Information Problem-Solving: The Big Six Skills Approach to Library & Information Skills Instruction
    Michael B. Eisenberg and Robert E. Berkowitz
The Role and Importance of Managing Information for Competitive Positioning in Economic Development
    Keith Harman
A Practical Guide to Managing Information for Competitive Positioning in Economic Development
    Keith Harman
Microcomputer Software for Performing Statistical Analysis: A Handbook for Supporting Library Decision Making
    Peter Hernon and John V. Richardson (Editors)
Public Access to Government Information, Second Edition
    Peter Hernon and Charles R. McClure
Statistics: A Component of the Research Process
    Peter Hernon
Statistics for Library Decision Making: A Handbook
    Peter Hernon et al.
Libraries: Partners in Adult Literacy
    Deborah Johnson, Jane Robbins, and Douglas L. Zweizig
Library and Information Science Research: Perspectives and Strategies for Improvement
    Charles R. McClure and Peter Hernon (Editors)
U.S. Government Information Policies: Views and Perspectives
    Charles R. McClure, Peter Hernon, and Harold C. Relyea
U.S. Scientific and Technical Information Policies: Views and Perspectives
    Charles R. McClure and Peter Hernon

In preparation
Organizational Decision Making and Information Use
    Mairead Browne
Technology and Library Information Services
    Carol Anderson and Robert Hauptman
Reshaping Librarianship: Advances and Decline in a Female Profession
    Roma Harris
Microcomputer Local Area Networks and Communications
    Thomas R. Kochtanek
Investigations of Human Responses to Knowledge Representations
    Mark E. Rorvig
Information Seeking as a Process of Construction
    Carol Kulthau
Assessing the Public Library Planning Process
    Annabel Stephens
Interpretations of Reference and Bibliographic Work
    Howard White, Marcia Bates, and Patrick Wilson

Library and Information Science Research: Perspectives and Strategies for Improvement

Edited by

Charles R. McClure
Syracuse University

Peter Hernon
Simmons College

ABLEX PUBLISHING CORPORATION
NORWOOD, NEW JERSEY

Copyright © 1991 by Ablex Publishing Corporation.

All rights reserved. No part of this publication may be reproduced, stored in a retrieval system, or transmitted, in any form or by any means, electronic, mechanical, photocopying, microfilming, recording, or otherwise, without permission of the publisher.

Printed in the United States of America

Library of Congress Cataloging-in-Publication Data

Library and information science research : perspectives and strategies
  for improvement / edited by Charles R. McClure, Peter Hernon.
    p. cm. — (Information management, policy, and services)
  Includes bibliographical references and index.
  ISBN 0-89391-731-1. — ISBN 0-89391-732-X (pbk.)
  1. Library science—Research—Methodology. 2. Information
science—Research—Methodology. I. McClure, Charles R.
II. Hernon, Peter. III. Series.
Z669.7.L476 1991
020'.72—dc20   90-25018
                                                              CIP

Ablex Publishing Corporation
355 Chestnut St.
Norwood, NJ 07648

P

> In order to keep this title in print and available to the academic community, this edition was produced using digital reprint technology in a relatively short print run. This would not have been attainable using traditional methods. Although the cover has been changed from its original appearance, the text remains the same and all materials and methods used still conform to the highest book-making standards.

Contents

List of Figures	*xi*
List of Tables	*xii*
Foreword	*xiii*
Preface	*xvi*

Part I: Overview of Research in Library and Information Science

1 The Elusive Nature of Research in LIS, *by Peter Hernon* — 3

Definition of Research	*3*
Types of Research	*5*
Types of Research Designs and Methods	*6*
Quality of Existing Base of Research	*6*
A Discipline, Profession, or Both?	*7*
A Paradigm or Unifying Principle	*9*
Selected Themes Underlying the Book	*10*

2 Guides to Conducting Research in Library and Information Science, *by Ronald R. Powell* — 15

Developing the Research Study	*16*
Basic Research Methodologies and Techniques	*18*
Applied Research Methodologies	*21*
Qualitative Research Methodologies	*22*
Analysis of Data	*23*
Conclusion	*25*

3 Impact of "National Research Agendas" on LIS Research, *by Charles Curran* — 31

Two Agenda Efforts	*32*
Other Than the Agendas	*36*
What Some Other Organizations Do about Topics	*37*
Conclusion and Recommendations	*38*

vi Contents

4 The Role of the U.S. Department of Education in Library and Information Science Research, *by Anne J. Mathews* — 45

- Federal Support of Library and Information Science Research — 46
- Developments, Issues, and Recommendations in the Library and Information Science Research Programs — 53
- Appendix A. Funding History of HEA II-B — 56
- Appendix B. U.S. Department of Education, Office of Educational Research and Improvement Library Programs. Chronological History of Library Research and Demonstration Grants under HEA Title II-B (1977–1989) — 57

5 International Aspects of LIS Research, *by Michael K. Buckland and John N. Gathegi* — 63

- Contexts and Comparisons — 64
- Difficulties in International Research — 65
- Comparative Studies — 68
- Conclusion and Recommendations — 69

6 The Role of Research in the Development of a Profession or a Discipline, *by Mary Biggs* — 72

- Neither a Discipline . . . — 72
- . . . Nor a Profession — 73
- The Role of Research in the Development of a Discipline — 74
- The Role of Research in the Development of a Profession — 75
- The Role of Research in the Development of Librarianship — 77
- "Technical Rationality" Versus "Reflection-in-Action" — 78
- New Research Styles for Librarianship — 79

7 Assessing the Quantity, Quality, and Impact of LIS Research, *by Nancy A. Van House* — 85

- Social Science Research — 86
- Research in the Professions — 88
- Research in LIS — 89
- Recommendations — 94
- Conclusion — 97

8 The Cross-Disciplinary Imperative of LIS Research, *by Robert Grover and Roger C. Greer* — 101

- The New Paradigm — 102
- Assessment of Current LIS Research — 106
- The Research That Is Needed — 109
- Conclusion — 112

9 Whither LIS Research: Ideology, Funding, and Educational Standards, *by Ellen Altman* — 114

- Differences in Ideology — 115
- The Agencies Funding Research — 117
- Accreditation and "Sustained Productive Scholarship" — 122
- Recommendations to Improve Research — 125

Contents vii

10 Library/Information Science Education: The Research Ethos,
    by Evelyn H. Daniel *128*

  Normative Expectations of Universities *129*
  Growth and Differentiation of Faculty *130*
  Growth and Differentiation of Students *132*
  Growth and Differentiation of Curriculum *136*
  Growth and Differentiation in Organizational Structures *137*
  Growth and Differentiation of Funding *139*
  Conclusion *142*

11 The Role of LIS Education, by Cheryl Duran *147*

  LIS Education *149*
  Knowledge Base of Students *150*
  Role of LIS Education within the Parent Organization *151*
  Critical Areas Meriting Future Research *151*
  Research—Who Conducts and Who Funds It *154*
  Looking to the Future *155*
  Introducing Research into the Curriculum *156*

Part II: Practical Context of Research
in Library and Information Science

12 The Role of the Library Administrator in Improving LIS
    Research, by Joe A. Hewitt *163*

  Require Reference to the Literature in Library Planning Documents and
    Committee Reports *166*
  Encourage Conscientious Response to Questionnaires and Other Surveys *167*
  Insist on High Quality in Surveys Conducted by Library Staff *168*
  Be Hospitable to Proposals to Conduct Research in the Library *169*
  Treat Major Operational Decisions as Field Experiments *169*
  Develop Automated Data Sources and Incorporate Them into Library Decision-
    Making Processes *170*
  Assert Commitment to Research as Part of the Library's Mission Statement *171*
  Exercise Influence on Library Organizations Conducting Research *172*
  Articulate the Research Needs and Concerns of the Practitioner Community *173*
  Support Ongoing Training in Research Skills *174*
  Provide Intellectual Leadership in the Library *175*
  Conclusion *177*

13 The Role of Practicing LIS Professionals, by Irene B. Hoadley *179*

  Issues Affecting Research *180*
  Constraints and Opportunities *182*
  Where We Should Go from Here *184*
  The Next Step *186*

14 The Role of Professional Associations, by Julie A.C. Virgo *189*

  Some Realities *190*
  Driving Forces *192*

viii **Contents**

Roles for Associations	193
Recommendations	195

15 The Role of Editors and Editorial Boards in Journal Publishing,
by Dorothy L. Steffens and Jane B. Robbins   197

Research Production and the Role of Editors	198
The Role of the Editorial Board	198
Criteria for Selecting Editorial Board Members	199
The Refereeing Process	199
The Role of Editors and Editorial Board Members in Improving the Quality of Research in Library and Information Studies	201
Conclusion	202

16 The Secret Science: The Role of Consulting and LIS Research,
by Douglas L. Zweizig   204

Defining LIS Research	204
Consulting	206
Contrasts between Research and Consulting	207
Summary	211

17 The Role of Private Funding Agencies, *by Peter R. Young*   214

Statement of the Issues	214
Importance of Private Agency Funding for LIS Research	219
Strategies for Private LIS Research Funding	221
Enhancing Research Support	224

18 The Role of Networks and Consortia in Library Research,
by Michael Koenig   227

Research about Networks and Their Role	227
The Role of Networks in Undertaking and Promoting Research	235
Conclusion	237

19 The Role of the Information Industry, *by Candy Schwartz*   240

The Information Industry	240
Current Support for LIS Research	241
Remaining Problems	246
Conclusion	248

Part III: Issues and Concerns Related to Research in Library and Information Science

20 Communicating Applied Library/Information Science Research to Decision Makers: Some Methodological Considerations,
by Charles R. McClure   253

Conflicting Perspectives	254
Competing Frames of Reference	257
Strategies and Techniques	260
Making Adjustments	264

21	**Opportunities and Challenges for LIS Research in Academic Libraries: Elements of Strategy,** *by Charles T. Townley*	**267**
	Rationale for LIS Research in Academic Libraries	267
	LIS Research Opportunities in Academic Libraries	268
	Research Challenges in Academic Librarianship	269
	Components for Strengthening Academic Library Research	271
	Building Your Strategy	274
	Appendix. ACRL Research Agenda	277
22	**Research Needs in Public Librarianship,** *by Joan C. Durrance*	**279**
	Context for Needed Research in Public Librarianship	279
	Barriers to the Creation of a Public Library Research Culture	280
	Public Library Leaders and Research	282
	Information Needs Research—A Key to Understanding Societal Needs	283
	Advances in Planning and Evaluation of Public Library Services: Toward More Effective Library Services	285
	Promising Research in Reference Effectiveness	288
	Development of a Research Infrastructure Which Will Foster Public Library Research Production and Consumption	289
23	**Research Needs and Issues in School Librarianship,** *by Shirley Fitzgibbons and Daniel Callison*	**296**
	Background	297
	Current Study	298
	What the Reviews of Research Tell Us	299
	Dissertation Studies Related to School Librarianship (1927–1988)	305
	Conclusion and Recommendations	312
24	**Research Needs and Issues in Special Librarianship,** *by James M. Matarazzo*	**316**
	Special Libraries Association	316
	Faculty Involvement with SLA	318
	Task Force on the Value of the Information Professional	320
	Valuing Corporate Libraries	321
	Issues	322
25	**Research Needs and Issues in State Librarianship,** *by Robert E. Dugan and Jane Ouderkirk*	**326**
	Importance of Research	327
	Issues and Constraints	329
	Opportunities and Strategies	332
	A Commitment to Research	334
26	**Paradigmatic Shift in Library and Information Science,** *by Martha L. Hale*	**336**
	Key Questions for a Discipline	337
	Change and Shift from the Old Paradigm	338
	Library Science	339
	Conclusion	343

x Contents

27 Becoming Critical: For a Theory of Purpose and Necessity in
American Librarianship, *by Michael H. Harris and
Masaru Itoga*   347

28 Research, Theory, and the Practice of LIS, *by Beverly P. Lynch*   360

    Research Agendas   *360*
    Research Questions   *362*
    Research Methodology   *362*
    Theory   *363*
    Concerns   *364*
    Final Comment   *365*

    Contributors   367

    Author Index   375

    Subject Index   *382*

List of Figures

1-1	Attributes of a Discipline and a Profession	*8*
1-2	Northwestern University's Criteria for Investing in an Academic Department	*11*
8-1	Dominant/Emergent Paradigms and Associated Beliefs	*104*
11-1	Objectives and Topical Areas Covered in a Course on the Role of Research in LIS	*157*
18-1	Comparison of Developmental Stage Hypotheses for Information Management	*230*
18-2	Ratios for Information Technology Capabilities	*233*
19-1	The Information Industries	*242*
19-2	Information Industry Support for LIS Research	*243*
19-3	Research Centers Involved in LIS-Related Research	*245*
20-1	Researchers' and Decision Makers' Frames of Reference (FOR)	*259*
20-2	Propositions for Improving the Communication of Research to Decision Makers	*263*
24-1	SLA Research Agenda	*319*

List of Tables

9-1	Research Grants Awarded by the National Library of Medicine	*119*
9-2	Research Grants Awarded by the National Science Foundation, Division of Information Science and Technology	*121*
9-3	Publication Records of LIS Faculty in the 10 Years Prior to COA Appointment	*124*
9-4	Rankings of Journal Prestige by LIS Deans Compared with Publication Records of Faculty on COA	*124*
10-1	Allocation of Faculty Time	*132*
10-2	LIS Research Funding	*140*
17-1	1985 R&D Expenditures by Sector and Character of Work	*220*
17-2	The Role of Private Funding Agencies	*221*
23-1	Reviews of Research in School Librarianship	*300*
23-2	Type of Research Publication Included in Research Reviews	*301*
23-3	Various Research Methods Used in Dissertations Related to Library Science in General or School Libraries in Specific	*306*
23-4	Comparison of Research Methods in Ed.D. to Ph.D. Dissertations with Emphasis on School Libraries, 1980–1988	*307*
23-5	Percentage by Types of Doctoral Degrees Granted for Dissertations Related to School Libraries, 1927–1988	*307*
23-6	Percentage of School Library-Related Doctorates Granted by Institutions Associated with ALA Accredited Master's Degree Programs	*309*
23-7	Institutions Most Frequently Granting Doctorates Related to School Librarianship, 1927–1988	*309*
23-8	Level of Library Programs Emphasized in Dissertations Concerning School Libraries, 1927–1988	*310*

Foreword

Librarians have long enjoyed a love-hate relationship with research. On the one hand, we have a great respect for the life of the mind which leads to and informs research, and many of us manage agencies filled with the results of that activity. On the other hand, we must be pragmatic in our use of scarce resources to satisfy multiple demands, and many of us come to our jobs having had little or no experience with the methodologies appropriate to conducting research on the complex dimensions of the information life-cycle which is the essential subject matter of our field. Thus, we recognize and respect the need for research, but few of us do it and, of those who do, the quality of the result is mixed. Over the years, many have criticized our field for these failings, but few have suggested remedies. The essays in this book fill that gap. All of the authors offer perspectives on the question of how to improve the quantity of research in our field and many suggest specific strategies for doing so. Two problematic aspects of that effort are constant themes in these essays: The possibility and proper role of research in a field dominated by practitioners and the appropriate philosophy or paradigm that should inform research in library and information science (LIS). The essays in this book do not solve those problems. But they do present thoughtful and intelligent arguments that clarify the issues.

This book is closely connected with the Library Research Round Table (LRRT) of the American Library Association. When Nancy Van House became chair-elect of LRRT in June 1989, she decided that her theme for the year would be a consideration of how to improve the quantity and quality of library research. She asked Charles R. McClure to plan a program on that topic for the 1990 Annual Conference and McClure, together with Peter Hernon, decided to do something bigger—to invite a group of nationally known leaders and researchers to produce papers that would offer perspectives and strategies for improving various aspects of the research enterprise in our field. Five of those papers would be selected for presentation at a LRRT program during the 1990 Annual Conference. All of the papers would appear in a published book, and *all* royalties from the sale of the book would be added to the endowment that supports LRRT's Jesse H. Shera Award for Research.

The first result of those plans was a very successful LRRT program in Chicago at the 1990 ALA Annual Conference. Five of the papers were presented to a large audience and stimulated considerable discussion. This volume completes those plans and presents a multitude of ideas for consideration by everyone concerned about research in library and information science.

Part One of this book includes 11 essays providing an "Overview of Research in Library and Information Science." Papers by Peter Hernon, Mary Biggs, and Robert Grover and Roger C. Greer address the nature of the enterprise. Ellen Altman addresses another dimension of that topic, comments on Federal funding for LIS research, and proposes changes in the makeup of ALA's Committee on Accreditation that would help to improve faculty research. Ronald R. Powell presents a very practical guide to the literature on how to conduct research in our field. Charles Curran comments on the impact of several agendas for LIS research that have been proposed recently by different groups, Michael Buckland and John Gathegi discuss international aspects of LIS research, and Nancy Van House assesses its quantity, quality, and impact. Evelyn Daniel and Cheryl Duran present ideas about library education in general and library educators in particular. Anne J. Mathews presents the role of the U.S. Department of Education's Office of Library Programs with a focus on funding provided since 1967 by the Title II.B of the Higher Education Act.

In Part Two, eight experts comment on the role of different agents in improving LIS research. Joe Hewitt suggests 11 practices that library administrators can institute in order to integrate research products and process into the ongoing operation of libraries. Irene Hoadley also makes recommendations regarding the role of practitioners. Julie Virgo analyzes the limited but critical role of professional associations. Dorothy L. Steffins and Jane Robbins describe the role of journal editors and editorial boards. Douglas Zweizig contributes an insightful analysis of the difference between consulting and research with recommendations about how the process and results of consulting could make a greater contribution to research. Michael Koenig describes the role of networks as both subjects for and tools of research. Candy Schwartz describes the role of the information industry in LIS research—a role that is primarily indirect. Peter Young explains why funding from private sources is needed and suggests how to frame LIS questions in ways that might attract such funding.

Part Three begins with an essay by Charles McClure suggesting how library researchers can design and execute applied research projects to ensure that the results will be used by library decision makers. The next five essays focus on research conducted in and about different components of the LIS community. Shirley Fitzgibbons and Daniel Callison assess past research on school librarianship by analyzing several reviews of the research literature and conducting their own analysis of a search of *Dissertation Abstracts International*. They then make recommendations for the future. Charles Townley takes a very different approach for academic librarianship. His comments are addressed to the practitioner and describe both the opportunities offered by research and challenges to getting it done. He then makes general recommendations for improving research in academic librarianship and recommendations for the individual who wants to get involved. Joan Durrance discusses barriers to the creation of a "research culture" in public librarianship and describes several areas where research could play a major role in helping public libraries be more responsive to societal needs. In his chapter on special librarianship, James Matarazzo focuses on the role of the Special Libraries Association (SLA) in fostering research and on the problem of low involvement in SLA or special librarianship by library school faculty. Robert Dugan and Jane Oederkirk identify potential research roles for state library agencies, explain why research has not been a priority for those agencies, and suggest strategies for change.

The last three essays deal with very broad issues. Marty Hale considers the meaning of the phrase "paradigm shift," describes the recent shift in the paradigm of LIS, and indicates what it means for research in our field. Michael Harris and Masaru Itoga argue that LIS research should be based not on its own paradigm, but on paradigms drawn from the social sciences. They suggest that this strategy "will support librarians in their pursuit of a critical understanding of the structural and functional characteristics of libraries, while at the same time allowing librarians to contribute to the corpus of knowledge about cultural institutions in general." Finally, Beverly Lynch concludes the volume with an essay noting that "the ongoing development of theory and the design of research cannot be divorced from the profession as it is practiced."

Jesse H. Shera would be proud of this book. He believed strongly in the importance of research to the continued vitality of librarianship and would be pleased that 34 experts were willing and able to produce challenging papers filled with strategies for improving research in our field. It is very appropriate that royalties from the sale of this volume will be added to the endowment fund established several years ago when LRRT renamed its 12-year-old research award in honor of Jesse H. Shera. The award is given annually to an excellent paper presenting the results of library research. By giving that award each year, LRRT has recognized and encouraged excellent research. In sponsoring this book, LRRT makes a different and perhaps larger contribution toward its objectives. The many actionable ideas presented here are a challenge to LRRT itself and to the many other groups and individuals in the library and information science community who share Shera's belief in the importance of research.

Mary Jo Lynch
Director
Office for Research
American Library Association
50 E. Huron St.
Chicago, IL 60611

Preface

The role and importance of research in librarianship, and later in library and information science, have been controversial. Some maintain that research is important to professional practice and the theoretical base of the profession/discipline, while others disagree. As library and information science matures as a profession and a discipline, there is increased interest in how that role can be strengthened, how the profession/discipline can enhance its research base, and how practicing librarians and other information professionals, might become more aware of the role and importance of research.

The research basis of any profession and discipline merits regular and careful scrutiny and review. That assessment should stimulate thinking about the role of research and the opportunities for the conduct of research. Such an assessment also provides ideas, approaches, and strategies that can assist the advancement of the profession or discipline and improve the overall quality, quantity, and impact of that research.

Any in-depth discussion of research in library and information science should involve individuals from various backgrounds and work-related situations. Such discussions illustrate that research is not the province of any one group and that research plays an important role in the larger context of scientific inquiry.

The 28 chapters in this book provide a forum for individuals from different backgrounds to present their unique perspectives. The chapters offer an overview and perspective on research in library and information science; identify key issues, constraints, and opportunities affecting research; suggest areas of agreement and disagreement among contributors; and offer specific strategies to improve research in library and information science.

As editors, our original intent was for each chapter to comprise a position paper of approximately 15 manuscript pages. However, as is evident, most contributors could not limit their assessment to our page expectations. Nonetheless, the contributors admirably accomplish the four objectives of the monograph:

- Provide a state-of-the-art assessment, discussion, and overview of research in library and information science;
- Offer specific recommendations and strategies for resolving issues related to research in library and information science and for improving the quality, quantity, and impact of that research;

- Increase the profession's (and library school students') awareness of the role and importance of research in library and information science; and
- Identify and analyze key issues and topics from a broad perspective cutting across a number of groups within library and information science.

The book should appeal to anyone interested in library and information science research and the conditions as well as strategies for improving that research. In particular, the monograph should appeal to members of professional library and information-related associations, individuals associated with private and public funding organizations, library school educators and students, and others interested in issues related to library and information science and its cross-disciplinary base.

Charles R. McClure
Peter Hernon
July 1990

part i
Overview of Research in Library and Information Science

chapter one

The Elusive Nature of Research in LIS

Peter Hernon

This chapter offers a general definition of research, one that accommodates different types of research activities and highlights the steps involved in the research process. The chapter also explores the types of research, research designs, and methodologies. After noting examples of works discussing the quality of the existing base of research, the chapter identifies the components of a profession and a discipline. Library and information science can be both, assuming that there is a sufficient body of theory and that the discipline is research oriented. The chapter concludes by noting some of the themes discussed in the monograph.

Research is something that we all know when we see it. Unfortunately, the attempts to define it are often misleading and incomplete. The purpose of this introductory chapter is to offer a general definition and to identify types of research. Furthermore, the chapter discusses the importance of research to library and information science (LIS) as both a profession and a discipline. The chapter also introduces selected themes discussed elsewhere in the monograph.

DEFINITION OF RESEARCH

There is no single, widely accepted definition of research, "in part because there is more than one kind of research" (Powell, 1985, p. 1). Following Goldhor's definition (Goldhor, 1972, p. 7), "research is any conscious premeditated inquiry—any investigation which seeks to increase one's knowledge of a given situation." "Given that definition, it is clear that people doing many different things are justified in calling their activity research" (Lynch, 1984a, p. 367).

For the purposes of this monograph, it might be useful to offer a more focused definition, one that covers the types of research in LIS. Research is an inquiry process that has clearly defined parameters and has as its aim, the:

- Discovery or creation of knowledge, or theory building;
- Testing, confirmation, revision, refutation of knowledge and theory; and/or
- Investigation of a problem for local decision making.

The inquiry process encompasses five activities:

- Reflective inquiry (identification of a problem, conducting a literature search to place the problem in proper perspective, and formulation of a logical or theoretical framework, objectives, and hypotheses/research questions);
- Adoption of appropriate procedures (research design and methodologies);
- The collection of data;
- Data analysis; and
- Presentation of findings and recommendations for future study.

Attempts to ensure reliability and validity should guide the second and third steps. Reliability is the extent to which the same results are produced on repeated samples of the same population. Reliability is concerned with replication and the consistency, stability, or accuracy from measurement to measurement.

Basically, there are two fundamental types of validity—internal and external. Internal validity concerns itself with the extent to which researchers measure what they intend to measure. Internal validity "is essentially a problem of control"—eliminating those variables which suggest alternative explanations or which prevent the identification of causal relationships (Ary, Jacobs, and Razavieh, 1985, p. 261). External validity, which is concerned with the generalizability or representativeness of study findings, addresses the question: "To what extent are the findings generalizable to the population, within known limits of sampling error?"

Krathwohl (1985, pp. 42, 49) views *good* research as those instances in which sound reasoning bonds each of the five components together. There are no significant conceptual or practical weaknesses in the bonding process. Few published studies, however, include all five components and supply indicators of reliability and validity. Moreover, in the case of historical research, some of the parts of a component might be inappropriate. For example, historical research may not engage in hypothesis testing.

Research cannot be viewed solely as an investigation testing hypotheses. Definitions of *scientific* research focusing on hypothesis testing (e.g., Martell, 1988) typically ignore other types of research, the context in which hypotheses are set, and the role of research design. A definition, such as the one proposed in this chapter, must be broad enough to encompass the different types of social science research. Apparently many definitions concentrate on one type of research (see Swisher and McClure, 1984; and Hernon, Bryant, De, Farah, Golub, Hwang, and Kuo, 1989).

TYPES OF RESEARCH

In the social sciences (of which library and information science is a part), there are different types of research. *Basic* research concerns the pursuit of knowledge for its own sake and may or may not immediately contribute to a theoretical base of knowledge. Basic research may engage in theory building, or the placement of abstract ideas, concepts, principles, and propositions that exist outside of a set of circumstances or empirical referents in some order, structure, or relationship. The purpose is to either construct new theories or produce new generalizations by adapting existing theories. Theories are abstract and, at times, open to interpretation. Nonetheless, they explain existing generalizations and predict new ones (see Van De Ven, 1989). Of course, not all concepts and propositions are measurable and testable.

Unless theory and the body of existing practice provide a framework for collecting and interpreting data, researchers might base their conclusions on the idiosyncratic characteristics of the dataset. Researchers often want to understand some phenomenon and to generalize beyond a dataset derived from either probability or nonprobability sampling.

Applied research validates theory and may result in the revision of theory. According to Kaplan (1964, p. 322), "a theory is validated, not by showing it to be invulnerable to criticism, but by putting it to good use, in one's own problems or in those of coworkers." Moreover, "that a theory is validated does not mean that it is probable . . . but only that it is more probable than the other possible explanations" (Ibid., p. 315). The testing of theory often involves hypothesis testing.

Action research is usually applied research directed to an immediate problem. Librarians often conduct action research to generate data useful for local decision making. The potential weakness of action research therefore is that it tends to focus on local problems to the exclusion of a broader context—theory building. Nonetheless, such research might demonstrate in *business terms* the value of services provided (Matarazzo and Prusak, 1990, pp. 8 and 10).

The above-mentioned definition addresses the three types of research. Basic research is the discovery of knowledge and theory building, while applied research includes the testing, confirmation, revision, and refutation of knowledge and theory. And, action research is the investigation of a problem as an aid for local decision making.

The distinctions among the types of research are not always clear. Basic and applied research, at some point, may be practical and useful. As both Powell (1985, p. 2) and Mouly (1978, p. 43) indicate, basic and applied research have a practical aspect; such research leads "to the solution of man's problems." The crucial factor therefore is whether research is "relevant" (Powell, 1985, p. 3). Of course, relevancy is open to differing interpretations. Complicating matters, research might be linked to demonstration, modeling, and development. Perhaps a close identification of research with demonstration and development undermines the expansion of basic research efforts in LIS.

TYPES OF RESEARCH DESIGNS AND METHODS

Each type of research lends itself to various types of research designs and methods of data collection. The types of designs include, for instance, experimental, quasi-experimental, and descriptive. The choice of an appropriate design depends on the reflective inquiry, constraints of time, finances, human and material resources, and perhaps political concerns. An experimental design aids in ruling out rival explanations and extraneous variables, and is the most likely to protect against threats to internal validity.

Many descriptive designs involve *case studies*, which represent an intensive, in-depth investigation of an individual, practice, or procedure to discover those variables important to the history or development of that individual, practice, or procedure. Researchers can take the results gathered from case studies and see if their interpretation is applicable to other situations.

Hernon and McClure (1990, Chapter 5) discuss different designs and methods of data collection that can be used with each type of research. Historically, much research in library and information science has been descriptive and has used a survey method, predominantly a mailed questionnaire. Such an observation underscores the broad base of existing action research.

QUALITY OF EXISTING BASE OF RESEARCH

An article in *The Chronicle of Higher Education* (Moffatt, 1989, p. B2) claimed that "a great deal of published academic writing in any field is mediocre and pedestrian." Presumably this indictment applies to published research as well. Quoting from Ennis (1967), Schlachter (1989, p. 293) declares that LIS research is still "fragmented, noncumulative, generally weak, and relentlessly oriented to immediate practice." McClure and Bishop (1989, p. 136) note that LIS research might be repetitive. Furthermore, it might deal with trivial problems, "fail to integrate or build on findings from other studies or basic knowledge from other disciplines," and lack essential components of the research process. Katzer (1989, p. 83) is even stronger in his indictment of the literature: the quality of the LIS research literature is "like nuggets in a sparse vein."

Despite these notes of pessimism, there are signs that the quantity and quality of the published research is improving. As Johnson (1988, p. 670), a former editor of *College & Research Libraries*, noted, "the quality of manuscripts is improving, and librarians are using more sophisticated methodologies in their research."

An issue of *Library Trends* (Lynch, 1984b) discusses "research in librarianship" and how theories and techniques have assisted researchers in formulating and addressing key questions. The 12 essays also identify "major contributions to research in librarianship during the past twenty years which have used theories or techniques" from the profession (Ibid., p. 363). This issue serves as a reminder that LIS has a body of basic and applied research, useful in advancing LIS as both a profession and a discipline.

The nationally known researchers interviewed by McClure and Bishop (1989, p. 138) expressed "guarded optimism" regarding the future status of LIS research for the next five years. They predicted that "an increasing amount of applied research would eventually have a greater impact on the profession" and discipline. Such optimism suggests that LIS has not matured as either a profession or a discipline. There are excellent opportunities to advance the image and theoretical base of LIS, thereby moving LIS to a higher conceptual level and linking it with fields such as records management and information resources management.

A DISCIPLINE, PROFESSION, OR BOTH?

The literature discussing the attributes of a profession and a discipline is substantial. There is also vast literature on librarianship as a profession,[1] but far fewer writings on it as a discipline. Simply stated, "the purpose of the discipline is the pursuit of knowledge," while a profession uses "theory and knowledge to serve—to respond to vital needs of individuals" (Spring, 1988, pp. 8–9). Figure 1-1 summarizes general attributes of both a discipline and a profession, but does not "score" or rate LIS as either.

Discussions of a *learned* profession typically revolve around medicine or law. Apparently, there is some disagreement as to whether librarianship, nursing, and social work, for instance, are professions or "semi-professions (Heim, 1979).[2] Presumably each of these occupations meets fewer attributes than does medicine. Because "the professions are more like a family than a conceptual group" (Spring, 1988, p. 2), they should be expected to meet the attributes depicted in the figure to varying degrees.

Robbins (1990), who evaluates librarianship as a profession, notes that "the critical components in professional competencies are those related to theoretical foundations, societal context, ethics, adaptability, professional improvement,

---

[1] See, for example, Asheim (1978).

[2] Etzioni (1969, pp. v–viii) refers to "semi-professions" as occupations requiring shorter periods of training and having less legitimate status, a less established right to privileged communication, "less of a specialized body of knowledge," and "less autonomy from supervision or societal control."

Figure 1-1. Attributes of a Discipline and a Profession.*

DISCIPLINE

1. A recognized area of study;
2. Departmental status, autonomy, and formal recognition in academe;
3. A substantial body of knowledge and theory;
4. A "common state of mind," including a sense of agreement on areas of inquiry and methods for studying problems, and a common belief that extending the discipline's insights is a worthy endeavor;
5. A belief that the continued development of the discipline depends on the generation of basic and applied research;
6. A number of people, well known within and outside the discipline, revered as contributors to knowledge, research, and practice;
7. Support from a national learned society;
8. Its age; and
9. A number of people interested in its study.

PROFESSION

1. A body of knowledge and theory essential for professionals to master;
2. A knowledge base resulting from prolonged study or training, or socialization in the profession;
3. Application of knowledge and services to human problems;
4. Service orientation "based on some theoretical structure or department of learning" and "practical experience" (Spring, 1988, p. 5);
5. A demand for the service and a willingness to help others;
6. Practitioners are recognized as professionals and as meeting a need; "practitioners are clearly distinguished from non-practitioners" (Ibid.);
7. New professionals receive training and education;
8. Professional organizations exist;
9. The organizations identify professional functions and set norms of professional conduct;
10. Practitioners render impartial services to the public;
11. Society holds the profession in esteem;
12. Sense of community, commitment, and autonomy—belief that one's work is a life-long calling and does not require supervision from someone outside the work group or profession;
13. A relationship with academe;
14. Professional-client relationship;
15. Expected level of educational attainment;
16. Expected norms for entrance into the profession;
17. A system of rewards;
18. Certification of competence and high level of professional standards;
19. Criteria for evaluating achievement and excellence;
20. "Practice of the profession is a full-time commitment" and "involves a life-time commitment" (Ibid.); and
21. "Practitioners have a monopoly on the right to deliver their particular service," and "practitioners hold that only practitioners are competent to judge the services delivered" (Ibid.).

*Adapted from Peter Hernon, "Government Information: A Field in Need of Research and Analytical Studies," in *United States Government Information Policies*, edited by Charles R. McClure, Peter Hernon, and Harold C. Relyea (Norwood, NJ: Ablex, 1989), pp. 10–13.

and professional growth within the profession as a whole" (p. 210). Spring (1988, p. 5) maintains that the central facets of a profession are:

> specialized intellectual training, . . . practitioners . . . highly committed to service, . . . practice . . . directed toward individuals, . . . practitioner[s] normally function(sic) apart from an organized structure, and . . . high status associated with the practice.

Although he does not mention it, research can be a critical aspect of any facet.

Where work is primarily intellectual and draws more on thinking processes than manual processes and routines, research can play an important role. Librarianship, as a profession, is more than the completion of daily tasks and routines. It involves planning, management, decision making, and other intellectual activities aimed at the resolution of specific information needs and, ideally, providing the best service possible.

A field of inquiry might be both a discipline and a profession. Political science and history are two examples. A central theme of this chapter and the book is that we should not be satisfied with the status of library and information science as a profession. Recognition as a discipline should provide LIS with increased recognition and nurturing by other disciplines and professions. More importantly, a discipline only grows and thrives if its body of basic and applied research increases. Such research may sustain a discipline, provide a basis for the development of new fields of inquiry, and suggest approaches for studying problems.

On the negative side, disciplinary-based research requires a critical mass of researchers able to conduct experimental, quasi-experimental, descriptive, and other kinds of research. Library and information science lacks such a critical mass. Complicating matters, there will be a separation, perhaps a severe one, between practitioners of the profession and the conduct of research having value for local decision making. At this time, the majority of research studies can be characterized as action, lacking a theoretical base. Katzer (1989, p. 28) inserts a useful caution: "too great a separation, without adequate spanning mechanisms, is not healthy for either research or the practitioner."

A PARADIGM OR UNIFYING PRINCIPLE

Bierbaum (1990, p. 18) argues that LIS "needs a unifying principle," or paradigm, to guide "research and applications of professional practice." Having such a paradigm would help "us ask the right questions," summarize "truths," and unite research and practice. Her candidate principle is the Principle of Least Effort, as formulated by Zipf (1949).[3]

---

[3] The *principle of least effort* "governs the use made of libraries and other sources of information and is, in fact, a major determinant of their use." Furthermore, this principle should be "taken into

Bierbaum assumes that this one principle can adequately capture the essence of library and information science, as a discipline and a profession. Other assumptions are that it is important for research to be practice-based and to be conducted as part of "a unifying principle." Others might prefer another principle as the unifying concept for practice and theory, or practice and research. Nonetheless, the critical question should be "Is library and information science a discipline, a profession, or both?" Bierbaum seems to answer the question favoring a profession and action research—having utility for local decision making.

SELECTED THEMES UNDERLYING THE BOOK

Further development of the research potential of library and information science as a discipline requires a "multi-faceted effort combining the many suggestions already proposed . . . in the literature" (Katzer, 1989, p. 84). The temptation is to conclude there are simple solutions to a complex problem.

Rethinking the Library in the Information Age (1989) offers some additional insights useful for readers of the other chapters. First, ". . . we [need to] create research opportunities for those in the profession and reward individuals who contribute to our base of research" (Ibid., p. 49). Second, the study of library and information science must attract researchers outside of the discipline. The purpose is to bring different insights and approaches to the investigation of problems. Third (Ibid., p. 51),

> The professionals . . . need to be targeted by a program geared toward raising the level of their understanding of and proficiency in the research enterprise in general; experimental design, including hypotheses generation, descriptive and inferential statistics, and ways and means for presenting findings and conclusions; and the pursuit of specific projects which will improve the quality of research in librarianship and information science.

Fourth (Ibid., p. 56),

> researchers in librarianship have not asked the questions that would excite their colleagues; and they have not approached the questions that they do ask with a rigor that wins the respect of more discipline-oriented colleagues.

Fifth (Ibid., p. 51),

> Few programs of library and information science have the breadth and depth to respond to large-scale research projects: they are too small, isolated from other

---

account in the planning of library buildings, in the allocation of storage space, and, perhaps most importantly, in the planning of new and innovative services" (Lancaster, 1977, p. 319).

units of their universities, and subject to heavy demands to educate Masters level students. Even the larger schools have too few specializations, and their faculty have substantial administrative responsibilities and commitments to doctoral or certificate level education.

To this list, one might add that when the research focuses on minute problems and issues, and does not address larger issues and problems, some knowledge may nonetheless result. The theoretical underpinnings of a profession or discipline, however, are sacrificed. Although a large part of the research is action oriented, one might wonder what role such research actually plays in local decision making. Can a majority of practicing libraries appreciate, understand, and apply research findings?

By approaching LIS as both a discipline and a profession, there is an opportunity to set even higher aspirations and expectations for theory, research, and practice. Clearly, LIS education must be a part of graduate programs in academe, and these programs should have high visibility within and outside the institution.

Northwestern University developed four criteria to identify which academic departments will receive increased financial support (see Figure 1-2). These

Figure 1-2. Northwestern University's Criteria for Investing in an Academic Department.*

I. Centrality to the Purpose of a Distinguished University
- The department is important to the intellectual climate of the University;
- Strengthening the department contributes directly to the academic reputation of the University;
- The cutting edge of the field should be identifiable, thereby allowing targeting of the investment and clarifying the risks associated with that investment; and
- The field must have an important teaching role at the undergraduate and/or graduate level.

II. Visibility
- The field must have broad visibility within academe;
- A substantial external constituency benefits from using the emerging research and scholarship; and
- Other distinguished universities maintain a similar field; there is a collective realization of the "worth" of the field.

III. Potential
- The potential for intellectual development and vitality is substantial. The area has growth potential;
- The potential for external funding is significant but is not an essential condition for selection; and
- Research benefits other disciplines and fields within the University.

IV. Present Status
- The University is presently active in the field; an increased investment will enable the University to be recognized as one of the leading institutions in that field.

---

*Source: *Strategies for Excellence: A Report of the Faculty Planning Committee* (Evanston, IL: Northwestern University, 1980, pp. 58–59).

criteria (centrality, visibility, potential, and present status) serve as a beginning model to advance the development of the disciplinary base of library and information science. Strategies to address each criterion are needed. Cross-disciplinary research efforts will have to be better supported, more funding made available, and scholars encouraged to investigate a wider variety of conceptual and practical issues. The foundation for a challenge is there.

The future requires a commitment on the part of researchers and practitioners to accept LIS as a discipline and a profession, to better define the discipline of LIS, and to demonstrate that disciplinary base. If some progress can be made in these areas, there will be a better understanding of problems within LIS amenable to research and the value of having such research conducted, whether that research is basic, applied, or action. There must be better use and integration of theoretical and other types of research into the practice of LIS. Researchers must be better able to articulate research findings and their importance to library decision makers ("Crunching Numbers Creatively," 1989). Finally, the research infrastructure in LIS must be strengthened and the critical mass of nationally recognized researchers to guide future generations must be increased.[4]

Research in LIS, or any profession for that matter, should encourage practitioners to ask why and not merely to do something. Greater attention to high quality basic and applied research focusing on theory building and modeling provides a key link in the transition of LIS from a profession to a discipline. Subsequent chapters expand on this and other issues and indicate the importance of research to the present and future development of LIS.

Research makes LIS into a *mature* profession and discipline, one that has broad societal recognition and meets the criteria specified in Figure 1-2, for "excellence" in academe. Discussions defining research therefore are not mere academic exercises. They focus national and international attention on research and the differences between it and other types of activities and publications. The standards and expectations for research in LIS should not remain static or decline; rather, they should continue to evolve and challenge us to improve.

The problems and obstacles to viewing LIS in the context of a discipline and profession are significant but not insurmountable. An edited volume such as this serves an important purpose. It draws attention to the role and importance of research, and presents the views of 34 people from diverse backgrounds about key issues. Moreover, it offers strategies for improving the quality of the research and developing the disciplinary base of LIS.

---

[4] A careful examination of *Rethinking the Library in the Information Age* (1989) underscores the problems discussed in this section. The recommendation, ironically, does not correspond to the problems identified. In fact, the strategies discussed cannot be implemented given the underlying problems identified. Because of this deficiency, it is important that this book offers practical and realistic solutions to the complex problems discussed in the various chapters.

REFERENCES

Ary, Donald, Lucy C. Jacobs, and Asghar Razavieh. *Introduction to Research in Education.* 3rd ed. New York: Holt, Rinehart and Winston, 1985.
Asheim, Lester. "Librarians as Professionals," *Library Trends*, 26 (Winter 1978): 225–257.
Bierbaum, Esther G. "A Paradigm for the '90s," *American Libraries*, 21 (January 1990): 18–19.
"Crunching Numbers Creatively" (a collection of eight articles), *Library Administration & Management*, 3 (Fall 1989): 170–212.
Ennis, Philip H. "Commitment to Research," *Wilson Library Bulletin*, 41 (May 1967): 899–901.
Etzioni, Amitai. *The Semi-Professions and Their Organization.* New York: The Free Press, 1969.
Goldhor, Herbert. *An Introduction to Scientific Research in Librarianship.* Urbana, IL: University of Illinois, Graduate Library School, 1972.
Heim, Kathleen. "Professional Education: Some Comparisons," in *As Much to Learn as to Teach: Essays in Honor of Lester Asheim*, edited by Joel M. Lee and Beth A. Hamilton. Hamden, CT: Linnet Books, 1979, pp. 128–176.
Hernon, Peter. "Government Information: A Field in Need of Research and Analytical Studies," in *United States Government Information Policies*, edited by Charles R. McClure, Peter Hernon, and Harold C. Relyea. Norwood, NJ: Ablex, 1989, pp. 10–13.
——— and Charles R. McClure. *Evaluation and Library Decision Making.* Norwood, NJ: Ablex, 1990.
———, Pat K. Bryant, Maya De, Barbara D. Farah, Andrew J. Golub, Hae-young Rieh Hwang, and Li-ling Kuo. *Statistics for Library Decision Making.* Norwood, NJ: Ablex, 1989.
Johnson, Richard D. "Current Trends in Library Journal Editing," *Library Trends*, 36 (Spring 1988): 659–672.
Kaplan, Abraham. *The Conduct of Inquiry.* San Francisco, CA: Chandler Publishing Co., 1964.
Katzer, Jeffrey. "ALA and the Status of Research in Library/ Information Science," *Library & Information Science Research*, 11 (April-June 1989): 83–87.
Krathwohl, David R. *Social and Behavioral Science Research.* San Francisco, CA: Jossey-Bass, 1985.
Lancaster, F.W. *The Measurement and Evaluation of Library Services.* Washington, D.C.: Information Resources Press, 1977.
Lynch, Mary Jo. "Research and Librarianship," *Library Trends*, 32 (Spring 1984a): 367–383.
———, Ed. "Research in Librarianship," *Library Trends*, 32 (Spring 1984b), entire issue.
Martell, Charles. "Editorial: What Is Research?," *College & Research Libraries*, 49 (May 1988): 183–184.
Matarazzo, James M. and Laurence Prusak. *Valuing Corporate Libraries: A Senior Management Survey.* Washington, D.C.: Special Libraries Association, 1990.

McClure, Charles R. and Ann Bishop. "The Status of Research in Library/Information Science: Guarded Optimism," *College & Research Libraries*, 50 (March 1989): 127–143.

Moffatt, Michael. "If Peer Review Is Acceptable for Evaluating Research, Why Shouldn't It Also Be Used to Evaluate Teaching," *The Chronicle of Higher Education*, 36 (October 4, 1989): B2.

Mouly, George J. *Educational Research*. Boston, MA: Allyn and Bacon, 1978.

Powell, Ronald R. *Basic Research Methods for Librarians*. Norwood, NJ: Ablex, 1985.

Rethinking the Library in the Information Age. Vol. 3. Prepared by the Department of Education, Office of Educational Research and Improvement, Office of Library Programs, Washington, D.C.: GPO, 1989.

Robbins, Jane. "Master's Degree from a Program Accredited by the American Library Association Required," *Journal of Education for Library and Information Science*, 30 (Winter 1990): 206–217.

Schlachter, Gail. "Research: One Step at a Time," *RQ*, 28 (Spring 1989): 293–294.

Spring, Michael B. "The Profession of Information Science," *MBS:DIS:Pittsburgh* (January 1988), pp. 1–18.

Strategies for Excellence: A Report of the Faculty Planning Committee. Evanston, IL: Northwestern University, 1980, pp. 58–59.

Swisher, Robert and Charles R. McClure. *Research for Decision Making: Methods for Librarians*. Chicago, IL: American Library Association, 1984.

Van De Ven, Andrew H. "Nothing Is Quite So Practical as a Good Theory," *Academy of Management Review*, 14 (1989): 486–489.

Zipf, George. *Human Behavior and the Principle of Least Effort*. Cambridge, MA: Addision-Wesley Press, 1949.

chapter two

Guides to Conducting Research in Library and Information Science*

Ronald R. Powell

> An overview of guides to conducting library and information science research is presented. Included are publications about the development of research studies, basic research methods and techniques, applied research methods, qualitative research, and data analysis. The cited works are intended for both the practitioner and the consumer of research and are drawn from the library and information science and the behavioral and social sciences literatures.

This chapter introduces active or would-be library and information science (LIS) researchers to resources that can facilitate their research activities. The chapter cites over 90 works, but in no way is it exhaustive, especially with regard to the nonlibrary and information science literature. The list includes works that the author has found useful in his own research, that have proven to be helpful in teaching research methods courses, and that have been cited by other researchers and authors. The review covers both monographs and journal articles. It emphasizes relatively recent publications, but includes older standards or classics where appropriate.

Other emphases of the review tend to reflect "what is out there" in the literature. For example, there are more guides to research in library science than in information science. More titles deal with quantitative research than with qualitative methods, though several cover both. More attention is given to basic research than to applied research.

The majority of the works cited in this chapter are aimed at the research practitioner. A smaller number of guides emphasize only what the consumer of research reports needs to know. Most of the titles should be helpful for both audiences.

---

*The author is indebted to Lori Siegel for her assistance in collecting the documents reviewed in this chapter.

The preponderance of the literature identified in this review was written primarily for the LIS researcher or practitioner. But several nonlibrary and information science works, particularly standard textbooks, were included when needed to supplement the library and information science literature. The consideration of guides to obtaining funding for research and reporting results was left to other chapters in this book. But here again, categories of resources may overlap and some of the more comprehensive works include sections on funding and writing and publishing research reports.

DEVELOPING THE RESEARCH STUDY

The development of most basic research studies, and many applied research studies, involves such steps as the identification of problems, theories, hypotheses, and assumptions; the consideration of validity and reliability; and the writing of a proposal. Some works on research methods give considerable attention to these issues; others are mostly, if not exclusively, concerned with the methodologies and techniques used in actually conducting the research.

General Guides to Social Science Research

A number of standard texts are useful for the development of research studies in the social and behavioral sciences. And in spite of their lack of examples directly applicable to library and information science, they can be very helpful to persons planning to conduct LIS research.

Babbie (1986) is a well-known social sciences text that is particularly strong on the conceptual development of a research study. His book introduces the reader to the logic, as well as the skills, of social science research. It also encourages readers to be responsible consumers of social science research. The appendices explain how to use the library and write the research report, as well as contain a glossary.

Other standard texts on social science research include Nachmias and Nachmias (1987), Kidder and Judd (1986), Gay (1981), Mouly (1978), and Kerlinger (1986). These works cover the basic steps involved in planning and conducting social science research, but they also exhibit somewhat different perspectives, emphases, and strengths. Kidder and Judd (1986), for example, is particularly strong in its coverage of research in the behavioral sciences. The book's central theme is causal analysis. It provides good coverage of survey methods and also addresses evaluation research, archival data, and ethics.

Gay (1981) is another good, basic introduction to research, particularly educational research. "The purpose of this book is to aid students in the acquisition of the skills and knowledge required of a competent consumer and producer of education research, primarily the former" (p. v). Gay also covers statistical analysis, tests, and research critiques. Mouly (1978), though now out-of-print, remains another standard text on research. Useful sections explain historical research and the research report.

The goal of Nachmias and Nachmias (1987, p. v) is "to offer a comprehensive, systematic treatment of the scientific approach in the social sciences." The contents emphasize the relationship among theory, research, and practice. There are helpful definitions throughout the text and sections on data analysis, including secondary data analysis and qualitative research.

Leedy (1985), Isaac and Michael (1981), and Sproull (1988) place an extra emphasis on the practical aspects of doing research. Isaac and Michael (1981) is a concise handbook used by many doctoral students over the years. Sproull (1988) leads the reader, step by step, through the research process and provides a number of examples, definitions, sample forms, and flow charts.

Leedy (1985) is an oft-cited, practical guide to research, though not as comprehensive as some of the other standard works. It does include useful examples, checklists, etc., plus a sample research proposal with a "running commentary" or critique. Leedy (1981) is also the author of a guide aimed primarily at the research consumer. One chapter, for example, is devoted to the reading of graphs, charts, tables, and other nonverbal presentations.

General Guides to Library and Information Science Research

A smaller number of general texts have been written from a library and information science perspective. Goldhor (1972) was one of the earliest and most influential books on basic research in library science. While this work is now a bit dated and has always suffered from a lack of an index, it is still a useful guide to the conceptual development of a research study.

More recent texts on library and information science research include Busha and Harter (1980), Powell (1985, 1991), Martyn and Lancaster (1981), and Moore (1987). The Busha and Harter (1980) text has been widely used; among its features are descriptions of illustrative studies and extensive bibliographies. About 40 percent of the work is devoted to statistics. Powell (1985) presents the material that he has found to be appropriate for an introductory course on research methods. It covers the major basic methodologies, research proposals and reports, and gives considerable attention to the development of a research study. The revised and updated second edition includes additional information on library history and bibliographical, comparative, and qualitative research. Moore (1987) is less comprehensive than the two previous titles, but two chapters offer useful practical advice on initiating and conducting a research project. These chapters include information about staffing, finances, facilities, progress reviews, etc.

Martyn and Lancaster (1981) is, to a great extent, based on the personal experiences of the authors. One of its major features is the coverage of less familiar techniques, such as the Delphi study, user panels, diaries, critical incident techniques, sociometric analysis, bibliometrics, cost-benefit evaluations, and document-availability studies.

Since 1964, two issues of *Library Trends* have been devoted to basic research methods. They are not so much how-to-do-it guides as they are reports on the state of the art. One issue (Garrison, 1964) covers basic methodologies and has a still useful chapter on some of the most common inadequacies of research proposals. It also includes a classic piece by Jesse Shera entitled "Darwin, Bacon, and Research in Librarianship." The other issue (Lynch, 1984) emphasizes the relationships between other disciplines and research in library science. For example, there are chapters on the application of sociological methods to library research and on the use of psychological concepts in library research.

BASIC RESEARCH METHODOLOGIES AND TECHNIQUES

Major elements in the research process are, of course, the methodologies and data collection techniques employed. What follows are brief descriptions of some selected publications that focus on specific methods and techniques commonly used in basic quantitative research (though they certainly have applications for applied and qualitative research as well). Of course, many of the general works discussed above also cover these methods and techniques.

Survey Research and Sampling

The preceding statement is particularly true with regard to survey research, so only a few additional works will be discussed here. Benson and Benson (1975) provide a fairly old, but still useful overview of survey research. It includes a glossary of survey research terms. Golden (1982) prepared another general overview of survey research for an ACRL workshop. This manual has good information on designing questionnaire items and on precoding and coding, and there is a lengthy bibliography.

Readers wanting more guidance on some specific data collection techniques often, but not exclusively, used in survey research may refer to Wurzburger (1987), Kidston (1985), and Bookstein (1985) for questionnaires; Backstrom and Hursh-Cesar (1981, Chapter 5) for interviews; and Glazier (1985) and Newhouse (1989) for observation.

Individuals wanting to read about the application of sampling techniques to library problems may refer to Drott (1969). He discusses accuracy and sample size, describes a method of selecting a random sample, and presents three examples illustrating the use of sampling techniques. Persons wanting more advice on how to determine optimum sample size (a common question) can turn to Kraemer and Thiemann (1987). It is a somewhat advanced, but useful, guide for determining the sample size for a particular study as affected by the research design being used.

Experimental Research

Cook and Greco (1977) authored a two-part article that presents the fundamentals of experimental design, discusses library-related examples, examines major factors affecting the validity of designs, and emphasizes the strengths and weaknesses of experimental comparisons. Campbell and Stanley (1963) is the longtime standard guide for selecting specific experimental and quasi-experimental research designs. The authors identify and describe about 20 of the most frequently used designs, provide some illustrative studies, and discuss the threats to the validity of the designs.

Historical and Bibliographical Research

In contrast to survey and experimental research methods, which have been given relatively little attention outside of the general texts, historical research, often referred to as "library history," is more often treated separately. However, few of the works on library history actually describe how to conduct historical research. For example, a chapter by Shiflett (1984) in *Library Trends* describes the possible interactions between historical research and other research approaches to library and information science, describes the value of historical research, and makes suggestions for improving historical research in librarianship.

Kaser (1978) provides a state-of-the-art overview of American library history and a lengthy bibliography. Marshall (1966) brought together 14 papers presented at the Second Library History Seminar. At this time his work is most useful for its sample studies. Another resource that is rather dated now is Harris' (1974) annotated bibliography of 650 master's theses and doctoral dissertations on American library history.

A somewhat more practitioner-oriented guide to library history is Stevens (1971). It includes chapters on primary sources, archives, oral history, textual criticism, and descriptive bibliography. A chapter by McCombs and Busha (1981) focuses exclusively on oral history in librarianship, but includes a lengthy bibliography on library history. Eaton (1964) discusses bibliographical research—i.e., descriptive and analytical, not enumerative, bibliography. Some interesting examples illustrate the methods of bibliographical research.

Shafer (1980) represents a readable, nonlibrary and information science introduction to conducting historical research. The work provides definitions of historical concepts, methods, and literature. It also covers problems encountered by historical researchers, proof and probability, historical evidence, internal and external criticism, analysis and synthesis, and communicating findings.

The Delphi Study

A less frequently used methodology, but one that has many applications to library and information science research, is the Delphi study. It is a procedure designed to generate consensus opinions by systematically refining responses from a group of experts. Again, the LIS literature describes the method and its applications more than it explains how to conduct such a study. Reilly (1973) gives a brief background of the Delphi technique and then discusses studies that utilized it. Dyer (1979) provides mostly a description and history of the Delphi method, along with a section on library applications and a bibliography. In a similar fashion, Fischer (1978) describes the method, gives a hypothetical example of its use, and reviews four Delphi studies. Hayes (1982) discusses a single Delphi study in considerable detail and provides samples of five questionnaires used in the study.

Bibliometrics

Library and information science publications on bibliometrics, which is concerned with the quantitative analysis of literature, also include relatively few how-to-do-it works. Wallace (1987), for example, discusses the use of bibliometrics, especially the concepts of scatter and obsolescence, in collection management. Bensman (1982) includes an extensive bibliography on bibliometrics and related techniques. Smith (1981) and White (1985) discuss citation analysis, which is a type of bibliometrics.

Two textbooks that might be useful for the bibliometrics researcher are those by Pao (1989) and Martyn and Lancaster (1981). The former work is intended for an introductory course in document-based information retrieval, not research methods, but the second chapter covers bibliometrics, including citations. Martyn and Lancaster devote considerable attention to the analysis of records, including bibliometrics and citation analysis.

Comparative Librarianship

Some view comparative librarianship, often referred to as international librarianship, as a topic, and others see it as a research method. Collings (1977) offers a good definition of comparative librarianship. Those wanting to conduct comparative research should see Simsova (1982), which is intended for use either as a class textbook or a teach-yourself manual. MacKee (1983) complements Simsova by identifying sources of data available to support research in comparative librarianship.

APPLIED RESEARCH METHODOLOGIES

Many of the works cited elsewhere in this chapter have substantial implications for applied research studies. For example, survey research methods, sampling techniques, and statistical analysis programs are often used in applied research. Therefore, this section discusses a small number of titles that deal almost exclusively with applied research methods. Two general works that fall into this category are Swisher and McClure (1984) and Powell (1989).

Swisher and McClure "provide an introduction for the practicing librarian and graduate student that explains the essential elements of statistics and how they may be directed toward decision making. This process is known as 'action research'" (p. xiii). Their work "stresses the importance of developing a research plan and analyzing data in such a way that practicing librarians can better make decisions and improve the overall effectiveness of their libraries" (pp. xiii–xiv). The book is also designed to assist librarians in becoming informed consumers of relevant research reports. It covers planning and designing action research, gathering data, sampling, data analysis, and statistical decision making.

A recent issue of *Library Trends* (Powell, 1989) is a festschrift for Herbert Goldhor and is devoted to problem solving in libraries. It emphasizes applied research with chapters on evaluative research, performance/output measures, cost analysis, managerial accounting, and other approaches to solving problems in library settings.

Operations Research

"Operations research (OR) is the use of scientific methods to study the functions or operations of an organization so as to develop better ways of planning and controlling changes" (Leimkuhler, 1977, p. 412). Leimkuhler (Ibid.) presents a brief history of the methodology, describes its use, and discusses applications to libraries. His work also covers models or modeling and systems analysis—two techniques closely related to operations research.

Rowley and Rowley (1981) provide a relatively comprehensive text on OR for both students and library managers. Their work (p. v):

> is an introductory account of operations research and its application to research and management in library and information science. Emphasis is on the problem, the way that it is tackled and the interpretation of the solution rather than the mathematical techniques involved in the solution.

It covers models, probability, simulation, queuing, resource allocation, networks, games, transportation, and inventory control. Other publications giving some attention to OR include Adeyemi (1977), Dougherty and Heinritz (1982), and O'Neill (1984). The last work also addresses models.

Evaluation Research

Evaluation research is another methodology often viewed as a type of applied research. Lancaster (1977) is a frequently cited, comprehensive guide to the measurement and evaluation of library services. But as Lancaster states, his work "should be regarded largely as a survey and synthesis of, as well as a guide to, published literature in the field" (p. ix). It does not take the place of a textbook on evaluation research. A second edition (with Sharon Baker) is in progress and, according to the preface, will serve as more of a guide to performing evaluations. Lancaster (1988) is a supplement/complement to the 1977 work. The newer publication serves as more of a practical guide to the actual conduct of library evaluations. It covers document delivery, reference, resource sharing, and cost studies. Numerous "exhibits" and a long bibliography enrich the text.

Hernon and McClure (1990) is intended for practitioners engaged in evaluation research. The *Library Systems Evaluation Guide* (1983–1987) is an eight-volume set that describes methodologies for evaluating serials control, circulation, public service, acquisitions, management services, interlibrary loan, cataloging, and system integration.

Standard, nonlibrary and information science texts on evaluation research include Weiss (1972) and Suchman (1967). They both illustrate how the basic methods and techniques of social science research can be employed in applied research. A more recent work by Rossi and Freeman (1989), now in its fourth edition, "provides an introduction to the broad set of research activities essential for designing, implementing, and appraising the utility of social programs" (p. 9).

A special type of evaluation research receiving a lot of attention today is performance or output measurement. A landmark study in this area was the one conducted by De Prospo and others at Rutgers University in the early 1970s. This project resulted in the publication of *Performance Measures for Public Libraries* (De Prospo, Altman, and Beasley, 1973) and a manual a year later. Van House, Lynch, McClure, Zweizeg, and Rodger (1987) is a newer manual on output measures for public libraries. It describes standardized procedures for assessing common public library services and includes instructions for collecting, analyzing, and interpreting data.

Van House, Weil, and McClure (1990) is a comparable manual for academic libraries. Kantor (1984) and Cronin (1985) have written less comprehensive performance measures manuals for academic libraries. The latter work is restricted to the performance measurement of public services.

QUALITATIVE RESEARCH METHODOLOGIES

Qualitative research methods and techniques, which have traditionally been associated with social anthropologists, are becoming increasingly popular with other social scientists, including LIS researchers. Historically, qualitative research involved the data collection techniques of participant observation and/or intensive interviewing, but it has come to encompass a variety of other methods as well. In fact, to the extent that historical research and case studies can be considered qualitative research, this approach has been evident in library science research for years. It is also worth noting that some of the techniques associated with qualitative research, such as observation and interviews, are regularly used in quantitative research, though usually in a more structured manner.

Qualitative research is also referred to as interpretative research, ethnography, and field research. A standard work using the last terminology is Burgess (1982, p. xi):

> The specific aims of this book are to indicate the diverse approaches involved in doing field research, to examine a range of research techniques that have been used in field research (participant observation, informal/unstructured interviewing and documentary materials), to examine the problems that arise in the course of doing field research and the ways in which these problems have been handled by experienced field researchers.

Chapters cover sampling strategies, recording field data, and analyzing and reporting field research.

Lofland and Lofland (1984) emphasize the data collection and analysis stages of qualitative research. Budd, Thorp, and Lewis (1967) explain content analysis, which they define as "a systematic technique for analyzing message content and message handling" (p. 2). Patton (1990) focuses on qualitative methods as they relate to evaluation.

Library and information science literature pertaining to qualitative research is relatively sparse at this time. Grover and Glazier (1985) present a rationale for the use of qualitative research methods in theory building and compare quantitative and qualitative research methods. They also review a study that utilized structured observation. A collection of papers (Glazier and Powell, 1991) will discuss observation, mechanical recording, interviews, case studies, sense making, and computer-aided qualitative research. Fidel (1984) describes the procedures followed and the types of analyses performed in a case study and discusses problems typical of that method.

ANALYSIS OF DATA

There are, of course, a number of standard, nonlibrary and information science texts on the statistical analysis of data. Over the years many researchers have used Blalock (1979). Also, several of the comprehensive guides to social science research cover statistics as well as research methodologies. Instead of reviewing those works, this chapter identifies several "consumer guides" to statistics, statistics texts aimed at the library and information science researcher, two works on computer-aided analysis, and one guide to qualitative analysis.

Looking first at the "consumer guides," Jaeger (1983, p. 9)

> is designed for those who simply want to *understand* statistics, as they appear in the research and evaluation reports of educators, social and behavioral scientists, business and government reports, and so on. Those who want to learn how to *compute* statistics should seek some other text.

Rowntree (1981), too, attempts to teach the reader how to understand the key concepts of statistics and how to use them in thinking about relevant real-world problems. The goal of Jaffe and Spirer (1987) is to help the reader "to be a critical observer of the statistical scene" (p. v). Dozens of examples of misuses of statistics are presented.

The University of Michigan's Survey Research Center (Andrews, Klem, Davidson, O'Malley, and Rodgers, 1974) published a booklet intended for researchers who have "some knowledge" of social science statistics, but who want a concise guide for selecting a particular statistic or statistical technique. Comparable computer programs perform much the same function.

Moving to statistical guides written for library and information science researchers, Carpenter (1978, p. xiii) attempts "to give a basic understanding of statistics, statistical analysis, and its usefulness in library science." This work covers descriptive statistics, inductive statistics, sampling, correlation and regression, and nonparametric tests and measures. It uses library-related examples and assumes minimal mathematical background. More recent texts in this area include Ravichandra Rao (1983), Simpson (1988), and Hafner (1989). Special features of these three books include a chapter on techniques, such as benefit-cost analysis in Hafner, a chapter on qualitative data in Simpson, and a chapter on bibliometrics in Ravichandra Rao.

A recent publication by Hernon, Hwang, Farah, Golub, Bryant, Kuo, and De (1989) is not intended as a basic text on statistics, but rather to assist researchers "in better understanding statistics and the types of decisions that the selection of a test entails" (p. xv). It attempts to place "selected statistical applications in the context of the research process and library decision making" (p. xv). Barnes (1985) is another work that is not intended as a basic text on data analysis, but it does contain useful chapters on coding data and preparing tables (as well as sampling).

Many researchers choose, of course, to analyze their data with the aid of a computer. The *SPSSx User's Guide* (1986) is a good example of a manual for one of the widely available statistical software packages for mainframe computers, in this case, the *Statistical Package for the Social Sciences.* Similar manuals exist for comparable statistical programs, such as *SAS* (Statistical Analysis System),

BMDP (Biomedical Computer Programs), and *OSIRIS* (Organized Set of Integrated Routines for Investigation of Social Science Data).

However, more and more researchers are analyzing their data with the somewhat more convenient, but less comprehensive, statistical programs written for microcomputers. Hernon and Richardson (1988) identify, evaluate, and compare more than 70 such programs; give a step-by-step tutorial on the use of one general purpose software package; illustrate the application of certain statistical tests to specific library problems; and discuss spreadsheet and data management software.

And, finally, readers wishing to consult a work devoted exclusively to the qualitative analysis of data can refer to Strauss (1987). This work introduces qualitative analysis, gives two illustrations, and covers specific techniques, such as open coding and memo writing, while emphasizing the generating and testing of theory.

CONCLUSION

The preceding review of the research methods literature is not exhaustive. It is particularly selective regarding the nonlibrary and information science literature. ture. While each work was assigned to only one category, many of them (especially the general texts) include information pertinent to more than one type of research activity.

The researcher looking for guidance on the use of methodologies and techniques, especially qualitative ones, would be well-advised to consult both the general social science research literature as well as those works aimed at researchers in library and information science. While few of the latter works have achieved the status of several of the standard social science texts, and while few of them are as comprehensive, they do offer certain advantages. For example, they generally provide the reader with examples and applications relevant to the library and information environment. Also, they probably make more accurate assumptions about the level of research expertise that their typical reader possesses.

However, there continues to be a need for more how-to-do-it guides to LIS research. Whether justified or not, many aspiring LIS researchers seem to be less intimidated by research texts aimed at the library and information professional rather than at the scholar in the behavioral or social sciences. Some of the LIS research guides that do exist need to be updated or supplemented by works that reflect some of the newer methods. Additional information about conducting qualitative research in library and information science is also needed. But the body of literature on LIS research methods is growing and has more advice than ever to offer the reader planning to conduct research, or read research findings, about library and information related problems.

REFERENCES

Adeyemi, N.M. "Library Operations Research-Purpose, Tools, Utility, and Implications for Developing Libraries," *Libri*, 27 (1977): 22–30.
Andrews, F.M., L. Klem, T.N. Davidson, P.M. O'Malley, and W.L. Rodgers. *A Guide for Selecting Statistical Techniques for Analyzing Social Science Data*. Ann Arbor, MI: Survey Research Center, Institute for Social Research, The University of Michigan, 1974.
Babbie, E. *The Practice of Social Research*. 4th Edition. Belmont, CA: Wadsworth, 1986.
Backstrom, C.H. & G. Hursh-Cesar. *Survey Research*. 2nd Edition. New York: John Wiley & Sons, 1981.
Barnes, A. *Social Science Research: A Skills Handbook*. Bristol, IN: Wyndham Hall, 1985.
Bensman, S.J. "Bibliometric Laws and Library Usage As Social Phenomena," *Library Research*, 4 (1982): 279–312.
Benson, D.K. and J.L. Benson. *A Benchmark Handbook: A Guide to Survey Research Terms*. Columbus, OH: Academy for Contemporary Problems, 1975.
Blalock, H.M. *Social Statistics*. Revised 2nd Edition. New York: McGraw-Hill, 1979.
Bookstein, A. "Questionnaire Research in a Library Setting," *Journal of Academic Librarianship*, 11 (1985): 24–28.
Budd, R.W., R.K. Thorp, and D. Lewis. *Content Analysis of Communications*. New York: Macmillan, 1967.
Burgess, R.G., Ed. *Field Research: A Sourcebook and Field Manual*. London, England: George Allen & Unwin, 1982.
Busha, C.H. and S.P. Harter. *Research Methods in Librarianship; Techniques and Interpretation*. New York: Academic Press, 1980.
Campbell, D.J. and J.C. Stanley. *Experimental and Quasi-experimental Designs for Research*. Boston, MA: Houghton Mifflin, 1963.
Carpenter, R.L. *Statistical Methods for Librarians*. Chicago, IL: American Library Association, 1978.
Collings, D.G. "Comparative Librarianship," in *Encyclopedia of Library and Information Science*, Edited by A. Kent and H. Lancour. Volume 5. New York: Marcel Dekker, 1977, pp. 492–502.
Cook, K. and C.M. Greco. "The Ugly Duckling Acknowledged: Experimental Design for Decision-Making. Part I," *Journal of Academic Librarianship*, 3 (1977): 23–28. "Part II," *Journal of Academic Librarianship*, 3 (1977): 85–89.
Cronin, M.J. *Performance Measurement for Public Services in Academic and Research Libraries* (Occasional Paper Number 9). Washington, D.C.: Association of Research Libraries, 1985.
DeProspo, E.R., E. Altman, and K. Beasley. *Performance Measures for Public Libraries*. Chicago, IL: American Library Association, 1973.
Dougherty, R.M. and F.J. Heinritz. *Scientific Management of Library Operations*. 2nd Edition. Metuchen, NJ: Scarecrow, 1982.
Drott, M.C. "Random Sampling: A Tool for Library Research," *College & Research Libraries*, 30 (1969): 119–125.

Dyer, E.R. "The Delphi Technique in Library Research," *Library Research*, 1 (1979): 41–52.
Eaton, J. "Bibliographical Research," *Library Trends*, 13 (1964): 42–53.
Fidel, R. "The Case Study Method: A Case Study," *Library and Information Science Research*, 6 (1984): 273–288.
Fischer, R.G. "The Delphi Method: A Description, Review, and Criticism," *Journal of Academic Librarianship*, 4 (1978): 64–70.
Garrison, G., Ed. "Research Methods in Librarianship," *Library Trends*, 13 (1964) (1).
Gay, L.R. *Educational Research; Competencies for Analysis & Application*. 2nd Edition. Columbus, OH: Charles E. Merrill, 1981. (A 3rd ed., 1987, was not examined.)
Glazier, J. "Structured Observation: How it Works," *College & Research Libraries News*, 46 (1985): 105–108.
_____ and R.R. Powell, Eds. *Qualitative Research in Information Management*. To be published by Libraries Unlimited, 1991.
Golden, G. *Survey Research Methods*. Chicago, IL: Association of College and Research Libraries, 1982.
Goldhor, H. *An Introduction to Scientific Research in Librarianship*. Urbana, IL: University of Illinois, Graduate School of Library Science, 1972.
Grover, R. and J. Glazier. "Implications for Application of Qualitative Methods to Library and Information Science Research," *Library & Information Science Research*, 7 (1985): 247–260.
Hafner, A.W. *Descriptive Statistical Techniques for Librarians*. Chicago, IL: American Library Association, 1989.
Harris, M.H. *A Guide to Research in American Library History*. 2nd Edition. Metuchen, NJ: Scarecrow, 1974.
Hayes, R.M. *Use of the Delphi Technique in Policy Formulation; A Case Study of the "Public Sector/Private Sector Task Force."* Unpublished manuscript, University of California, Los Angeles: Graduate School of Library & Information Science, 1982.
Hernon, P. and C.R. McClure. *Evaluation and Library Decision Making*. Norwood, NJ: Ablex, 1990.
Hernon, P. and J.V. Richardson, Eds. *Microcomputer Software for Performing Statistical Analysis: A Handbook Supporting Library Decision Making*. Norwood, NJ: Ablex, 1988.
Hernon, P., H.R. Hwang, B.D. Farah, A.J. Golub, P.K. Bryant, L. Kuo, and M. De. *Statistics for Library Decision Making: A Handbook*. Norwood, NJ: Ablex, 1989.
Isaac, S. and W.B. Michael. *Handbook in Research and Evaluation*. 2nd Edition. San Diego, CA: Edits Publishers, 1981.
Jaeger, R.M. *Statistics; A Spectator Sport*. Beverly Hills, CA: Sage, 1983.
Jaffe, A.J. and H.F. Spirer. *Misused Statistics: Straight Talk for Twisted Numbers*. New York: Marcel Dekker, 1987.
Kantor, P.B. *Objective Performance Measures for Academic and Research Libraries*. Washington, D.C.: Association of Research Libraries, 1984.
Kaser, D. "Advances in American Library History," in *Advances in Librarianship*, Edited by M.H. Harris. Volume 8. New York: Academic Press, 1978, pp. 181–199.
Kerlinger, F.N. *Foundations of Behavioral Research*. 3rd Edition. New York: Holt, Rinehart & Winston, 1986.

Kidder, L.H. and C.M. Judd. *Research Methods in Social Relations*. 5th Edition. New York: Holt, Rinehart and Winston, 1986.

Kidston, J.S. "The Validity of Questionnaire Responses," *Library Quarterly*, 55 (1985): 133–150.

Kraemer, H.C. and S. Thiemann. *How Many Subjects? Statistical Power Analysis in Research*. Newbury Park, CA: Sage, 1987.

Lancaster, F.W. *If You Want to Evaluate Your Library...* Champaign, IL: University of Illinois, Graduate School of Library and Information Science, 1988.

———. *The Measurement and Evaluation of Library Services*. Washington, D.C.: Information Resources Press, 1977.

Leedy, P.D. *How to Read Research and Understand It*. New York: Macmillan, 1981.

———. *Practical Research; Planning and Design*. 3rd Edition. New York: Macmillan, 1985.

Leimkuhler, F.F. "Operations Research," in *Encyclopedia of Library and Information Science*, Edited by A. Kent and H. Lancour. Volume 20. New York: Marcel Dekker, 1977, pp. 412–439.

Library Systems Evaluation Guide. Volumes 1–8. Powell, OH: James E. Rush Associates, 1983–1987.

Lofland, J. and L.H. Lofland. *A Guide to Qualitative Observation and Analysis*. Belmont, CA: Wadsworth, 1984.

Lynch, M.J., Ed. "Research in Librarianship," *Library Trends*, 32 (1984): 361–577.

MacKee, M. *A Handbook of Comparative Librarianship*. 3rd Edition. London, England: Clive Bingley, 1983.

Marshall, J.D. (Ed.). *Approaches to Library History. Proceedings of the Second Library History Seminar*. Tallahassee, FL: Journal of Library History, 1966.

Martyn, J. and F.W. Lancaster. *Investigative Methods in Library and Information Science: An Introduction*. Arlington, VA: Information Resources Press, 1981.

McCombs, C. and C.H. Busha. "Historical Research and Oral History in Librarianship," in *A Library Science Research Reader and Bibliographic Guide*, Edited by C.H. Busha. Littleton, CO: Libraries Unlimited, 1981, pp. 72–111.

Moore, N. *How to Do Research*. 2nd Edition. London: The Library Association, 1987.

Mouly, G.J. *Educational Research; The Art and Science of Investigation*. Boston, MA: Allyn and Bacon, 1978.

Nachmias, D. and C. Nachmias. *Research Methods in the Social Sciences*. 3rd Edition. New York: St. Martin's Press, 1987.

Newhouse, R.C. "Librarian-Researchers: Perspectives on a Methodology," *Library Quarterly*, 59 (1989): 22–26.

O'Neill, E. "Operations Research," *Library Trends*, 32 (1984): 509–520.

Pao, M.L. *Concepts of Information Retrieval*. Englewood, CO: Libraries Unlimited, 1989.

Patton, M.Q. *Qualititative Evaluation and Research Methods*. 2nd Edition. Newbury Park, CA: Sage, 1990.

Powell, R.R. *Basic Research Methods for Librarians*. Norwood, NJ: Ablex, 1985, 1991.

———., Ed. "Problem Solving in Libraries," *Library Trends*, 38 (1989): 153–325.

Ravichandra Rao, I.K. *Quantitative Methods for Library and Information Science*. New York: John Wiley & Sons, 1983.

Reilly, K.D. "The Delphi Technique: Fundamentals and Applications," in *Targets for*

Research in Library Education, Edited by H. Borko. Chicago, IL: American Library Association, 1973, pp. 187–199.
Rossi, P.H. and H.E. Freeman. *Evaluation; A Systematic Approach.* 4th Edition. Newbury Park, CA: Sage, 1989.
Rowley, J.E. and P.J. Rowley. *Operations Research; A Tool for Library Management.* Chicago, IL: American Library Association, 1981.
Rowntree, D. *Statistics Without Tears; A Primer for Non-mathematicians.* New York: Charles Scribner's Sons, 1981.
SPSSx User's Guide. 2nd Edition. Chicago, IL: SPSS, 1986.
Shafer, R.J., Ed. *A Guide to Historical Method.* 3rd Edition. Homewood, IL: Dorsey, 1980.
Shiflett, O.L. "Clio's Claim: The Role of Historical Research in Library and Information Science," *Library Trends,* 32 (1984): 385–406.
Simpson, I.S. *Basic Statistics for Librarians.* 3rd Edition. London: Library Association, 1988.
Simsova, S. *A Primer of Comparative Librarianship.* London: Clive Bingley, 1982.
Smith, L.C. "Citation Analysis," *Library Trends,* 30 (1981): 83-106.
Sproull, N.S. *Handbook of Research Methods—A Guide for Practitioners and Students in the Social Sciences.* Metuchen, NJ: Scarecrow, 1988.
Stevens, R.E. (Ed.). *Research Methods in Librarianship: Historical and Bibliographical Methods in Library Research.* Urbana, IL: University of Illinois, Graduate School of Library Science, 1971.
Strauss, A.L. *Qualitative Analysis for Social Scientists.* Cambridge: Cambridge University Press, 1987.
Suchman, E.A. *Evaluative Research; Principles and Practice in Public Service & Social Action Programs.* New York: Sage, 1967.
Swisher, R. and C.R. McClure. *Research for Decision Making; Methods for Librarians.* Chicago, IL: American Library Association, 1984.
Van House, N.A., M.J. Lynch, C.R. McClure, D.L. Zweizig, and E.J. Rodger. *Output Measures for Public Libraries.* 2nd Edition. Chicago, IL: American Library Association, 1987.
Van House, N., B. Weil, and C. McClure. *Measuring Academic Library Performance: A Practical Approach.* Chicago, IL: American Library Association, 1990.
Wallace, D.P. "A Solution in Search of a Problem: Bibliometrics & Libraries," *Library Journal,* 112 (1987): 43–47.
Weiss, C.H. *Evaluation Research; Methods for Assessing Program Effectiveness.* Englewood Cliffs, NJ: Prentice-Hall, 1972.
White, E.C. "Bibliometrics: From Curiosity to Convention," *Special Libraries,* 76 (1985): 35–42.
Wurzburger, M. "Conducting a Mail Survey: Some of the Things You Probably Didn't Learn in Any Research Methods Course," *College & Research Libraries News,* 48 (1987): 697–700.

ADDITIONAL READINGS

Berdie, D.R., J.F. Anderson, and M.A. Niebuhr. *Questionnaires: Design and Use.* 2nd Edition. Metuchen, NJ: Scarecrow, 1986.

Bogdan, R. and S.J. Taylor. *Introduction to Qualitative Research Methods: A Phenomenological Approach to the Social Sciences.* New York: John Wiley and Sons, 1975.

Chatman, E.A. "Field Research: Methodological Themes," *Library & Information Science Research,* 6 (1984): 425–438.

Cobb, A.K. and J.N. Hagemaster. "Ten Criteria for Evaluating Qualitative Research Proposals," *Journal of Nursing Education,* 26 (1987): 138–143.

Dale, D.C. "Content Analysis: A Research Methodology for School Library Media Specialists," *School Library Media Quarterly,* 18 (1989): 45–46.

Davis, Donald G., Jr. and John Mark Tucker. *American Library History: A Comprehensive Guide to the Literature.* Santa Barbara, CA: ABC-CLIO, 1989.

Krueger, R.A. *Focus Groups: A Practical Guide for Applied Research.* Newbury Park, CA: Sage, 1988.

Line, M.B. *Library Surveys: An Introduction to Their Use, Planning, Procedures and Presentation.* 2nd Edition. London: Clive Bingley, 1982.

Nicholas, D. and M. Ritchie. *Literature and Bibliometrics.* London: Clive Bingley, 1984.

Norman, G.R. and D.L. Streiner. *PDQ Statistics.* Toronto: B.C. Decker, 1986.

Robbins, J.B. and D. Zweizig. *Are We There Yet? Evaluating Library Collections, Reference Services, Programs, and Personnel.* Madison, WI: School of Library and Information Studies, University of Wisconsin-Madison, 1988.

chapter three

Impact of "National Research Agendas" on LIS Research

Charles Curran

Political processes produce agendas, and political processes have lives and impacts of their own. So whatever *conceptual* influences national agendas have, they have *decision-making* influences also. Who creates such agendas? What study topics receive official sanction? How much funding is available? Researchers respond to agendas on the basis of how satisfied they are with answers to these questions, and researchers who agree that research priorities do have to be established and funding does have to be provided may find the National Commission idea attractive.

Burlesque Straightperson: How's your significant other?
Burlesque Comedian: Compared to what?[1]

There is much to be studied in library and information science.[2]

Exploring a question about the impact of one thing upon another requires an explorer to define some terms. For example, what is *impact*? *The American Heritage Dictionary* (1981, p. 658) provides some interesting assistance in this regard. "The striking of one body against another; a collision" is the first offering. Many researchers, especially those who have had difficulty winning support or respect for their projects, would agree with the "collision" idea. "The effect of one thing upon another" (Ibid., p. 658) is the second suggestion. *Effect* is the concept which applies here. So the question about impact can be rephrased: What has been the *effect* of the "National Research Agendas" on LIS research?

---

[1] This is an old burlesque schtick, degenderized for the liberated 1990s. Paul C. Janaske (1975) used the unlaundered version. Both versions make the appeal for comparisons in context.

[2] This is an old library saying, undoctored for the 1990s, and extracted from a conclusion appearing on p. 66 of *Building an Infrastructure for Library Research*, which is the third volume of *Rethinking the Library in the Information Age* (1989).

An *agenda* is "a list of things to be done" (Ibid., p. 24). Now, a *National Agenda* is a list of things to be accomplished on some grander scale, either for the nation, by the nation, or with the nation's permission, encouragement, and support. A *really* pivotal issue here is not so much definition, however, as it is ownership. In the library and information research community, a key question is: Whose agenda is it? If it is one's agenda for oneself, then that is a rather standard, nonthreatening concept. If it is one's list of things to do, things to be assigned to someone else, then that is quite a different situation, especially to the *someone else*. When they are members of the *someone else* corps, researchers may interpret an agenda thusly:

> Here is a list of research topics. Choose from these, or don't research anything. Don't expect support unless you select an approved topic. And just as this year's list differs from last year's, so will next year's differ from this one.

The next definition problem—What does library and information science (LIS) mean?—and the companion problem—What does library and information science research mean?—will be handled without a lexicographer's intervention. Library and information science is what those having such words in their titles or job descriptions say it is. Research is what those who have questions and who endeavor to answer those questions systematically say it is. When they systematically look for questions and answers about LIS, whether they are, librarians, information scientists, or anthropologists, they are doing LIS research.

Why would they do such things? Well, as one National Research Agenda reminds us, "there is much to be studied."

As the burlesque performer has indicated, however, there is more to the question of *impact* than mere definition can explain. Impact, or effect, compared to what? A time when there were no "Agendas"? The time after the "Agendas"? An effect directly attributable to the "Agendas"? An effect directly attributable to something other than an "Agenda"?

As this chapter explores the question of how the national agendas have influenced the conduct of inquiry, the chapter considers two efforts to produce such national agendas and some of the results judged to show the impact or "effect" of the agendas. Next, in order to place this effect in a context for comparison, the chapter examines the impact of some *extra-agenda* research activity. The chapter concludes with some recommendations for inspection by agenda advocates, agenda followers, and research administrators.

TWO AGENDA EFFORTS

Number 1: The 1980s Agenda

In February 1982, Cuadra Associates (1982) issued a *Summary Report* which gave the details of the construction of a research agenda. The project had been funded by the Department of Education, Office of Libraries and Learning Technologies, and it involved 26 researchers and practitioners, including one researcher/nonparticipant. They constructed a list of important, researchable ideas for librarians and information scientists to consider. The document's preface (Ibid., p. 1) states:

> The purpose of this summary report is to help disseminate the "Library and Information Science Research Agenda for the 1980s" widely throughout the library and information science community and to other interested organizations and agencies, as well. The 20 projects that comprise the Research Agenda and the issues that have been raised in the course of our work can, we hope, stimulate productive discussion and debate about the type of research that can have the greatest impact on future library and information services. This report can also be used by library and information science organizations to convey to potential sources of research funding a sense of the exciting potential of future library and information services and the ways in which research can contribute to that future.

The list was the result of the study group's attempt to present 20 projects which emerged from scrutiny of and debate about 90 project ideas assembled for consideration.

By definition, then, we had a National Agenda. It was national because it was a federally funded effort involving participants from all over the country. It was an agenda because it posted a list. It was important because it was "an attempt to decide what research ought to be done during the rest of the decade" (Lynch, 1982, p. 305).

Impact

The impact took several forms, two of which will be discussed here. One is *fire*, both enemy and friendly. Another is *effect upon research production*.

Fire. Reaction to the *Agenda* was soon forthcoming. A "Symposium" published in 1982 (Curran, 1982) addressed, in particular, the process which produced the list. Symposium participants registered several points about a so-called committee approach to identifying ideas for other researchers to pursue. In short, they had little confidence in such a group process. Some were especially alarmed that the *Agenda* would be used as a want list, a list of topics bearing some kind of stamp of approval for funding. *Discussion* of the *Agenda* topics they welcomed; "Anointing" of the *Agenda* topics they feared (Ibid.).

Symposium participant Leslie Morris called the *Agenda* "totalitarian" (Ibid., p. 388). Participant Charles R. McClure added (Ibid.): "In short, the committee methodology used for the *Agenda* largely prescribes its products," and he contended that the *Agenda* process could not produce the "creative tension" researchers need. The list could "straight-jacket mind-sets, serve only to put 'blinders' on funding agencies and discourage innovative, non-traditional heuristic research in library/information science," observed McClure (Ibid.).

Participant Douglas Zweizig was equally direct. He claimed that it was "unrealistic to hope that researchers show interest in working with others' ideas" (Ibid., p. 389). He found (Ibid.):

> fault with the *Agenda* on two major and related counts. First is the flaw in the basic assumption that researchers will respond to a call to address problems which they themselves did not identify. Second is the absence in the *Agenda* procedure of what he sees as necessary combinations of the four elements which spawn and nourish research endeavors.

Zweizig had identified the four elements as "the proper combination of . . . need, interest, resources and prior work in the area" (Ibid.).

Not all the participants offered negative reviews. Wayne Wiegand (Ibid., p. 387) saw the *Agenda* as presenting a "range of choices," not a "dictated list of mandated projects."

Symposium participants obviously saw the need to engage in serious and spirited discussion of the *Agenda*, but few foresaw much hope for the list to have a positive impact on research production.

Effect upon Research Production. While it may be possible to name research projects which were identified, proposed, and funded as a direct result of the 1980s *Agenda* recommendations, it would be very difficult to measure the total impact of that *Agenda* upon scholarly output.

Insofar as funded studies directly related to that list of topics in the national agenda are concerned, three RFPs were issued; one was withdrawn; and two studies were funded (Mathews, 1989, p. 253): *Diffusion of Library Innovation*, and *Library Networks Study*. It would be dangerous to assert that no other activity was influenced by the *Agenda*. It would be just as dangerous to search for matches between the *Agenda* and every Post-*Agenda* Title II-B topic, or between the *Agenda* and every Post-*Agenda* LIS dissertation topic, and then claim that each hit represented evidence of the direct influence of the *Agenda*.

In view of the results—two funded studies—*modest* would appear to be a generous word to use in assessing the observable direct influence of the *Agenda* on research in library and information science. True, support issues should be factored. Indeed, the absence of a support mechanism weakened the *Agenda*.

Leery of lists appears to be a good descriptive phrase to use in assessing the observable influence of the *Agenda* on the way some researchers react to national agenda-making activities. The appearance of lists raises antennae.

Why Listaphobia? There is something inherently intelligent about making lists. Shoppers do better with lists. Teachers perform better with outlines. Time Managers tout the making of lists as the single most important practice in their arsenal of time management devices and methods. Orchestras rely heavily upon a list of notes to play in sequence, and so do their audiences and their critics. We demand that political candidates have agendas and that political parties have platforms—lists of priorities. Moses received a list of ten suggestions which continue to influence some of us some of the time.

The problem seems not to be with the *list* as an artifact, but with the complexities of the organizations and associations for whom lists are made, the uses to which lists will be put, the motives and identities of the list makers, the methods employed in list construction, and the sanctions and enjoinders implied or mandated in the lists.

Altman and Antieau (1988, pp. 54–55) provide an interesting and insightful comment on the difficulties inherent in governmentally influenced priority selection when the priorities shift from year to year, as they tend to do when personnel shuffles occur:

> It would be unrealistic to expect a coherent research agenda with this constant ferment of reorganization, name changes, personnel changes, and shifting priorities. Still curiosity prompts asking: Which of those projects have proven worthwhile?

By "projects" the authors were referring to Title II-B studies, not to *Agenda* studies, but their point is well taken. Agenda makers sometimes sacrifice continuity.

Number 2: The 1990s Agenda

The three-volume *Rethinking the Library in the Information Age* (1988–1989) represents the second of the national research agendas under consideration here. The process which produced the three documents was more gradual than the one employed for setting the 1980s agenda. The process began in 1986 with an attempt to identify likely contributors to a research agenda effort, and continued through 1988 when Volume 1, *A Summary of Issues in Library Research*, presented a summary of essays by the chosen contributors. Volume II, *Proposals for the 1990s*, contains the full text of those essays. Volume III, *Building an Infrastructure for Library Research*, the product of a fall 1988 session devoted to discussion of a possible component to support research in LIS, concludes this phase of the 1990s agenda.

This second effort at a national agenda appears to have calmed some fears about list construction at the national level. The process seems to be reasoned, democratic, and substantially more decentralized than its predecessor. There are higher hopes for this agenda and it has met with fewer major complaints than the 1980s agenda.

Impact. This second effort has not attracted the volume of immediate unfriendly fire than its predecessor had. Robbins (1987) noted that the preparers of the 1990s plan seemed not to have heeded the comments which were directed at the 1980s attempt. While she acknowledges that the 1990s version seems improved with respect to "both the process and the proposed product" (Ibid., p. 141), Robbins observes that the fundamental point—that agendas created by others seldom appeal to researchers—has been ignored.

This *political* point bears consideration. There is a seed in this 1990s agenda effort that may sprout and if it does, it may carry the political solution to the political problem of who makes what decisions about which research topics will be pursued by whom. This "political solution" will be considered in the conclusions and recommendations section of this chapter.

A point about funding needs to be made also. If, as Lynch (1988, p. 335) indicates, the 1990s project results "will be used to direct the distribution of dollars to support research," then the agenda will most certainly have an enormous impact.

OTHER THAN THE AGENDAS

In terms of numbers of opportunities for researchers to report their projects, the American Library Association's Library Research Round Table (LRRT) has performed steadily. Each year the LRRT conducts a research competition, and the annual Research Forums enable researchers to present papers.

The Council on Library Resources has funded and helped disseminate the findings of research activity. The Association for Library and Information Science Education (ALISE) conducts annual research competitions and includes forum presentations in its annual convention. The American Society for Information Science engages in similar efforts, and several divisions of the American Library Association also sponsor research activities.

Other associations provide regular forums for research communication through conferences, published proceedings, and journals. While the 1980s *Agenda* created quite a stir, its impact, three RFPs and two funded studies, has been less than that of these associations, insofar as providing numbers of opportunities for researchers to air their findings is concerned.

Interestingly, several of these associations have constructed or are in the process of constructing their own *research agendas* (see Chapters 21 and 24)! This bears watching, too.

Of course, a core of journals publishes research findings, and there are those who claim that this cadre of journals constitutes the steadiest, most accessible outlet for systematic inquiry. They argue that researchers aim for publication in these journals because the journals are perceived to be the most likely vehicles of expression for their ideas. The journal influences research production more than any other single force. Keeping the journals healthy and flourishing should be a major strategy for researchers who want their findings published and disseminated.

The subject of *impact* has been brought into still sharper focus by Altman and Antieau (1988), who defined *impact* as the act of being cited. They looked at the research and demonstration projects funded from 1965 to 1980 under Title II-B of the Higher Education Act. During the period under investigation, 312 projects were funded. To date, two 1980s *Agenda*-related projects were funded. That is a difference of 310. That is a noticeable difference. Their examination of a sample of projects also showed that of "163 projects analyzed 77 were never cited in serials indexed by *Social Sciences Citation Index*" (Ibid., p. 48).

The implications of their findings extend beyond the purposes of this chapter, but their points are well taken. If citation patterns indicate impact of thought, then those studies which are never completed (for lack of support), or which do not get cited, may have little if any impact.

Certainly the roles of the ALA and the Public Library Association have to be acknowledged when one considers the impact of "extra-agenda" influences on research activity. Perhaps "output measures movement" is too grandiose a term to describe the impact of *Output Measures* documents (Van House, Lynch, McClure, Zweizig, and Rodger, 1987; McClure, Owen, Zweizig, Lynch, and Van House, 1987) on the planning, research, and problem-solving efforts which that PLA project has spawned, but the planning process has caught on, both at state and local public library levels, and it spreads to other information agency environments.

It has not been the purpose here to provide an exhaustive list of funding sources, government and foundation, and then to chart the full impact of each episode of support. This sketch, however, may provide a picture of the extent to which previous and current national agendas can effect the conduct of inquiry in library and information science. "Not very much" is the suggestion about the 1980s effort, and "wait and see" is the fairest comment that can be made about the 1990s attempt. If the "research roundtable" or "commission" idea, support for which is explicit in the 1990s agenda itself (see *Rethinking the Library in the Information Age,* 1989, Volume III), and in the expressed thinking of many observers, takes hold, the 1990s agenda will have had substantial impact. This "commission," however, must not accept as its charge the administration of "somebody else's" agenda, however, for that would not solve the political problem with national agendas.

WHAT SOME OTHER ORGANIZATIONS DO ABOUT TOPICS

That the LIS profession seems to be conducting a love affair with agendas and lists is but a minor overstatement. Yet, it is no secret that librarians have greeted agendas with considerable negative enthusiasm. Why then this affair? Do others share our affection for *the ten most important* priorities?

The American Medical Association (AMA) is as concerned with *hot topics* as any professional/research organization is. Their Council for Scientific Affairs meets six times a year and identifies areas for research efforts. Unlike the librarians who motivate themselves to perform this identification behavior at irregular intervals, the medical doctors perform an ongoing monitoring of the research topic landscape.

A Social Work Research Task Force funded by the National Institute of Mental Health helps discover research needs in social work areas and assists practitioners of the social work arts in identifying the research productivity in their field.

Other organizations identify research topics on a need-to-know basis. When the National Football League (NFL) needs to know something, usually because the Commissioner or the Vice President of Communications and Development decides so, the League will conduct a study. *Realignment and Expansion* are current research priorities of the NFL. The Players Association employs a Head of Research who conducts research for that organization, and an aide in the Association office reports that most of the topics researched are identified by the Head of Research.

Though agenda making may not be confined to the LIS establishment, it is most definitely *not* a rule-of-thumb practice in other disciplines. True, health organizations identify current concerns—the AIDS problem, for example—and issue calls for proposals. National association officers questioned about agenda activity among the groups which their associations fund seemed amused to learn about LIS agendas. Several counseled the author of this chapter that agendas do not achieve a fit with the kinds of personal prerogatives that are essential for the conduct of inquiry. Where have LIS researchers heard that before?

Clearly the ALA, AMA, National Association of Social Workers (NASW), and the NFL are hardly comparable organizations. Each, however, shares an obvious interest in conducting inquiry into those areas of crucial concern to their respective constituencies. Of these groups, only the librarians seem to want to draw up "lists that last."

CONCLUSION AND RECOMMENDATIONS

The problem is that indeed "there is much to be studied," but the way to go about doing the studying is not always clear, or if clear, not always satisfactory. This is not a reference to problems of definition, research design, or motivation. It is a comment about the impact of national research agendas on the conduct of inquiry in library and information science. More specifically, this is a reference to research administration—that collection of decisional and functional processes that *enable* researchers to do what they do.

Researchers conduct research because they *want* to and *get* to, and perhaps some *have* to. Researchers research because questions needing answers are there, and they are driven to explore possibilities. Researchers research because the environment is hospitable and because they enjoy support and encouragement.

Some researchers research because they must. In fact, government, industry, and education employ people under "research or perish" agreements.

And yet there is a problem. Even with *want to*, *get to*, and *have to* factors in place, some researchers do not respond positively to lists of approved topics unless they are the ones who helped make the list. To label this as petulant and immature behavior may satisfy the scolding parent in all of us, but it will not solve our problem.

While the problem has economic, intellectual, and experiential properties, the main ingredient is political. The chief flaws in national agenda approaches are rooted in dissatisfaction about who makes the decisions about eligible research topics and not in the actual make-up of such lists. Researchers with no input to the topic identification process, and no direct access to those who make lists, balk at invitations to pursue inquiries selected by others.

Moreover, some of those who balk do so not only because they feel disenfranchised, but because they resent the specter of government decree. They fear government interference with personal research prerogatives. They recoil. They are staunch believers in what they hold to be a steadfast principle of political science: Control follows the dollar.

Even when some researchers enter the competition in response to RFPs, they frequently harbor a mistrust of the award process. They sometimes focus upon what they identify as defects in the jury or reader process, and they may become vocal critics of the politics involved.

The Politics Involved

The main complaints about national agendas are political complaints focusing on the nature of the decision process, the identity of the deciders, and the locus of control. It is not an oversimplification to assert that since the problem is a political problem, the solution must be a political solution.

A National Commission or Roundtable as a Solution

In "The Status of Research in Library/Information Science," a collection of "assessments of leading researchers," McClure and Bishop (1989, p. 140) relay an interesting recommendation:

> Establish a national commission of LIS researchers and practitioners to articulate the importance, role and impact of research in LIS (not to be confused with establishing a *national agenda* [italics added] for research).

This is an interesting suggestion for several reasons. One is that the recommendation contains still another negative expression about the concept of a national agenda. Another is that the suggestion hints at the required political solution to a political problem. Because there now stands a collection of parts awaiting assembly and charge (see Volume III, *Rethinking the Library in the Information Age,* 1989), the ingredients for a Commission infrastructure *already exist.* Pat Molholt, of the Rensselaer Polytechnic Institute's Folsom Library, has criticized librarianship for "lacking both the 'research mindedness' and an infrastructure capable of coordinating any research agenda" (Lynch, 1989, p. 344). The conceptual framework she poses as a remedy to this problem fits well with the requirement to develop a political solution. Molholt should be included in arranging the Commission or Roundtable.

Some Arrangements to Work Out

Giving operational expression to this abstraction will be a complicated and laborious task. Major issues of composition and charge loom. Indeed, this is an appropriate subject for a Department of Education RFP. This chapter author calls for the issuance of such an RFP.

For the purposes of this chapter, this writer will offer several suggestions that address the composition and charge issues.

Composition. Since a democratic or representative model is likely to have the best chance to succeed where models perceived to be less democratic have failed, the composition of a Commission should be answerable to the profession, and especially to the *sending bodies.* Among the groups which might supply elected Commissioners are ALA's the Library Research Round Table, and some of the divisional research bodies—the Research Committee of the Association of College and Research Libraries, for example. The American Society for Information Science research arm could elect Commissioners, as could the Association for Library and Information Science Education's Research Committee. ALA could be represented by the Office for Research. The Council on Library Resources should be represented; so should the National Commission on Libraries and Information Science, research centers, foundations, universities, and private industry. Some membership would be elected and subject to recall. Some Commissioners would serve, with voting privileges, in *ex officio* capacities, such as one each from the Office for Research and the Office of Library Programs, U.S. Department of Education.

Designers of the Commission will want to establish reasonable limits on membership number, to construct a procedural mechanism that is democratic and workable, and to structure a system of accountability which mandates communication with constituencies.

Charge. While the quoted suggestion indicates a mission to "articulate the importance, role, and impact of research in LIS," the assertion here is that a Commission whose role is merely articulation:

- .Underplays its truer, more important role;
- Spends too much of its time convincing persons who are already convinced; and
- Falls short of addressing the political problems that make the Commission necessary in the first place.

If the Commission were to adopt a charge to articulate research needs to the financial and bureaucratic powers that control and administer funding, however, that would be a worthwhile role—that of convincing the unconvinced.

What the Commission should do is work within the established structure, *with* the Office of Library Programs to promote funding, oversee the preparation and *distribution* of RFPs, democratize the review process, participate in the award process, assist in the monitoring of projects, and aid in the dissemination of results.

Other charges may be appropriate. Certainly the review and selection process may be amenable to revision along lines which will make those who perform it more directly accountable to the profession.

"Doability" and Realism. The problem with national agendas is that they can be perceived as Big Brotherish, even totalitarian, both terms have antecedents in the political process. Resolving such a problem requires a political solution, but not one which superimposes an assortment of unrealistic expectations and requirements upon a system already firmly, and legitimately, in place.

The Federal government is unlikely to look kindly on a suggestion which infringes on its prerogatives. So the Laws of Constraint and of the Situation may have to be observed. That does not mean they cannot be reinterpreted, only that they must be part of a remedial equation. If the Office for Library Programs and the Department of Education were to view the Commission as a useful and legitimate partner in the government's effort to identify, support, and monitor research activity, then they might agree to issue the RFP to design it. They should do so.

Also, since this is an imperfect world, researchers should not expect the Commission to provide conflict-free solutions to the problem of identifying topics and selecting recipients. They should expect the workings of the Commission to be relatively open and their activities and decisions subject to review. These and other advantages associated with a democratically formed Commission could effectively eliminate criticisms aimed at list-producing enterprises, such as national agendas constructed by appointed experts operating in work retreats at resort hotels.

To expect a Commission to do away with lists is unrealistic. For one thing, "congressional mandate [requires] the secretary of education to publish proposed research priorities in the *Federal Register* every two years" (Mathews, 1989, p. 253). In addition to being unrealistic, a suggestion that the Federal bureaucracy should surrender all its prerogatives is probably unwelcome.

Research in the 1990s

The observation here is that the national agenda for the 1980s had little impact on library and information science research production. Only two major studies were funded. It had considerable impact upon the thinking about agenda-driven priorities, however, as it has made researchers leery of a national agenda approach to topic identification.

Whether the current agenda effort, "'An agenda for the 1990s' and HEA II-B," do, in fact, "constitute the missing link" (Mathews, 1989, p. 256), by providing dollars for individuals or groups wishing to do research, remains to be seen. The process which produced issues for study was substantially democratic and the process of prioritizing topics was at least representative. If, as suggested in a recent issue of *Library & Information Science Research*, it is too early to comment upon the impact of this second national agenda on library and information science research and the effort deserves a chance to succeed before agenda watchers have at it (Curran, 1988, p. 217), it is *not* too soon to observe that some of the same criteria for selecting the participants in the agenda for the 1990s could be employed in forming the Commission. In this connection, the papers of Volume III of *Rethinking the Library*, especially the "Overview" by Robert M. Hayes (1989), warrant inspection.

In fact, it is the explicit attention devoted to the issue of research infrastructure and to the need for coordination that a commission might supply which earns this 1990s agenda effort its stripes. With due respect to the participants who wrote fine essays which identify researchable topic areas, there is no shortage of topics. What is in short supply is the management of research policy. Volume III, *Building an Infrastructure for Library Research*, of the 1990s agenda effort gives the enterprise its soul, and LIS researchers some hope and direction.

Concluding Thoughts about Possible Future Prospects

"Commission" or "Committee" groups manage research policy in other associations. LIS researchers who study the manner in which the American Medical Association operates its research management may identify in the doctors' methods some very useful, adaptable strategies and tactics. This suggestion is fraught with peril, however, for there are legions who will claim that comparisons between medical and information professions are odious. Most are. Certainly the amount of funding available to the AMA is greater than that available to the LIS researcher. There is no discounting that tremendous difference. This "Commission" idea is going to come to pass. It will come to be because parties to the research process demand a workable, accountable system for encouraging, supporting, and reporting research activity. No human institution will ever achieve an absolutely smooth, conflict-free operation, but the partners in the research process—researchers, research administrators, universities, funders, and the Federal bureaucracy—have reached an understanding: The present way does not work.

A "Commission" will help insure that the conduct of inquiry, itself, does not become so highly politicized and "agendized" that observers perceive the research process to be driven exclusively by special or governmental interests.

The "Commission" will not, nor should it, put an end to agenda activity, for list making is not a culprit here. The beat goes on, by the way. The Association of College and Research Libraries' Research Committee has recently announced its new research agenda ("ACRL Research Agenda," 1990, pp. 317–319; see also Chapter 21).

The "Commission" will not, nor *may* it, interfere with the prerogatives of private funders, but it might help funders in the private sector connect with a broader assortment of research talent.

Finally, the "Commission" can empower the researcher without infringing on the powers of government to suggest, support, and demand accountability. In so doing, it will place the responsibility for identification, design, and execution exactly where it belongs—in the research community; and it will calm the fears of research administrators, especially at the university level, that the only supportable research is "government" research.

This will happen because it must.

REFERENCES

"ACRL Research Agenda," *College & Research Libraries News*, 51 (April 1990): 317–319.

Altman, Ellen and Kim Antieau. "Dissemination and Impact of U.S. Department of Education's Library Research and Demonstration Projects: A Citation Analysis," *Government Information Quarterly*, 5 (1988): 45–56.

The American Heritage Dictionary of the English Language. Atlanta, GA: Houghton Mifflin Co., 1981.

Cuadra Associates, Inc. *A Library and Information Science Research Agenda for the 1980s*. Santa Monica, CA: Cuadra Associates, Inc., 1982.

Curran, Charles C. "A Symposium on a Library and Information Science Research Agenda for the 1980s," *Library & Information Science Research*, 4 (1982): 385–400.

———. "Extra Contextual Encounters," *Library & Information Science Research*, 10 (1988): 217–219.

Hayes, Robert M. "Overview of Position Papers and Discussion," in *Rethinking the Library in the Information Age*. Vol. 3, edited by Anne J. Mathews. Washington, D.C.: GPO, 1989, pp. 1–17.

Janaske, Paul C. "Federally Funded Research in Librarianship," *Library Trends*, 24 (July 1975): 101–114.

Lynch, Mary Jo. "Research on Libraries and Librarianship in 1981," *The Bowker Annual*, 27th Edition. New York: Bowker, 1982, pp. 305–308.
———. "Research on Libraries and Librarianship in 1987," *The Bowker Annual*, 33rd Edition. New York: Bowker, 1988, pp. 335–345.
———. "Research on Libraries and Librarianship in 1988," *The Bowker Annual*, 34th Edition. New York: Bowker, 1989, pp. 343–354.
Mathews, Anne J. "An Overview of Issues, Proposals and Products in Library/ Information Research," *Journal of Education for Library and Information Science*, 29 (1989): 251–261.
McClure, Charles R., Amy Owen, Douglas L. Zweizig, Mary Jo Lynch, and Nancy A. Van House. *Planning and Role Setting for Public Libraries*. Chicago, IL: American Library Association, 1987.
McClure, Charles R. and Ann Bishop. "The Status of Research in Library/Information Science: Guarded Optimism," *College & Research Libraries*, 50 (1989): 127–143.
Rethinking the Library in the Information Age. 3 volumes. Prepared by the U.S. Department of Education, Office of Educational Research and Improvement. Washington, D.C.: GPO, 1988–1989.
Robbins, Jane. "Another! Research Agenda," *Library & Information Science Research*, 9 (1987): 141–142.
Van House, Nancy A., Mary Jo Lynch, Charles R. McClure, Douglas L. Zweizig, and Eleanor Jo Rodger. *Output Measures for Public Libraries*. 2nd editon. Chicago, IL: American Library Association, 1987.

chapter four

The Role of the U.S. Department of Education in Library and Information Science Research

Anne J. Mathews

The U.S. Department of Education has taken a leadership role in library and information science research since 1965 when Title II of the Higher Education Act was first funded. In addition to providing an overview of the two grant programs—HEA II-B and D—administered by the Department's Office of Library Programs, this chapter addresses the Office of Library Programs' role in research, identifies key developments and issues, and makes recommendations for the future role of the Department in supporting research, including the creation of a research roundtable.

> Research pursuits. . . will make the library community more cognizant of current realities. Armed with the results and benefiting from prototype programs in the field, librarians can move with much more assurance into the increasingly strenuous tug-of-war among many agencies for the support of the American people.

This quote, from the U.S. Department of Education's *Alliance for Excellence: Librarians Respond to A Nation at Risk* (1984, pp. 35–36), raises several questions about the research programs administered by the Office of Library Programs:

- Are the results of research making their way into the hands of library practitioners?
- Are research conclusions packaged in a way that encourages their use by practitioners?
- Are results of research endeavors being used for decision making by practitioners and policy makers?

45

- What impact has research had on actual library practices?
- What impact has research had on library and information science education?

A current review of major library journals and newsletters reveals a number of articles citing the budget crises of public, academic, and school libraries across the country. What could be learned from research that would help those libraries whose budget woes are reported in the literature? The writers of *Alliance for Excellence* suggest that research results could make libraries more powerful in their efforts to compete for local dollars. Houser and Schrader (1978) suggest that schools of library and information science have traditionally taught a non-research, experience-based approach to program development, and library practitioners simply are not tuned into applying research. If, indeed, this be the case, library practitioners need to become convinced of the benefit, not to mention the power, of research.

Simply stated, research is critically important to practitioners. Through collaboration, practitioners and researchers can better identify research needs and disseminate research findings. This chapter reviews Federal support for libraries and information science research and discusses several ways of improving the research environment, including opportunities for practitioners to become more involved in library and information science research.

FEDERAL SUPPORT OF LIBRARY AND INFORMATION SCIENCE RESEARCH

In 1965, Congress included library and information science research as a part of the Higher Education Act, Title II-B program administered by the U.S. Department of Education. With the creation of this program, the Federal government assumed a role in library and information science research (see Appendix A).

The Department of Education is responsible for some of the most important Federal funding programs for libraries. Over the years Congress has appropriated more than $2 billion for Titles I, II, and III of the Library Services and Construction Act (LSCA), which supports public libraries and interlibrary cooperation; $14.2 million for Title IV of LSCA, Library Services for Indian Tribes and Hawaiian Natives Program; $19.2 million for Title VI of LSCA, Library Literacy Program; and over $163 million for Title II of the Higher Education Act, which supports academic and research libraries (HEA II-C, $75.6 million; HEA II-D, $10.9 million), training and retraining of librarians (HEA II-B, $50.6 million), and research in library and information science (HEA II-B, Research and Demonstration Program, $26.6 million). In addition, funds from a variety of programs, including Chapters I and II of the Education Consolidation and Improvement Act, have gone to support school library media programs.

Although Federal support for the nation's school, public, and academic library programs addresses many aspects of librarianship, this chapter is limited to the funding for library and information science research. The research programs are administered by the Office of Library Programs (OLP) within the Office of Educational Research and Improvement (OERI). Title II of the Higher Education Act includes two programs that fund research—Library Research and Demonstration Program (HEA II-B) and College Library Technology and Cooperation Grants Program (HEA II-D). In addition to an overview of these grant programs, this chapter addresses the role of the Office of Library Programs in library and information science research, identifies key developments and issues, and makes recommendations for the future of library and information science research.

Responsibility

The mission of the Office of Library Programs is to provide leadership for the nation's libraries and to administer the congressionally mandated priorities of the Library Services and Construction Act and Title II of the Higher Education Act. This includes program oversight as well as establishing research priorities. There are other influences within the Federal government that affect the Office of Library Programs. These include the:

- Priorities of the President and the Secretary of Education, which are most recently expressed in the goals resulting from the 1989 Education Summit with the governors in Charlottesville, VA;
- Mission of the Department, which includes as a goal, improving the quality and usefulness of education through federally supported research, evaluation, and sharing of information; and
- Mission and priorities of the Office of Educational Research and Improvement of which the Office of Library Programs is part and which directs the Office of Library Programs to strengthen the library as a national resource for education and literacy by promoting excellence in programs.

A closer look at the mission of the Office of Educational Research and Improvement (OERI) reveals that its chief function is to furnish Americans with information on the condition and progress of education, one of the most central responsibilities of the Department itself and one defined by Congress in 1867. Since its reorganization in 1985, the OERI has striven to accomplish this mission through:

- Upgrading the nation's statistical database, with emphasis on filling gaps in available data;
- Supporting basic and applied research, evaluations, and analyses, and resolving issues and problems of greatest concern in education; and
- Improving dissemination and application of education information among practitioners, policy makers, parents, and the public.

Library Research and Demonstration Program, Before HEA II-B

The Library Research and Demonstration Program provides grants to institutions of higher education and other public and private organizations for research and demonstration pertaining to library improvement, experimental and/or theoretical research, and training in librarianship, and for the dissemination of information resulting from these projects.

As noted earlier, HEA II-B, Library Research and Demonstration Program, has been funded for 24 years. An analysis of the research projects funded between fiscal years 1977 and 1989 shows that 92 projects were funded, covering five major topics: planning/development, institutional cooperation, reader services, education, and technology (see Appendix B).

Nearly one-fourth of these studies were concerned with policy issues relating to the effects of technological applications on the management of libraries and information centers, on one hand, and the development of multitype library networks and cooperative endeavors, on the other. Both of these developments, which have been gaining momentum since the 1970s, have forced librarians and information center managers to reallocate resources, to reevaluate and reexamine programs, in many cases to restaff, and, in all cases, to review and rethink ways of managing their institutions to serve their changing publics and clients.

Research and demonstration products from this period include commercially published books, research reports, unpublished studies, and pamphlets—most of which are in the Educational Resources Information Center (ERIC). Some of the better known publications have included *Alliance for Excellence*, referred to earlier, along with five position papers on libraries and the learning society related to *A Nation at Risk*. The research reports include: *A Library and Information Science Research Agenda for the 1980s* (Cuadra Associates, 1982), the *Diffusion of Innovations in Library and Information Science* (King Research, 1986), and *New Directions in Library and Information Science Education* (King Research, 1985).

From a historical perspective, one of the most dramatic of HEA II-B's products was the Online Computer Library Center (OCLC). Started in 1969 as an experimental step in automation among and supported by 40 Ohio colleges, OCLC has developed into an international bibliographic utility with more than 10,000 libraries as clients in the United States and abroad. Federal encouragement for OCLC began in 1970 with HEA II-B support of slightly under one-quarter of a million dollars ($215,135). Today OCLC itself is supporting a significant number of research projects.

The 92 projects funded between fiscal years 1977 and 1989 received more than $5.9 million. This represented a dramatic decrease from the nearly $20 million in funding available between 1967 and 1976 (see Appendix A). As we look to a future of continued tight budgets for library and information science research, it is critical to assess the condition of our research so that the areas with the greatest need receive funding.

Setting Research Agendas

In the beginning of the last decade, Cuadra Associates (1982) set a research agenda for the 1980s. The report states that the 1980s agenda was not intended to lock a funding program into a fixed set of objectives. However, it did "represent a carefully considered statement of proposed research priorities" (Ibid., p. 6). Four broad areas were identified:

- Information generation and provision of library and information services;
- Information users and uses;
- Economics of information and of library and information services; and
- Education and professional issues.

As a result of the Cuadra recommendations, two major studies were funded: the *Diffusion of Innovations in Library and Information Science* (King Research, 1986) and *Libraries and Literacy Education* (Zweizig, Robbins, and Johnson, 1988).

In 1986, the Office of Library Programs launched a project entitled "Issues in Library Research—An Agenda for the 1990s." There were several reasons for developing another research agenda. First, it was time to establish priorities that reflected emerging needs. Second, the Cuadra list required updating in order to take into account the many changes that had taken place in librarianship over the past decade. It is interesting to note that although some of the issues identified in the new research agenda were quite different from those contained in the Cuadra report, other issues were repeated in the new agenda. This confirmed and emphasized those areas still in need of attention. A third reason for a new agenda was that the Cuadra report was predicated on a pre-set list of topics, while an Agenda for the 1990s was based on open discussions with no predetermined issues.

The development of the 1986 Research Agenda project involved more than 200 librarians and laypersons with an interest in libraries and information science. This mix of participants included a larger and more varied selection of nonlibrary professionals and laypersons than was the case when the Cuadra report was developed.

In essence, the project addressed the future of libraries. It identified researchable issues that can help libraries attain—or maintain—a position of leadership in the information society. The major issues generated by the project include:

- Library funding and economics;
- Libraries and education;
- Information users and needs;
- Access to information;
- Policy issues: Federal, state, and local roles and responsibilities;
- Education and training of librarians;
- Archives and preservation;

- Organizing, indexing, and retrieving materials;
- Role of the public services librarian; and
- Library models for the future.

The first four issues in this list were identified as those of highest priority. The issues, including the more than 200 identified researchable topics, represent problems and challenges that are viewed as the most important for the future of libraries in this country. While the Cuadra report focused more on operational or functional aspects of the problems to be researched, the Agenda for the 1990s leans more toward an analytical or philosophical approach to the issues. In either case, the purpose of identifying the issues is to stimulate researchers, generate additional questions, and further the discussion of library and information science research.

A final recommendation of the Agenda project focused on establishing a Research Roundtable within the Office of Library Programs. The Roundtable would be drawn from leaders in the business, education, and library communities who will focus on the issues in library and information science research, and be the catalyst for ongoing research initiatives.

A complete summary of the Agenda meetings, the commissioned papers, and the recommendations are available in the three volumes: *Rethinking the Library in the Information Age* (1988–1989) (Volume I, *Issues in Library Research: Proposals for the 1990s: An Executive Summary*; Volume II, *Issues in Library Research: Proposals for the 1990s* (Commissioned Papers); Volume III, *Building an Infrastructure for Library Research*).

In 1987, OLP issued a notice for applications for HEA II-B—the first such notice for field-initiated proposals since fiscal year 1979—in response to the library profession's request for flexibility in the research program. Beginning in 1988, the top four priorities from the Research Issues project were announced in the *Federal Register*. Of the 13 field-initiated projects funded since 1987, three focused on evaluation, three on accessing information electronically, three on information needs of users, two on policy, one on censorship, and one on demonstrating collaboration of teachers, researchers, librarians, geographers, and archaeologists. All proposals were scored by peer review panels and awards were made based on their recommendations.

Publications resulting from the 1987 field-initiated projects included *The Public Library Effectiveness Study* by Nancy Van House and Thomas Childers (Drexel University, 1989), *Facilitating Information through Cognitive Models of the Search Process* by Carol Kuhlthau and Betty Turock (Rutgers University, 1989), and *Libraries and Literacy Education* by Jane Robbins and Douglas Zweizig (University of Wisconsin-Madison, 1988). Written reports have not yet been received from the 1988 and 1989 projects, and the 1990 projects have not yet been announced. The Chronological History of Library Research and Demonstration Grants under HEA II-B (1977–1989) (see Appendix B) contains a complete list of funded projects to date. The list also reflects the decrease in funding over the past decade. However, as Fitzgibbons (1984, p. 551) notes:

> Though NSF and NLM appear to be the most important research funding sources in terms of total amounts, their emphases on either scientific information or health sciences information make their funds available only to researchers interested in those areas. The same can be said for CLR (Council on Library Resources) with its focus on academic and research libraries. Consequently, even though the HEA Title II-B has been the smallest program and increasingly so, it has held the most promise for researchers seeking funding for research in other areas of the profession.

The HEA II-B program has made possible the exploration of a wide range of issues. It has also generated many new questions. Recent competitions for HEA II-B research dollars exceeded by a factor of four-to-one the amount available for funding. This is a hopeful sign, as a viable profession must produce a body of substantive research.

By the end of the 1970s, the emphasis in research and demonstration projects indicated that two significant developments were making an impact on libraries: technology and networking. In response to requests for funding to examine the problems and possibilities of technological advances and networking capabilities, Congress authorized a new program in 1986.

College Library Technology and Cooperation Grants Program, HEA II-D

The College Library Technology and Cooperation Grants Program, enacted by Congress under the Higher Education Amendments of 1986, assists libraries in higher education institutions to acquire the resources necessary to institute or improve their networking capabilities. Technological advances in academic library resource sharing, networking, and information transfer pose new problems that need to be researched in depth and new alternatives that need to be tested.

Initial funding for HEA II-D was provided in Fiscal Year 1988 with an appropriation of $3.59 million. There are four types of grants awarded: networking, combinations of institutions of higher education, services to institutions, and research and demonstration. Authorized activities for all four types of grants include:

- Buying access to networks;
- Acquiring additional equipment and supplies to assist in achieving the purpose of the project;
- Paying staff;
- Paying for telecommunications expenses;
- Evaluating the project; and
- Disseminating information about the project.

A one-third matching requirement is a key program factor, and grants are awarded for a period of up to three years.

For HEA II-D Research and Demonstration grants, institutions of higher education may apply to conduct research or demonstration projects to meet specialized national or regional needs in utilizing technology to enhance library and information science. During the first two fiscal years of the program (1988 and 1989), applications presented a broad variety of innovative ideas and approaches. Over 20 research and demonstration projects were funded during these first two years of the program, for a total of $2,336,715. In the initial funding year, there were 53 requests, totaling $6,864,000, for research and demonstration projects. Now in its third year, requests for funding for research and demonstration projects continue to exceed by several million dollars the total dollars available for all four types of HEA II-D grants.

An analysis of the funded projects show three general categories of research activity:

- *Computer-Assisted Instruction Projects.* These projects develop methods to raise the level of computer competence among library users and staff, to instruct users on alternate computerized information databases, and to measure the impact of computer-assisted user instruction programs on the academic performance of students and researchers.
- *Current Technology Impact Studies.* These projects analyze and evaluate the effects of library technology currently in use. The projects also measure the variables involved in utilizing library technology, including cost factors, effects on users and staffs, and the feasibility of expanding the current systems for different uses.
- *Advanced System Design.* These projects develop advanced information gathering and analysis systems to increase productivity for researchers and improve interlibrary loan functions for resource-sharing networks, among other things.

At least one important conclusion can be drawn from the projects funded so far: funds allocated for research and development projects are making a significant contribution to those studying new and better methods of networking leading to increased and more affordable methods of library cooperation.

Since HEA II-D is a relatively new program and since projects can be funded for up to three years, there have as yet been no final reports or publications by grantees. Several grantees have indicated in their interim reports the preparation of journal articles and conference presentations about their projects. However, as a number of these projects are on the "cutting edge" of the application of new technologies, they are worthy of the profession's attention.

Considering the importance of technology to many aspects of library development, the creation of the HEA II-D program could not have come at a better time. Its funding level for research and demonstration, which was $1,010,061 in

1988 and $1,326,654 in 1989, is greater than that of the HEA II-B program. With the addition of the HEA II-D program to the already existing HEA II-B program, the Federal funding for library and information science research has been greatly strengthened and more responsive to today's research environment.

DEVELOPMENTS, ISSUES, AND RECOMMENDATIONS IN THE LIBRARY AND INFORMATION SCIENCE RESEARCH PROGRAMS

Reviewing the library and information science research funded through HEA II-B and D reveals two key elements that further contribute to the strength of the programs—vision and flexibility. What the Cuadra report did for the 1980s, the Research Issues project will do for the 1990s; that is, to identify issues and provide direction, but within a framework that allows the field to initiate specific research activities to address the issues.

The Research Issues project appears to have given other organizations in the field of library and information science the impetus to develop their own research agendas. As expected, some issues raised by these agendas overlap with those of the Research Issues project. This is only natural as common concerns exist across the profession. It is also important to note that these agendas reflect the specific interests of the organizations that developed them. Again, this is as it should be as different organizations have different interests. Nevertheless, it is the commonality of issues that is important, binding together the organizations that represent the field.

The dissemination of the products of the Research Issues project seems to have been successful, but a recurring problem in the research program is that of effective dissemination of the research findings to practitioners and decision makers. Over the years, the Office of Library Programs has been more successful in disseminating research results to the research community and to schools of library and information science than to practitioners. Although much of the funded research has been published as research reports or placed in ERIC, there needs to be a more specific effort to promote research findings to library practitioners and decision makers by designing products that would be useful to them.

The Office of Library Programs recognizes this problem and is studying ways of reaching these important audiences, through targeting dissemination activities, examining current products and designing new ones, and encouraging collaborative research. The Office of Library Programs continues to seek more effective methods for disseminating ideas and products: suggestions and comments from colleagues are welcomed. As we plan for the future, practitioners need to know what works. Research results and applications can tell them this.

The Office of Library Programs encourages dialogue among the members of the research community and practitioners; and shares with library scientists information from other parts of OERI. Although informal communication is helpful, a more formalized approach would improve communication, foster collaboration, garner support, maximize funding, and lend greater direction to research and researchers.

A Research Roundtable

In focusing on how to improve the quality of research and provide continuity for long-term research efforts, the participants in the 1986 "Issues in Library Research: Proposals for the 1990s" project recommended the creation of a Library and Information Science Research Roundtable to be administered by the Office of Library Programs. They believed a Research Roundtable could provide an ongoing forum where library and information scientists, scholars, practitioners, and policy makers from both the private and public sectors could meet and discuss issues of mutual interest.

Following up on this recommendation, the Office of Library Programs invited representatives from universities, industry, and foundations to an all-day meeting in 1989, chaired by Dr. Maurice Mitchell of the Annenberg Foundation. The group defined further the purposes and structure of the Research Roundtable.

The report from this meeting described the roundtable primarily as a mechanism for the Office of Library Programs to:

- Collaborate with other agencies, institutions, and individuals involved in library and information science research;
- Focus the limited amount of available funds for research;
- Leverage the HEA II-B and D funds with other Federal monies and/or industry funds;
- Exchange information about current projects underway; and
- Identify significant issues needing to be addressed.

The organization would include representatives from the various public and private constituencies in the library and information research community.

A model for such a research roundtable exists in the structure of the National Academy of Science/National Academy of Engineering/National Institute of Medicine's National Research Council's Government–University–Industry Research Roundtable. This Roundtable was created in 1984 to serve as a forum where scientists, engineers, administrators, and policy makers assemble to explore ways to improve the productivity of the nation's research enterprise. The Roundtable provides an opportunity to understand issues, to inject imaginative thought into the system, and to provide a setting for seeking common ground. It neither makes recommendations nor offers specific advice, but develops options and brings all interested parties together. Its strength rests in its breadth of membership and in the continuity with which it can address issues.

The Office of Library Programs is interested in hearing comments from the field about the application of this model to library and information science. The model represents one possible avenue worthy of further exploration.

Reviewing Library and Information Science Research

Another, but very different, avenue to consider may be a review of the research administered by the Office of Library Programs in the context of education research efforts nationwide. Library research has never been included in this kind of review. Since most of the research supported by HEA II-B and D is field-initiated, it could shed some light on the impact of these research efforts as compared to other research programs in the education field.

Such a study could answer questions about library and information science research that have been looming in some researchers' and policy makers' minds for some time: Although field-initiated research is beneficial to individual institutions in terms of practices and applications, is it making enough of an impact to be continued? Could limited Federal research dollars be better used? And if so, what direction should the research initiatives take?

As the prime sponsor of Federal library research, the Office of Library Programs will benefit from the forthcoming National Research Council study that will review the terrain of education and improvement efforts in the United States and the role of OERI and the Department of Education in research and improvement. The results of this study would be beneficial to the library research program for three reasons. The study would:

- Put the library research programs in the context of all of the research efforts mounted by the Department of Education which should glean more realistic findings than an isolated study of these programs;
- Offer recommendations for better ways of targeting research funds to impact actual practices; and
- Provide guidance in determining ways practitioners could be better integrated into the research process and the application of research findings.

Research is an essential part of any profession's environment. It is a major contributor to its health and well-being. As part of the infrastructure of library and information science research, the Office of Library Programs actively seeks ways of strengthening the research environment. It believes that making research more responsive to the needs of the profession and targeting research to critical areas of library development are two ways of accomplishing this.

REFERENCES

Cuadra Associates, Inc. *A Library and Information Science Research Agenda for the 1980s*. Santa Monica, CA: Cuadra Associates, Inc., 1982.

Fitzgibbons, Shirley. "Funding of Research in Librarianship," *Library Trends*, 32 (1984): 537–556.

Houser, Lloyd and Alvin M. Schrader. *The Search for a Scientific Profession: Library Science Education in the U.S. and Canada*. Metuchen, NJ: Scarecrow Press, 1978.

King Research. *Diffusion of Innovations in Library and Information Science.* Rockville, MD, 1986.

―――. *New Directions in Library and Information Science Education.* 13 volumes. Rockville, MD, 1985.

Rethinking the Library in the Information Age. 3 volumes. Prepared by the U.S. Department of Education. Washington, D.C.: GPO, 1988–1989.

U.S. Department of Education. *Alliance for Excellence: Librarians Respond to A Nation at Risk.* Washington, D.C.: GPO, 1984.

Zweizig, Douglas L., Jane Robbins, and Debra W. Johnson. *Libraries and Literacy Education.* Madison, WI: University of Wisconsin-Madison, School of Library and Information Studies, 1988.

Appendix A. Funding History of HEA II-B.

Fiscal Year	Appropriation	R & D Grants and Contracts	
		Amount Awarded	Number Awarded
1967[1]	$3,550,000	$3,381,052	38
1968	3,550,000	2,020,942	21
1969	3,000,000	2,986,264	39
1970	2,171,000	2,160,622	30
1971	2,171,000	2,170,274	18
1972	2,750,000	2,748,953	31
1973	1,785,000	1,784,741	24
1974	1,425,000	1,418,433	20
1975	1,000,000	999,338	19
1976	1,000,000	999,918	19
1977	1,000,000	995,193	18
1978	1,000,000	998,904	17
1979	1,000,000	980,563	12
1980	1,000,000[2]	319,877	4
1981	1,000,000[2]	239,954	12
1982	1,000,000[2]	243,438	1
1983	1,000,000[2]	237,643	4
1984	1,000,000[2]	240,000	2
1985	1,000,000[2]	363,900	3
1986	1,000,000[2]	345,126	3
1987	1,000,000[2]	326,176	3
1988	718,000[2]	306,303	5
HEA II-D[3]	3,590,000	1,010,061	9
1989	709,000[2]	297,325	5
HEA II-D	3,651,000	1,326,654	13

[1] indicates initial year of funding for HEA II-B.
[2] indicates HEA II-B Research and Demonstration monies included in the HEA II-B Training appropriation.
[3] indicates initial year of funding for HEA II-D.

Appendix B. U.S. Department of Eduction, Office of Educational Research and Improvement Library Programs. Chronological History of Library Research and Demonstration Grants under HEA Title II-B (1977–1989).

Date	Institution	Title	Cost
1977	American Library Association	The Process of Standards Development for Community Library Services: A Proposed Research Study	$140,000
1977	City University of New York, Herbert H. Lehman College	Development of a Model System for Bilingual Subject Approach in a Minority-Oriented Information Center	$35,590
1977	Drexel University	Survey of Public Library Information and Referral Services	$45,000
1977	Elgin Community College	Research and Demonstration for a Comprehensive Package of Computer Programs to Serve the Community College Learning Resource Center	$70,500
1977	Mitre Corporation	The Role of Microcomputers in Library Automation	$64,000
1977	New England Board of Higher Education	Implementation of a Computerized Interlibrary System to Provide Market Value Information for Resource Sharing to a Multi-type Regional Library Network	$94,460
1977	Oakland University, Rochester, Michigan	A Study of the Relationship between the Intermediary Searcher and the System User and the Assessment of Search Results as Judged by the User	$23,600
1977	Oklahoma State Department of Education	Library Media Specialists: Leadership Training (A Model)	$54,500
1977	South Dakota Department of Education and Cultural Affairs	Training Program for Library Media Specialists to Serve the Handicapped Student	$28,100
1977	State University of New York–Albany	Development of a Responsive Library Acquisitions Formula	$90,000
1977	State University of New York–Buffalo	The Design and Testing of Values to Be Derived in the Training of Librarians through a Systematic Data Gathering Project on Graduates of a Program in Education for Librarianship	$15,150
1977	University of California–Los Angeles	The Use of On-line Microfiche Catalogs for Technical Service and Retrieval of Bibliographic Data	$76,361
1977	University of North Carolina at Greensboro	Children's Media Data Bank and Information Center: A Library Research and Demonstration Project	$69,100

(continued)

58 Mathews

Appendix B. (Continued)

Date	Institution	Title	Cost
1977	University of Pittsburgh	Resistance to Technological Change in Libraries, Part I	$98,700
1977	University of South Carolina	Information Needs Assessment of Rural Groups for Library Program Development (A Model)	$17,398
1977	Virgin Islands Department of Conservation and Cultural Affairs	Virgin Islands Demonstration Library Network Study	$31,100
1977	Washington State Library	A Network Management Tool: Computer Simulation	$20,934
1977	Western Michigan University	Early Childhood Library Programming: Identification and Demonstration of Competencies Needed	$20,000
1978	American Library Association	The Process of Standards Development for Community Library Services	$37,968
1978	Dallas Municipal Library Department	Special Information Services	$69,852
1978	Drexel University	A Quantitative Inventory of Resource Development and Utilization for Metropolitan High School Students	$62,500
1978	Eastern Michigan University	Library Services for Nontraditional Students	$40,890
1978	Educational Testing Service	The Impacts of Automation on Libraries and Information Services	$86,850
1978	Florida State University	A Survey of the State of Public Library Services to the Blind and Physically Handicapped	$45,392
1978	Indiana Department of Public Instruction	Demonstration of Cooperative Development of a Machine-Readable Nonprint Media Base for School Library Media Centers	$149,000
1978	Mitre Corporation	A Guide to Automation for Libraries	$74,370
1978	North Texas State University	The Olney Experiment: A Venture in Coordination and Merger of School and Public Libraries	$39,999
1978	Northern Virginia Training Center for the Mentally Retarded	Model Library Programs for Institutionalized Mentally Retarded and Multiple Handicapped Persons	$17,020
1978	Portland State University	Educational Media for Handicapped Students in Regular K-12 Schools	$69,987
1978	Seattle University	Information for Community Action: A Demonstration of University/Public Library Cooperation in Meeting Community Group's Information Needs	$57,516 '

Appendix B. (Continued)

Date	Institution	Title	Cost
1978	State University of New York–Buffalo	Storage and Care of Nonbook Materials	$14,202
1978	Syracuse University	Developing Alternative Strategies for Evaluating Competencies of Library Media Personnel in Competency-Based Programs	$35,435
1978	Temple University	Nontraditional Acquisitions Models for College Libraries	$58,387
1978	University of North Carolina	Children's Media Data Bank and Information Center	$69,000
1978	University of Pittsburgh	Library Education and Resistance to Technology	$79,966
1978	Western Michigan University	Early Childhood Library Programming: Measurement and Evaluation	$30,569
1979	American Library Association	Curriculum Materials for Library Services to Jail Populations	$41,000
1979	Catholic University of America	Development and Demonstration of Criteria & Guidelines for Quality Control in Continuing Education for Library/Information/Media Personnel: A Provider Evaluation and Approval Program	$90,000
1979	Contract Research Corporation	Libraries in Literacy	$189,193
1979	Drexel University	Survey of Public Library Information & Referral Service: Phase II—Organizational Context & User Reactions	$57,000
1979	Elgin Community College	Research and Demonstration for a Comprehensive Package of Computer Program to Serve Community College Learning Resource Centers—Phase II	$145,000
1979	Gallaudet College	Development of a National Center on Deafness	$28,368
1979	Portland State University	Educational Media for Handicapped Children in Regular K-12 Schools—Phase II	$80,200
1979	Seattle University	Information for Community Action: A Demonstration of University/Public Library Cooperation in Meeting Community Group's Information Needs	$82,457
1979	Simmons College	A Regional Investigation of Citizen's Information Needs in New England	$99,806
1979	Temple University	Alternative Publications in College Libraries: An Evaluative Model	$55,000
1979	University of California–Los Angeles	A Survey of and Guide to Abstracting and Indexing Services for Current Black Periodical Literature	$55,040

(continued)

Appendix B. (Continued)

Date	Institution	Title	Cost
1980	Bibliographic Center for Research, Rocky Mountain Region, Inc.	New Methods for Tracking Online Searching of Computerized Data Bases	$57,125
1980	Contract Research Corporation	Libraries in Literacy: Redesign and Implementation of School Library Section	$49,151
1980	King Research	1981–1982 Library Human Resources: Study of Supply and Demand	$176,151
1980	North Texas State University	Evaluation and Assessment of the Olney Community Library (Continuation)	$36,619
1981	Cuadra Associates	National Research Agenda for the 1980's: Final Report	$127,354
1981	Donald Foos	The Changing Institutional Role of the Public Library	$5,000
1981	King Research, Inc.	New Technology and the Public Library	$5,500
1981	Marilyn Gell Mason	Federal Role in Library Networking	$5,000
1981	Marilyn Gel Mason	Public Library Finance	$5,000
1981	Nina Martin	State Educational Agency Responsibilities and Services for School Media Programs	$7,500
1981	V. Mathews	Libraries: Aids to Life Satisfaction for Older Women	$5,000
1981	Simmons College	Criteria of Effectiveness for Network Delivery of Citizens' Information through Libraries	$56,888
1981	Abigail Studdiford	History of HEA Title II-C, Strengthening Research Library Resources	$9,420
1981	Mary Trochim	The Effect of Membership in Bibliographic Utilities on Interlibrary Loan Trends	$4,850
1981	Betty Turock	Public Library Services to the Aging in the Eighties	$4,993
1981	Blanche Woolls	The Use of Technology in School Library Media Administration	$3,449
1982	King Research, Inc.	New Directions in Library & Information Science Education—Final Report	$243,438
1983	E. H. White Co.	Libraries and the Learning Society (Alliance for Excellence)	$79,000
1983	King Research, Inc.	Diffusion of Innovations in Library and Information Science	$78,643
1983	Lawrence Johnson Associates, Inc.	Role of Libraries in Creating and Providing Viewtext Information Services	$60,000
1983	St. John's University	Historical Review of HEA Title II-B Fellowships	$20,000
1984	American Library Association	Accreditation: A Way Ahead	$45,764
1984	E. H. White Co.	Libraries and the Learning Society	$173,500
1984	Library of Congress Center for the Book	Books in Our Future	$20,000

Appendix B. (Continued)

Date	Institution	Title	Cost
1985	American Library Association	The Cooperative System for Public Library Data Collection (includes $30,000 from Center for Education Statistics)	$57,460
1985	University of Oklahoma	Leadership Training, Guidance, & Direction for the Improvement of Public Library Services to Native Americans	$209,227
1985	University of Wisconsin–Madison	Libraries and Literacy Education	$148,037
1986	American Library Association	The Cooperative System for Public Library Data Collection (includes $30,000 from Center for Education Statistics)	$57,460
1986	Betty Turock	Public Library Services to the Aging in the Eighties: Update	$22,674
1986	Washington Consulting Group	Issues in Library Research—Proposals for the Nineties	$304,339
1987	American Library Association	The Cooperative System for Public Library Data Collection (includes $30,000 from Center for Education Statistics)	$57,460
1987	Drexel University	The Effectiveness of Libraries: The Public Library	$132,000
1987	Library of Congress Center for the Book	Leaders Are Readers	$13,000
1987	Rutgers University	Facilitating Information through Cognitive Models of the Search Process	$94,703
1987	University of Wisconsin–Madison	Evaluating Adult Literacy Projects	$52,969
1987	Washington Consulting Group	Issues in Library Research—Proposals for the Nineties	$44,627
1988	University of Alaska	Demonstrating the Use of Multi-disciplines in Studying and Analyzing Specific Aspects of Life in the Circumpolar North	$63,646
1988	University of Chicago	Medical Literature As a Source of New Knowledge	$41,248
1988	Clarion University	Assessing Information Needs of Rural Americans	$59,443
1988	Indiana University Foundation	To Determine Extent of Dissemination of Public Library Planning Process and the Effect on the Use of Administrative Innovations	$57,143
1988	Rutgers University	Nature and Improvement of Libraries—User Interaction and On-Line Searching for Information Delivery in Libraries	$84,823
1989	City University of New York, Baruch Colleges	Hypermedia and Research Methodology: An Associative Research Model	$55,500

(continued)

Appendix B. (*Continued*)

Date	Institution	Title	Cost
1989	Indiana University	Local Implementations of the Public Library Planning and Role Setting Process	$45,700
1989	Louisiana State University	Age Analysis of Public Library Collections	$66,875
1989	Ohio State University	Developing a Prototype System for Intelligent Information Retrieval	$63,500
1989	University of Wisconsin—Madison	Factors Influencing the Outcome of Challenges to Materials in Middle, Junior, and Senior High School Libraries	$65,750

chapter five

International Aspects of LIS Research

Michael K. Buckland
John N. Gathegi

Research done or reviewed across national frontiers acquires international aspects. Three important characteristics of international research are reviewed: (1) An emphasis on the context and varieties of context of the LIS phenomena being examined; (2) Significant practical difficulties (e.g., distance, language, culture, and bibliographic resources); and (3) A conscious emphasis on comparison. Recommendations include more attention in LIS research to the relationships between information services and their contexts.

Most libraries and information services are abroad, whatever country you happen to live in. Further, foreign library and information services are more or less different from those at home. To ignore foreign libraries and information services is to ignore most of the field and most of the variety within the field. Each country has its own laws, customs, and government practices, many of which affect the flow of information—intentionally or otherwise. Since knowledge and access to information affect the distribution of political power and economic resources, information studies need to be very sensitive to the ideological and political situation in each country. LIS examples include research on intellectual property legislation, regulation of mass media, science policy, and censorship, as well as library service.

The purpose of this chapter is to examine international aspects of LIS research: the characteristics, the benefits, the difficulties, and the remedies. Research acquires international aspects whenever the attention of the doer or the reviewer of research crosses national frontiers.

LIS research includes scholarly studies of library services, librarianship, related retrieval-based information services, information use, and information policies. Chapters 1, 7, and 9 define research and the research found in LIS. This is the sort of investigation undertaken by faculty and advanced students in schools accredited by the Committee on Accreditation of the American Library Association and comparable institutions abroad. This chapter discusses research in the sense of seeking to discover what was (apparently) not previously known.

The purpose of research is to improve and extend our understanding. We seek better theory, i.e., better descriptions of whatever it is. Descriptions and definitions are expressed in terms of relationships: Similarity and various sorts of dissimilarity compared with other things. Further, descriptions need to explain relationships, especially the cause and nature of changes and variations. All of these considerations are based on comparison. In general, the greater the variety of evidence that can be compared, the better the basis for research, for improved understanding.

The characteristic features of LIS research when it has international aspects are: The importance of context, a set of practical difficulties, and an emphasis on comparison. These characteristics are not unique to international studies, but are strongly marked. For example, not all comparative studies are international, but all international studies are comparative, at least implicitly.

CONTEXTS AND COMPARISONS

LIS research acquires international aspects when the doers or the reviewers of research cross national frontiers. To cross a national frontier is to move from one context to another: To a different economy, a different political system, a different educational system, a different commercial and technological infrastructure, and, in particular, a different culture.

The contrast in contexts may be striking, as when traveling from, say, the United States to Ethiopia. Even when the contrast is less dramatic, as when traveling from the Republic of Ireland to the United Kingdom, the differences in infrastructure and culture are nevertheless substantial (Swank, 1963).

Attention to contexts is important for LIS research because, just as flora and fauna are sensitive to their habitat, so also the development of library and other information services is sensitive to their context. Most obviously the publishing, telecommunications, economic, and educational infrastructure varies. So not all patterns of library provision can be quite the same. There is no reason why we should expect them to be the same in different contexts.

Benge (1978) wrote that "basic theory is international, its interpretation is not." We suggest that the situation is more complex. First, theory is not universal. At least, theory is not evenly distributed around the world. Not everyone or every center is equally interested in theory or in the same theories. Different theories tend to arise in different localities, for example, the Prague school of linguistics or the Riga school of semiotics. Within LIS, for example, British and Indian views of classification have a different flavor from U.S. views. For decades the French-language literature on information retrieval has contained theories about the nature of information retrieval that are absent from the English-language literature, defining "document" more broadly to include museum objects and equating documents with evidence (Buckland, forthcoming).

Second, library and information services depend for their existence on the allocation and deployment of resources. Hence, the existence, deployment, and detailed provision of services will depend not only on there being resources to allocate, but also on the social values of those in a position to allocate them (Buckland, 1988; Gathegi, forthcoming). Even if the economic and technological resources were the same, one would not expect the same collections, services, and priorities in Iran, Albania, California, and Guatemala. The variation extends beyond languages to differences in perceptions and values.

For example, the *Encyclopedia of Library and Information Science* (1970, vol. 3, p. 279) states that

> The aim of the British Council has always been the long-term one of promoting cultural exchange and understanding between Britain and other nations. It has deliberately stayed out of the political arena. . . . As a result, over the years, the Council has been able to establish its reputation as a reliable, politically disinterested, cultural organization.

However, another encyclopedia, the *Lexikon des Bibliothekswesens* (1974, vol. 1, pp. 302–303) states that

> In practice the libraries of the British Council serve the imperialistic foreign policy of Great Britain by spreading the point of view of the ruling circles of monopolistic capitalism, through the ideological fight against Marxism-Leninism and against the national liberation movements as well as by influencing some classes of the newly independent countries into the bourgeois, capitalist path of development. (Translation MKB)

Which encyclopedia are we to believe?

One might expect a librarian in Iran to be less likely to select *Satanic Verses* than a librarian in the United States. However, the effects of local cultural context can be very marked in less obvious cases as is shown in a comparative study of protestant clergy in Britain and Germany at the outbreak of the First World War. Both were professionals dedicated to the same branch of Christian theology. Further, at that time the British and the Germans saw themselves as much more closely related, ethnically and culturally, than they do now. However, their reactions to the outbreak of the Great War and the advice and explanations that they preached to their congregations were dramatically and diametrically different (Hoover, 1989).

DIFFICULTIES IN INTERNATIONAL RESEARCH

Certain difficulties are characteristic of international research. These difficulties are not unique to international research, but, cumulatively, they make international research distinctive. (This categorization is based on Clow, 1986, pp. 115–116.)

Language

In spite of its wide usage, the English language is not as pervasive as we might at first presume. International research commonly necessitates working in a foreign language. Even when the language is officially the same, there are subtle differences in meaning. One has to deal not only with the language in general terms, but also with specialized and local vocabulary. The solution is not simply a matter of literal translation. Language is culture-based. One is dealing with nuances of cultural differences embedded in the nuances of language (Sable, 1978; Dickson, 1979).

Distance

Much can be done from the comfort of one's armchair or library table, but serious international research requires traveling and communicating over significant distances. It is not simply a matter of miles, but of inconvenience, effort, costs, and formalities. There are substantial practical problems in trying to live and work in an alien environment.

Culture

As Clow observes (1986, p. 115), "The cultural barrier is perhaps the least feared by intrepid researchers, from whichever zone, though in reality it is the most serious obstacle to meaningful research." The real complexities of cultural differences are below the surface, not readily visible at first inspection.

Politics

Political considerations affect international studies in a variety of ways. Civil wars kill research projects as well as people. In some countries research may be discouraged as a matter of policy. John Gathegi had to redesign his doctoral research because, having traveled from California to East Africa, he was denied a permit to conduct research in one of the two countries he had traveled to study. In other countries a research report construed as critical of the country can be very damaging to an academic career.

Interest

Choice of research is shaped by fashions and interests which, with hindsight, are not always the topics most likely to advance our understanding. LIS *research*, as distinguished from LIS *practice*, would be better served if some of this attention were diverted to some less-studied areas. In particular, there has been relatively little serious analysis of LIS in socialist countries and right-wing dictatorships. These are particularly interesting *because* they are different. What did the Italian fascists see as the mission of popular libraries? How were their views different from those of the Nazis, Soviets, and modern Italians? Much LIS research can be characterized as having a local problem-solving orientation and/or as technique-driven inquiry. The "international" literature appearing in LIS journals is often of a purely descriptive, "tourist-type" report lacking critical analysis. It tends to be read for curiosity and not given much serious scholarly attention. The risk is that unless a distinction is made between "tourist" reports and scholarly analysis, the latter is likely to be undervalued.

Scholarly international research in LIS needs to be distinguished from other international writing if international research is to receive due credit, as in larger disciplines, such as political science and sociology, where this type of scholarship is better established and with which LIS shares much in common. Much LIS research is oriented towards technique and has an emphasis on technology. Studying "how" to do things can be less complicated than studying "why." There are endless opportunities for "how" studies. International LIS research generally requires not just "how" but also "why."

Bibliographic Control

Effectiveness and efficiency in research depend on being able to identify relevant vant materials. However, in some countries bibliographic control is deficient, making it difficult to identify or locate relevant literature. This problem is more marked in developing countries, where bibliographic control, like much else, remains underdeveloped. (See Buckley, 1983, for a discussion of bibliographic control in LIS.)

Resources

Good research depends on evidence. Foreign materials, especially in foreign languages, are difficult to identify, difficult to evaluate for selection, and likely to be little-used. For these reasons, foreign materials needed to support research are less likely to be selected even by North American libraries. Publishing in developing countries is problematic (Altbach, 1987). Trying to use libraries in developing countries is further handicapped by these libraries' chronic shortage of funds (Crowder, 1986).

Foreign doctoral students in U.S. LIS programs commonly and very reasonably do research relating to their home country. Such work is easily regarded as location specific research designed to solve problems unique to the foreign countries (Gathegi, forthcoming). But this view fails to recognize that the research has been accomplished while the student was in *this* country and not in the foreign one, requiring the student to transcend the constraints noted above (Rochester, 1986). These difficulties are, in fact, compounded because the same difficulties also apply, more or less, to faculty members responsible for providing guidance and evaluation. There are significant limits to the extent to which faculty should supervise students' work concerning topics, languages, and contexts with which they are not familiar.

COMPARATIVE STUDIES

Concepts and comparing are foundations upon which scholarship is based. As Bunge (1967, p.74) notes,

> Regarded from a methodological viewpoint concepts are tools for distinguishing items and grouping them: they enable us to perform conceptual and empirical analyses and syntheses. In particular, individual concepts help us to discriminate among individuals. Certain relation concepts make comparison and ordering possible; and quantitative concepts are the core of measurement.

Comparing is basic to sorting, ordering, and systematic arrangement and quantification. Trying to describe anything in terms of itself does not get one very far. In practice things are described by reference to (i.e., comparison with) other things. Less formally one can say that one's understanding of the characteristics and behavior of something is increased by observing it in a diversity of circumstances. One will have a better understanding concerning a class of phenomena if one examines not one example in one circumstance, but numerous examples in a diversity of circumstances.

Studying public libraries in Austria, Hong Kong, and Indiana is likely to provide a more complete understanding of the nature and functioning of public libraries, than would studying public libraries in only *one* of these places. One might be interested in public libraries in only one of these places, Austria perhaps, but, even here, reference to other manifestations is likely to provide additional insights into the Austrian scene. It is an important feature of international studies that they involve a high degree of variety and, therefore, comparison.

Use of the term "comparative librarianship" should not be taken to imply that there are any other studies in librarianship that do *not* involve comparison, only that in some studies, those identified as "comparative," the comparison is more explicit and more self-conscious. Self-consciously "comparative" approaches have proved particularly useful when attempts were made to bring order and understanding to problem areas that seemed, at the time, to be lacking in systematic explanation: comparative anatomy, comparative law, and comparative linguistics.

We speculate that, after comparison, if progress has been achieved in developing plausible theoretical explanations of the diversity, then those theories form the basis for subsequent investigation and the self-conscious comparison can be allowed to recede into the history of the discipline. With this view, "comparative librarianship" is best seen as an important, but transitional, intermediate stage in LIS research.

International studies have a challenging advantage in that they present a great deal of diversity that needs to be noticed, appreciated, and explained. In this sense international studies have an important role to play in the development of theory quite independent of any interest one may have in any particular country. *Library Services in Theory and Context* (Buckland, 1988), an examination of the nature of library services in general terms, was written in Austria and was based, to a significant degree, on a need to explain why library services in Austria differed from library services elsewhere.

CONCLUSION AND RECOMMENDATIONS

LIS research that has international aspects tends to be more complex than research that does not have international aspects because it involves the study of context-sensitive phenomena in different contexts. Generally, there are additional difficulties, notably language and distance. In consequence, the results of research with international aspects are likely to appear cruder than the results of research conducted on phenomena that are better-defined and where the complexity and difficulties are less. The advantage is that, when international research is successful, the results are likely be more powerful because they deal with greater variety.

Despite the difficulties noted above, LIS research with international aspects is well established (Fang, 1981; Smith, 1986). We recommend a number of developments that, in addition to more money and more talent, would lead to improvement in international research in LIS.

First, there should be a greater emphasis on research that, while not necessarily international, addresses areas important in international research, in particular, the mutual interaction between library and information services and their cultural context. In particular, we would recommend more investigation of:

- The politics of library service and information issues (e.g., Hennessy, 1981; Harris, 1986);
- The intellectual history in LIS. Where did ideas come from and how? Who influenced whom? (e.g., Machlup and Mansfield, 1983, Section 5); and
- The cultural roles of information-related institutions that serve to transmit culture selectively and yet are products of their cultures (e.g., Sherman, 1989).

Our impression is that these areas have been receiving increased attention and that even more attention would be better.

Second, examiners of dissertations and reviewers for scholarly journals should expect some reference to foreign work and should be willing to ask for an explanation of its absence whether or not the topic is international.

Third, international studies should not be permitted as doctoral dissertations unless it is clear that dissertation committee members have (among them) sufficient familiarity with the languages, cultures, and contexts involved to provide adequate guidance, supervision, and evaluation.

Fourth, interpretative reviews of foreign developments should be sought by journal editors and conference organizers, especially when they can identify a means of obtaining a report on an area that has been unfashionable and neglected.

Fifth, LIS collections should be surveyed to see what gaps in coverage emerge when these collections are viewed together. Some cooperative collection development might lead to an LIS "Farmington Plan" scheme that could make a significant difference in the long term to the completeness of holdings nationwide where items of marginal interest to any one school are concerned. This is all the more important now that the catalog records of all libraries are becoming accessible from all libraries.

Sixth, whatever can be done to strengthen LIS research and LIS schools abroad would benefit everyone.

Seventh, writings on comparative and international studies in LIS have been accused in the past of a lack of rigor (Danton, 1973). They are not unique in this, but the fact that the accusation has been made in itself reduces the excuses for sloppiness.

There is, perhaps, a certain mystique about international and comparative LIS research. It has, to some extent, been treated as a separate field within LIS. However, as LIS develops, and especially as our understanding of the relationship between information services and their contexts is strengthened, we may not only hope for international studies to become better, but also expect international studies to appear less exotic.

REFERENCES

Altbach, P.G. *The Knowledge Context: Comparative Perspectives on the Distribution of Knowledge.* Albany, NY: State University of New York Press, 1987.

Benge, R.C. "Library Studies and Indigenisation," *Library Scientist*, 5(1978):65–67.

Buckland, M.K. "Information as Thing," *Journal of the American Society for Information Science*, forthcoming.

———. *Library Services in Theory and Context.* 2nd Edition. New York: Pergamon, 1988.

Buckley, B.J. "The Coverage of Library/Information Science Periodicals from the Developing Countries by the Major Abstracting and Indexing Services," *Information and Library Manager*, 2(1983):119.

Bunge, M.A. *Scientific Research I: The Search for System*. New York: Springer Verlag, 1967.

Clow, D. "British-based Research in International and Comparative Librarianship," in *Developments in International and Comparative Librarianship, 1976-1985*, edited by I.A. Smith. London: Library Association, 1986, pp. 103-122.

Crowder, M. "The Book Crisis: Africa's Other Famine," in *Africa Bibliography, 1985*, edited by H. Blackhurst. Manchester, England: Manchester University Press, 1986, pp. xvi-xxi.

Danton, J.P. *Dimensions of Comparative Librarianship*. Chicago, IL: American Library Association, 1973.

Dickson, A.J. "Librarians and the Language Barrier," *Aslib Proceedings*, 31(1979):488-494.

Encyclopedia of Library and Information Science. Vol. 3. New York: Marcel Dekker, 1970.

Fang, J.R. "International and Comparative Librarianship: A Current Assessment," *Bowker Annual*. New York: Bowker, 1981, pp. 366-375.

Gathegi, J.N. "Trailing Technology: Problems in the Application of Contemporary Library Education in Developing Countries," in *Translating an International Education to a National Environment*, edited by J.I. Tallman and J.B. Ojiambo. Metuchen, N.J.: Scarecrow, forthcoming.

Harris, M. "State, Class, and Cultural Reproduction: Toward a Theory of Library Service in the United States," *Advances in Librarianship*. Vol. 14, edited by W. Simonton. New York: Academic Press, 1986, pp. 211-252.

Hennessy, J.A. "Guerilla Librarianship? A Review Article on the Librarianship of Politics and the Politics of Librarianship," *Journal of Librarianship*, 13(1981):248-255.

Hoover, A.J. *God, Germany, and Britain in the Great War: A Study in Clerical Nationalism*. New York: Praeger, 1989.

Lexikon des Bibliothekswesens. 2. Aufl., herausg. von H. Kunze u.G. Rückl. Leipzig, GDR: VEB Verlag für Buch- und Bibliothekswesen, 1974, Bd. 1, pp. 302-303.

Machlup, F and U. Mansfield, Eds. *The Study of Information: Interdisciplinary Messages*. New York: Wiley, 1983.

Rochester, M. *Foreign Students in American Library Education: Impact on Home Countries*. New York: Greenwood Press, 1986.

Sable, M.H. "Language Problem in Comparative and International Librarianship," *Herald of Library and Information Science*, 17(1978):139-141.

Sherman, D. *Worthy Monuments: Art Museums and the Politics of Culture in Nineteenth-Century France*. Cambridge, MA: Harvard Univ. Press, 1989.

Smith, I.A., Ed. *Developments in International and Comparative Librarianship, 1976-1985*. Birmingham, U.K.: International and Comparative Librarianship Group of the Library Association, 1986.

Swank, R.C. "Six Items for Export: International Values in American Librarianship," *Library Journal*, 88(February 15, 1963): 711-716.

chapter six

The Role of Research in the Development of a Profession or a Discipline

Mary Biggs

> The argument is made and defended that librarianship is neither a discipline nor a profession, as that term is defined traditionally. Given this, what types of research are likely to be useful to librarians, and how can it be generated, communicated, and applied in practice? These questions are discussed, and new "research styles" for librarianship are proposed.

Librarianship is neither a discipline nor a profession as traditionally defined, and it has no real prospects of becoming either one.

NEITHER A DISCIPLINE . . .

At the 1990 conference of the Association for Library and Information Science Education (ALISE), Beverly Lynch, long-time university librarian and newly appointed dean of the UCLA library school, stated straightforwardly that she did not consider the field a "discipline" in itself, but rather the product of contributions from many different disciplines. Surprisingly, this stirred no vocal controversy, no objections from the floor, so perhaps it is now an accepted view among library educators. Yet, for decades, writers have referred to "the discipline," and schools have been founded and research programs designed on the apparent assumption that a unified, coherent body of knowledge and system of methodology underlies, or might be developed to underlie, the practice of librarianship.

Scholars' hopes for a definitive intellectual approach have fastened on varying themes. The early faculty of librarianship's first research-minded school, at the University of Chicago, saw the study of reading processes as its natural center. Others have considered "bibliography," variously interpreted, the proper base of the field. Most recently and compellingly, information "science" (or "studies" or "management") has been touted as the likeliest progenitor of a body of theory and fact sufficiently rigorous, broad, and profound to inform wide-ranging practice and elevate it to the status of profession, as well as to support library schools' claims that they house academic disciplines. But just what "information science" encompasses is unclear at best, and its relationship to practice is murkier yet.

In the final analysis, what is taught in library schools and passed off as the field's research base is a pastiche drawn from history, sociology, psychology, economics, mathematics, literature, law, logic, computer science, "product development" in the information industry, etiquette, and common sense. What comes to be applied in practice emanates largely from the last three, floated on the rich stew of each librarian's unique blending of general education, experiences, and interests.

Among the field's most respected writers and faculty members are many whose doctoral degrees, if they have them, were earned not from library schools, but in departments of history, philosophy, physics, sociology, education, or technology. To these "terminal degrees" may or may not have been added training or experience in librarianship. There is no describable discipline and what is sometimes called "the discipline" is, in fact, remarkably chaotic.

. . . NOR A PROFESSION

Discussions of whether librarianship is a profession, of what in fact a profession is, and of what, for that matter, librarianship is, have become overextended and tedious beyond bearing. Like "What is reality?" or "What is love?," if these questions were susceptible to final answers, someone would have come up with them by now. But the durability of the questions confirms their continuing significance for librarians.

In the practical and minimal sense that they do a job usually requiring a college education, librarians are professionals. But against nearly all traditional, more rigorous measures of professionalism, librarianship falls short. It lacks "ownership" of a substantial, coherent, and esoteric body of specialized knowledge; it has succeeded only partially in restricting its practice to people trained in its accredited schools; and it has failed to win community sanction of its claims to professional status. The only test that librarianship meets—and, interestingly, that occupations better-established as professional, such as law and medicine, are failing increasingly often—is the test of altruism, of the subordination of personal goals to client welfare.[1] But this is at least partly a by-product of what

---

[1] The characteristics of a profession have been the subject of many publications. Among the most important and illuminating recent works written from a broad perspective are: Jencks and Riesman (1968, pp. 199–256); Bledstein (1976); Schön (1983); Freidson (1986); and Abbott (1988). Among the significant analyses focused on librarianship are: Ennis and Winger (1962); Hanks and Schmidt (1975); Asheim (1979); Reeves (1980); and Winter (1988).

librarianship lacks. When status and money are hopelessly out of reach, one is unlikely to be seen as grasping.

Librarians probably resemble editors or journalists more closely than doctors or lawyers. Like these "idea people" in publishing, librarians need a good liberal arts education, an interest in ideas, and the ability to communicate. Like them, librarians must have certain skills and command of a unique jargon, and schools must exist to impart them. There are, however, other routes into all three lines of work and considerable evidence that a bright, motivated person can be trained on the job, though graduation from a good occupational school or program may remain the ideal means of entry. Reeves (1980) speculates that librarians cannot achieve recognition as full professionals in the larger society because they cannot claim to monopolize a significant knowledge base. Within the library, however, they may arrange the work so that those tasks they find fundamental to their professional self-image are carefully guarded and neither explained to the non-librarian staff and patrons nor, under any circumstances, turned over to them. Reeves's research (Ibid., p. 137) disclosed that: "Because librarians . . . tended to enjoy a monopoly over relevant information within the library, the question of whether or not their occupation also possessed a societal monopoly on knowledge was never raised as an issue."

THE ROLE OF RESEARCH IN THE DEVELOPMENT OF A DISCIPLINE

Assuming that all of the above is true (and many would disagree), is there reason for us to be concerned further with "the role of research in the development of a discipline or a profession"? The answer is yes, because its role has been rather different from what is generally assumed. This casts the accepted professions in a new, harsher light and carries implications for librarianship.

Research is necessary, of course, for without it, there is only unsystematic observation, intuition, and superstition—no body of trustworthy knowledge, no data to support or challenge explanatory theories and promote their extension or their demise. Two great theoretical sociologists of opposite political persuasions have pointed this out: "No theorist . . . can any longer carry on his work without feeling that the empirical sociologists are looking over his shoulder and that sooner or later he must answer to them," wrote Shils (1980, p. 142). "He knows now that his work can no longer be self-sustaining but that it must justify itself by what it contributes to research" (Ibid.). And Mills (1959, p. 70), deploring "abstracted empiricism," nonetheless observed that "social research," though "advanced by ideas," is "disciplined by fact." Without discipline, there is no discipline.

Once a firm disciplinary floor has been established—basic legal principles, a set of writings accepted as sacred, a hard core of knowledge about the human body and the etiology of disease—intellectual agreements are reached that permit communication and development. Appropriate means of investigation and presentation are designed and systematized; student successors are trained and socialized; theories are formulated and probed using the by-now-understood methods and language of the discipline. Eventually, as more is known and greater specialization becomes necessary, fertile subdisciplines sprout on the one side, while on the other, knowledge overgrows boundaries and intellectual collaborations become irresistible. Sometimes these lead to the development of rather formal interdisciplines and later, perhaps, to accepted new disciplines whose adventuresome, "illegitimate" origins are virtually forgotten.

Today, these processes of definition and development through theoretical analysis and research take place largely within the academy. Here is the time; here are the libraries and labs; here are the trained researchers, "enrollees" in the crucial "invisible colleges." Here, despite academe's financial links to industry and government and academicians' intellectual investment in established paradigms, is thought to reside the necessary spirit of scholarly disinterestedness and valuation of "pure" knowledge.

In an explicitly work-related academic field, such as medicine or law, the question becomes whether and how disciplinary development undergirds and elaborates practice.

THE ROLE OF RESEARCH IN THE DEVELOPMENT OF A PROFESSION

Again, research is necessary, for without it, there can be no articulation of practical procedures that are sufficiently consistent, efficient, specialized, and mystified to win society's recognition that they add up to a "profession." In his social history of American medicine, Starr (1988) shows that until scientific research yielded knowledge that led to uniform, effective therapies, the public resisted doctors' claims to professional status and they could not secure a monopoly on medical treatment.

The basic knowledge shaping professional practice is generated largely by researchers and theoreticians somehow associated, by employment or training, with universities. But it does not follow that all scholarly work carried out in professional schools is communicated to practitioners and used by them or is even potentially helpful to them. Nor are all useful developments in professional practice necessarily stimulated by research or engendered in academe. Nor is everything taught in professional degree programs relevant to practice or *believed* to be relevant. Professional education serves some unacknowledged purposes that have nothing to do with readying students for jobs.

First, it provides congenial employment for intellectuals fascinated by intrinsically intriguing problems. The resulting studies may or may not be able to advance the profession to which these faculty are ostensibly dedicated; and even if they are able to, the faculty may or may not succeed in communicating their findings in comprehensible form—and may or may not even try. A call to relevance by Lynton and Elman (1987) asserts that the academic world as a whole has the responsibility to *share* its knowledge, to see that it is *used*. For this to happen, they conclude ironically and accurately, it would require a major overhaul of the scholarly reward system—which suggests just how remote the "ivory tower" has become.

Starting from the premise that application of professional knowledge is its "main purpose," Abbott (1988) points out that "a profession's formal knowledge system is ordered by abstractions alone." Within the academic sector, he says, this knowledge exists "in a peculiarly disassembled state that prevents its use:" "The entities of diagnosis are disassembled into their components in order that those components may be rationally theorized" (Ibid., p. 57). Drawing an example from librarianship, he notes that the work of the "indexing theorist" typically offers the practicing librarian little (Ibid., p. 53). The same might be said of any other "information scientist," of the classification theorist, the economist of information, the empirical researcher evaluating services, or, for that matter, the library historian. Although some of these people may eventually influence practice by contributing to the development of useful *products*—automated systems, reference works, classification schedules, and the like—in fact, these usually follow on highly applied, commercially funded research. When the "academic knowledge system" fails to provide "new treatments, diagnoses, and inferences for working professionals," Abbott (Ibid., p. 57) finds, "professional jurisdictions gradually weaken"—or never emerge at all.

Jencks and Riesman (1968, pp. 252–253) are also concerned with how professional school curricula relate to practice. They hypothesize:

> As a general rule it is probably fair to say that professional schools cultivate a narrower range of talents than the professions themselves reward, but that they cultivate these talents more deeply. . . . Engineering professors, for example, are usually interested in turning out men with skills appropriate to teachers of engineering; they simply take it for granted that these skills will also be appropriate to the practice of engineering. In many cases, of course, they are right. But in many cases they are probably wrong. . . . What both the young engineer and his employer really want, beyond a minimal level of technical skill, is often a set of human skills, which few engineering professors have and even fewer try to teach.

It is not surprising, then, that studies have shown low or no correlation between students' professional school grades and their subsequent levels of professional success. Either faculty are not teaching critical substance at all or they are not teaching it well. In any case, write Jencks and Riesman (Ibid., p. 206), "the primary role of the professional school may . . . be socialization, not training."

Another significant function of schools is to control entry to occupations, protecting their middle-class status and pay scales by throwing up the obstacle of prolonged, allegedly difficult study, and (at least in theory) preventing labor oversupply. That is, whether or not the material taught must really be known, a profession cannot, "politically," maintain its elevated social position without its program of academic study. This is entirely as important, from the professional's standpoint, as knowing enough to do the job.

Ehrenreich (1989, pp. 80–81) observes that organic chemistry and calculus, which are notorious "screening" courses for pre-med students, have almost nothing to do with treating patients. And Jencks and Riesman (1968, p. 255) speculate:

> The world of [professional] work may not be a pyramid . . . the right metaphor may rather be a factory surrounded by a wall. The gates through the wall are watched by educators, who admit would-be workers only if they perform certain exercises that the educators think good for character, or at least think reliable signs of good character. Like most gatekeepers, these educators are an independent lot, keeping their own hours, making their own judgments, consulting occasionally with one another but almost never with the management inside the walls. They turn away some people whom the management would admit if asked, and they let in others who were neither invited nor wanted.

THE ROLE OF RESEARCH IN THE DEVELOPMENT OF LIBRARIANSHIP

Certainly, research and scholarly analysis have contributed to librarians' knowledge base, supporting the need for specialized training and promoting a sense of professionalism. Our classification schedules and cataloging rules are based on logic, were devised painstakingly, and require training and experience to implement expertly. They may, in fact, comprise librarians' entire cache of unique expertise.

Extracting information from reference books and computerized databases takes knowledge, but it is not knowledge "owned" by our occupation. The needed strategies are designed by librarians reacting passively to the tools given them. In the creation and revision of those tools, librarians may have no role at all, or only an advisory one.

Collection development, another task often seen by librarians as "professional," is perhaps the one least demanding of library-school education. It requires some degree of subject knowledge, an interest in intellectual materials, and a good idea of the library's strengths and mission and of its clients' needs. This has much to do with being a broadly educated person with good judgment, but nothing at all to do with "library science."

Arguing along the same lines, one can dismiss each of librarianship's other traditional tasks: bibliographic instruction, community outreach, storytelling, circulation, resource sharing, and certainly library administration. This is not to say that they represent work that is trivial or easy or takes no training. But neither need they be the exclusive province of a particular "profession." While library schools may offer students valuable introductions to these functions, they are often carried out by librarians who never heard them mentioned in school, for they do not derive from a necessary base of esoteric knowledge, and research contributes little or nothing to their successful performance.

In an article tellingly entitled "Conflict, Interdependence, Mediocrity: Librarians and Library Educators," Rayward (1983), who was then dean of the University of Chicago library school, criticized faculty members for continuing to identify themselves primarily as librarians and thus failing to construct research agendas: "The ethos of the academy remains foreign to them." But he implied that even if research were performed and a core of basic knowledge developed, practitioners would pay no heed (Ibid., pp. 1317, 1313): "They tend to be skeptical of theory. In the face of the daily exigencies of practice they are irreducibly pragmatic." Rayward does not consider the possibility that conventional academic research is simply not applicable to library practice—and that library practice not only falls outside of classic professionalism (a charge he makes), but that this is *right*, *appropriate*, to be expected, to be desired, given what librarians are hired to do.

"TECHNICAL RATIONALITY" VERSUS "REFLECTION-IN-ACTION"

On the reasons for this, Schön (1983, pp. 21–69) is particularly enlightening. He posits two models of practice. The first, which he calls "technical rationality," describes the way an established profession (e.g., medicine) is usually understood to operate. It presupposes clearly identified clients with highly specific needs—leading to a professional practice with fixed, unambiguous ends. *Who* the professional is serving at any one time is clear (the sick patient); *what* must be done for that person is clear (cure the sickness); and *how* to do it can be readily determined from a body of concrete technical knowledge (there are certain drugs, certain surgical techniques, etc., and for the great majority of ailments, which to use and their likely effectiveness have been pretty well established by research).

There is also a built-in accountability, a way to assess *whether* the professional's expertise has value. As Starr (1988) shows, when medical practice seemed ineffective, with no apparent expert base and unreliable results, doctors were not considered professionals. Schön (1983) emphasizes that even physicians sometimes combat the unfamiliar, their technical backgrounds offering little guidance. One thinks, for instance, of those doctors who first encountered AIDS. Still, comparatively speaking, the way that they work fits the "technical rationality" model.

But for many occupations, ends are shifting and ambiguous. The identity of the clients may be uncertain, especially if they do not hire and pay the practitioners directly. Exactly what they need may be hard to tell; the clients themselves may not know clearly, or may believe they have no needs the practitioner can satisfy when in fact they do. Harder still is assessing whether the needs that *can* be identified or inferred have been met. For example, is the collection as well selected as possible? How fully and accurately are reference questions answered? How effective is bibliographic instruction, story hour, The Book Chat Club, or the literacy program? How can we know these things definitely? How can we demonstrate success? We try, but our answers are not as clear-cut and persuasive as a patient living or dying, a case won or lost, a bridge holding or giving way.

Schön (1983, pp. 21–69), therefore, proposes an alternative model of practice: "Reflection-in-Action." Most people who regard themselves as professionals, he says, learn *as* they practice. Rather than pluck knowledge from a static store to apply to a clear and static problem, they must adapt what they know to a situation rife with uncertainties and, through the *process* of dealing with it, add to their knowledge. According to this model, librarianship, for example, would develop practitioner-by-practitioner in an informal, highly dynamic, and rather accidental way. Librarians have often been faulted for writing and reading "how we do it good" articles rather than research, and for emphasizing professional association service over scholarly activities. But if practical knowledge grows most usefully *through* practice, then anecdotal information from other practitioners, communicated through articles, conference programs, and hallway chitchat, quite properly takes priority.

NEW RESEARCH STYLES FOR LIBRARIANSHIP

Librarianship is neither a discipline nor a profession, but rather an occupation grounded in techniques and personal "arts." I have defended this statement partly by referring to librarianship's lack of a coherent body of esoteric and unique basic knowledge, and to the possible irrelevancy of such a body of knowledge, even if it existed, to library practice. While the field's comparative indifference to research is censured, librarians putter along rather well without it. True, they have not succeeded in gaining societal recognition as prestigious professionals, and they regularly receive more meager resources than they think they and their clients need. Yet, in fact, libraries appear to be well regarded on the whole. They receive few complaints. Often they seem more self-critical than criticized by others. This may be because they envision their potential more clearly than outsiders can, or it may be that their standards are unrealistic or pitched higher than their patrons consider necessary. But we might at least consider the possibility that most of the time, we do *well enough*.

In one of his more provocative passages, Bledstein (1976, pp. 99, 102) points out that after the "culture of professionalism" developed:

> Practitioners succeeded by playing on the weaknesses of the client, his vulnerability, helplessness, and general anxiety. . . . Professionals not only lived in an irrational world, they cultivated that irrationality . . . an irrational world, an amoral one in a state of constant crisis, made the professional person who possessed his special knowledge indispensable to the victimized client.

Librarians' essentially decent concern about the informational impoverishment of the public and, by implication, their own failings, may be overheated and perversely self-interested.

This is not to say, however, that there is no research to be done, no analysis to be carried out, that would be useful. Elsewhere, I have argued that we should discard the notion of library "science" as itself a cohesive research field and instead draw to us experts from appropriate disciplines and work with them to explore the problems of technology, communication, economics, politics, sociology, and cognition that affect libraries and information transfer generally (Biggs, in press). This might be done in at least three ways.

First, and most obviously, library school faculty members and doctoral students could collaborate much more closely and frequently than they do now with scholars fully trained in the research methods of relevant disciplines and daily immersed in those disciplines. For example, a problem of library economics might be tackled by a research team comprising a library school professor, who would bring to it his understanding of libraries, and an economist expert in economic theory and methodology. Such collaboration could be formally encouraged in various ways—for instance, through a funding effort analogous to the Cooperative Research Grants awarded by the Council on Library Resources (CLR) to library practitioner-educator pairs. To have real impact, however, they must be more numerous and provide much larger amounts of money. Also, one or more interdisciplinary research centers or "institutes" could be established in research universities blessed with strong, ambitious, extroverted library school faculties and interested scholars in related fields. Administered by the library schools, these might cost little in actual cash, but they would provide structure, space, and equipment for researchers, both student and faculty, from across campus and even from different institutions to meet, talk, write grant proposals, and mount research projects together. Speakers, seminars, and cross-listed courses could also be sponsored by these centers, but always with the purpose of stimulating research on questions of interest to librarians.

Ideally, a grant program or research center (which could function in tandem) would generate a well-edited, -promoted, and -respected "occasional paper" or "report" series. A great incentive to research teaming across divisional boundaries would be interdisciplinary journals and other publication efforts sufficiently comprehensible and interesting to scholars generally, and so intellectually sound, as to be widely credible and widely read. Librarians talk too much to one another, too little to those in other fields.

A second means of building more effectively on the ideas of developed disciplines requires pulling up the doctoral programs by the roots and totally redesigning them. Except, perhaps, for some communal seminars dealing with the problems of librarianship, the new programs would be tailored to students' individual research interests, their requirements worked out in accord with the requirements of doctoral programs in appropriate disciplines. Thus, the student intent on studying, say, the sociology of public library use might take a seminar or do structured independent reading on public libraries, but most of his class time would be spent in graduate sociology courses, and at least one of his principal advisors would be a sociologist. Before embarking on a dissertation, he would have acquired at least as much knowledge of sociological theory and research methods as his counterparts in the sociology department.[2] Some library school faculty may declare that this is already true—that their methods classes, or their requirements that courses be taken extradepartmentally, or that "outside readers" sit on doctoral committees, add up to graduate education that compares well with what the disciplines offer. But this was certainly not true of the two doctoral-granting library schools in which I taught, prestigious though they were. My impression, confirmed by most of the library dissertations I have read, is that the "historians," "sociologists," etc., trained in library schools are simply not as expert in those fields, and are advised by faculty who are not as expert, as are their peers in departments of history and sociology.

A third possibility, of course, is to abandon the library school Ph.D. altogether, replacing it with the degree of the discipline appropriate to the student's research interest. This is basically the second model with its emphasis shifted and might sometimes result in a nearly identical program of study. Librarianship would be a specialty *within* the program, pursued through optional coursework or perhaps just independent study, consultation with at least one librarian advisor, and, of course, the choice of dissertation topic. No longer would advanced research directly pertinent to libraries be confined to the few universities with doctoral-granting library schools. The Ph.D. in a discipline with specialization in librarianship could be earned through any suitable, receptive doctoral program of any university so long as an acceptable library specialist could be persuaded to advise. This makes more sense than continuing to grant doctorates of dubious definition in a nondiscipline. The important thing, however, is not the name of the degree, but the theoretical and methodological sophistication it denotes.

But no matter how researchers are trained, they should form partnerships with practitioners: The practitioners communicating concrete problems of practice, the researchers devising ways to study and solve them, and the practitioners then

---

[2] I am indebted to Abraham Bookstein for this idea.

testing and applying the solutions. Following this research style, which Schön (1983, p. 325) calls "reflective research:" "The roles of practitioner and researcher will have permeable boundaries, and research and practice careers will intertwine as a matter of course."

Again, a grants program resembling, but elaborated far beyond, CLR's modest offering would be helpful. But as crucial as involving practitioners directly in research is successfully communicating research results to them, obtaining their responses, and using these to guide further investigation. The present isolation of academic research from the field must be overcome; one can imagine several mechanisms.

First, library school training in empirical research methods for Master's degree students, which should be mandatory, needs to be expanded, stiffened, and made more exciting. Its goal should be not necessarily to produce researchers, but to prepare new librarians who will be critical, imaginative *consumers* of research findings and research *partners*, capable of formulating investigable questions and addressing them analytically.

Second, we need more formal means of mingling practitioners and scholars, as equals, expressly to discuss research. Individual library schools, the Association for Library and Information Science Education (ALISE), Beta Phi Mu, and other appropriate organizations could adopt and pursue this goal together or singly.

Finally, library and library school directors must provide time for their people to explore common interests together. Lynton and Elman (1987) call for universities to advance in a "new direction" that moves them toward the larger society in order to enrich it with the fruits of their discoveries. But to do this, universities' reward structures must accommodate and encourage professorial consultancies, civic and professional association involvements, writings designed to "popularize" scholarly knowledge or facilitate its teaching, and, indeed, teaching itself: resourceful, inventive, up-to-date, time-consuming, and effective teaching. Presently, all of these are discouraged by universities, the great majority of which recognize only research, grant-getting, and scholarly publishing when promotions and tenure are dispensed. Difficult though it would be to change this system, it may be easier now than at any time in the past 20 years.

An anticipated shift in the faculty labor market will favor job seekers over employers, reducing universities' ability to impose rigid requirements. (Despite the closing of several library schools, there seems *already* to be a faculty shortage in this field.) More significant yet is the recent spate of demands—from laypeople, government officials, and educators themselves—that higher education become more accountable to its constituencies.[3]

---

[3] Notable among many recent examples are: Bennett (1984); Association of American Colleges (1985); Lynton and Elman (1987); Boyer (1987); Cheney (1988); Sykes (1989); Smith (1990); Schaefer (1990); and, from librarianship, Gorman (1990).

However it were to be carried out, under the "reflective research" model scholarly investigation would tangibly *aid* practice, but not necessarily fuel its development into a "profession" as traditionally defined. What matters, however, is not becoming indisputably "professional," whatever that might mean, but finding out how to fulfill our unique mission as well as we can. Research can figure prominently in the process of discovery, but it is unlikely to be conventional research carried out independently by academicians and communicated principally through scholarly journals.

REFERENCES

Abbott, Andrew. *The System of Professions: An Essay on the Division of Labor.* Chicago, IL: University of Chicago Press, 1988.

Asheim, Lester. "Librarians as Professionals," *Library Trends*, 27 (Winter 1979): 225–257.

Association of American Colleges. Project on Redefining the Meaning and Purpose of Baccalaureate Degrees. *Integrity in the College Curriculum: A Report to the Academic Community.* Washington, D.C.: Association of American Colleges, 1985.

Bennett, William J. *To Reclaim a Legacy: A Report on the Humanities in Higher Education.* Washington, D.C.: National Endowment for the Humanities, 1984.

Biggs, Mary. "The Scholarly Vocation and Library Science," *Advances in Librarianship*, in press.

Bledstein, Burton J. *The Culture of Professionalism: The Middle Class and the Development of Higher Education in America.* New York: W. W. Norton, 1976.

Boyer, Ernest L. *College: The Undergraduate Experience in America.* New York: Harper & Row, 1987.

Cheney, Lynne V. "Text of Cheney's 'Report to the President, the Congress, and the American People' on the Humanities in America," *Chronicle of Higher Education*, 35 (September 21, 1988): A17–A23.

Ehrenreich, Barbara. *Fear of Falling: The Inner Life of the Middle Class.* New York: Pantheon Books, 1989.

Ennis, Philip H., and Howard W. Winger, Eds. *Seven Questions about the Profession of Librarianship.* Chicago, IL: University of Chicago Press, 1962.

Freidson, Eliot. *Professional Powers: A Study of the Institutionalization of Formal Knowledge.* Chicago, IL: University of Chicago Press, 1986.

Gorman, Michael. "A Bogus and Dismal Science, or The Eggplant That Ate Library Schools," *American Libraries*, 21 (May 1990): 462–463.

Hanks, Gardner and C. James Schmidt. "An Alternative Model of a Profession for Librarians," *College & Research Libraries*, 36 (May 1975): 175–187.

Jencks, Christopher and David Riesman. *The Academic Revolution.* Garden City, NY: Doubleday, 1968.

Lynton, Ernest A. and Sandra E. Elman. *New Directions for the University: Meeting Society's Needs for Applied Knowledge and Competent Individuals.* San Francisco, CA: Jossey-Bass, 1987.

Mills, C. Wright. *The Sociological Imagination.* New York: Oxford University Press, 1959.
Rayward, W. Boyd. "Conflict, Interdependence, Mediocrity: Librarians and Library Educators," *Library Journal,* 108 (July 1983): 1313–1317.
Reeves, William Joseph. *Librarians as Professionals: The Occupation's Impact on Library Work Arrangements.* Lexington, MA: Lexington Books/D. C. Heath, 1980.
Schaefer, William D. "Much 'Scholarship' in the Humanities Is Done Badly and Probably Shouldn't Be Done at All," *Chronicle of Higher Education,* 37 (March 7, 1990): B1–B3.
Schön, Donald A. *The Reflective Practitioner: How Professionals Think in Action.* New York: Basic Books, 1983.
Shils, Edward A. "The Confluence of Sociological Traditions," in *The Calling of Sociology, and Other Essays on the Pursuit of Learning,* edited by Edward A. Shils. Chicago, IL: University of Chicago Press, 1980, pp. 134–164.
Smith, Page. *Killing the Spirit: Higher Education in America.* New York: Viking, 1990.
Starr, Paul. *The Social Transformation of American Medicine.* New York: Basic Books, 1988.
Sykes, Charles J. *ProfScam: Professors and the Demise of Higher Education.* Washington, D.C.: Regnery Gateway, 1989.
Winter, Michael F. *The Culture and Control of Expertise: Toward a Sociological Understanding of Librarianship.* Westport, CT: Greenwood Press, 1988.

chapter seven

Assessing the Quantity, Quality, and Impact of LIS Research

Nancy A. Van House

This chapter assesses the quantity, quality, and impact of research in library and information science (LIS). It places LIS research in the larger context of social science and professional research. After reviewing some of the functions of research, it demonstrates that more, but not necessarily better, LIS research is being published. LIS research suffers from serious, but not fatal, methodological and content problems. Some possible causes and solutions are discussed. Notably, the field must broaden its scope, reduce its focus on current practice and institutions, and increase its contact with other social science disciplines.

In recent years, a number of LIS writers have discussed the state of LIS research and offered suggestions for improvement; among them are Katzer (1989), McClure and Bishop (1989), Lynch (1984b), and Odi (1982). This chapter too will assess the quantity, quality, and impact of research in library and information science (LIS). Rather than repeat the arguments of other authors, however, this chapter will try to build on them.

This chapter will also attempt to place LIS research in its larger context. LIS has much in common with other professions whose research uses the concepts and methods of the social sciences. It is reassuring to see that other professional schools are grappling with some of the same issues; these are common problems with no simple solutions. Looking to other fields may help LIS researchers to see the problems afresh and to generate new solutions by "borrowing perspectives from other fields, which encourages altering our metaphors and gestalts in ways that challenge the underlying rationales supporting accepted theories" (Whetten, 1989, p.493).

This chapter begins with a recap of the purposes of social science research in general, and research in professional schools in particular. It then evaluates the quantity, quality, and impact of LIS research, and attempts to determine some of the causes of the problems identified. It concludes by offering suggestions for further development of LIS research.

SOCIAL SCIENCE RESEARCH

The traditional pattern of scientific (including social scientific) research is the generation and testing of formal theories.

Theory Building

A social science theory is "a systematic explanation for the observed facts and laws that relate to a specific aspect of life" (Babbie, 1989, p. 46) and a "powerful generalization about recurrent human behavior" (Mohr, 1982, p. 5). A theory is powerful if it is "accurate with respect to a large and well-defined scope of important human behavior" (Ibid.). Social science theories are not descriptions of immutable laws of human behavior, but rather mutable generalizations about observed regularities in behavior, intended to organize our experience in ways that aid understanding (Durbin, 1978).

Whetten (1989), the editor of the *American Management Review*, a preeminent journal of theory-building in management, has defined the elements of good theory as:

- *What*: Which factors are part of the explanation of the phenomenon of interest? A good theory should be parsimonious but comprehensive;
- *How*: How are these factors related? "What" and "how" together define the domain of the theory;
- *Why*: What are the underlying factors that justify the selection of variables and proposed causal relationships?
- *Who, where, and when*: The temporal and contextual limits on the generalizability of a theory. The larger its range, the more powerful the theory.

Theory does not simply describe regularities of behavior or correlations among factors. It attempts to explain "how" and "why." A theory is evaluated according to:

- How good is the logic underlying the theory;
- Does the theory describe phenomena of interest;
- Is its range sufficiently large to be of general interest; and
- How accurately does it describe the phenomena of interest.

Not all theoretical research consists of the construction of new theory; indeed, if it were, research would be fragmented and noncumulative. Theory advances through incremental refinements. Whetten (1989) describes what makes a theoretical contribution:

- Important changes in a theory's "what" and "how"—frequently stimulated by surprising research results;

- Changes in "why" are probably the most fruitful, but also the most difficult avenue of theory development; and
- Changes in "who," "when," and "where:" Testing the applicability of a model in a new setting. New applications are of greatest value when they contribute to a refinement of the theory, that is, when tests of new "who," "when," and "where" refine the "what" and "why."

Theory Testing

Theories are tested against empirical observations. Much of social science research methodology is concerned with this stage of research. Do data support the theory? Are the observations made in such a way that the theory is tested thoroughly and objectively? Are there other logical explanations for the data?

Durbin (1978) says that theorizing is an integral part of empirical investigation, just as empirical analysis has meaning only by reference to the theory from which it is generated. Without theory, empirical investigation is simply description. Without empirical observation, theories cannot be tested.

Some of the criteria by which theory testing is evaluated include:

- The validity and reliability of the research design, including the adequacy of the sample, if any; the validity of the operationalization of the constructs; and the credibility of the statistical analyses;
- The generalizability of the findings; and
- The stability or replicability of the findings.

It is important to note that the positivist epistemology and its associated research methods have recently come under examination by social scientists. Some (e.g., Harris, 1986) have argued that the positivist epistemology is not appropriate for LIS. These criticisms require careful consideration. However, the positivist method remains the most widely accepted in the social sciences and LIS. The issue addressed here is not whether the positivist method is appropriate, but whether LIS researchers who have adopted it are using it capably and appropriately.

Other Functions of Social Science Research

Much of social science research is not aimed at developing cumulative theory, but rather such research fulfills one of the following other functions (Mohr, 1982):

- *Description:* Collecting information about a phenomenon of interest. Good descriptive data can aid theory and decision making. However, description of professional practice and conditions is temporally and contextually con-

strained, and does not explain; it only describes. Information gathered for its own sake is reporting. Gathering information to describe and understand the relationships among phenomena is science (Durbin, 1978);
- *Forecasting*: Forecasting can be done without theory by finding regular patterns of behavior or of relationships between variables. Without theory, however, without an explanation of the "why" and "how," the temporal and contextual limits of the forecasting model are unknown;
- *Evaluation:* Evaluation research uses many of the same methods as other social science research to evaluate specific organizations or programs. By its very nature, however, it tends to be fragmented and noncumulative (Childers, 1990) and the generalizability of its findings is unclear;
- *Understanding current affairs and institutions:* Understanding specific recent events or institutions helps decision making by learning from past mistakes; and
- *Arousing the interest of the investigator and other social scientists*: Mohr (1982, p. 32) suggests that "an empirical discipline will suffer in prestige and accomplishment if the major part of research within it is merely interesting to the investigator and a few colleagues and goes no further in the short run."

"Interest" refers back to Whetten's criteria for theory: Research that tells us something that we did not know before, particularly about the why, but also the what and how, or that extends the who, where, and when, is of most interest because the results are likely to be of interest to more people.

RESEARCH IN THE PROFESSIONS

In his classic discussion of organizational research, Simon (1976) warns that a professional school that depends on practice as its sole source of knowledge becomes, not an innovator, but a slightly out-of-date purveyor of almost-current practice. Research in the professions should be grounded in two areas: professional practice and social science theory (Simon, 1976; Van de Ven, 1989; Schön, 1983). Theory provides the underlying concepts and methods for diagnosing and solving problems; practice supplies the problems and tests the utility of results. Innovation consists of bringing these two areas together: Looking to the profession for new questions to be answered using the methods and concepts of the social sciences; or starting with social scientific knowledge and looking for new applications in the professions.

In an article titled "Nothing Is Quite So Practical As a Good Theory," Van de Ven (1989, p. 486) describes the relationship between theory and professional practice: "Good theory is practical precisely because it advances knowledge in a scientific discipline, guides research toward crucial questions, and enlightens the profession."

Assessing the Quantity, Quality, and Impact of LIS Research 89

Where does theory come from? Simon (1976) did not advocate the building of a theory of management *per se*, but rather the linking of management with theory from other fields. Whetten (1989) advocated borrowing perspectives from other fields.

The function of research in professional schools, then, is to combine knowledge about the problems and practices of the profession with a range of social science disciplines to understand and extend professional practice. The relationship is bi-directional: Practice provides the setting to test theory against behavior, to test the "why" and "how," and discover and extend the "who," "what," and "where."

RESEARCH IN LIS

How much research is being done in LIS? How good is it, according to the standards of social science research? What is the impact of LIS research on both professional practice and our understanding of larger questions? What is the relationship between research in LIS and other social science disciplines?

Quantity of LIS Research

Quantity of research is easier to assess than quality. What is most easily quantified is not research *per se* but publications. The evidence is fragmentary, but it appears that the quantity of published LIS research has been increasing.

Among 23 active researchers interviewed by McClure and Bishop (1989) on the state of LIS research, three out of four believed that the quantity of research was increasing. Most believed that more journals, though not necessarily more good ones, were being published. McClure and Bishop also cite evidence that the ERIC database, which includes both published and unpublished literature, grew during the 1980s.

Feehan, Gragg, Havener, and Kester (1987) found that in 1984, 91 LIS journals met their criteria for research journals. They cite earlier studies using the same criteria which found 39 journals in 1977, 41 in 1981, and 62 in 1983, a marked increase.

Articles in research journals, however, are not necessarily research articles. Among 520 articles randomly selected from the 91 journals, Feehan et al. (Ibid.) classified 23.6 percent as "research." They do not define "research," but it appears that one criterion was the inclusion of data. They conclude that the proportion of research articles in their sample was less than that found in earlier, comparable studies.

Among these "research" articles, 50.5 percent addressed applied concerns, 16.2 percent professional concerns, and only 13 percent theory. ("Theory" is not defined. This figure may be an underestimate since "research" articles were apparently required to report data, eliminating any that were purely theoretical.)

From the data of Feehan et al. (1987) and McClure and Bishop (1989), it appears that:

- The number of LIS research journals and articles is increasing, but the proportion of articles that are research-related is decreasing; and
- Most of what is published addresses applied concerns.

These findings serve to temper somewhat any enthusiasm about the increased number of journals and articles. It is likely that nonresearch articles contribute significantly to the LIS profession. But for LIS *research*, the impact of an increasing number of nonresearch articles is neutral or even negative. LIS has traditionally used the term "research" rather loosely; in particular, both bibliographic searching and the development of new knowledge have been called "research" in LIS (Lynch, 1984a). This mixing of research and nonresearch articles in research journals may further confuse members of the LIS profession about what is and is not research.

Quality of LIS Research

Evaluation of the *quality* social science research is based on two sets of criteria. One has to do with the conduct of research: Its underlying logic and methodology, and the validity and robustness of its conclusions. The other has to do with the topic of the research: Does it address questions that are useful, interesting, or important?

Research cannot be of good quality in the second sense and not the first. If the results are not valid, then whether or not the purported findings are interesting is irrelevant. However, research can be good in the first sense and not the second. For example, there might be a careful and believable study of uninteresting or trivial phenomena.

The first set of criteria cut across the social sciences. The second are more specific to each discipline: What are the important questions? What does a particular piece of research tell us that is new and interesting?

Research in LIS is frequently criticized. Katzer (1989, p. 83), for example, states:

> Research in this field has been criticized for using inappropriate statistics, for being too applied, for using the wrong methods, for not being current, for approaching problems too simply, and for a variety of other weaknesses.

The majority of researchers interviewed by McClure and Bishop (1989) felt that the quality of LIS research had improved in recent years. However, problems remain: "The profession as a whole is poorly equipped to recognize and strive for research quality" (Ibid., p. 135). Summarizing much of the recent literature on LIS research, McClure and Bishop quote complaints about the simplicity of the methods used and of misuse of statistics.

The last 10 years or so has seen a marked increase in both the extent of and variety of statistical and research methods used. Hernon et al. (1989), for example, present an array of statistical methods and cite LIS literature using each. A few years ago they would undoubtedly have found many fewer articles to cite.

Kinnucan, Nelson, and Allen (1987) reviewed the statistical methods used in information science (not including library) research. It is indicative that such a review was even done, limited as it was to examples of standard statistical methods, not innovative ones. Although they do not share others' dismay about the infrequent use of statistics (perhaps because their sample was limited to the information science literature), they did find examples of the misuse of statistics—and in refereed journals, where such misuses should have been caught before publication.

Why the methodological problems? There are several possible reasons. One is that these methods are still fairly new to LIS. Many LIS faculty received their doctorates before quantitative social science methods became common in LIS. They were trained in a research tradition closer to that of the humanities.

Another reason may be that the number of journals has increased faster than the pool of good research articles, so that more lesser-quality articles are being published. Another explanation for methodological problems is suggested by an examination of journal authors and referees. LIS appears to have an unusual (among professions) preponderance of practitioners publishing in the research literature. The plurality of authors are academic librarians, mostly without doctorates, who generally rely on descriptive statistics. Library school faculty, who are more likely to use inferential statistics, account for a much smaller proportion of the published literature (Enger, Quirk, and Stewart, 1989). No comparable data exist for other professions, but in management, for example, the literatures of research and practice are clearly differentiated, presumably with a recognition of the distinct virtues of each.

The editorial boards of most LIS journals are composed largely of practitioners. Most have national reputations as librarians, but have little or no research training or experience. They may be well-qualified to judge the importance to the practice of the subjects of research, but not the quality of the research methods.

Why the involvement of practitioners in research? And why not?

McClure and Bishop's (1989) respondents believed that a major reason for the increase in research publications was the pressure on academic librarians to publish. For many, academic status has brought with it publication as a criterion for advancement, without either training or institutional support.

Ironically, another source of difficulty may be that the profession is doing more training in "research methods." Many library schools now offer—even require—courses on research methods at the master's level. Conference programs and preconferences on doing research are common. This training is commendable but mislabeled.

Quantitative approaches to problem solving are taught in many professional schools, but not as "research methods." Research methods—not quantitative problem solving, but *research* methods—cannot be mastered in one MLS course or a one-day preconference. But this minimal training, combined with pressure to publish, may result in poor (as well as, of course, good) "research," primarily in-house studies, submitted to research journals.

There is much to be commended about librarians using quantitative problem-solving methods and sharing their findings. Not all research must use sophisticated methods and statistical tests. A piece of research on an interesting and significant problem using simple but appropriate methods may be elegant and understandable, and have great impact.

Problems arise when the goal is merely to publish, not to solve an interesting problem; when a simple, clean in-house study is presented as more than it is so as to get published; when methods are used inappropriately; or when authors do not fully understand their own methods and findings and misinterpret their results. And, unfortunately, all these problems appear frequently in the LIS literature.

Significance and Impact of LIS Research

Daft, Griffin, and Yates (1987) asked a group of prominent organizational researchers what makes research significant. They concluded: "[R]esearch is significant because it reaches into the uncertain world of organizations and returns with something clear, tangible, and well-understood" (p. 783). They found that significant studies addressed important problems, challenged previously held assumptions, and produced results that were concrete and understandable. Schön (1983) suggests that, to have impact, professional research should answer interesting questions, change practice, and/or generate further research.

LIS practitioners commonly criticize the research in LIS, particularly that done by nonpractitioners, as irrelevant, while researchers criticize practitioners for ignoring research (McClure, 1989).

Much of LIS literature is designed to aid specific management decisions and change practice. Feehan et al. (1987) found that "applied topics" accounted for 50 percent of the research articles in their sample. Applied research includes action research (Swisher and McClure, 1984), service studies (Goldhor, quoted by Brookes, 1989), evaluation research (Childers, 1990), and consulting and demonstration projects (Katzer, 1989). We will refer to this constellation of types of applied research as "action research" to emphasize their common goal of providing a basis for action.

One effect of the field's growing interest in action research and in "research" training is that the quality of action research has improved. The field has become more knowledgeable about measurement and quantitative problem solving. One sign of this is that library associations have sponsored several measurement manuals for practitioners: Kantor (1984) (sponsored by the Association of Research Libraries), Zweizig and Rodger (1982) (Public Library Association); Van House, Lynch, McClure, Zweizig, and Rodger (1987) (Public Library Association), and Van House, Weil, and McClure (1990) (Association of College and Research Libraries).

Action research in LIS can have significant impact when it meets Thomas and Tymons' (1982) criteria for research relevant to practitioners:

- *Descriptive relevance:* The accuracy of research findings in capturing phenomena encountered by practitioners;
- *Goal relevance:* The correspondence of outcome (or dependent) variables to things that practitioners wish to influence;
- *Operational validity*: The extent to which research addresses factors that are under the practitioners' control;
- *Nonobviousness:* The research meets or exceeds the complexity of common-sense theory already used by practitioner; and
- *Timeliness*: The results are available to practitioners in time to use them to deal with problems.

Taken together, these criteria suggest that research that is of interest to practitioners tells them more than they already knew and in such a way that they can act on the findings to bring about desired changes.

Action research, however, is of limited applicability beyond the local library:

- Most action research studies address a single, short-term problem with, in Whetten's (1989) terms, a limited "what" and "how;"
- Their "who," "where," and "when" are limited to a single library at a point in time; even minimal cross-library comparisons are rarely done, and studies are rarely replicated;
- Their "why" consists primarily of unproven (often unprovable) conjecture, or correlations confused with causality;
- The use of earlier LIS research is often hit or miss. Even less use is made of research from other disciplines or professions. The findings are thus noncumulative and useful earlier methods and findings are inadequately disseminated and tested; and
- Most studies are strictly limited to *current* library practice, rendering them rapidly obsolete.

A recent federally funded attempt to develop an LIS research agenda (*Rethinking the Library in the Information Age*, 1988–1989) produced a list of over 100 questions for research. The topics proposed focused on applied topics and current practice and institutions. None addressed the underlying information-seeking behavior that results in library use. Many were questions of policy choices based on values for which research is of little help, indicating a misunderstanding of the role of research in policy making. Overall, the questions showed a limited concept of the field, and emphasized present applications over long-term understanding.

Some see the solution to the limitations of LIS research in increased theory building (e.g., Brookes, 1989; Houser and Schrader, 1978; Odi, 1982). For example (Brookes, 1989, pp. 238–239),

> at present there is no dominant theoretical research framework in library and information science. . . . [L]ibrarianship is not yet a science because its central theoretical problems remain unsolved. . . . [L]ibrarianship is thus orbiting a theoretical black hole. . . . Many other academic disciplines have found themselves in a similar situation. The common solution is to apply the precepts and methodologies of the sciences to solve fundamental theoretical problems.

There is indeed a paucity of theory building in LIS. Critics, such as Brookes, however, founder when they start listing the "fundamental theoretical problems" to be solved. Despite some interesting and thought-provoking attempts (e.g., Buckland, 1988), there is no general agreement on the beginnings of such a theory, nor even on the topics to be addressed.

RECOMMENDATIONS

There is no quick fix, no shortcut to a robust field with a strong research tradition. Some possible future directions, however, can be suggested.

Theory Building and Borrowing

Theory building is difficult. And repeated attempts at new theory building are not cumulative. Whetten (1989, p. 492) notes that most scholars "are not going to generate a new theory from scratch, but are going to work on improving what already exists."

What to do in a field where little exists? Rather than beginning with the attempt to develop sweeping new theories, it makes sense, as Simon (1976) suggests, to: (1) start with interesting LIS questions and look for methods and concepts from other social sciences to answer them; or (2) start with social scientific knowledge and look for LIS applications. For example, this author used the concepts of Segment Labor Markets to analyze the market for librarians (Van House, 1987) increasing our understanding of both the library labor market and of how labor markets work in general.

Building on other fields requires, of course, knowledge of other fields. Harris (1986) points out that the first University of Chicago GLS faculty were drawn from other fields, had had recent exposure to current developments in those fields, and pursued an interdisciplinary approach. But in time, he says, LIS faculty were graduates of LIS programs which drew back into themselves so that eventually the field suffered from "rigid isolation."

An issue of *Library Trends* on research edited by Lynch (1984b) features several chapters, each describing the application of a particular social science field to LIS. These authors present interesting possible links between these fields and LIS, but they cite surprisingly few studies that have made those links. And when LIS researchers have "borrowed" from other fields, it has often been short term and superficial: One cannot dabble in another research tradition and immediately understand its nuances and complexities. The borrowing of which we speak needs to be truly interdisciplinary research.

Simon (1976) points out that two sets of social systems possess the knowledge needed by professional schools—practitioners and scholars in the relevant disciplines. He says that the main way to get access to the information and skills stored and transmitted in a social system is to participate in it. He recommends that professional schools participate in both. This means that LIS faculty need ties both to practitioners and to scholars in related disciplines: Ties forged on their own campuses and at meetings and conferences of these related disciplines.

This contact should begin in Ph.D. education, where LIS students should be encouraged—required—to take courses and consult with faculty in other disciplines as well as LIS. This contact should be extensive, not just an occasional course. It may even consist of a second Master's or a Ph.D., not in LIS, but in a related field with LIS as its application.

Education and Training

Discussions of the quality of LIS research always emphasize the need for improved education in research methods. However, Ph.D.-level research methods training needs to be distinguished from MLS-level "research methods." The latter is aimed at quantitative problem solving, the former at bringing students into the world of scholarship.

Research methods should not be confused with research. Better training in research methods will help people to carry out research, but will not teach them what research needs to be done.

Practice and Research

Practice and research need to be seen as distinct and interacting components of the LIS field. Research should not be judged exclusively by its contribution to immediate practice. And quantitative decision making should not be confused with research.

The role of practitioners in research needs to be clarified. Requiring academic librarians to publish without the training and institutional support afforded faculty does them a disservice. Presenting in-house management studies to the university community as research on a par with that done by social science faculty discredits the library profession. More insidiously, however, applying publish-or-perish to academic librarians devalues their role as librarians. The implication is that it is better to be pseudo-faculty, than genuine librarians with their own distinct expertise and unique contribution to the university community. This is damaging to the profession's image within the university and to its self-image as well (Wilson, 1979).

One place where this distinction between research and quantitative decision making must be made is in the journals. If action studies are to be published (and often they should be), they should be in different, practitioner-oriented journals if possible. Many disciplines have an array of journals, each with its own niche; such differentiation would be useful in LIS. If the market cannot support such diversity, then distinctions should be made within the journals as to the type of article.

Increased Research

Daft et al.'s (1987) sample of prominent researchers often did not know in advance which projects would be significant. This suggests that the more research there is, the more likely that something will be interesting. The less research people do, the less likely they are to take a "flying leap" on a study that may give unexpected results (or may crash).

Budd (1989) says that, to increase the amount of research done by its faculty, Rutgers University had to change its notion of workload to value research on a par with teaching, administrative activity, and professional service. It is disappointing that this would constitute a *change* for a library school in a research university like Rutgers, but they are not unique. To do research, faculty need support, time, and rewards. It is difficult to include research in the time left over from a high teaching load and a heavy commitment to administration and professional service. More importantly, the values that are transmitted to faculty under such circumstances do not promote research.

Many in the field blame the lack of research on the lack of funding. Funding certainly helps. And funding is much harder to come by in LIS than in many other disciplines. But LIS will not increase its research funding simply by complaining about what it could have done if only it had the opportunity. A track record of interesting, creative research is necessary to attract research support. Research projects designed to be carried out with available resources—including creative use of such resources that exist, such as partnerships, with libraries—can demonstrate that the field has interesting questions and capable researchers who merit further funding.

More (Good) Researchers

The creeping crisis in library research and education is the growing shortage of new faculty. Library schools find it increasingly difficult to fill positions, and a large number of faculty will retire soon. At the same time enrollments in Ph.D. programs are not strong. And many new Ph.D.s are going into library administration where they will do action research, or no research at all.

The problems of library education are beyond the scope of this chapter. But because faculty are a major source of research, especially that which is not action research, the number and quality of people getting Ph.D.s, especially those going into library education, are important here.

One problem is that faculty salaries are often low, especially when one compares what talented people earn as beginning faculty versus as experienced librarians. Another is that, to the extent that library schools emphasize practice and not research, talented students will be drawn to practice and not research. The best way to infect someone with the excitement and challenge of research is to expose them to exciting and challenging research.

The solution to the salary problem is complex, since in most cases it is a university-wide problem. However, LIS faculty often earn even less than their colleagues in other departments. The solution to exciting people about research is perhaps clearer: Increased faculty involvement in research will spill over to students.

Cumulative Research

Much of the research in LIS is episodic. Rarely do researchers build a continuing series of projects so that their own work is a coherent whole. Nor do they often build on one another's work. Fragmentation of research efforts reduces the overall impact of the work that is done.

CONCLUSION

The field of LIS research has problems, but they are not unique:

> Because of its orientation toward applications, we are told, [this field] does not lend itself to systematic inquiry and theoretical testing. Many leading programs . . . do not have as strong a commitment to research as they could, compared to other

disciplines. The field, consequently, must often rely upon scientific findings from other areas. (McCurdy and Cleary, 1984, p. 49)

Is this yet another indictment of LIS? No, it is one of public administration. LIS' problems are shared by other professions.

LIS research has problems, which will not be solved by doing more of the same, only harder and faster. Instead, the field has to consider the factors that have gotten it to this point. Mohr (1982) was quoted above as saying that a field's research needs to be of interest beyond its own boundaries. Schools of LIS are housed in universities, upon whose support the schools and ultimately the profession depend. LIS research needs less inward examination and more outward linkages, both to learn from other fields and to communicate to them the value of LIS and the importance of the questions to be addressed in this growing age of information. The quality of research in LIS needs to be improved through attention both to method and to the nature of the questions that are asked. In particular, LIS research needs to move beyond an understanding of current institutions and research aimed at immediate practice to address broader issues of information and its use drawing on the whole range of social sciences.

REFERENCES

Babbie, Earl. *The Practice of Social Research*. 5th Edition. Belmont, CA: Wadsworth Pub. Co., 1989.

Brookes, Terence A. "The Model of Science and Scientific Models in Librarianship," *Library Trends*, 38 (1989): 237–249.

Buckland, Michael. *Library Services in Theory and Context*. 2nd Edition. Oxford, England: Pergammon Press, 1988.

Budd, Richard W. "Recruiting, Retaining, and Rewarding Research Faculty: Art or Atmosphere?," *Journal of Education for Library and Information Science*, 30 (1989): 83–89.

Childers, Thomas. "Evaluative Research in the Library and Information Field," *Library Trends*, 38 (1990): 250–267.

Daft, Richard L., Ricky W. Griffin, and Valerie Yates. "Retrospective Accounts of Research Factors Associated with Significant and Not-So-Significant Research Outcomes," *Academy of Management Journal*, 30 (1987): 763–785.

Durbin, Robert. *Theory Building*. New York: The Free Press, 1978.

Enger, Kathy B., Georgia Quirk, and J. Andrew Stewart. "Statistical Methods Used by Authors of Library and Information Science Journal Articles," *Library & Information Science Research*, 11 (1989): 37–46.

Feehan, Patricia E., W. Lee Gragg II, W. Michael Havener, and Diane D. Kester. "Library and Information Science Research: An Analysis of the 1984 Journal Literature," *Library & Information Science Research*, 9 (1987): 173–185.

Harris, Michael. "The Dialectic of Defeat: Antimonies in Research in Library and Information Science," *Library Trends*, 34 (1986): 515–531.

Assessing the Quantity, Quality, and Impact of LIS Research 99

Hernon, Peter, Pat K. Bryant, Maya De, Barbara D. Farah, Andrew J. Golub, Hae-young Rieh Hwang, and Li-ling Kuo. *Statistics for Library Decision Making*. Norwood, NJ: Ablex, 1989.

Houser, Lloyd, and Alvin M. Schrader. *The Search for a Scientific Profession: Library Science Education in the United States and Canada*. Metuchen, NJ: Scarecrow Press, 1978.

Kantor, Paul B. *Objective Performance Measures for Academic and Research Libraries*. Washington, D.C.: Association of Research Libraries, 1984.

Katzer, Jeffrey. "ALA and the Status of Research in Library/Information Science," *Library & Information Science Research*, 11 (1989): 83–87.

Kinnucan, Mark T., Michael J. Nelson, and Bryce L. Allen. "Statistical Methods in Information Science Research," *Annual Review of Information Science and Technology*. Vol. 22, edited by Martha E. Williams. New York: Elsevier, 1987, pp. 147–178.

Lynch, Mary Jo. "Research and Librarianship: an Uneasy Connection," *Library Trends*, 32 (1984a): 367–84.

———, Ed. "Research in Librarianship," *Library Trends*, 32 (Spring, 1984b), entire issue.

McClure, Charles. "Increasing the Usefulness of Research for Library Managers: Propositions, Issues, and Strategies," *Library Trends*, 38 (1989): 280–294.

———, and Ann Bishop. "The Status of Research in Library/Information Science: Guarded Optimism," *College & Research Libraries*, 50 (1989): 127–143.

McCurdy, Howard E. and Robert E. Cleary. "Why Can't We Resolve the Research Issue in Public Administration?," *Public Administration Review*, 44 (1984): 49–55.

Mohr, Lawrence B. *Explaining Organizational Behavior: The Limits and Possibilities of Theory and Research*. San Francisco, CA: Jossey-Bass, 1982.

Odi, Amusi. "Creative Research and Theory Building in Library and Information Sciences," *College & Research Libraries*, 43 (1982): 312–319.

Rethinking the Library in the Information Age. 3 vols. Prepared by the Department of Education, Office of Educational Research and Improvement, Office of Library Programs. Washington, D.C.: GPO, 1988–1989.

Schön, Donald A. *The Reflective Practitioner: How Professionals Think in Action*. New York: Basic Books, 1983.

Simon, Herbert A. "The Business School: A Problem in Organizational Design," *Administrative Behavior: a Study of Decision-Making Processes in Administrative Organizations*. 3rd Edition. New York: Free Press, 1976, pp. 335–356.

Swisher, Robert, and Charles McClure. *Research for Decision Making: Methods for Librarians*. Chicago, IL: American Library Association, 1984.

Thomas, Kenneth W. and Walter G. Tymon, Jr. "Necessary Properties of Relevant Research: Lessons from Recent Criticisms of the Organizational Sciences," *Academy of Management Review*, 7 (1982): 345–352.

Van de Ven, Andrew H. "Nothing Is Quite So Practical as a Good Theory," *Academy of Management Review*, 14 (1989): 486–489.

Van House, Nancy A. "Labor Market Segmentation and Librarian Salaries," *Library Quarterly*, 57 (1987): 171–189.

———, Mary Jo Lynch, Charles R. McClure, Douglas L. Zweizig, and Eleanor Jo Rodger. *Output Measures for Public Libraries: A Manual of Standardized Procedures*. 2nd Edition. Chicago, IL: American Library Association, 1987.

———, Beth Weil, and Charles R. McClure. *Measuring Academic Library Performance: A Practical Approach*. Chicago, IL: American Library Association, 1990.

Whetten, David. "What Constitutes a Theoretical Contribution?," *Academy of Management Review*, 14 (1989): 490–495.

Wilson, Pauline. "Librarians as Teachers: The Study of an Organizational Fiction," *Library Quarterly*, 49 (1979): 146–162.

Zweizig, Douglas and Eleanor Jo Rodger. *Output Measures for Public Libraries*. Chicago, IL: American Library Association, 1982.

chapter eight

The Cross-Disciplinary Imperative of LIS Research

Robert Grover
Roger C. Greer

> Contemporary society is complex, global, and conducive to holistic thinking. A new paradigm has emerged, characterized by such traits as recognition of complex and heterarchic views of phenomena, of an indeterminate future, of a mutual view of causality, and of perspective research. This emerging paradigm suggests that LIS research must be cross-disciplinary in order for the library and information profession to provide meaningful contributions to society. This chapter describes the emerging new paradigm, presents trends and needs in LIS research, and suggests strategies to integrate a broader context for LIS research.

The technology which brought about the "Information Age" has melded the disparate elements of society which the industrial age separated. While industrial society divided the whole into parts for assembly line production, contemporary society looks at "the whole." A "new paradigm" has arisen, and it promotes holistic thinking and recognition of multiple options for our dealings with the world.

Naisbitt and Aburdene (1990) describe the next decade as one which will encounter a variety of forces, integrated, in large part, by technology. A global economy will be fueled by telecommunications networking made possible by fiber optic cable spanning the globe. Commerce has become international to the extent that American chains are found in the Orient, South America, and Europe; the Big Mac and Kentucky Fried Chicken are favorites everywhere. Western dress and the English language are integral to the culture of people throughout the world; at the same time, there is a countertrend to maintain nationalistic cultures in the context of a global economy.

This merging of cultures, governments, and economies is paralleled by the corresponding dismantling of intellectual barriers which existed during the industrial age. As the Berlin Wall toppled in 1989, enabling a rush of Germans to advocate unification, so too are the barriers to intellectual inquiry collapsing, enabling cross-disciplinary exchange of ideas and a wider sharing of research methods.

The thesis of this chapter is that library and information science (LIS) research *must* be cross-disciplinary in order for the library and information profession to progress in contemporary society. Because the library and information profession is a product of society, it must meet societal needs and effectively contribute to that society in order to flourish. The role of LIS research is to provide a framework for the library and information profession which:

- Articulates the function of this discipline (information science) and the library and information profession in society;
- Identifies the position of these fields in the context of intellectual endeavors (positions it within the intellectual and social framework in society); and
- Provides direction, parameters, guidance, and values for the practicing information professional. Because of the central role of information transfer in the affairs of humankind, and the ubiquitous nature of information, LIS research must take a holistic approach to problems and cross discipline boundaries in its search for understanding.

This chapter describes the new paradigm which influences the thinking and direction of our society, presents cross-disciplinary trends and needs in LIS research, and suggests what should be done to integrate a broader context for LIS research.

THE NEW PARADIGM

Contemporary society may be characterized by complexity and rapid change, propelled by new technologies. Society demands new approaches to solve new problems. Capra (1982, p. 25) pointed out that the crises in our society, e.g., pollution, chemical contamination of our food supply, nutritional and infectious diseases, and the energy crisis, cannot be addressed by academics who "subscribe to narrow perceptions of reality which are inadequate for dealing with the major problems of our time." Another manifestation of the need for new solutions were the events in Eastern Europe during the latter part of 1989—a complete surprise to every element of our political, academic, and communication communities. The fact that existing theories, research, and forecasts failed to even approximate a prediction of the cascade of political upheavals among the nations of the Warsaw Pact is perhaps the most visible evidence of the inadequacies of the dominant paradigm as a framework to view today's reality.

Capra (Ibid.) observed that during the 16th and 17th centuries the machine became the dominant metaphor for viewing the world. According to the Cartesian view (Ibid., p. 66), "the world was believed to be a mechanical system that could be described objectively, without ever mentioning the human observer, and such an objective description of nature became the ideal of all science." However, atomic physics created a new basis for science and a new world view which required a holistic perspective. As other disciplines and professions (e.g., biology, psychology, medicine, and education) have moved inexorably toward a new perspective in understanding contemporary society, so must LIS.

Characteristics of the New Paradigm

This paradigm shift from the mechanistic to the holistic has been explored by Ferguson (1980), Schwartz and Ogilvy (1979), and Lincoln and Guba (1985). A paradigm, a lens through which a community views the world (Achleitner and Hale, 1990, p. 3), filters the thoughts of the researcher. The new paradigm recognizes a greater complexity of relationships among phenomena, denying the possibility of directional cause and effect relationships of isolated variables. There may be no hierarchial order to the world as once believed.

Figure 8-1 provides a synthesis by Achleitner and Hale (1988, pp. 4–5) of work by Schwartz and Ogilvy (1979, p. 13) and Lincoln and Guba (1985, pp. 51–56). Displayed are the characteristic shifts from the dominant to the emerging paradigm, followed by a description of associated beliefs.

These seven characteristics are not isolated variables; they are intertwined, forming a synergetic relationship. In the library and information profession, the influence of the new paradigm is most evident in the value shift that is emerging. Traditionally, the dominant value was related to quantity. The new paradigm, on the other hand, places a higher value on quality. The most prestigious libraries were those with the largest collections, the largest staff, the largest budgets, the largest buildings, etc. This value system ignored the most important factor, the user. Prestige accrued from the mere possession of these quantities with the unspoken implication that they were used. In fact, evidence of use, user satisfaction, even user needs remained outside the measures associated with prestige.

As in other sectors of society, management, for example, the paradigm shift has provoked a concern for people. Size, if a factor at all, is very likely valued for its smallness which enables a closer link with the consumer, customer, or client. Libraries are also affected by this societal about face, but have been further confronted with their own success in creating networks for information transfer and compact means of storage and retrieval of information. It is commonplace for the professional press to boast that access to the world's knowledge base is available to even the smallest library or information service agency because of the successful creation of an information transfer infrastructure. Given the fact that every library has the potential of every other library, regardless of size, a value system indexed by size becomes meaningless.

Figure 8-1. Dominant/Emergent Paradigms and Associated Beliefs.

Dominant/Emergent Paradigms	Associated Beliefs
From simple toward complex views of phenomena being investigated	Diversity, interaction, and open systems are symptoms of the emerging reality. An entity cannot be separated from its interactive environment. Complex systems develop "unique properties" and a system can no longer be perceived as the "sum of its parts."
From hierarchic toward heterarchic views of order in the world being studied	The old notion of order was based on the concept of hierarchy. God was seen as the Prime Mover. The emergent concept is that there may be no natural order, that orders exist side by side.
From mechanical toward holographic metaphors used to describe the phenomena being studied	The machine (Newtonian mechanics) metaphor is replaced by the hologram. Images in the hologram are created through a dynamic process of interaction. Information is distributed throughout the image. Pieces of the whole are evident throughout the system.
From a view that the unknown can be determined toward an acceptance that the future is indeterminate	Heisenberg's Indeterminacy Principle states that at a subatomic level the future state of a particle is in principle not predictable. In complex systems the future cannot be predicted.
From linear toward a mutual view of causality	Distinction between cause and effect is meaningless. The new paradigm adds positive feedback and feed-forward.
From a view of change as a planned assembly of events toward change morphogenetically	A system that functions under conditions of openness, diversity, complexity, and indeterminacy changes morphogenetically. Change occurs unpredictably.
From objective research toward perspective research	Perception, instruments, and disciplines are not neutral.

A shift in focus from the collection, organization, etc., of the physical or electronic record to a concern for the user in the record is consistent with other factors in society. In addition, an awareness that the primary distinction between the services of a professional and those of a technician is a matter of customization. Each provides a service, but the professional diagnoses the nature of the needs and fashions a customized response. The technician diagnoses the need and provides a standard response based on the application of learned formulas, techniques, and procedures. The clients' satisfaction is presumed to increase with the quality of the customized response provided by the professional. A major thrust for future research must focus on the user of information and the diagnostic phase of professional service. This research must necessarily draw upon diverse fields and disciplines to fashion a new theory base for this major step forward for the information professions.

In summary, the new paradigm is characterized by ambiguity, interconnectedness, complexity, and recognition of constant change. The new paradigm is consistent with the general systems theory of von Bertalanffy (1956), recognizing the importance of a holistic approach to understanding phenomena, and it complements the beliefs associated with positivism. The new paradigm eschews the notion that research must be objective in favor of a recognition that naturalistic or qualitative forms of perspective inquiry are also valid.

Implications for LIS Research

The emerging paradigm, outlined above, implies that research in library and information science must recognize the complexity of the society in which library and information professionals work. Following are implications for research drawn from Lincoln (1985, pp. 141–156):

- Research must be conducted in a natural setting, diminishing the possibility that the controlling of variables in an experimental study could influence results of a research project. A problem must be studied in its context in order to be fully understood
- Researchers must be satisfied with an emergent research design. Because of the complexity of societal problems, it is not possible to formulate in advance a complex research design which will enable collection of data to address a problem. People are unpredictable, and researchers must allow sufficient flexibility in the research design to allow the scope of the problem to unfold unpredictably
- The human is a plausible research-gathering instrument who can understand the emotional, or irrational, elements of a problem
- Qualitative methods of data gathering are most appropriate for accommodating complex social issues involving multiple, sometimes conflicting, realities. Such methods include interviews, observations, content analysis, and various unobtrusive measures. Qualitative measures are also very useful in social problems for which little is known. For a more complete analysis of qualitative methods, see Grover and Glazier (1985) and Glazier (1985)
- Utilization of tacit knowledge, including impressions and intuition. Data gathering may include data collected by the researcher which may be collected through the recognition of nonverbal cues or responses to "hunches" or "gut reaction." These intuitive responses, part of the holistic approach to problem solving, may lead to the discovery of new relationships, resulting in new theory. For a discussion and comparison of intuitive, impressionistic, systematic, and scientific data gathering methods, see Hale (1986).

- Data analysis is usually accomplished with inductive reasoning. Use of qualitative methods results in the collection of large quantities of rich data. By pouring over the data, trends and relationships tend to emerge through inductive analysis, resulting in discoveries which had not been anticipated
- Purposive or theoretical sampling replaces random samples in research projects. In-depth study of a small sample, using qualitative methods, requires a sample which is representative of a special population under study. The sample is selected specifically to represent the problem under study
- Boundaries for the study are determined by the problem under investigation. Because there are no hypotheses to provide limitations for data collection, the nature of the problem, the subjects, and limitations of time, resources, and energy of the researcher impose boundaries on the study
- Application of findings must be done tentatively. Because of the limited scope of a study, a small purposive sample, and the contextual nature of the inquiry, generalizability must be carefully and tentatively considered. Generalizations are best applied in numerous contexts and the theory restated and refined in order to fit the definitions imposed by the new context
- The case study takes on new importance. Careful and detailed description of a context for purpose of analysis results in a thoroughly implemented case study which provides the circumstances for participants to react to the context of their environment. The case study method is an important vehicle for gaining that understanding required for theory building.

The complexity of social research, required for new understandings in library and information science, implies study in a diverse body of knowledge to understand the human condition. Because the focus of LIS research must include human behavior in its myriad manifestations relating to information and information transfer, research models must draw upon the disciplines within the family of social and behavioral science for methodologies which can generate applicable theory. Human behavior can be better understood through the study of such social science disciplines as history, anthropology, psychology, sociology, communication, ethnography, and linguistics. The study of information systems can build upon theory from management, engineering, physics, systems theory, organizational theory, and other applied areas of inquiry. Theory can be borrowed from a variety of other disciplines, grounded in library and information practice, and restated for application in the library and information profession. Hence, the thesis that library and information science research must be cross-disciplinary in nature.

ASSESSMENT OF CURRENT LIS RESEARCH

The main body of LIS research to date has not reflected new paradigm thinking. LIS research has been characterized as fragmented, noncumulative, pragmatic, and methodologically primitive. While the authors do not profess to present a comprehensive assessment of library and information science research analysis, we present selected studies which have addressed the state of existing research and suggest the need for cross-disciplinary research in library and information science.

Analysis of LIS Research

Childers (1984, pp. 524–525) cited numerous studies which characterized research in the field as "noncumulative and episodic." Furthermore, he concluded that many (p. 526)

> library school faculty are not fully socialized into their role as the academic segment of a profession and as a university faculty—that, rather, they play the role of professional librarian, rather than professional academic.

Childers' conclusion apparently is reinforced by the results of Hayes' (1983) study of faculty members' publication patterns, which found that many faculty members in library schools, even senior faculty, published relatively little, an average of only 7.85 articles per person during the 15-year period of the study.

The focus of LIS research often has been on the technologies of the profession rather than on the clientele. While surveys and experiments on the processes of the profession make up a substantial part of the research published, studies of the public are less frequent. An analysis of articles in library professional journals published during the years 1950, 1960, 1965, 1970, and 1975 resulted in the following observation by Peritz (1980, p. 264): "The papers seem to be more process oriented than client oriented, and they are more concerned with the needs of the professional community than with the needs of any other group." In addition, Peritz (Ibid., p. 265) noted few studies on the handicapped, minorities, the aged, disadvantaged users, and the subject of reading.

Feehan, Gragg, Havener, and Kester (1987) corroborated the Peritz findings and concluded (1) there is a need for more theoretical research in library and information science; (2) historical, survey, and other descriptive research methods were dominant data-gathering techniques; and (3) descriptive analytical techniques dominate over the predictive and inferential.

A recent study of 165 research articles randomly selected from 37 LIS refereed journals published during the years 1981–1985, found that 30 percent of the references cited were from other disciplines, and the articles reporting research lacked conceptual structure and rigor (Grover, Glazier, and Tsai, 1990).

These findings suggest that many faculty members of library and information science schools, who represent the core of the scholarly community of the profession, are not productive researchers who actively investigate the social context of the library and information professions. While there is evidence that some attempt to adapt theory from other disciplines is emerging, it is essential that this trend increases dramatically in order to frame LIS research conceptually.

Recommendations to Improve Research

Harris (1986), and McClure and Bishop (1989), have assessed research in the field and suggest new approaches to improve research in the profession. Harris (1986, p. 525) noted that "nearly all of our research is policy oriented, designed for immediate professional consumption." Furthermore, "All too frequently the emphasis is on professionally palatable findings. Most of the work is quite expert, but it is also unwilling to challenge conventional wisdom."

Harris (Ibid., pp. 522–523) suggested that, to be meaningful to the profession, research should be holistic, reflexive and empirical, and dialectical. In other words, researchers should investigate problems in library and information science by basing the research on social science theory and relating the problems being addressed to their broader social context. By reflexive and empirical, Harris meant that researchers should recognize that the goal of objectivism supported by positivists is not possible, and it should be recognized that the researcher shares the world of the subjects being studied. The intent is not to slide back into a nonscientific subjective appraisal of a problem, but to attempt to synthesize both empiricism and reflection in research. Researchers should recognize the subjectivity inherent in social science research, and they should recognize change and instability in the library and information profession and in society.

McClure and Bishop (1989) interviewed leading researchers in library and information science in an effort to assess the quality of research and to make recommendations. Among the strategies for improving LIS research they offered were the following (Ibid., p. 140):

- Encourage faculty at schools of LIS to take refresher courses in research methods from related disciplines, e.g., education, public administration, psychology, sociology, and/or communication; and
- Encourage LIS researchers to work on cross-disciplinary research teams or obtain the involvement of researchers outside LIS.

A recent research agenda published by the Office of Library Programs, U.S. Department of Education, proposed a series of research questions intended to address issues facing libraries and information agencies in the future (*Rethinking the Library in the Information Age*, 1988–1989). The questions address a multitude of problems, including social, economic, technological, psychological, educational, management, cultural, and policy issues. The magnitude and breadth of the research agenda would indicate a need to borrow from the theory base of other disciplines in order to address these areas of concern.

It seems clear that the current status of research in LIS and the needs of the profession would urge the application of cross-disciplinary research in the field.

THE RESEARCH THAT IS NEEDED

A chasm exists between the research that is needed and the research that has been produced to date. While the literature for years has professed a need for broadly theoretical research, that research has not been forthcoming on a broad scale, as evidenced by the assessments referred to above. The section which follows will suggest a direction for cross-disciplinary research.

The Library and Information Profession

A profession may be viewed as a social group with a shared knowledge relating to the resolution of a societal need. This shared knowledge includes a theory base (science) which provides a framework for analysis and appraisal of individual needs, a technology (procedures and practices) employed to satisfy a need, and an art which embodies the values, limitations, attitudes, and motivations for integrating the theory and technology on behalf of a client, client group, or society. The objective of professional practice is a customized resolution of a diagnosed need. The fundamental role of research within a profession is to increase understanding of the context of professional practice by providing a theoretical framework for diagnosis (analysis), prescription (recommendation), treatment (implementation), and evaluation for the purpose of facilitating information transfer.

The so-called "mature professions" (Larson, 1977, p. 55) have developed academic disciplines which provide a broad theoretical base for professional practice. The nature of that body of knowledge shared by library and information professionals has been identified by Butler (1933), Shera (1972), and Greer (1987), among others. These views have prescribed a multidisciplinary theory base for the library and information profession.

In his *Introduction to Library Science*, Butler (1933, p. xi) articulated the social role of the library, claiming that it is a "necessary unit in the social fabric." He probed the psychological, sociological, and historical dimensions of library science. Shera (1972), in his exploration of the theory base for the profession, outlined the central area of study as "social epistemology." Recognizing the contributions of psychology to librarians, he also cited the need to study the nature of knowledge as it influences social organizations. Shera (Ibid., p. 112) described social epistemology and its purpose:

> —a study of the ways in which society as a whole achieves a perceptive relation to its *total* environment. It should lift the study of intellectual life from that of a

scrutiny of the individual to an inquiry into the means by which a society, nation, or culture achieves understanding of stimuli which act upon it. The focus of this new discipline should be upon the production, flow, integration, and consumption of communicated thought throughout the social fabric. From such a discipline should emerge a new body of knowledge about, and a new synthesis of, the interaction between knowledge and social activity.

Greer (1987) has provided a conceptual framework for the discipline of information science which is multidisciplinary. This discipline is based upon the common features of the diverse roles in the library and information profession.

Information professionals, in their variety of roles, working in a variety of environments, have in common four characteristics. Those characteristics, common to librarians, information managers, archivists, records managers, and information specialists by any other name, are as follows:

- Responsibility for the design and management of an information base, whether packaged (books, serials, software, etc.) or unpackaged (electronically stored, locally produced database in a variety of formats);
- Responsibility for the design and management of an information organization, consisting of staff, an information system, equipment, space, and financial resources which enables delivery of information from the information base to clientele;
- Responsibility for identifying and accommodating the information needs and unique cognitive and behavioral styles of individuals among the information system's clientele; and
- Responsibility for identifying the information needs of client groups and facilitating the information transfer process to those groups.

The Discipline of Information Science

Addressing these four characteristics is the basis for the knowledge base which supports the library and information profession. Study of these four areas comprises the theoretical foundation for the education and research required for maintenance and advancement of the profession.

Greer (1987) suggested that information science must develop the broad discipline supporting the information professions. This discipline must inventory and extrapolate theory, methodologies, and constructs from other disciplines to develop a research base for the library and information profession. The fields of analysis encompassed by the discipline of information science, and addressing the common roles of information professionals are:

- *Sociology of information*—how society creates, produces, disseminates, organizes, diffuses, utilizes, preserves, or discards information (information is defined as recorded knowledge);

- *Information psychology*—how individuals seek, acquire, organize, process, utilize, and store information;
- *Information organization management*—how to create and manage an organization designed to support and enhance the information transfer process; and
- *Information engineering*—how to design databases, library collections, and other information systems customized to meet the needs of a client population.

Although each of these fields of study is distinctive enough to be considered separately, interrelationships among the four fields are profound, and no field can be understood without consideration of the impact by the other fields.

A Proposed Research Model

Research must examine the influence of environmental and policy contexts—economic, cultural, technological, political, legislative, etc.—on each of the four fields and the influences of each of the fields on the others. These societal factors must be considered along with the processes required in the management of a library/information system. This environmental context includes the following:

- *Culture*—language, philosophical and moral values, history, and all of those valued characteristics developed over time by the clientele, considered as an entity, or by the constituent groups served by the information agency;
- *Geography*—aspects such as climate and topographical characteristics;
- *Political structure of society*—the system for governance and underlying values regarding the role of government in the society served by the information agency;
- *Legislation and regulations* issued by legislative and regulatory agencies of the government which influence operation of the information agency;
- *The economic system* under which the information agency functions;
- *Technology infrastructure* as it is utilized within the agency and by the clientele; and
- *Information policy*—such as copyright laws, policies regarding secrecy, censorship, privacy, the public's right to know, government responsibility to inform, and those policies which influence the transfer of information to a clientele.

This mutually interdependent, multidisciplinary, holistic perspective of the role of the information professions suggests that information science must emerge as a new social science discipline. Research to create new knowledge in this discipline must build upon the knowledge base and research of such disciplines as psychology, economics, intellectual history, political theory, cultural anthropology, ethnography, cybernetics, and bibliometrics.

This discipline which supports practice in the library and information profession is cross-disciplinary, and the research which contributes to this discipline must also be cross-disciplinary.

CONCLUSION

Given the importance of information and knowledge to the economic, political, and social well-being of contemporary society, research which creates new knowledge enabling the more effective creation, recording, production, organization, storage, retrieval, and diffusion of information is critical. Also critical is the application of new theory to the practice of the library and information profession. The new paradigm which is influencing research and thought implies that research in LIS should study information in its context and apply innovative, even intuitive, methods to explain the human condition in this complex society. In order to address the need for more holistic, broadly theoretical research, the cross-disciplinary nature of information science must be recognized, and theory must be borrowed from other disciplines, applied to library and information settings, and refined for the library and information profession. Both theory and research methods must be borrowed from other disciplines from the sciences, social sciences, and humanities in order to infuse new ideas into the rapidly expanding profession and the dynamic discipline of information science. If the library and information profession is to remain a vital force in society, the research conducted for the profession *must* be cross-disciplinary. To foster meaningful research in the society characterized by an emerging new paradigm, a holistic, cross-disciplinary approach is indeed an imperative.

REFERENCES

Achleitner, H. and M.L. Hale. "Dissolving Certainties: Managing Information in the New Information Environment," in *Information Literacies for the Twenty-first Century*, edited by V.L.P. Blake and R. Tjoumas. Boston, MA: G.K. Hall, 1990, pp. 253–262.

―――― & M.L. Hale. "Information Transfer: Educating Information Professionals in the Emergent Paradigm," in *Bridging the Gap between Theory and Practice; Proceedings of the First Joint Meeting between the Association Internationale des Ecoles de de Sciences de l'Information (AIESI) and the Association for Library and Information Science Education (ALISE)*, edited by R. Savard. Montreal: AIESI and ALISE, May 25–27, 1988, pp. 1–12.

Butler, P. *An Introduction to Library Science*. Chicago, IL: University of Chicago Press, 1933.

Capra, F. *The Turning Point*. New York: Simon & Schuster, 1982.

Childers, T. "Will the Cycle Be Unbroken?" *Library Trends*, 32 (1984):521–535.

Feehan, P.E., W.L. Gragg II, W.M. Havener, and D.D. Kester. "Library and Information Science Research: An Analysis of the 1984 Journal Literature," *Library & Information Science Research*, 9 (1987): 173–185.

Ferguson, M. *The Aquarian Conspiracy*. New York: St. Martin's Press, 1980.

Glazier, J. "Structured Observation: How It Works," *College & Research Libraries News*, 46 (1985):105–108.

Greer, R.C. "A Model for the Discipline of Information Science," in *Intellectual Foundations for Information Professionals*, edited by H. Achleitner. New York: Columbia University Press, 1987, pp. 3–25.

Grover, R., and J. Glazier. "Implications for Application of Qualitative Methods to Library and Information Science Research," *Library & Information Science Research*, 7 (1985):247–260.

_____. J. Glazier, and M. Tsai. "An Analysis of Research in Library and Information Science," Unpublished manuscript, Emporia State University, 1990.

Hale, M.L. "Administrators and Information: A Review of Methodologies Used for Diagnosing Information Use," in *Advances in Librarianship*. Vol. 14, edited by W. Simonton. Orlando, FL: Academic Press, 1986, pp. 75–99.

Harris, M.H. "The Dialectic of Defeat: Antimonies in Research in Library and Information Science," *Library Trends*, 34 (1986):515–531.

Hayes, R.M. "Citation Statistics as a Measure of Faculty Research Productivity," *Journal of Education for Librarianship*, 23 (1983):151–172.

Larson, M.S. *The Rise of Professionalism: A Sociological Analysis*. Berkeley, CA: University of California Press, 1977.

Lincoln, Y.S. "The Substance of the Emergent Paradigm: Implications for Researchers," in *Organizational Theory and Inquiry: The Paradigm Revolution*, edited by Y.S. Lincoln. Beverly Hills, CA: Sage Publications, 1985, pp. 137–157.

_____. and E.G. Guba. *Naturalistic Inquiry*. Beverly Hills, CA: Sage, 1985.

McClure, C.R. and A. Bishop. "The Status of Research in Library/Information Science: Guarded Optimism," *College & Research Libraries*, 50 (1989):127–143.

Naisbitt, J. and P. Aburdene. *Megatrends 2000: Ten New Directions for the 1990's*. New York: William Morrow, 1990.

Peritz, B.C. "The Methods of Library Science Research: Some Results from a Bibliometric Survey," *Library Research*, 2 (1980):251–268

Rethinking the Library in the Information Age: Issues in Library Research, Proposals for the 1990s. Prepared by the U.S. Department of Education. 3 volumes. Washington, D.C.: GPO, 1988–1989.

Schwartz, P. and J. Ogilvy. *The Emergent Paradigm: Changing Patterns of Thought and Belief* (Analytical Report 7). Menlo Park, CA: SRI International, Values and Lifestyle Program, 1979.

Shera, J.H. *The Foundations of Education for Librarianship*. New York: Becker and Hayes, 1972.

Von Bertalanffy, L. "General System Theory," *General Systems*, 1 (1956):1–10.

chapter nine

Whither LIS Research: Ideology, Funding, and Educational Standards

Ellen Altman

Lack of agreement about what the focus of LIS research should be and the appropriate methodologies to employ have fragmented the research community into several ideological camps. This lack of focus combined with the broadened definition of "information" and interest in studying it has created opportunities for researchers in other disciplines to garner a larger and larger share of federally funded research grants. The research infrastructure cannot be improved unless prominent researchers oversee educational standards.

What qualifies as library/information science research? Is it any type of investigation conducted by people who call themselves librarians or information scientists? Or, must the investigation focus solely on matters closely related to libraries, their users, and containers of information such as books and databases. Or, would the research be "better" if it were more cross-disciplinary or interdisciplinary? Should it be based on a theory? Must the theory fit a particular paradigm? Must hypotheses be stated and tested? Does research require the collection of data that can be counted? Must those data be subjected to statistical testing? Is discovering new knowledge a requisite? Does the investigation have to prove something? Are the findings more important if they help solve practical problems?

All these questions, and more, have been raised in the professional literature by proponents or opponents of various sides. The very fact that these questions can be raised is itself an indication that there is no overarching paradigm, no consensus within the discipline. The objectives of this chapter are to describe the ideological differences that hinder progress in the discipline, to document the decline of interest in research by Federal funding agencies, and to demonstrate the failure of the profession's leadership to provide affirmation of the importance of research.

DIFFERENCES IN IDEOLOGY

Traditionally, research conducted by librarians has been bibliography-related. However, the focus and types of research have shifted rather dramatically in the past 60 years, or so, from bibliography and historical descriptions of libraries (the preponderance of the dissertations done in the early years at the University of Chicago) to a greater number of studies based on the counting of phenomenon and then subjecting those counts to statistical testing. One factor contributing to this shift has certainly been the efforts by some in the academic community to emulate the methods of scientific research—hypothesis testing and the use of inferential statistics—to demonstrate the "science" in library and information science. Yet, almost everyone who has written about research in librarianship agrees that it could be better. They disagree over what constitutes better, about how to make it better, and for whom to make it better.

As in all academic areas, library and information science (LIS) researchers fall into distinct clusters, with yet finer distinctions within clusters. The major division in LIS is between the *Quals* and the *Quants*. Naturally, both groups disagree about the importance of mathematics, especially statistics, in research. But they differ even more over the problems to be investigated and the methods to be employed. The *Quals* tend to use social science methods, such as historiography, ethnography and qualitative sociology, to study the "library" and its users in terms of social phenomenon. Their approach is inductive in that they use documents, observations, and interviews to build their conclusions. The *Quants* are interested in finding, if not laws, at least patterns to predict how phenomenon will behave. Their approach is deductive in that they specify what they are attempting to prove and what variables will be used before any data are collected. They are adherents of what is popularly known as the "scientific method."

The first researchers in the field (that is, in Librarianship, long before there was an Information Science) were *Quals*. They were primarily historians—of books, libraries, librarians, bibliography, and publishing; and all the ancillary elements of the book trade. David Kaser and Haynes McMullin are examples of contemporary *Quals*. One characteristic of the historians is that, alone among the LIS researchers, they seldom write introspective pieces about the nature of LIS research. They simply continue their historical projects in their own individual ways.

The Social Theorists represent a newer contingent of *Quals*. They insist that research must not ignore the historical and cultural factors in society at large which have exerted, and continue to exert, great influence over the library as an institution. The most persuasive proponent of the social theorists is Harris (1986a, 1986b). In a *Library Trends* paper, he argues that research ought to focus on what Shera (1965, p. 29) called "social epistemology," "the analysis of the production, distribution, and utilization of intellectual products in much the same fashion as that in which the production, distribution, and utilization of material products have long been investigated."

Contemporary research, Harris (1986b, p. 217) believes, has instead concentrated on finding solutions to internal administrative problems of "performance, productivity, and usefulness." He claims the "scientific" approach has led to "a body of literature that is fragmented and reductionist" (p.222).

Further, he charges that researchers have "fallen prey to the siren called 'positivism,'" undue concentration on observable phenomena and facts without any inquiry into causes (p. 218). In an earlier paper (1986a, p. 522), he dismisses the scientists' contributions by charging that "a positivist approach has proven of little value as a means of producing knowledge of social reality. It seems equally clear that library physics is not about to begin."

He charges (1986b, p. 222) that although LIS research is "increasingly technically sophisticated, it is also increasingly trivial." Harris maintains that the search for a paradigm in the social sciences has been fruitless and mostly abandoned since the 1960s.

The *Quants*, in contrast to the *Quals*, are vastly more concerned with numbers, statistics, probabilities, and paradigms. Despite their reliance on quantitative methods, the *Quants* are also split into two disparate camps—the *Scientists* and the *Engineers*. Houser is a leading proponent of the view that *library* research should adhere to the scientific method as described by Kuhn (1962). According to Houser (1988), the point of research is to test theory which fits within a disciplinary paradigm. The theory should be tested by verifying hypotheses. Such an approach would permit explanation and prediction of phenomenon, which in turn would build our knowledge base in a coherent manner. He says unless these things are done, librarianship cannot claim to be a discipline. He argues that the proper focus of library research is the study of literatures.

His own analysis of the papers published in the *Journal of the American Society for Information Science* denies the existence of an information science. Houser (1988, p.3) claims that what is called information science is

> merely library science. . . . There is no scientific community of information scientists. In fact, there is no justification for naming a new branch of science information science. . . and no justification for people to term themselves "information scientists."

Contrasting with Houser's *Scientist* view are the opinions of the *Engineers*—those who actually call themselves "information scientists." A former president of the American Society for Information Science (Williams, 1988, pp. 17–18) readily conceded that the group is an amalgam of many disciplines. She acknowledges that information science "uses the theories, principles, techniques and technologies of a variety of disciplines toward the solution of information problems." This liberal view can be considered eclectic, or as evidence that the entire field is in disarray. Some evidence for the latter view is indicated by the diversity in educational preparation and programs in "information science," with students enrolled in library schools, business schools, and engineering departments.

The outstanding characteristic of the *Engineers* is their emphasis on pragmatic problem solving. At the more mundane level, they attack problems of organization, management, and control in "conventional" libraries. At a more complex level, they are attacking, in bits and pieces, the problem of designing an "information retrieval" system that actually retrieves data of interest to an inquirer. Ideally, they strive for a system which gets past the black marks on the paper to uncover meaning. If technology is not the solution to all problems, it is certainly the first place they look. The solution to problems is defined as the need to make the technology better or to learn how to use it better. They tend to write terse, equation-laden papers for the *Journal of the American Society for Information Science* and *Information Processing and Management*. One sometimes wonders about the substantive value of these efforts. When reviewing a group of papers in information science, Robert Fairthorne supposedly remarked: "It is not a question of the emperor having no clothes, but of some very elaborate clothes covering no emperor."

This lack of consensus about what problems to study and what methods to employ has perhaps contributed to a declining interest on the part of major agencies in funding proposals submitted by LIS researchers. These agencies are turning to researchers in other disciplines for new approaches to the study of information problems. This intellectual disarray, at least in part, stems from the apparent lack of interest on the part of those who approve educational standards, such as the American Library Association's Committee on Accreditation, to insist on setting any standards for scholarship.

THE AGENCIES FUNDING RESEARCH

Library researchers, whether *Quants* or *Quals*, have been getting a progressively smaller and smaller share of the Federal research dollar. Cuadra Associates' (1982) *A Library and Information Science Research Agenda for the 1980s: Final Report* identified 600 projects funded through the 1970s. The report determined that most of the money for research support, $51.5 million, came from three Federal agencies. These were the National Science Foundation's Division of Information Science and Technology, $33 million; the Department of Education's Office of Libraries and Learning Resources, $10.5 million; and the National Library of Medicine (NLM), $8 million. Although these same agencies were also the major sources of funding during the 1980s, their funding patterns have undergone substantial change.

Despite the Federal deficit and the widespread impression that the Reagan administration was not supportive of research, the money allocated to LIS research rose dramatically during his two terms. For fiscal years 1980 through 1988, the National Library of Medicine spent $22,038,253 for research projects.[1] This amount was $14 million more than NLM's extramural research budget in the previous decade. The National Science Foundation's (NSF) allocation of $84,992,490 was $52 million more than the agency had received in the 1970s.

Despite these impressive gains, LIS researchers garnered only a small fraction of that money. Of the more than $22 million in grants awarded by NLM, LIS researchers received $801,000; that represents 3.63 percent of all awards. Their share of awards from NSF was 3.2 percent, or somewhat less than $3.5 million out of approximately $85 million awarded since 1980 for research in information science and technology.

The data in the following tables were taken from the *ALA Yearbook* (1976–1989), the *Bowker Annual of Library and Book Trade Information* (1980–1989), and the *National Library of Medicine News* ("Grant Awards," 1988). These sources give the names of the principal investigators and their institutional affiliations. The names of the investigators were checked against the directory issues of *Journal of Education for Library and Information Science* (1979–1987) and the *Directory of Library and Information Professionals* (1988) to determine how many worked in library environments or held degrees in the discipline. The grants to LIS researchers were separated into three groups: those to LIS faculty, those to LIS consulting firms, and those to LIS researchers in other information agencies. No published data are available on the number of proposals submitted but not funded, so it cannot be determined if the proportion of unsuccessful proposals submitted by librarians is higher than those submitted by researchers in other disciplines. Yet, the data in the tables indicate that researchers from other disciplines are winning a larger and larger slice of the research-related dollars and proportion of projects funded.

Table 9-1 shows that the National Library of Medicine awarded 174 grants during the 1980s. Library researchers received only 15 of them. Their best year at NLM during the decade was 1980 when they won 9.4 percent of grant monies allocated. Even so, that figure represented a sharp drop from the 18.5 percent and 31.59 percent they had received in the two years preceding. In fiscal year 1988 they did not receive a single award.

The situation is even more dismal at NSF as indicated by Table 9-2. That agency awarded 1,156 grants from fiscal years 1980 through 1988. Yet, library-oriented researchers won only 42 (3.63%) of them. Of the nearly $85 million disbursed for these projects, librarians received less than $3.5 million. Table 9-2 shows that the

---

[1] This does not include funding for either the Integrated Academic Information Management Systems demonstration projects or the Resource Improvement grants for hospital libraries.

Table 9–1. Research Grants Awarded by the National Library of Medicine.

Fiscal Year	1980	1981	1982	1983	1984	1985	1986	1987	1988	Total
Total Grants Made	11	19	20	27	18	32	29	10	8	174
Awarded to										
Library Schools		1	2	4	1	2	1	3	0	14
Consulting Firms										
Other Library	1									1
% to LIS Researchers	9.09%	5.26%	10.00%	14.81%	5.56%	6.25%	3.45%	30.00%	0.00%	8.62%
Total Library Related (000)	$88	$105	$110	$235	$32	$107	$53	$71	$0	$801
Total $ Awarded (000)	$936	$2,136	$2,170	$3,057	$2,129	$4,753	$4,368	$1,480	$1,009	$22,038
% of $ to LIS Researchers	9.41%	4.90%	5.08%	7.67%	1.49%	2.26%	1.22%	4.81%	0.00%	3.63%

proportion of research dollars received by librarians dropped from a high of 10.19 percent in 1980 to slightly over 1 percent by the end of the decade.

Why the decline? One likely reason is that these agencies have broadened their definition of "information" to embrace a wide variety of approaches. The Division of Information Science and Technology at NSF was reorganized in 1986 and renamed Division of Information, Robotics and Intelligent Systems. As a result, its research interests shifted toward engineering. Nevertheless, NSF appears to have decided to reserve a share of its funds specifically for library/information science studies. Since 1982, the agency has released a special list to the *Bowker Annual of Library and Book Trade Information*, which it calls "Library-Related Research." That term has been stretched to include topics such as artificial intelligence, relational databases, and parallel computation. The data compiled from those lists of "Library-Related Research" show that over the seven years covered by these figures, library/information scientists have won 16.8 percent of the grants and 19.62 percent of the dollars. Considering that these awards are categorized as "Library-Related," it is discouraging that LIS researchers have not been more successful in competing for these grants.

Another reason for the decline in awards to LIS researchers is tougher competition. According to Brownstein (1986, p. 17), former Director of the Division of Information Science and Technology, NSF sees information science as

> changing from an applied service-oriented activity to a basic research discipline. . . . Applied work is supported only if it has broad generic application potential. It [information science] interacts dynamically with rapidly advancing high technology and with socio-technical trends in advanced industrial economies.

Clearly, NSF sees information science in a broad context and expects the proposals that it funds to be on the cutting edge.

The story is similar at NLM. From firsthand experience as a member of NLM's interdisciplinary review panel from 1981–1985, the author is aware that the competition is formidable. Many of the proposals are submitted by physicians who are developing expert systems to diagnose symptoms, suggest treatments, or train medical school students. Many of these physicians know quite a lot about computers; some even hold Ph.D.s in computer science. The sophistion of most of the proposed work recommended for funding is high. The review panels' expectations for the quality of proposals submitted are equally as high.

In contrast to NSF and NLM, the Office of Library Programs in the Department of Education, once a prime source of funding for LIS, has fallen on hard times. Since 1980, it has received slightly more than $2.5 million for R&D efforts. That figure represents only 17.5 percent of the more than $15 million it had spent during the 1970s for research and demonstration. Between fiscal years 1981 and 1986, the office awarded no competitive research grants. Funding for the R&D program has been continually threatened over the past decade. This agency has become essentially a bystander insofar as LIS research is concerned.

Table 9–2. Research Grants Awarded by the National Science Foundation, Division of Information Science and Technology.

Fiscal Year	1980	1981	1982	1983	1984	1985	1986	1987	1988	Total
Total Grants Made	60	67	57	85	117	150	148	264	208	1156
Awarded to										
Library Schools	1	4	1	2	3	6	4	5	3	29
Library Consulting Firms		4		3	3					10
Other Library	2		1							3
% to LIS Researchers	5.00%	11.94%	3.51%	5.88%	5.13%	4.00%	2.70%	1.89%	1.44%	3.63%
Total Library Related (000)	$523	$485	$280	$486	$357	$443	$378	$210	$222	$3,383
Total $ Awarded (000)	$5,129	$5,719	$4,758	$6,589	$8,332	$11,274	$10,037	$16,775	$16,380	$84,992
% of $ to LIS Researchers	10.19%	8.48%	5.88%	7.37%	4.32%	3.93%	3.77%	1.25%	0.93%	3.20%

ACCREDITATION AND "SUSTAINED PRODUCTIVE SCHOLARSHIP"

Katzer (1989, p. 85) has taken ALA's Committee on Accreditation (COA) to task, claiming that the self-study that the schools must complete every seven years asks nothing "about the research productivity of faculty or the development of research skills or appreciation in its students" and thus, communicates "that research is not a high priority" (p. 87). The Committee on Accreditation (1989, p. 89) responded, in part, that "the *Standards for Accreditation 1972* state that the 'faculty as a group should evidence. . . a record of sustained productive scholarship.'" "Instructions specifically request that schools 'list research published and grants received during the past year.'"

The committee evaluating the role of professional associations for the Office of Library Programs supported Katzer's position. Their conclusions ("Building an Infrastructure for Library Research," 1989) are included in the final report of the research agenda for the 1990s, *Rethinking the Library in the Information Age* (1989, p. 27):

> Because one of the largest populations of current and future researchers is located in the schools of Library and Information Science, ALA's accreditation role can be used more effectively to support the development of a research infrastructure for this field. Ideally, what is needed is the development of a "research ethic" in the schools. . . . ALA can significantly accelerate the development of this research ethic . . . through its accreditation process.

To accomplish this acceleration, the committee recommended that the importance of research be "emphasized from the top" with a policy statement, that questions about research be included in the self-study report, and that "reminders" be included in the annual reports submitted by the schools.

COA, and by extension the American Library Association (ALA), has taken the position that "sustained productive scholarship" is important. Because of this, it would be reasonable to expect those persons appointed to the Committee to judge the scholarship of others themselves to have compiled such a record. Two studies—Hayes (1983) and Varlejs and Dalrymple (1986)—provide data on the productivity of LIS faculty. Hayes' data are based on the publications of, and citations to, 411 associate professors and professors at accredited programs listed in the directory issue of the *Journal of Education for Librarianship*. His data, taken from both the citation and source indexes in *Social Sciences Citation Index* (*SSCI*), cover a 15-year span, from 1965–1980. However, Hayes cautions that *SSCI* does not index many of the journals in which LIS faculty might publish. Nor does *SSCI* attempt comprehensive coverage of citations in monographs. His ranking of the "top 40" faculty is based on a "normalized number of citations in 'substantive' articles (p. 153)"—not the actual number of publications produced

LIS Research: Ideology, Funding, and Educational Standards   123

by each faculty member, nor the number of actual citations. Although one might disagree with the premise and the process of how the data were "normalized," the paper does indicate productivity. Only three persons who have ever served on COA since the adoption of the new standards are on the list. They occupy positions 26, 39, and 40. In their study, Varlejs and Dalrymple (1986) counted the publications of LIS faculty for only the year 1983. Among the 15 individuals who produced the most publications, only one had served on COA.

If scholarship, especially for faculty members, is a prerequisite for service on the Committee on Accreditation, then the research record *prior to appointment* should reflect that qualification. To determine if it did, the names of faculty who served on the Committee and dates of their terms were taken from the *ALA Yearbook*, the *ALA Handbook of Organization* (1989), and periodical articles about the committee. These names were checked in *Library Literature* (1962–1989) to identify all their publications, not just those reflecting research. Book reviews, *ALA Yearbook* summaries, and articles about them were excluded. The journal articles were categorized as refereed or nonrefereed based on surveys of journal policies by Budd (1988) and Fraley and Via (1985).

Table 9-3 ranks the total number of publications by LIS faculty *prior to* their appointments to COA. The records for some members after their appointment are considerably more impressive. As Table 9-3 demonstrates, the publications are unevenly distributed among the group. Six persons account for 90 of the 185 publications. The median for the group is 6. One faculty member had no publications in the 10 years prior to appointment. More disturbing is that the preponderance of the faculty publications appeared in nonrefereed journals.

An examination of the titles of the journals in which the faculty had been published revealed *no* articles in 13 of the 31 journals which are considered most important by LIS deans as reported by Kohl and Davis (1985). Table 9-4 reproduces the top journals on the list of deans' preferences and compares them with the journals in which these faculty actually were published.

A Spearman-rank correlation coefficient was computed to measure the relationship between the two sets of rankings. The r' value of -2.47 indicates a negative relationship. A z test was applied to determine if that negative correlation was significant. A z value exceeding 2.58 means that the probability of the magnitude of this negative correlation being attributable to chance is 1 in 100. The calculated value for $z = -7.83$, which indicates that the likelihood of chance accounting for the discrepancy between the two groups is negligible.

Over the past 18 years, only one article by a COA faculty member has appeared in *Library Quarterly*, the *Journal of the American Society for Information Science*, or *College & Research Libraries*. Yet, the deans ranked these three journals first, second, and third in importance. The two articles in *Library & Information Science Research* were written by the same person. Although 12 articles appeared in *Library Journal*, two people wrote 11 of them. These same two account for four of the six articles in *American Libraries*.

124 Altman

Table 9-3. Publication Records of LIS Faculty in the 10 Years Prior to COA Appointment.

Faculty Member	Books	Chapters	Refereed Articles	Nonrefereed Articles	Bibliographies	Total Publications
1	1	5	1	24		31
2		1	9	9		19
3	1	5	2	11		19
4		1	1	13		15
5		2	7	4		13
6		1	8	3		12
7	3	1	3	2		9
8	1	3	2	2		8
9	1	3		4		8
10		2	3	2		7
11		1	2	4		7
12	1		2		3	6
13	1	1	1	2		5
14				4		4
15	1	1		2		4
16				2	1	3
17			2	1		3
18		1	1	1		3
19				2		2
20		1	1			2
21			1		1	2
22			2			2
23				1		1
24						0
Totals:	10	29	48	94	4	185

Table 9-4. Rankings of Journal Prestige by LIS Deans Compared with Publication Records of Faculty on COA.

Journals Preferred by Deans	Most Papers by COA Faculty
Library Quarterly	Special Libraries
Journal of the American Society for Information Science	Library Journal
	Drexel Library Quarterly
College & Research Libraries	School Library Journal
Library Trends	RQ
Journal of Education for Library & Information Science	Wilson Library Bulletin
	American Libraries
Library Resources & Technical Services	School Library Media Quarterly
Drexel Library Quarterly	Journal of Academic Librarianship
Special Libraries	Journal of Education for Library & Information Science
Information Technology & Libraries	
Library & Information Science Research	Library Trends
Journal of Academic Librarianship	

The publication patterns of the COA members become even more curious when compared against Watson's (1985) data tabulating articles by LIS faculty who had published in "eleven major library science periodicals" between 1979 and 1983. Watson found that over 50 percent of the articles in *Library & Information Science Research* had been written by LIS faculty. They wrote over 40 percent of the papers in both *Library Quarterly* and the *Journal of Library History*, and nearly 30 percent of those in *Library Trends*. Although LIS faculty wrote nearly 12 percent of the articles appearing in *College & Research Libraries*, COA members wrote no papers for *College & Research Libraries* during that time. Clearly, a record of "sustained productive scholarship" has not been a requisite for appointment to the Committee on Accreditation.

RECOMMENDATIONS TO IMPROVE RESEARCH

This chapter has focused on three issues: the ideological differences among LIS researchers, the declining level of Federal support for their proposals, and the profession's failure to set a standard for scholarship. Of these three, the latter is the only one which can be directly and effectively altered. The strong ideological differences that separate various LIS researchers are no stronger (or weaker) than those that separate various other disciplines. Both *Quals* and *Quants* need to recognize that their respective methods have their strong and weak points. As for obtaining increased funding, lobbying and complaints that we are not getting our "fair share" will be of little avail. Innovative proposals on the cutting edge are needed instead.

The first step is to put our own house in order. In looking over the list of those appointed to COA since the adoption of the 1972 standards, one might conclude that "balance" has been the primary criterion for selection. Balance has been in terms of practitioners and professors, ethnicity, type of library or service interest, geography, and gender. So long as COA and ALA posture and make pronouncements regarding the importance of research, but continue by their actions to demonstrate that research is really not a significant factor in accreditation, library schools—home of most of the researchers—will have little incentive to encourage their faculties toward greater research productivity. However, if the Committee on Accreditation wants to push the schools to emphasize the role of research, it needs to make certain that its own credibility can withstand challenge. That means selecting people, both faculty and practitioners, with more of an emphasis on professional accomplishments, rather than just representatives of particular groups.

COA should take a positive stance on the importance of educating students about research. Historically, the schools themselves have decided if a course in research methods is required. If not, many students opt out. Merely presenting different methodologies, as many of these courses presumably do, is insufficient.

Students need a framework in which to understand the appropriateness of those methodologies. These courses should give more emphasis to explaining the purposes of research, defining paradigms, theories, and hypotheses, and explaining inferential statistics at a level beyond simple correlation. Instructors should include examples of findings that will be valuable to practitioners.

Finally, COA should begin to examine doctoral programs. Since future LIS researchers will be graduates of these programs, it is important to ensure that their education in research is rigorous and that those who supervise their dissertations are qualified to do so.

Alleviating the problem of diminished funding for research is difficult. Sophisticated competitors from computer science, linguistics, psychology, and electrical engineering have discovered "information" as a source of research grants. If alliances cannot be forged with scholars in those disciplines, LIS researchers might study the papers resulting from the grants to see how their own interests could be incorporated with the types of proposals of interest to the funders.

It is unlikely that only one methodological camp has the correct approach to problem solving. As Mellon (1990, p. 19) points out, the quantitative and qualitative methods "might more appropriately be considered as opposite ends of a research spectrum that combines varying amounts of descriptive and statistical data." Both approaches have something to offer—the insights gained from small-scale intensive studies, rich in detail, might be used in designing larger more predictive studies. If the *Quals* and *Quants* could team up on projects some breakthroughs might be achieved. What might emerge could be the new discipline that Shera (1965, p. 7) envisioned. That discipline would focus "upon the production, flow, integration, and consumption of all forms of communication throughout the entire social pattern" (Ibid.).

REFERENCES

ALA Handbook of Organization. Chicago, IL: American Library Association, 1989.
ALA Yearbook. Chicago, IL: American Library Association, 1976–1989.
Bowker Annual of Library and Book Trade Information. New York: Bowker, 1980–1989.
Brownstein, C.N. "NSF Support for Information Science Research," *Bulletin of the American Society for Information Science*, 12 (1986): 17.
Budd, J. "Publication in Library & Information Science: The State of the Literature," *Library Journal*, 113 (September 1, 1988): 125–131.
"Building an Infrastructure for Library Research," in *Rethinking the Library in the Information Age*. Vol. 3. Washington, D. C.: GPO, 1989, pp. 19–31.
Committee on Accreditation. "Response to Jeffrey Katzer," *Library & Information Science Research*, 11 (1989): 89.
Cuadra Associates. *A Library and Information Science Research Agenda for the 1980s: Final Report*. Santa Monica, CA: Cuadra Associates, Inc., 1982.

Directory of Library and Information Professionals. Woodbridge, CT: Research Publications, 1988.
Fraley, R. and B. Via. "Survey of Library & Information Science Journal Publishers," in *Librarian/Author: A Practical Guide on How to Get Published*, edited by B.C. Sellen. New York: Neal-Schuman, 1985, pp. 120–212.
"Grant Awards," *National Library of Medicine News* (December 1988), pp. 10–12.
Harris, M.H. "The Dialectic of Defeat: Antimonies in Research in Library and Information Science," *Library Trends*, 34 (1986a): 515–531.
———. "State, Class, and Cultural Reproduction: Toward a Theory of Library Service in the United States," in *Advances in Librarianship*. New York: Academic Press, 1986b, pp. 211–252.
Hayes, R.M. "Citation Statistics as a Measure of Faculty Research Productivity," *Journal of Education for Librarianship*, 23 (Winter 1983): 151–172.
Houser, L.J. "A Conceptual Analysis of Information Science," *Library & Information Science Research*, 10 (1988): 3–34.
Journal of Education for Library and Information Science (Directory Issue, 1979–1987).
Katzer, J. "ALA and the Status of Research in Library/Information Science," *Library & Information Science Research*, 11 (1989): 83–87.
Kohl, D.F. and C.H. Davis. "Ratings of Journals by ARL Directors and Deans of Library & Information Science Schools," *College & Research Libraries*, 46 (1985): 40–47.
Kuhn, T.S. *The Structure of Scientific Revolutions*. Chicago, IL: University of Chicago Press, 1962.
Library Literature. New York: H.W. Wilson Company, 1962–1989.
Mellon, C.A. *Naturalistic Inquiry for Library Science*. New York: Greenwood Press, 1990.
Rethinking the Library in the Information Age. Prepared by the Department of Education. Vol. 3. Washington, D.C.: GPO, 1989.
Shera, J.H. *Libraries and the Organization of Knowledge*. Hamden, CT: Archon Books, 1965.
Varlejs, J. and P. Dalrymple. "Publication Output of Library and Information Science Faculty," *Journal of Library and Information Science Education*, 27 (1986): 71–89.
Watson, P.D. "Production of Scholarly Articles by Academic Librarians and Library School Faculty," *College & Research Libraries*, 46 (July 1985): 334–342.
Williams, M.E. "Defining Information Science and the Role of ASIS," *Bulletin of the American Society for Information Science*, 14 (December/January 1988): 17–19.

chapter ten

Library/Information Science Education: The Research Ethos

Evelyn H. Daniel

Strategies to create a more facilitative environment for research in library/information schools are presented. Suggestions are drawn from a study of changes in higher education that have strengthened university-provided support for research. Particularly important are suggestions that relate to the teaching—research balance. These include differentiation of staff, use of financial aid as an investment tool, and strengthening the research aspects of the master's curriculum, among others.

> . . . scientific progress is not quite what we had taken it to be
> —Thomas S. Kuhn

McClure and Bishop (1989) find occasion for "guarded optimism" in their assessment of the state of research in library and information science (LIS). The researchers they interviewed emphasized the importance of internal or personal motivation in carrying out research. They asserted the importance of institutional and professional factors, either in kindling or maintaining personal motivation. They saw a "broad landscape of opportunities" for improving the status of research.

This stance is congruent with that espoused in this chapter. The argument here will hinge on the importance of certain motivating factors in the environment in which LIS schools find themselves. A supportive environment can spur faculty on to embrace ever more explicit, more rigorous, more productive, and more ambitious research goals than done previously. It is probably true that many individuals among the faculty have read the environment accurately and responded more rapidly to the demands of today's research universities than have their schools. The schools have moved, albeit slowly and haltingly, to respond to the research expectations held by their parent institutions. This chapter will outline some strategies LIS schools can pursue to increase the level of support provided for research.

"Who/what/why should a library educator be?," asks Biggs (1985) in a recent article. Chief among her conclusions is that the library educator should be an educator. Biggs asserts that LIS faculty have shifted from a primary identification with the profession of librarianship to a closer affiliation with their university and faculty colleagues from other fields. Library educators are a part of a faculty profession that holds values, norms, and goals that are in essence different from those held by the library profession.

"Up until 1928," writes Biggs (Ibid., p. 264), "the scholar would have been a misfit on any library school faculty." She calls the early decision of the LIS schools to locate in the colleges and universities, a "fateful decision" that led to an "inexorable shifting from faculty identification with the field to their integration into the academy" (Ibid., p. 273). Budd (1989), in his tough-minded article on the management of faculty, echoes this view. He says we who are on faculties of LIS schools must recognize "who we are and where we are." He continues, "The reality is that we are academic programs situated in the context of universities" (Ibid., p. 84). To Budd, this carries the fundamental requirement for LIS faculty to produce meaningful and significant research.

NORMATIVE EXPECTATIONS OF UNIVERSITIES

Not only are LIS schools firmly ensconced in higher education, the vast majority of LIS schools are in doctoral-granting universities, the most prestigious higher education group (Daniel, 1986). In these universities, research is an axiomatic part of the university's purpose. Further, it is through the products of its research efforts that the university gains its prestige (Shils, 1979). Pedagogic activities result in few easily and widely recognizable marks of accomplishment in contrast to research where the audience and the visibility is national and international. Thus, universities demand scholarly outputs from their members.

The long and frequently bitter controversy over which of the dual goals of the university should have ascendancy—teaching or research—remains an issue in delicate equilibrium. In one of the first salvos in this long-enduring battle, Charles Pierce, defending his dictionary definition of "university" in 1891, argued that a university had nothing to do with instruction at all (Hawkins, 1979, p. 285). Charles Eliot (1898, p. 13), then president of Harvard, however, reminded his faculty that "the University does not hold a single fund primarily intended to secure to men of learning the leisure and means to prosecute original researches." In fact, for much of the early history of the university in the United States, faculty were given "freedom" to investigate, but were "obligated" to teach. This is still true today for many smaller colleges and universities, and for many LIS schools as well.

The tension between teaching and research persists. As Hawkins (1979, p. 288) points out, the two elements "could follow each other tidily in a statement of purpose, but were clearly entangled in relationships of considerable ambiguity." Although university administrators like to emphasize the beneficial and mutually supportive nature of teaching and research, many liberal arts faculty, at least, choose their profession to continue the study of their specialty. They bemoan the lack of time to do their "own work" (meaning their research work) and decry those "other tasks" (primary teaching and committee work) that keep them from it. One professor, distressed over the pressures of these "other" activities, claimed his tombstone would read: "He learned much that other men had discovered and conveyed much of this to others" (Ibid., p. 289).

Hawkins (Ibid., p. 291) suggests that one explanation of the organizational elaboration of universities lies in how the deliberate complexity of design aids in working out tensions between the teaching and research functions. Certainly the growth and differentiation of the university have provided several mechanisms by which those faculty with the strongest motivation for research have been assisted and supported in their aims. The differentiating strategies followed by the universities that have helped to nurture and protect the primacy of research will be examined in the next section of this chapter. The extent to which LIS schools have availed themselves of these strategies also will be assessed. Further expansion of these organizational mechanisms may be a productive strategy for LIS schools to follow in attempting to strengthen their research stance. The growth and differentiation of five aspects of the educational programs will be discussed under the major categories of faculty, students, curriculum, organizational structure, and funding.

GROWTH AND DIFFERENTIATION OF FACULTY

Academic faculty form a separate professional group that have more in common with each other than they do with those who practice within the discipline or profession that is the faculty member's specialty. Just as librarians are identified with (and defined by) the libraries that employ them, faculty have become identified with their employing institutions and perceive themselves as part of a professional collectivity (Bowen and Schuster, 1986).

Mintzberg (1979, pp. 348–379) describes the characteristics of professional bureaucracies, such as universities. He notes that coordination in such places inheres in the standardization of skills, training, and indoctrination, particularly the latter. He says the environment (rather than the age or size of an institution) is the chief contingency factor (Ibid., p. 366). The degree of autonomy granted may be perceived as exceptional because control systems are internalized and normative, and perhaps held the more strongly because of this. The growing similarity of the rank and tenure process among academic units at universities and among similar universities is striking. Demonstrated scholarly productivity of sufficient quantity and recognized quality, as determined by peer faculty from across the campus, is essential for tenure and promotion at all major research universities today. Because less prestigious colleges and universities look to the major institutions as models, there is remarkable consensus on what constitutes scholarly productivity and what might be expected of an individual faculty member.

The school that attempts to substitute professional service (or administrative contribution) for research productivity loses status within its university home. LIS schools that have aligned their policy and procedures for faculty appointment, promotion, and tenure with the established standards of the university will stress the importance of research productivity and assure that the clear message of its necessity is transmitted to junior faculty.

To enable faculty to spend the amount of time necessary to produce competent research and yet still meet the school's teaching commitment responsibly, the university has quietly and substantially differentiated its teaching and research staff. For one thing, there is a firm line of demarcation between graduate and undergraduate faculty responsibilities, recognized in workload, of which more will be said below under the sections dealing with students and curriculum. Teaching assistants, adjunct faculty, staff with some teaching responsibilities, visiting teaching appointments, site supervisors for on-site instruction in practical skills, all can provide much first-level fundamentals and skills teaching, freeing faculty to teach courses more attune to their research specialties.

LIS schools are often constrained by the degree to which they can take advantage of a differentiated teaching strategy for several reasons. Some universities (mine is one) will not allow doctoral students to teach graduate master's students without regular faculty oversight and acceptance of final responsibility. LIS schools may not have sufficient flexibility in faculty lines and discretionary personnel budget to enable them to build a corps of reliable adjunct faculty. Sometimes, the advancement of new knowledge in certain areas of the curriculum has been so rapid that practitioners may not be knowledgeable in the breadth and depth considered necessary by the school. Deliberate strategies to shift some of the teaching burden, however, can be explored in the expectation that the shift will allow the school to support both its teaching and research responsibilities in a creditable way.

Harvard created the sabbatical year in 1880 as a tactic to lure a "star" faculty member from Johns Hopkins (Hawkins, 1979, p. 292). This popular innovation is often perceived as a right by militant faculty to the dismay of some administrators. LIS schools have been somewhat slow to recognize the practice of sabbaticals, but the practice has gained momentum in the last decade. Even where a formal sabbatical may not be possible, most LIS schools grant "released time" as an administrative prerogative to encourage or reward greater attention to research. Although released time is more often granted to senior faculty, the University of North Carolina at Chapel Hill, for one, recently adopted a

Table 10–1. Allocation of Faculty Time.*

	All Faculty %	Public Research Univ. %	Private Research Univ. %	Public Comprehensive Univ. %	Private Comprehensive Univ. %	Liberal Arts Colleges %
Teaching	56	43	40	62	62	65
Research	16	29	30	11	9	8
Admin.	13	14	14	13	14	14
Other	15	14	16	14	15	13

*Source: *The Chronicle of Higher Education* (1990a).

university-wide policy of providing junior faculty one semester free of teaching obligations between his or her fourth and sixth years to permit strengthening the individual's research portfolio before the tenure decision.[1]

Faculty time is usually calculated in terms of teaching load, which varies considerably. Smaller colleges and universities that regard teaching as their primary mission may set a teaching load as high as five or six courses per semester. Within a large research university, the teaching load will vary from department to department, as a function of the level of instruction and the wealth of the department. Generally, graduate units require no more than five, or at the most, six courses per year, and sometimes, only two courses per semester. LIS schools do not provide this information in their annual statistical report unfortunately (see Association for Library and Information Science Education, 1980-), but it is unusual for a course load to be more than six courses a year and five is probably more suitable for true graduate teaching.

Budd (1989, p. 87), in a significant departure, describes how Rutgers has shifted from a *teaching load* to a *workload* concept, asserting that the former relegates research to time left over, or "released." He believes the workload measure permits differential assignment among faculty and "lays to rest the myth of equal teaching loads (Ibid.)." The *Chronicle of Higher Education* reports aggregate statistics in terms of workload. For the fall of 1987, the allocation of faculty time to various work responsibilities was reported in the *Chronicle* (see Table 10-1). The differing tradeoffs between teaching and research at various institutions are striking.

GROWTH AND DIFFERENTIATION OF STUDENTS

After the Second World War, all LIS schools moved in a very short period from offering fifth-year baccalaureate degrees to graduate programs leading to the

---

[1] Unfortunately the policy carried no financial support and left this aspect to the academic units to work out. In practice, this has meant less than universal action on the policy. But, on the positive side, an important goal has been set.

master's degree. In retrospect, this concerted action may have had some dysfunctional consequences. Some professionals, during the same period, notably counseling psychologists, chose the Ph.D. degree as their terminal degree instead of the Master's. If LIS had taken this course, the research elements essential for a Ph.D. would doubtlessly have inculcated stronger respect and support of research from the field and perhaps also accorded the profession a higher status relative to others. These research elements were not included in the abbreviated and practically oriented master's degree that was adopted.

The other decision that might have been made would have been to retain the undergraduate program as preparation for information workers and as a prerequisite for master's degree work which would prepare the information managers. The retention of a strong undergraduate program might have forced our graduate master's programs to a more theoretical stance and obviated the need for so much first-level skill training within the graduate degree.

In any event, undergraduate library science education until recently has been nearly unanimously regarded by LIS schools with accredited master's programs as inappropriate and unsound.[2] Yet, within the past decade several leading schools—Pittsburgh, Syracuse, Drexel, and Western Ontario—have developed undergraduate programs (and Rutgers acquired one in a merger) that emphasize disciplinary rather than professional aspects of information work, often not focusing on librarianship as much as information science, information systems, or communication (Daniel, 1987, p. 64).

The rise of the Ph.D. degree in research universities was a creative response to the functional interconnectedness of teaching and research. Doctoral students were not only the objects of teaching, they were also neophyte researchers. Universities often tend to idealize these students and their work, perhaps because they can be presented to the outside world as meeting both aspects of the teaching/research mission. At the turn of the century when the Ph.D. degree began to become widely accepted, William James (1906), in protest against its proliferation, branded doctoral education as the "Mandarin disease" and spoke of the "Ph.D. octopus." He observed that the doctorate offered no guarantee that the recipient would be an effective teacher. James may have misperceived the intent of the degree, which had little or nothing to do with teaching, but was intended to strengthen the research thrust of the university. This strategy has been a highly successful one.

The doctorate serves several purposes for LIS schools. Budd (1989, p. 85) observes, "the environment of recruiting is immeasurably enhanced by the presence of a national research-oriented Ph.D. program." Doctoral programs have the effect of upgrading faculty research efforts, creating an intellectually

---

[2] This attitude has caused substantial difficulties for one constituency, the school library media specialists, who are the chief group now educated in undergraduate training programs, almost all within schools of education.

challenging milieu, and making the school a more accepted part of the university. Many LIS schools have recognized the advantages of the Ph.D.

The doctoral program in library science at the Graduate Library School at the University of Chicago was the only one until 1948 when both Illinois and Columbia began offering one. By 1976, however, 17 LIS schools offered the doctorate in library science. In 1977, there were 23 schools with doctorates; in 1989, there were 25. The increase in doctoral-granting programs has provided a greater number of faculty with doctorates. The ALISE reports show a steady increase in the percentage of faculty in LIS schools holding the doctorate. Selected years are shown below:

- 1977: 61.8%
- 1980: 68.5%
- 1983: 71.5%
- 1986: 79.9%
- 1989: 85.8%.

Heim (1989, p. 224) reported in 1989 that of 16 schools, all the faculty held earned doctorates.

A decade ago White and Momenee (1978) commented that the growth of doctoral degrees in the field had been "startling." Through 1975, they identified 662 doctorates (from 308 six years earlier). They anticipated that more than 1,000 will have been granted by 1980. Between 1985 and 1989, nearly 2,000 students have been enrolled in LIS doctoral programs. The number of students shows a steady progression from 299 in 1985 to 421 in 1989. It is interesting that the group showing the largest proportion of increase during this period was the group of males between the ages of 20 and 39. This group made up 26.8 percent of the 1989 group. Despite the growth, the number of Ph.D. degrees granted is still very small in comparison to master's degrees granted. Seventy Ph.D. degrees were granted by 19 reporting schools for the calendar year 1988 (Association for Library and Information Science Education, 1989).

Hayes (1983), in a citation study of associate and full professors of ALA accredited programs, found that faculty in schools with doctoral programs were more productive of published articles than those in schools without one. He further found that those faculty specializing in information science were more productive than those specializing in library science. Many LIS schools lacking doctoral programs are exploring the possibility of adding such a program. If the school is in a research university, this strategy is particularly appealing.

The fellowship as an award to attract resident graduate students, says Hawkins (1979, p. 295), was a crucial institutional invention that succeeded and was widely imitated despite early grumblings from critics about "hiring students." Fellowships allow mature students to be in residence in a school on a full-time basis as junior colleagues, where they are to spend their time in study at an advanced level and in conversing with faculty about mutual research interests. This has the advantage of encouraging faculty to concentrate on research problems and helps faculty to keep up to date on new questions, new methodologies, and research design issues.

Granted that fellowships and assistantships are useful mechanisms to strengthen a school's research orientation, to what extent have LIS schools used financial aid for this purpose? The ALISE statistical report (Association for Library and Information Science Education, 1989, p. 113) provides data on scholarship aid awarded at the doctoral level by 19 reporting schools, as follows:

- Total Amount Awarded: $798,001
- Range of Totals: $1,194 to $252,000
- Average for 19 Schools: $42,000
- Total Number of Awards: 199
- Average Award per Student: $4,010.

Comparative statistics for five years earlier (Ibid., 1983, pp. 556–558) were as follows:

- Total: $369,113
- Range of Totals: $960 to $47,061
- Average for 17 Schools: $21,712
- Total Number of Awards: 98
- Average Award per Student: $3,767.

Although it is good to see the increase in the total amount and the doubling of the number of students provided some assistance, the average award is far below the amount sufficient to allow a student to pursue full-time study. Perhaps fewer more substantial awards would attract stronger students. Clearly the most attractive strategy would be to increase the total pool of funds available for fellowships and assistantships.

Title II-B of the Higher Education Act of 1965 makes available funds dedicated for library career training in the form of fellowships. The current level of award for 12 months of full-time study is $14,800 for tuition and living expenses. The customary university award for doctoral study at the University of North Carolina is $9,000 for an academic nine-month year plus tuition. These two figures suggest an appropriate level of financial support for graduate doctoral study. Lesser sums, while no doubt helpful, fail to provide sufficient support. Ideally, such support should be provided to a student for three to four years. Realistically, most LIS schools do not have the resources to attain this goal, nor can they expect much assistance from their parent institutions. The need, combined with the unlikelihood of getting it elsewhere, argues powerfully for the pursuit of research funding and the inclusion of research assistantships on proposals submitted for funding. Faculty involvement in team research in other departments and interdisciplinary units may also admit the opportunity to recommend doctoral students for research assistantships.

Academic librarianship might benefit from a shift to the Ph.D in the terminal degree required. Those academic librarians aspiring to top-level administrative positions often do pursue the degree; the rank and file do not. A second master's degree in a subject field will never equate, in the minds of most academic faculty, with the Ph.D. With the requirement for academic librarians at all ranks to show some research productivity, there is validity for considering the more rigorous preparation requirement.

GROWTH AND DIFFERENTIATION OF CURRICULUM

Among the strategies used by universities to embed a stronger research orientation in the curriculum are such innovations as honors classes at the undergraduate level, research paper requirements, seminars in the faculty members' specializations, courses in the methodology of research and research design, laboratory courses, tutorial sections, independent study, and the master's thesis. As observed above in the section on faculty, some displacement of teaching responsibilities to other milieus allows faculty more opportunity for research. For example, fieldwork is an excellent way for a master's student to learn onsite skills and the daily work environment. Much of the skill learning is inappropriate for graduate classroom instruction and some skill learning is impossible out of context. It is also easier to discuss certain issues intellectually if some experiential groundwork has been laid.

On the issue of what the objectives should be in educating (master's) students for research, Childers (1984) identified three—"doing it, applying it and embracing a critical attitude (toward it)." More recently, Tague (1987) examined the role of research in LIS education and asked what part research plays in the curriculum of LIS programs. Although she cites several studies critical of the lack of research, content, and methodology in master's programs (notably Houser and Schrader, Zaariman and Saracevic), she also found that a course in research methods forms a part of the master's curriculum in most LIS schools and that this course is frequently required. Tague examined the contents of two popular research textbooks and commented on the increasing prominence of social science research techniques.

Some major textbooks intended for research methods teaching at the master's level have been identified. The earliest, published in 1971, focused on bibliographic methods (Wynar, 1971). A very well-known one by Goldhor (1972), published a year later, called an *Introduction to Scientific Research in Librarianship*, marked a major departure with its stress on logical study design and systematic collection and analysis of data. Busha and Harter (1980) devote more than one-third of their book to descriptive and inferential statistics. Swisher and McClure (1984) have focused on the practical outcomes of research, as has Powell (1985).

Although research may be regarded "as a frill, taking away valuable time that should be spent on amassing practical skills" (Tague, 1987, p. 127), there is increasing support for the practicality of learning analytical, data-gathering, and decision-making skills taught through participation in research at the master's level. Over time, it can have the effect of developing a corps of graduates more comfortable with research concepts and more aware of the power of research; it may ameliorate some of the more egregious complaints from the field about theoretical (as opposed to practical) teaching.

GROWTH AND DIFFERENTIATION IN ORGANIZATIONAL STRUCTURES

The academic department system, although perhaps first established as a means to help the student in choosing courses and areas of specialization, became a mechanism to represent the faculty's research specializations. Many critics of the departmental system charge that departments have become too powerful and rigid and that they create artificial boundaries and barriers that impede the fluid pursuit of knowledge. On the other hand, departments do create a human-sized body of individuals with common interests and sufficient expertise to judge research efforts. Departments also have been flexible in their accommodation of new specialties over periods of time (Ben-David, 1972, pp. 139–168).

LIS schools have not availed themselves of the power of the departmental mechanism to provide a home for like-minded researchers, but have frequently experienced only the more negative isolating tendencies. LIS schools, with few exceptions, form one department schools. Where more than one department exits within an LIS school, it is usually based on a degree orientation (undergraduate, second master's, or Ph.D.) instead of a research specialization. The small size of LIS schools works against the use of departments to identify, differentiate, and protect research specialties, but perhaps it may be a strategy worth exploring.

In pursuing interdisciplinary investigations, the dysfunctions of departmentation become significant. A variety of new organizational structures has been created to overcome this problem. Many of these newer units make little or no pretense that teaching is a goal, unless it is for an interdisciplinary doctoral degree or seminar. The "Curriculum in . . . " is a possible exception to this statement. These new organizational mechanisms, for example, centers, institutes, and the like, aim to bring together faculty with similar or complementary research interests.

Geiger (1990) argues that organizational research units separate from the basic departmental structure was an innovation of the American research university and enabled it to mediate in an effective way between the knowledge demands of society (particularly in the years after 1945) and the knowledge producing capabilities of university researchers. Before the end of the 19th century, only two research structures—observatories and museums—were common. The Hatch Act of 1887 established agricultural extension stations as a third structure. In the post-war period, some new entities have been created, largely to channel research funding from the government and other agencies into organizational structures more suitable than departments for performing the research task. These entities include research laboratories, centers, institutes, bureaus, and offices.

Geiger (Ibid., p. 9) identifies a continuum based on sponsored research as follows:

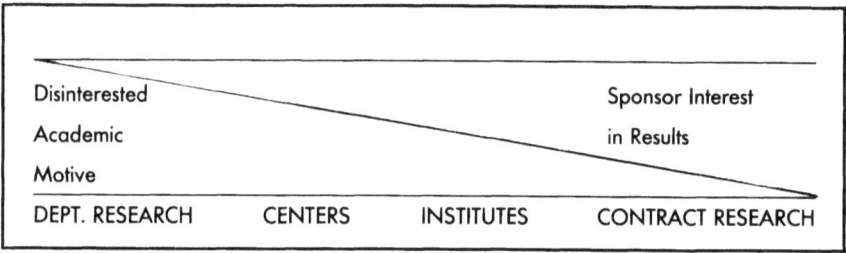

Centers are often used internally as a means of facilitating interdisciplinary investigations. Participation by faculty is sanctioned through the established departments. The research is predominantly academic but often supported by outside agencies for nonacademic reasons. Geiger (Ibid., p. 10) suggests centers "conduct academic research for ulterior motives" and "academic influences tend to overshadow the vested interests of their sponsors in the long run."

Research institutes were created more explicitly to provide utility for the sponsor. Although Geiger identifies the "fecundity" of the research program of an individual professor as the force behind the creation of some institutes, more often the university administration agrees to play host to externally supported institutes for a variety of reasons, including loyalty to key faculty, service to the government, and perhaps most of all, to enhance university prestige. Institutes provide graduate students with opportunities for training, employment, and dissertation topics; usually there is also some support for faculty research, although institutes often employ nonfaculty professionals as full-time researchers.

The distinctions between centers and institutes are not always as clear as they are set forth above, particularly in the LIS field. Illinois's research institute is the best known and longest enduring of such organizational structures within the LIS milieu. The Illinois institute provides applied research services to the state and a number of other contract research activities. Tennessee's LIS school under the influence of new faculty member Jose-Marie Griffiths, formerly of King Research, is involved in setting up a similar entrepreneurial institute there. Other schools have also made efforts in this direction.

The notion of a center as a multidisciplinary structure to carry out broad information-oriented research is an idea that has been proposed many times by the Council on Library Resources (1989, pp. 30-32) in documents and presentations by Director Jim Haas. The latest research agenda effort launched by the Office of Library Programs (OLP) (*Rethinking the Library in the Information Age*, 1989) also advocates this notion stressing an improved infrastructure for research. OLP recommends four general approaches, two that deal with professional associations and research library consortia respectively, and two that recommend the creation of "centers." The "library think tank" type of center would be an independent effort outside the aegis of LIS schools and higher education and modeled similarly to the Conference Board and the RAND Corporation (Eisenbeis, Lee, Markuson, Person, and Webster, 1988, pp. 33-34).

The university-based center proposed by the Office of Library Programs would (1) be interdisciplinary, (2) make use of a permanent group of faculty, (3) be set up in a well-established research university, and (4) be institutionally stable, among other aspects (Biggs, Marcum, Robbins, Bookstein, and Heim, 1988, pp. 55-67). OLP's report outlines a research program and identifies 10 major research areas. The establishment of this kind of center in one LIS school would give visibility to the field's research efforts and perhaps create a mecca for faculty from other schools to spend time in residence. The competition for such a center (if requisite funding is provided) would be keen. One outcome might be the emulation of the center concept through the establishment of several smaller centers in LIS schools not selected for this one.

GROWTH AND DIFFERENTIATION OF FUNDING

Before the Second World War, universities relied on the state and direct tuition support for all but a tiny part of their operating budgets. Some private universities had additional substantial endowments, but rarely did they have substantial amounts of discretionary money. "In essence, American society supported its universities for the instruction they provided, and the universities, in turn, paid their faculty to teach" (Geiger, 1990, p. 4).

The urge for research arose within the university and, although some amount of expenses for professional research could be sequestered from the general instructional budget, there was clearly a need for financial support from other sources. Not only was there a need for professional time for research, but also substantial other resources for laboratories, equipment, supplies, other personnel, and travel had also to be provided, although the laboratories and equipment

Table 10–2. LIS Research Funding.*

Selected Years	% of Funding for Research Reported by LIS Schools	% of all LIS Schools Reporting Funded Research
1974	3.0	2.1
1980	5.0	4.9
1984	2.4	4.3
1988	3.6	3.8

*Source: Association of Library and Information Science Report 1980—and Russell Bidlack's private 1974 compilation that preceded the ALISE data collection effort.

at least could do double duty for teaching as well as research. The dependence of universities on outside funds to sustain research activities has been, and continues to be, a major challenge of universities.

The great volume of Federal research funding began during the Second World War and grew into a flood in the heady years of post-war recovery with the promise of a Great Society to be achieved through the results of scientific research. Geiger (1990, p. 13) reports that university research and development funding, already rising "at a healthy rate" in the 1950s, increased nearly 20 percent per year from 1959 to 1966, then in the decade between 1958 and 1968, rose an astonishing 371 percent. Some 80 percent of these funds were from Federal sources and the vast majority was directed to basic research. University research funding as a percentage of Gross National Product declined steadily after 1968. In the late 1970s and early 1980s, the support for research received by universities surpassed that of the 1960s, but with a far smaller proportion of Federal funds. "The fastest growing component of the university research economy," writes Geiger (Ibid., p. 15), is "industry sponsored research, which is clearly programmatic in character."

Where are LIS schools in this shifting situation and what can be learned from these events? One message is clear: LIS schools will have to seek outside sources to support their research mission. Table 10-2 provides a picture of LIS research funding for selected years from 1974 to 1988. Neither of these two columns of figures is very encouraging. LIS schools typically report that 85 to 90 percent of their budget comes from their parent institutions. Given the predictions about the future expectations for any increases in university support (gloomy at best), LIS schools must develop better strategies to increase funds available for research, and these funds will almost certainly have to come from outside sources.

One potential source for both public and private universities is gift funding. LIS schools, as good citizens of the university, are expected to do their part in canvassing for funds, even though the LIS alumni community who are the chief targets of such fund-raising efforts are not a rich vein to tap. Fitzgibbons (1984) thoroughly investigated past funding for research in librarianship. The four major funding agencies for research (and development) that have provided the most stable funding for research, she reports, are the Department of Education through its HEA Title II-B Library Research and Demonstration Program,[3] the National Science Foundation,[4] the National Library of Medicine, and the Council on Library Resources. Fitzgibbons (Ibid.) also identifies several professional organizations that provide funding for research. The awards from these groups are usually quite small, but are growing in both number and quantity, and do provide a measure of recognition for the researcher that can result in additional support from the home institution.

Although universities cannot be expected to be the primary source of research funding, most set aside a portion of the overhead monies received from all funded projects and make it available on a competitive basis to university researchers. This is often a good source for summer or junior faculty grants and wins recognition for the school, as well as modest support for faculty. Universities also provide research offices that offer tracking and monitoring services for more elusive funding sources, such as foundations and state and local agencies, sources that may become more important as the competition for support from the large Federal agencies become more intense and the total amount diminishes.

Probably the biggest new target for research funding for all academic units will be industry support. This has both advantages and disadvantages. Industry support is usually provided in return for the price of control over the nature of the research projects undertaken. The degree to which such support represents "true" research (if such a thing exists) as opposed to consultant problem solving is also problematic. Perhaps one strategy to consider might be to create a center-like structure to which more than one corporation could be induced to contribute regularly in return for the opportunity to call upon the center for assistance in problem solving, and (no less important) to be able to offset profit for income tax purposes. A board consisting of representatives from the researcher group and from the industry managers would select appropriate projects. This sort of arrangement has been successful for some business schools and might be worth exploring.

---

[3] Fitzgibbons (1984, p. 546) notes that, over time, a trend in the Title II-B grant awards show that they are now used for a few large contracts in place of many small ones, that they are often designated for one topic determined by the administering office rather than researcher-generated topics, and that they are awarded to for-profit organizations rather than individual researchers. Matthews (1989) provides an update and a somewhat different and more abbreviated analysis. Her article provides a listing of all projects funded between 1977 and 1987. (See also Chapter 4.)

[4] NSF seems in a state of constant reorganization. As a result, it is often difficult to identify where current information science support lies. Fitzgibbons (1984, p. 547) quotes Atkinson who says NSF's investigators are usually from outside library science and clustered mostly in the disciplines of psychology, and computer and information science.

CONCLUSION

There is much more that might, and perhaps should, be said concerning research in LIS education. Very little attention here has been paid to the growth and differentiation of external factors that affect LIS research in education directly. Another substantial article might consider the relationship of LIS education to the research journals, to the associations (particularly the Association for Library and Information Science Education), and to its accrediting body which is currently being pressed to change its standards to accommodate new specializations and to strengthen requirements for demonstrated research.

While writing this chapter, the author was troubled by its seeming separation of research activity from teaching and service, as though it were a thing apart which, of course, it cannot be if the field is to remain healthy. The writer acknowledges the social importance of a broader definition of scholarship that would recognize and reward teaching, service, textbook writing, and other faculty activities, similar to that espoused by the Carnegie Foundation for the Advancement of Teaching and argued so forcefully by foundation president Ernest Boyer in the forthcoming report, "The New American Scholar" (The *Chronicle of Higher Education*, 1990b).

Still, there is stiff resistance to the broader definition—from research universities, from smaller universities seeking to become more prestigious, from academic disciplines, and from scholars themselves. Junior faculty would not be wise to base their career aspirations on an expectation that good work in teaching and in service will be sufficient to win tenure in the predictable future. Nor would it be wise for a small professional school to base its hopes for survival on a similar expectation. The LIS field has too many vivid and painful examples to the contrary to take such a risk. Columbia's difficulties provide the most recent example. The review committee of Columbia's LIS school asked rhetorically, "To what extent is professional education, in the absence of a strong scholarly orientation, an appropriate undertaking for research universities?" (Lee, 1990, p. B1).

We cannot accept ill-prepared teaching, poorly presented lectures, unimaginative assignments, disorganized syllabi, or a disjointed curriculum. We cannot neglect our responsibilities for service or turn our backs on the activities and interests of the professions for which we provide new entrants. But excellent teaching and important service contributions fail to be sufficient. We must establish our field in the eyes of our university peers as a scholarly one. No school can neglect its responsibility (1) to undertake and support a serious research effort by all members of its faculty, (2) to provide a facilitative environment to encourage and enhance faculty efforts, and (3) to publicize its research program aggressively.

This chapter has presented several strategies that suggest actions a school might take to create a more facilitative environment for research. Sometimes this means revamping a school completely. In others (happily the majority), the effort

Library/Information Science Education: The Research Ethos   143

involves strengthening current directions and exploring some new initiatives. Nine recommendations are synthesized from the chapter and are presented here in prescriptive fashion.

First, review the school's internal appointment, tenure, and promotion document to ensure that it is as rigorous as that used by those departments on campus deemed the most research-oriented. Provide every means of assistance possible to help faculty caught in a transition to more rigorous standards, but preserve the integrity of the process.

Second, examine total teaching responsibilities to ensure that faculty talent is not used in time-consuming and nonproductive (from a research standpoint) ways, such as running laboratories, installing and maintaining equipment, keeping routine fieldwork records and correspondence, spending time making decisions on a case-by-case basis instead of policy formulation for the general situation and delegation to administration. Consider whether any differentiation in staffing for teaching, advising, and supervising duties might be possible to enable faculty to concentrate more time on their research.

Third, reconsider the issue of faculty teaching load and explore the use of a workload concept. Whatever load allocation method is used, make sure the requirements and productivity expectations for LIS faculty are not less than those of other graduate academic units on campus that are recognized as productive research units.

Fourth, provide faculty with appropriate work tools and other necessary resources to enable them to accomplish their research without spending undue time and effort on the clerical aspects of the task.

Fifth, weigh the possible advantages of developing a doctoral program, if the school does not have one and if it is in an appropriate university environment. To be sure, the field does not need poorly conceived and inadequately supported new doctoral programs. Nor does it need programs that over-emphasize administrative skills as opposed to research skills at the doctoral level. However, a small but rigorously developed program can have a powerful impact on a school. The effort will almost certainly be viewed favorably by the university (although probably not to the point of providing sufficient resources, unfortunately). If a doctoral program exists, study possible ways of strengthening it, making it more rigorous and ensuring that it contributes to the overall research orientation of the school.

Sixth, deliberately use financial aid as a research investment tool, not only through support for doctoral students, but also in the activities assigned to aid recipients. Work to make the awards large enough so that students do not have to spend time working at other jobs that take away from the research community and reduce their ability to commit long hours and high energy to important scholarly tasks. Try to create a "critical mass" of doctoral students in some contiguous space so that they can support one another as they become socialized to the norms of research.

Seventh, strengthen the research aspects of the master's curriculum. Consider the adoption of a research paper or project if one is not now required. Group master's students into larger classes in first-level courses to allow a greater number of small advanced seminars in faculty members' research interest areas. Encourage independent study and spur faculty to share their enthusiasm and their research activities with the master's students. Ask for more research papers in classes and motivate students to think in terms of publication and presentation.

Eighth, reflect on the possibility of creating a center or institute, possibly as a collaborative undertaking with one or more other academic units, as a mechanism to focus attention on research, to attract paying projects that might allow students the possibility of practicing some research skills, and to serve as a focal point for publicizing the research activities of the school.

And, finally, articulate the importance of research in our field to the administration, to the students, and to each other. Study our growing body of current research literature and find opportunities for serious discussion of these questions. Be supportive of each other's research efforts and not harmfully critical. Prove by word and deed that LIS is an intellectually vital and scholarly field that investigates serious and important questions about the mysterious and centrally important phenomenon of information creation and use in our society.

REFERENCES

Association for Library and Information Science Education. *Library and Information Science Education Statistical Report*, 1980–.

Ben-David, Joseph. *Trends in American Higher Education*. Chicago, IL: University of Chicago Press, 1972.

Biggs, Mary. "Who/What/Why Should a Library Educator Be?," *Journal of Education for Library and Information Science*, 25 (Spring 1985): 262–278.

———, Deanna Marcum, Jane Robbins, Abraham Bookstein, and Kathleen Heim. "University-Based Models: Creating Centers for Research in Library and Information Science," in *Rethinking the Library in the Information Age*. Vol. 2. Prepared by the Department of Education. Washington, D.C.: GPO, 1988, pp. 55–67.

Bowen, Howard R. and Jack H. Schuster. *American Professors: A National Resource Imperiled*. New York: Oxford Univ. Press, 1986.

Budd, Richard W. "Recruiting, Retaining, and Rewarding Research Faculty: Art or Atmosphere?," *Journal of Education for Library and Information Science*, 30 (Fall 1989): 83–89.

Busha, Charles H. and Stephen P. Harter. *Research Methods in Librarianship: Techniques and Interpretation*. New York: Academic Press, 1980.

Childers, Thomas. "Will the Cycle Be Unbroken? Research and Schools of Library and Information Studies," *Library Trends*, 32 (Spring 1984): 521–535.

The Chronicle of Higher Education, (February 7, 1990a), p. A16.

———, (April 11, 1990b), p. A1, A16.

Council on Library Resources. *Thirty-Third Annual Report, 1989.* Washington, D.C.: Council on Library Resources, 1989.

Daniel, Evelyn H. "The Library/Information School in Context: The Place of Library/Information Science Education within Higher Education," *Library Trends,* 34 (Spring 1986): 623–643.

―――. "New Curriculum Areas," in *Education of Library and Information Professionals; Present and Future Prospects,* edited by Richard K. Gardner. Littleton, CO: Libraries Unlimited, 1987, pp. 53–70.

Eisenbeis, Kathleen, Sul Lee, Barbara Markuson, Ruth Person, and Duane Webster. "A Library Think Tank: Creating an Independent Center for Library-Oriented Information Research and Policy Studies," in *Rethinking the Library in the Information Age.* Vol. 2. Prepared by the Department of Education. Washington, D.C.: GPO, 1988, pp. 33–41.

Eliot, Charles William. "Inaugural Address as President of Harvard College," in *Educational Reform: Essays and Addresses,* Edited by C.W. Eliot. New York: Century, 1898, pp. 1–4.

Fitzgibbons, Shirley Grinnell. "Funding of Research in Librarianship," *Library Trends,* 32 (Spring 1984): 537–556.

Geiger, Roger L. "Organized Research Units—Their Role in the Development of University Research," *Journal of Higher Education,* 61 (January/February 1990): 1–19.

Goldhor, Herbert. *An Introduction to Scientific Research in Librarianship.* Urbana, IL: University of Illinois, Graduate School of Library Science, 1972.

Hawkins, Hugh. "University Identity: The Teaching and Research Functions," in *The Organization of Knowledge in Modern America, 1860–1920,* edited by Alexandra Oleson and John Voss. Baltimore, MD: Johns Hopkins University Press, 1979, pp. 285–312.

Hayes, Robert M. "Citation Statistics as a Measure of Faculty Research Productivity," *Journal of Education for Librarianship,* 23 (1983): 151–172.

Heim, Kathleen M. "Summary and Comparative Analysis," in *Library and Information Science Education Statistical Report, 1989.* Sarasota, FL: Association for Library and Information Science Education, 1989, pp. 223–231.

James, William. "The Ph.D. Octopus," *Harvard Monthly,* 36 (1906): 1–9.

Lee, Felicia R. "Librarians May Lose Oldest School," *New York Times* (April 17, 1990), B1, B4.

Matthews, Anne J. "An Overview of Issues, Proposals, and Products in Library/Information Research," *Journal of Education for Library and Information Science,* 29 (Spring 1989): 251–261.

McClure, Charles R. and Ann Bishop. "The Status of Research in Library/Information Science: Guarded Optimism," *College & Research Libraries,* 50 (March 1989): 127–143.

Mintzberg, Henry. *The Structuring of Organizations.* Englewood Cliffs, NJ: Prentice-Hall, 1979.

Powell, Ronald R. *Basic Research Methods for Librarians.* Norwood, NJ: Ablex, 1985.

Rethinking the Library in the Information Age. Vol. 3. Prepared by the Department of Education. Washington, D.C.: GPO, 1989.

Shils, Edward. "The Order of Learning in the United States: The Ascendancy of the

University," in *The Organization of Knowledge in Modern America, 1860-1920*, edited by Alexandra Oleson and John Voss. Baltimore, MD: Johns Hopkins Univ. Press, 1979, pp. 19–47.

Swisher, Robert and Charles R. McClure. *Research for Decision Making: Methods for Libraries.* Chicago, IL: American Library Association, 1984.

Tague, Jean. "The Role of Research in Information and Library Education," in *Education of Library and Information Professionals; Present and Future Prospects*, edited by Richard K. Gardner. Littleton, CO: Libraries Unlimited, 1987, pp. 121–134.

White, Herbert S. and Karen Momenee. "Impact of the Increase in Library Doctorates," *College & Research Libraries*, 39 (May 1978): 207–214.

Wynar, Bohdan S. *Research Methods in Library Science: A Bibliographic Guide with Topical Outlines.* Littleton, CO: Libraries Unlimited, 1971.

chapter eleven

The Role of LIS Education

Cheryl Duran

This chapter discusses three issues: Research on library and information science (LIS), research as a component in the curriculum of library schools, and research on LIS education. The chapter presents the second issue in greater depth. Research is an important component for making LIS both a profession and a discipline. Moreover, it should aid librarians in marketing, decision making, and planning. As a result, research merits inclusion in the core curriculum of LIS schools.

Based upon interviews conducted with three library school leaders, the chapter identifies critical areas of the past, present, and future meriting research. The discussion underscores the importance of information policy as a critical component of the curriculum of the future. Without effective spanning mechanisms, the gulf between theory and practice, or LIS education and the practice of librarianship, may widen. The chapter offers some suggested spanning mechanisms.

The purpose of library and information science (LIS) education "is to prepare students for a career, not for the performance of narrow tasks" (Robbins, 1990, p. 40). Schools of LIS should educate students to assume leadership and decision-making roles in libraries and information centers. Through their education, students acquire (Ibid., p. 42):

- Understanding of the theoretical foundations of the profession;
- Ability to meld theory into the practice setting;
- Ability to use written and oral communication effectively on behalf of the profession;
- Understanding of the societal context in which the profession is practiced;
- Internalization of the behaviors and norms (the ethics) of the profession;
- Ability to anticipate and adapt to changes important to professional practice;
- Scholarly concern for the improvement of professional practice; and
- Motivation to continue learning related to professional growth.

With the advent of the information age, the employment opportunities for graduates of LIS programs have greatly expanded into settings outside libraries and information centers. Schools of LIS are definitely not single-product organizations as their graduates now serve in a wide variety of information-related organizations (Stueart, 1981, p. 1992).

This chapter argues that coverage of the research process should be a component of the curriculum of schools of library and information science. Research-oriented courses and assignments at the master's level tend to focus on problem solving and teaching students to examine problems analytically. At the doctoral level, students should learn to become researchers, to engage in theory construction and testing, and to practice the conduct of different types of research.

When librarians discuss LIS as a profession, they tend to equate education with training and to identify specific skills and competencies that students should master (Powell and Creth, 1986; Powell, 1988). Such discussions do not place these skills and competencies in the context of particular work situations and job descriptions, downplay the importance of research to the advancement of the field, and may equate research with the mastery of reference search skills (Ibid.). Research is analytical and central to the development and testing of theory, and the placement of localized investigations in a broader and more meaningful context. Research plays an important role in defining both a *learned* profession and a discipline.

According to Hayes (1989b, p. 2),

> if one's field is regarded only as multi-disciplinary it is not treated with respect by the more focused fields and, especially, by the traditional academic fields. They will evaluate contributions from their own perspective; they will interpret value and significance in terms of their own discipline. The result is a failure to recognize the validity of the multi-disciplinary field, its problems and the significance of solutions to them. It is only if we can clearly articulate the specific discipline of our own field, independent of others, that we will have a solid basis for assessment of significance.

Viewing LIS as both a learned profession and a discipline places increased demands on the curriculum, recruitment of faculty, the selection of prospective students, and the expectations of those in and outside librarianship.

The norm has been for writers (and others) to equate research in LIS with research on LIS education and to less frequently treat research as a component of the curriculum. As a result, the profession has come to view research on LIS education as synonymous with research in library and information science and has only recently considered research in respect to its inclusion within the core curriculum. In fact, these issues are separate but related. Although the chapter considers all these issues, it places less emphasis on research in LIS. Other chapters in the monograph present this topic in greater detail. In effect, this chapter attempts to present aspects of the three issues not covered elsewhere in the book.

The chapter highlights the role of research for a disciplinary-based LIS educational program. It specifically discusses the curriculum, the knowledge base that students should have, and the role of library education within the parent organization and the profession itself. Furthermore, the chapter considers critical areas meriting research, and who will conduct and fund research in LIS. The chapter looks to the future and the necessity for having spanning mechanisms that lessen the differences between theory and practice. And, finally, there are some practical suggestions for covering research in the curriculum of master's-level courses.

LIS EDUCATION

Research as a Component of the Curriculum

Library schools differ in their treatment of research within their curriculum. Some schools have a required research methods course, while others either have an optional course or no research course offerings whatsoever. Those schools offering formal courses vary in the frequency with which they provide such courses, the experience of the faculty in teaching such courses and conducting research, and the topical areas covered. Some schools present the role of research, including the steps beginning with problem identification and ending with the reporting of study findings, and prepare students as consumers of research. Other schools might devote the entire course to a discussion of statistics, methodologies, or other specific components of the research process.

Other courses in the curriculum either reinforce the coverage of research provided in the one optional or required course, or they do not treat research at all. Another approach taken by some schools is to require that students have completed a research methods or statistics course prior to enrollment in the LIS program. Compounding the difficulty in creating a common set of graduate student expectations prior to entry into the program is the recognition that many students often choose librarianship as an alternative career. Historically, most students entering a LIS program come from a humanities background and therefore have had little or no exposure to the scientific method and the concomitant methods of problem solving. Clearly, no single undergraduate program adequately prepares students for entry into a LIS program in respect to the fulfillment of a set of specialized research requirements. Moreover, because LIS is a discipline that draws heavily upon other disciplines in the behavioral, social, and physical sciences, it is difficult to identify a common pool of research knowledge that students within the program should receive within the structure of a one- or two-year program.

Research on LIS Education

Hayes (1988, pp. 60, 73) has succinctly identified key research questions pertaining to library and information science. At least six of his questions have direct application to the role of research within the curriculum of schools of library and information science:

- How important is the professional librarian to society, and what is the evidence of that importance?
- What are the proper roles and responsibilities of various academic programs in meeting the needs for professional librarians?
- What is and, with the objective of excellence in library education, what should be the effect of societal changes on programmatic goals and objectives?
- How should specialization be dealt with in first professional degree programs?
- How can the quality of students best be advanced, considering recruitment, admission requirements, and recommended undergraduate preparation?
- To what extent should library education be responsible for the lifelong learning needs of the profession?

The premise of this chapter is that the graduate schools have a responsibility to ensure that students understand that research plays an important role in answering these (and other) questions and in respect to helping them develop a vision of the future.

KNOWLEDGE BASE OF STUDENTS

Griffiths and King (1986) identified a set of skills, attitudes, and knowledge needed for professional information work, in a variety of employment contexts. Building from their work, it can be suggested that, as information professionals, master's-level students would benefit from courses pertaining to research (specifically evaluation of library programs and services), statistics, and management. Together with the traditional core of reference services and the organization of knowledge, the aforementioned courses would round out a core curriculum. In respect to incorporating a distinct core course on technology, the assumption is that technology utilization is to be treated as an integral component of each course. It is also suggested that schools that do not offer course work on evaluation might substitute a course on systems analysis.

A combination of courses, such as the one proposed above, is necessary for educating high-quality graduate-level students. This combination would result in the matriculation of entry-level information professionals able to cope with change and complex managerial and policy issues. After all, "the objective of education is the training of the mind, and the professional degree must not stand as a denial of this objective" (Shera, 1972, p. 361). "The program of study must be intellectual" (Ibid.).

ROLE OF LIS EDUCATION
WITHIN THE PARENT ORGANIZATION

"Library schools are among the smallest of schools in almost any university" (Hayes, 1988, p. 55). Paris (1988) investigated the closing of four library schools and showed that the schools studied had become isolated within the university. Neither the LIS administration nor faculty engaged in cross-disciplinary research with other members of the university's faculty. The faculty also did not participate in university-wide committees and planning processes. Furthermore, the research conducted with the LIS programs was not on par with that produced by other units within the university.

According to Hayes (1988, p. 72),

> By closing library schools the universities have sent several messages. For instance: How does the quality of research in library schools compare with that in the university as a whole? What must we do to improve the image? Library schools with doctoral programs emphasize research; library schools with a terminal Master's degree emphasize service. Is there some way to incorporate service into the goals and mission of the university without jeopardizing research?

Where the mission of the parent institution involves the conduct of research, and the central administration expects all colleges and schools to meet that mission, it is critical that schools of library and information science accept an active role in the completion of basic and applied research. Moreover, there should be joint programs with other departments and schools within the university, and students in other programs should be encouraged to take LIS courses that have direct relevance to their academic and professional aspirations.

CRITICAL AREAS MERITING FUTURE RESEARCH

Almost 20 years ago, Borko (1973, pp. 216–221) rated topical areas meriting research in library education. The highest area of priority related to "improving and updating the skills of professional librarians." Having such a category underscores that LIS programs typically do not confine themselves to the preparation of entry-level librarians and expanding the critical mass of researchers. Functioning in the information age, many librarians need to update their knowledge base and obtain a better understanding of current and future issues. Kaser (1978, p. 195) points out that "too often we feel compelled to discover the wheel anew instead of improving upon and adjusting our inherited wheels in the light of changing environmental conditions." Furthermore (Ibid.), librarians may fail to recognize:

> the difference between transient and perpetual issues. Our responses to the former should differ from our responses to the latter. Too often the profession dissipates its energies and resources attempting to react to every meaningless blip that turns up on its radar screen.

Borko's other four priority areas include "library school educational planning and relevance," "administration of the library school and library with regard to specific courses, skills, and programs," "forms of instruction and supportive facilities for maintaining instruction," and "the role of professional associations and communication among librarians."

The author of this chapter interviewed three educators who helped to shape the direction that LIS education, for the past decade, has taken. She asked Harold Borko, Robert M. Hayes, and Beverly Lynch to characterize the most significant research issues for a decade ago, now, and 10 years hence.

Hayes and Lynch concurred that Borko's agenda presented the areas of research emphasis for the 1970s and much of the 1980s. According to Lynch, the research concentrated on attempting to determine the best methods for the accomplishment of specific tasks, for example, the best way to determine user needs. Hayes indicated that both researchers and funding organizations, such as Conant (1980), Griffiths and King (1986), and the American Library Association (1986), provided commentary on the nature of research and encouraged the setting of research agendas to guide the future.

In response to a characterization of the research of today, these three educators emphasized that the research is noncumulative; it does not build upon past studies, theories, findings, and methodologies. Clearly, they supported the findings of McClure and Bishop (1989). While funding organizations might set research agendas to guide present and future funding decisions, library school faculty should devote more time to the conduct of research, regardless of the topical area. They need to build upon past research endeavors and to advance the disciplinary base of LIS. Having a critical mass of active researchers is of more importance than trying to direct the scope, direction, and type of research that educators conduct.

The Council on Library Resources (1989, p. 31), as Hayes explained, identifies some examples of research areas in an effort to encourage more research that will impact both the profession and the direction that the educational programs at both the master's and doctoral levels take. The Council (Ibid.) believes that "there is great need to understand better:

- How information can best be described, analyzed, integrated, and organized for use;
- How certain policies, set at all levels of government, affect access to information;
- The effect of technology-based information systems on scholarship, learning, government, and the public well-being;
- The economics of information;
- The effect of organizational structure on information diffusion; and
- The constraints on effecting change."

Information policy is the common thread linking the six areas.

According to Hernon and Relyea (forthcoming), information policy is a field that encompasses information science and public policy. The field "treats information as both a commodity and a resource to be collected, protected, shared, manipulated, and managed." More specifically, information policy

> is a set of interrelated principles, laws, guidelines, rules, regulations, and procedures guiding the oversight and management of the information *life-cycle*: the production, collection, distribution/dissemination, retrieval, and retirement of information. Information policy also embraces access to, and use of, information.

Collectively, information policies form a framework that impacts the economic, political, and social choices available to individuals and a society itself (Mason, 1983, p. 93).

Hayes (1989a, p. 6) poses the question "How do we integrate into library education issues related to information policies, telecommunications policies, and the whole range of political decision making with respect to the allocation of resources to our field?" As he underscores, this is not a simple question to answer, in part because LIS educators should explore and evaluate the potential impact of their research on other disciplines and professions. Hayes (Ibid.) also asks the question "Are there aspects of such research that call for collaboration with colleagues on the campus in other disciplines who might contribute to it and benefit from it?"

When asked to identify the key research issues for the year 2000, Borko identified five major issues areas:

- Measuring the effectiveness of library services and programs, and improving these services and programs as necessary;
- Information policy, with its implications at the local, state, regional, national, and international levels;
- Information users and uses, as investigated through multi-method and cross-disciplinary research;

- Information-handling technologies emphasizing the role and uses of hypermedia for LIS education; and
- New applications of existing information retrieval mechanisms.

Hayes suggests that the aforementioned issues identified by the Council on Library Resources will still be investigated throughout the decade. Lynch underscored the continued need to examine information-seeking behavior of all segments of society, with special attention to the community of scholars.

To their list, we might append the need to investigate diverse methods for teaching students to understand and apply research, as well as to increase their problem-solving capabilities. As more library school graduates become information managers coping with a broad set of issues, more than ever they will need such an intellectual foundation (Lynch, 1988).

RESEARCH—WHO CONDUCTS AND WHO FUNDS IT

Numerous articles appearing in the *Journal of Education for Library and Information Science*, and elsewhere, have examined the adequacy of LIS education to meet present and future demands and expectations. The examination, however, tends to focus on LIS as a profession and practical expectations for graduates of the program (e.g., Conant, 1980). Library school educators, as the overwhelming response to the Conant report indicates, probably would argue that they should have primary responsibility for conducting research related to matters of professional education, including the content of the curriculum. Professional organizations and practicing librarians might somewhat disagree with the educators on this point. Perhaps, the important issue is less "who" does the research. Research should focus on LIS as a discipline and identify strategies whereby research can become an integral part of each course. A key question becomes "How do we teach research appreciation and application in a discipline that draws extensively upon other disciplines and professions?" In other words, the base of knowledge is extensive, often complex, and difficult to master in one- or two-year programs. At any rate, the purpose of research should be to challenge both practitioners and educators to improve the theory, practice, and disciplinary base of LIS.

The U.S. government should continue to support research on LIS education as well as issues related to practice. At the same time, professional organizations and groups, such as the Council on Library Resources, should encourage research on LIS education. Outside funding agencies tend to support action-oriented research that does not have an extensive theoretical base. Because of this, these organizations and groups should not dictate a research agenda for the discipline.

LOOKING TO THE FUTURE

Given the types of issues and problems that information managers and information access professionals face in the information age, library education must become more research- and theory-oriented. At the same time, practicing librarians must embrace both research and theory. Unless they do so, the gulf between library education and the practice of librarianship may increase. Any attempts to narrow the gap should not hold back LIS education, but should encourage practice to absorb more theory and research.

As more universities have higher research expectations for their departments, colleges, and schools, schools of library and information science that do not meet these expectations will be out of step with the parent institution. As a consequence, they might be subsumed by other units that are more aggressively pursuing research or the institution might decide that it no longer needs LIS schools and programs.

Clearly, there is a need for mechanisms narrowing the potential gulf between LIS education and practice, and ensuring that LIS becomes more disciplinary based. None of these spanning mechanisms can favor training over education; rather, they should promote theory and research. The Committee on Accreditation of the American Library Association might serve as a spanning mechanism, but only if: (1) accrediting teams better understand and support the need for disciplinary-based LIS education, and (2) the types of issues raised in this book are satisfactorily resolved.

Some practitioners assume that there is no connection between good research and good librarianship and that it is not important to make that connection (Lynch, 1988, p. 77). On the other hand, "generalizations, model building, and theory construction coming from such research would strengthen enormously our knowledge of libraries, information, and the users served by librarians" (Ibid., p. 87). The critical issue in LIS education for the decade is "How do we make that connection and simultaneously advance the theoretical base of LIS education?"

This chapter cannot offer simple strategies for answering this question. Library school educators, employers, funders, and students must all recognize that a theory-based and research-oriented education grounded in practice benefits everyone—including those financing and using libraries. Such education advances theory and underscores the value of the relationship between research and practice in areas such as the economics of information. Moreover, students who have gained a base of knowledge about research should receive opportunities, upon entry into the profession, to initiate investigations as part of their library responsibilities and activities.

In brief, a first step will be for the above-mentioned groups to stop reacting to every meaningless blip on the radar screen of LIS. We need to focus on the central issues and identify strategies for making students more effective consumers and conductors of research. That research should not be confined to the accomplishment of problem solving in a local context. We need more experimental and other types of basic and applied research that challenge and stimulate LIS as a discipline and a career (see Powell, 1989).

The chapter has assumed that the rapid advancement of LIS from a profession to a discipline should occur within the immediate future. The problem is that there must be a critical mass of high-quality researchers and that "too much change in too short a time would . . . upset the educational ecosystem, and, in all probability, alienate practitioners in 'libraryland'" (Cronin, 1983, p. 23). However, the increasing research and grantsmanship orientation of many universities might force rapid change, if LIS schools are to remain and flourish within that type of institutional environment.

INTRODUCING RESEARCH INTO THE CURRICULUM[1]

As already mentioned, schools of library and information science should offer a required course on the role of research. Such a course, supported by additional coursework on systems analysis and the evaluation of library services, provides a good foundation on which other courses can build.

Such a course, taught by faculty members active as researchers and able to draw upon diverse and rich experiences, might examine the need and opportunities for research in LIS, types of research studies, problem identification, and the execution of a research study. The course would examine the research process from conceptualization of a problem to publication of a study.

Figure 11-1 provides the objectives and topics covered in such a course. The purpose of this course is to provide students with an opportunity to gain a common understanding of the role of research in LIS. The course encourages students to develop a grasp of the fundamental structure of research, to understand the present state of knowledge on a topic, and to realize cross-disciplinary efforts on the research front. Central to the research process is the role of reflective inquiry, in particular, that part labeled the "logical structure." In this regard, research studies should expound the structure or framework within which the problem will be investigated, that is, studies should identify all relevant variables and relevant theory that guide data collection and interpretation (see Chapter 1). Application of the logical structure in the investigation of the problems is validated in terms of its anticipated advantages and consequences.

Given the wide range of purposes for which research is conducted, the specific needs of libraries, and the nature of library and information science as a social science discipline, not all research can meet the same standards of generality, prediction, or explanation. What is important, however, is that the course en-

---

[1] Peter Hernon, Simmons College, supplied the information for this section of the chapter.

Figure 11-1. Objectives and Topical Areas Covered in a Course on the Role of Research in LIS.*

Objectives
1. To develop an appreciation of the role of research in library and information science;
2. To encourage students to be intelligent consumers of research and to have general insights into the steps involved in the conduct of action research;
3. To teach students to read critically and interpret thoughtfully research findings, including the ability to recognize both strengths and weaknesses in research reports and writing;
4. To understand the role of reflective inquiry in developing research studies;
5. To be able to identify problem statements;
6. To understand selected methods by which research is conducted and data are gathered, tabulated, and analyzed; and
7. To apply the concepts of the research process to a library problem.

Syllabus
I. Introduction
A. General Research
1. What is research (characteristics and types)?
2. Role and function of research in society.
3. The distinction between research and publication.
4. The social responsibility/accountability of scholars.
5. The collegiality and community of academic scholarship.
B. Research in Library and Information Science
1. History of scholarship in library and information science.
2. Library and information science as a discipline and profession, with emphasis on the role of research
3. Perceived needs for research in library and information science (impact on decision making).
4. Current trends in research in library and information science.
5. Individual and team research.
6. Review of research opportunities (grants, contracts, and support)—Funded versus non-funded research.
II. Elements in the Research Process
A. Reflective Inquiry
1. Identification and statement of a reasonable problem.
2. Review and evaluation of related research (the context).
3. Logical structure and/or theoretical framework.
4. Objectives.
5. Hypotheses or questions.
B. Procedures
1. Research design or action plan.
2. Relevant methodologies (discussion of representative ones)—The application of these methodologies to library and information science.
C. Data Collection and Analysis
1. The role of statistics.
2. Canned statistical packages (e.g., StatPac).
D. The Writing of Research Reports
E. The Scholar/Publisher Interface
III. Conclusion

*Source: Peter Hernon, Simmons College, Boston, MA, 1990.

courages students to expand their understanding of the role of research in professional education and practice.

Such a course is designed for master's-level students. However, it can be adapted to meet the needs of doctoral students and practicing librarians able to enroll in a library school course. Most practicing librarians will have to rely on research methods and statistics courses taught at their academic (or a nearby academic) institution. Because of this, they will profit from the identification of the works listed in Chapter 2.

Perhaps the most fundamental task is to persuade entire faculties of schools of library and information science (or at least the voting majority) that knowledge about research, theory, and problem solving (see Biggs and Bookstein, 1988, p. 40) are important for students and librarians to grow professionally and to attack the type of problems that libraries of the present and future encounter.

REFERENCES

American Library Association. Committee on Accreditation. *Accreditation: A Way Ahead.* Chicago, IL: American Library Association, 1986.

Biggs, Mary and Abraham Bookstein. "What Constitutes a High-Quality M.L.S. Program? Forty-five Faculty Members' Views," *Journal of Education for Library and Information Science*, 29 (Summer 1988): 28–46.

Borko, Harold. *Targets for Research in Library Education.* Chicago, IL: American Library Association, 1973.

Conant, R. W. *The Conant Report: A Study of the Education of Librarians.* Cambridge, MA: MIT Press, 1980.

Council on Library Resources. *Thirty-Third Annual Report.* Washington, D.C.: Council on Library Resources, 1989.

Cronin, Blaise. *The Transition Years: New Initiatives in the Education of Professional Information Workers.* London, England: Aslib, 1983.

Griffiths, J. M. and Donald King. *New Directions in Library and Information Science Education.* Final Report. Rockville, MD: King Research, Inc., 1986.

Hayes, Robert M. "Education and Training of Librarians," in *Rethinking the Library in the Information Age.* Vol. 2. Prepared by the Department of Education, Office of Educational Research and Improvement. Washington, D.C.: GPO, 1988, pp. 43–74.

———. Memo to Jim Haas, Kathleen Heim, Deanna Marcum, and Bob Wedgeworth on "Comments on Four Objectives," unpublished, October 17, 1989a.

———. "The Science of Library & Information Science." Summary of remarks made at the meeting of the Board of the Council on Library Resources, unpublished, November 1989b.

Hernon, Peter and Harold C. Relyea. "Information Policy," in *The Encyclopedia of Library and Information Science*, edited by Allen Kent. New York: Dekker, forthcoming.

Kaser, David. "Advances in Library History," in *Advances in Librarianship*. Vol. 8. New York: Academic Press, 1978, pp. 181-199.

Lynch, Beverly P. "Education and Training of Librarians," in *Rethinking the Library in the Information Age*. Vol. 2. Prepared by the Department of Education, Office of Educational Research and Improvement. Washington, D.C.: GPO, 1988, pp. 75-91.

Mason, Marilyn Gell. *The Federal Role in Library and Information Services*. White Plains, NY: Knowledge Industry Publications, Inc., 1983.

McClure, Charles R. and Ann Bishop. "The Status of Research in Library/Information Science: Guarded Optimism," *College & Research Libraries*, 50 (March 1989): 127-143.

Paris, Marion. *Library School Closings: Four Case Studies*. New York: Scarecrow, 1988.

Powell, Ronald, Ed. "Problem Solving in Libraries: A Festschrift in Honor of Herbert Goldhor," *Library Trends*, 38 (Fall 1989): 153-325.

———. "Sources of Professional Knowledge for Academic Librarians," *College & Research Libraries*, 49 (July 1988): 332-340.

———. and Sheila D. Creth. "Knowledge Bases and Library Education," *College & Research Libraries*, 47 (January 1986): 16-27.

Robbins, Jane. "Yes, Virginia, You Can Require an Accredited Master's Degree for That Job!," *Library Journal*, 115 (February 1, 1990): 40-44.

Shera, Jesse H. *The Foundations of Education for Librarianship*. New York: Wiley and Sons, 1972.

Stueart, Robert D. "Great Expectations: Library and Information Science Education at the Crossroads," *Library Journal*, 106 (October 1981): 1989-1992.

part ii
Practical Context of Research in Library and Information Science

chapter twelve

The Role of the Library Administrator in Improving LIS Research

Joe A. Hewitt

Libraries are extraordinarily busy environments in which the struggle to provide high-quality services and collections on limited resources works against any activity which is not seen as directly supporting this effort. The primary contribution the library administration can make towards improving LIS research is to implement practices that work towards the integration of both the products and processes of research into the ongoing operation of libraries. These practices demonstrate the value of research in improving library services. This chapter presents and discusses 11 such practices.

The role of the library administrator in improving the status of library and information science (LIS) research is frequently addressed in terms of *support* for research conducted by the library's professional and/or academic staff. Commentaries on the topic tend to be presented in the context of the issues of academic status and professionalism, with research posited as an activity competing with the basic managerial and service functions of the library professional. Such commentaries also tend to focus on descriptions of strategies for eking out small measures of support from strained library budgets—support for released time and research leave, clerical and computing support, travel, and so forth. More often than not, these commentaries include an apology for the fact that the prevailing conditions in libraries allow for little more than token support of LIS research, if libraries are also to fulfill their fundamental missions and meet the needs of their users.

These are not insignificant concerns. In a broader cultural context, it has been suggested that a certain degree of slack or, to be more precise, opportunity for idleness, must exist in a culture before it can engage in the kind of speculative enquiry that yields new knowledge.[1] In the Western world, early science was

---

[1] I am indebted to Professor Gene V. Glass, Laboratory of Educational Research, University of Colorado, for his lectures and writings on the theme of use of research in education for several ideas used in the introductory section of this chapter (see Glass, 1971).

considered folly, a mere hobby of eccentric gentlemen, at least until the formation of the Royal Society of London in 1662. Vestiges of this stigma adhere even today to basic researchers in all applied fields in the eyes of those engaged in the daily struggle to deal with the immediate business at hand. And, the library is an extremely *busy* environment; it is an environment in which the urgent concerns of budgets, the press of users and workloads, staffing problems, political issues, meetings, planning and policy development, red tape, and the whole enterprise of running a complex organization with less than adequate resources, leaves little slack and no idleness. There is simply very little room in the modern library for basic curiosity to take root, to be nourished by speculative reflection, and to grow through disciplined and energetic inquiry, except on the part of a handful of extraordinarily committed individuals.

What then can library administrators do to improve the status of LIS research under these conditions? First, they can begin by acknowledging the reality that some current notions of *support*—four hours a week of released time to work on approved projects, a few hours each week of student assistant help, and/or a research committee to counsel professional staff interested in conducting research projects—will not measurably improve the quantity or quality of research on a broad scale.

Such support is no doubt beneficial as a staff development program and it may result on occasion in studies and professional contributions of real value, but it does not address the critical research concerns of the profession. Indeed, in some ways, this approach may do more harm than good; it serves to perpetuate the idea that research is an activity that stands apart from and competes with the ongoing business of managing the library and developing library programs and services. Second, these programs provide a comforting illusion of real support while there is in fact little possibility that sufficient "slack" can ever be carved out of the overburdened resources of the typical library to make a substantial contribution to the LIS research effort.

This chapter takes the position that the major contribution the library administrator can make to the improvement of LIS research is to make decisions and develop policies which work towards the integration of research into the operation of the library and to serve as a role model, opinion leader, and catalyst in an effort to change attitudes towards LIS research among staff. This view is based on an assumption that the potential of research for improving library services must be more widely recognized before the profession at large will support an effort to improve LIS research. Further, the key to recognizing that potential is to make greater use of both the results and the process of research in the *daily operation* of libraries, rather than to support research as a peripheral activity presumed to reinforce the librarian's claim for faculty status. The library administrator can play a key role in this process, which might be visualized as one of creating a discriminating demand for quality research that has actual value in operating libraries and information agencies.

But this will be no easy task. Research is not highly regarded among practitioners for its utilitarian value. The direct, explicit, and acknowledged influence of research on practical decision making in libraries is almost nonexistent. Mintzberg (1973, p.7) has asserted as one of the nine major conclusions of his own research: "There is no science in managerial work." Schön (1982) argues persuasively that the positivist model of technical rationality through which the systematic knowledge base of a profession is developed has little relevance to, indeed is antithetical to, the epistemology of practice. Thus, it will be no simple task to develop and implement management practices that attempt to integrate research into the ongoing operation of a library. Furthermore, it is not altogether clear to what extent it is appropriate to do so. Care must be taken not to disturb radically the balance in the library decision-making process with respect to contextual knowledge, intuition based on experience, philosophical conviction, common sense, political acumen, and knowledge of research-based findings. Yet, it is vitally important for LIS research, if it is to advance in part through the support of the profession at large, to become a more salient element in this equation.

There must be one final caveat regarding the intrusion of research into the world of practice in a prominent way. No less a figure than Alfred North Whitehead (see Glass, 1971, p.28) has observed:

> It is a profoundly erroneous truism, repeated by all copy-books and by eminent people when they are making speeches, that we should cultivate the habit of thinking about what we are doing. The precise opposite is the case. Civilization advances by extending the number of important operations which we can perform without thinking about them.

Translating this statement from the global terms of "civilization" to the bounded world of the library organization has a number of implications.

First, to operate without paralysis in the complex world of modern librarianship, it is necessary to accept some fundamental assumptions on which our operations are based without "thinking about them," or more accurately, without questioning them in the course of everyday decision making. This is not to say that traditional working assumptions of the profession cannot be invalidated or that there is no room for new knowledge. On the contrary, numerous "important operations" are rife with uncertainty and many long-standing operational assumptions and rules of thumb are known to be suspect in the changing world of library and information science. In this context, Whitehead's insight is relevant to the pace and method of the adoption of new knowledge into practice. *To become operative in the world of practice, research results need to become known and established to the point that large numbers of practitioners accept them as self evidently superior to those assumptions they now accept "without thinking about them."* This process of accepting and assimilating new knowledge is not something that happens merely by conducting research and reporting results. Systematic attention and effort must be applied to the process of assimilation if research is to have impact in a time frame that is anything less than geologic.

Second, the library administrator is perhaps critically positioned to play the chief mediating role in the process of utilizing research results and demonstrating their value in practice. The academic research community has not been particularly successful in influencing the practitioner community. This failure is sometimes attributed to a lack of interest on the part of researchers in problems considered significant and relevant by practitioners, to a failure to translate research results into the terms of practice, or to the possibility that the academic LIS research community simply does not have sufficient critical mass to conduct research of high quality and also take an active role in its application. All but the third of these explanations are probably superficial.

More fundamentally, perhaps, are explanations based on the theories of Schön (1982) and others that the world of research and the arenas of practice in all professions are based on such totally conflicting paradigms that there are inherent and seemingly intractable barriers to communication. An effective bridging mechanism must rest heavily on a committed group of professionals who are conversant in both worlds and positioned as decision makers in the arenas in which new knowledge is to be applied. Most importantly, they must be prepared to deal sensitively with the conditions, limitations, values, and complexities of the world of practice. Such requirements disqualify most academic researchers for a direct role in assimilation and point emphatically to the library administrative/manager as the key agent.

The following sections will suggest a few management practices and policies which, if adopted on a broad scale by library administrators, could serve over time to change the perspectives of practitioners toward research and improve the environment for the integration of research into practice. Many of these suggestions are small measures, but taken together, their cumulative effect could result in a dramatic enhancement in the synergy between research and practice in LIS.

REQUIRE REFERENCE TO THE LITERATURE IN LIBRARY PLANNING DOCUMENTS AND COMMITTEE REPORTS

The staffs of large academic libraries produce internal background papers, planning documents, committee reports, needs assessments, etc., in large numbers. All too frequently such reports reflect an intensive analysis of the local situation or problem, but ignore the larger context of the issue as it may be revealed in the literature. It is not suggested here that formal or comprehensive literature reviews are appropriate for such documents. However, those who prepare internal reports should be encouraged to show cognizance of directly related literature in order to provide context and perspective on issues as they are manifest locally. Such a practice would not only serve to increase awareness of and appreciation for the research literature among staff, but could reveal gaps in the literature on problems of immediate concern to the profession and improve the quality of decisions in the library in some cases.

ENCOURAGE CONSCIENTIOUS RESPONSE TO QUESTIONNAIRES AND OTHER SURVEYS

The survey is one of the most frequently used methodologies in LIS research. In unpublished work, Hewitt and Seibert have analyzed 175 questionnaires and telephone surveys directed in a single year to the Library at the University of North Carolina at Chapel Hill.[2] Although many LIS surveys leave much to be desired in terms of survey design and quality of instrumentation, in general, they represent a serious effort to improve the level of understanding of libraries through research. In order to achieve respectable response rates, LIS surveys depend heavily on professional librarians who are not subject to negative questionnaire bias.

It is not being suggested that library administrators decree that all questionnaires be completed without exception. Some are so poorly conceived and executed that participation not only wastes the time of the respondent, but contributes to the production of inaccurate and misleading research. In the case of reasonably competent surveys, however, the manager should encourage a thorough response and require it for those surveys that show promise of being especially valuable to the discipline and/or profession.

The administrator can encourage a mindset among professional staff to take advantage of the learning opportunities that questionnaires and other surveys provide to respondents. These include:

- Questionnaires provide insights into what is of current research interest and how others frame problems;
- Questionnaires can cue librarians to be attentive to potential problem areas in their own operations;
- Questionnaires may alert librarians to the need to keep statistics and other management information on their operations that they do not ordinarily maintain; and

---

[2] A report of this study is in preparation. The study analyzes 175 telephone and questionnaire surveys directed to the Academic Affairs Library at the University of North Carolina at Chapel Hill in 1988. Surveys are being analyzed by source, type of survey, topic, time required to complete, information in cover letter, judgments regarding value, and by other factors. Also being analyzed as part of the study are in-depth interviews with respondents regarding their perspectives of specific survey techniques, question types, and so on.

- Especially competent questionnaires can be retained as models both for the library's own surveys and as standards by which to judge other questionnaires received by the library.

INSIST ON HIGH QUALITY IN SURVEYS CONDUCTED BY LIBRARY STAFF

The most frequent source of the surveys analyzed in the Hewitt and Seibert study were other libraries, 46 (26%), as compared to only 7 (4%) from researchers based in library schools and 16 (9%) from practicing librarians conducting independent research projects. Apparently, practicing librarians frequently consider it necessary to survey other libraries to gather information in support of local decisions. The library manager should exercise quality control over this activity in his or her own library through measures such as the following:

- Insist that a literature search be done before a survey is conducted. In many cases redundant surveys can be avoided by making use of the published literature;
- Have the developer of the questionnaire review appropriate methods textbooks on questionnaire design and administration *before* the instrument is developed;
- Review the sampling plan and/or peer group definition to ensure that the questionnaire is being sent to appropriate respondents;
- Review the questionnaire to see that it meets high standards of quality. If it is a complex questionnaire, particularly one which makes use of scaled and/or rank order responses, insist that the instrument be reviewed by a specialist in questionnaire design; and
- *Require* that all questionnaires be pretested.[3]

These same measures are recommended even more emphatically for user surveys the library may conduct, as they generally pose greater problems in terms of sampling strategy and the translation of library terminology into lay terms. Much of the decision-oriented, in-house research conducted by libraries is not considered research by those who conduct it, but "information gathering." By applying higher standards to this activity, some of the "information gathering" could be improved to a level that it would represent a respectable research contribution. At the same time, professional staff could begin to appreciate the relevance of obtaining more highly developed research skills in fulfilling the practical dimensions of their work.

---

[3] Although it should go without saying that all questionnaires should be pretested, evidence being analyzed in the Hewitt and Seibert study referred to above suggests that this may not be the case.

BE HOSPITABLE TO PROPOSALS TO CONDUCT RESEARCH IN THE LIBRARY

Some administrators resist proposals by outside researchers to conduct studies in their libraries, sometimes for good reason, but often due to a basic mistrust of researchers and the research process. Many practitioners complain that researchers, like newspaper reporters, oversimplify the situations of practice. The manager should be prepared to accept the inherent limitations of research, which are always necessary in the process of constructing measures, defining categories, and making use of other devices required to bring order to observations of complex, interactive phenomena. In spite of these limitations, the administrator should attempt to be hospitable to reasonable proposals from qualified and objective researchers. More open, unrestricted research sites must be made available to researchers if certain types of LIS research are to advance significantly. The library administrator is the key to opening up such access for researchers.

This is not to suggest, of course, that all proposals to conduct research in an organization should be approved routinely. Qualitative research studies involving extensive interviewing and observations of staff, systems studies requiring staff to keep diaries and statistics, studies involving unobtrusive observations of staff and users, and many other types of research, may raise difficult questions with respect to costs to the library, disruptive intrusion into the workplace, and even ethical questions. The administrator must weigh these issues carefully with respect to each specific proposal. In doing so, however, the administrator should be conscious of an obligation neither to be controlled by a negative bias toward research or certain research methodologies, nor to be affected by fears that research will result in a judgmental finding reflecting negatively on the library or on individuals in the organization. Such an outcome rarely occurs with research conducted responsibly.

TREAT MAJOR OPERATIONAL DECISIONS AS FIELD EXPERIMENTS

Perhaps one of the most dramatic ways in which the library administrator can improve LIS research is to adopt a practice, when possible and appropriate, of treating major operational developments as field experiments. "Major operational developments" refers here to events in the life of the library such as the following:

- Establishing major new services, such as end-user searching, a machine-readable data file center, or a document delivery service;
- Instituting new policies with respect to loan periods, faculty fines, library hours, etc.;

- Making available new automated systems or subsystems;
- Occupying a new building or addition, or significantly reorganizing the physical environment of the library;
- Changing the organizational structure of the library; and
- Instituting major new collection development programs or approaches.

Briefly, "field experiment" in this operational context refers to a process of measuring effects in a planned and systematic way as part of the process of implementing the change itself. This involves, among other things, documenting preexisting conditions (using quantitative measures when possible), predicting outcomes based on stated assumptions, deciding beforehand how and by what criteria and measures the change will be evaluated, insuring that appropriate observations are made throughout the process of change, adjusting or manipulating variables to affect outcomes, and culminating the change in longitudinal evaluative analysis.

Treating selected library decisions as natural experiments may not involve as much additional work as it may appear on the surface. Descriptive studies containing largely *post hoc* analysis of major library developments are often prepared by library staff in any case. Introducing a stronger element of design into such evaluations can often be done with little or no incremental cost. Indeed, overall effort may be reduced by the focus and definition of a designed evaluation in that the reconstruction required of totally *ex post facto* analyses is often inefficient and time-consuming. Most importantly, the quality of the evaluation will be improved. However, it is impossible to estimate causal linkages without a controlled field experiment design and, second, the subjectivity so common in *ex post facto* evaluations by persons involved directly in the development of a program can be controlled only by a designed evaluative process.

Of all the recommendations presented in this chapter, this one may hold the greatest potential for affecting LIS research in a positive and fundamental way over the long term. A sustained, cumulative, developmental/evaluative applied research effort, which uses replicable research designs and takes advantage of the almost limitless opportunities to conduct field research in a variety of settings, would no doubt have a profound impact on practice and perhaps even on the development of grounded theory. If such an effort is to be mounted, its required scale and the organization of the profession dictate that the library administrator play the key role in initiating and sustaining it.

DEVELOP AUTOMATED DATA SOURCES AND INCORPORATE THEM INTO LIBRARY DECISION-MAKING PROCESSES

Machlup (1976) called librarians to task for not maintaining data on their collections and acquisitions programs adequate to support sophisticated analysis of the availability of scholarly research materials (see also Heron, 1977; Machlup,

1977). In the course of his study, *The Production and Distribution of Knowledge in the United States*, and its follow-up, Machlup (1962, 1980–1984) had found a paucity of information about library collections, especially with respect to their subject composition. Although Machlup's complaint was ill-tempered and not entirely fair to librarians in light of the technology at the time, his point is well taken. It is the responsibility of the library administrator to assure that adequate data and documentation are maintained to support analytical approaches to management, LIS research, and even mega-analyses of the scholarly communication system, such as that conducted by Machlup.

Automated systems in libraries have served not only to improve and extend information services, but have also greatly expanded libraries' capacity to gather information on collections, acquisitions patterns, collection use, user interaction with online catalogs, and so on. Functional specialists involved in the development and implementation of systems tend to concentrate on systems features that support specific operational activities. It is the role of the administrator to take a broad overview of automated systems as generators of management information and to ensure that appropriate data-generation capabilities are designed and implemented.

In spite of large amounts of data being generated by library systems and staff, in many libraries this information is virtually sterile in terms of its impact on decisions. According to some respondents in the research currently underway by this author, one problem expressed by administrators is that staff are frequently not capable of analyzing and interpreting such data in meaningful ways.[4] This is not an issue of inferential statistics in that the data in question describe populations rather than samples. There appears to be a lack of skill in techniques of aggregation, data reduction, graphic display, and other data-manipulation techniques for the *logical* analysis and sound interpretation of large, interrelated sets of descriptive, quantitative data. If the full potential of automated systems for analytical management information is to be realized, library administrators must play a key role in defining more precisely the skills that librarians need in this environment of expanded management information. Administrators must also take steps to provide these skills. Following that, the administrator should attempt to take measures that ensure that available quantitative data are given due consideration in the library's decision-making processes.

ASSERT COMMITMENT TO RESEARCH AS PART OF THE LIBRARY'S MISSION STATEMENT

A formal and potentially powerful way in which the administrator can improve LIS research is to see that a commitment to research is asserted in the library's

---

[4] The author has received a CLR Fellows Grant to study the organizational change process in research libraries. In the course of in-depth interviews with administrators in libraries which have recently undergone structural organizational change, management process involving the use of quantitative data are frequently discussed.

mission statement. This may be a purely symbolic gesture if resources are not available to pursue such a goal. Even so, it constitutes recognition of the value of research in developing library services and programs, and can serve to legitimatize requests for resources to conduct a research program. In academic institutions, it may be necessary for the library to have an acknowledged independent research agenda in order to qualify librarians for leaves and other research support from the institution. Even within the library, resources dedicated to research may be resented by staff who see research as a frill that detracts from the effort to provide day-to-day library services. By incorporating research into the library's formal statement of goals, research activities are supported by an enabling rationale that protects them from unfounded criticism.

The following is quoted from a goals, objectives, and strategies statement of the Health Sciences Library of the University of North Carolina at Chapel Hill (*Strategic Plan*, 1988, p. 10).

> *Goal IV:* The library conducts and promotes research in information and library science.
>
> *Objective A:* Establish a research agenda which focuses on increasing the effectiveness of systems and services, and on prototype research and development.

The statement itemizes strategies to attain this goal as well as other objectives and strategies related to research. This is an exemplary statement in that it ties research directly to the development and improvement of services to users and concentrates on the developmental/evaluative research strategies most appropriate for an operational setting.

A persistent, underlying theme in many resource allocation decisions in libraries is the tension between critical immediate needs and those of programs required to prepare the library for the future. In many respects the situation in libraries is comparable to that of American industry, which all to often has maximized short-term profits at the cost of research and development, retooling, and other forms of reinvestment required to maintain long-term competitive effectiveness. LIS research should be viewed by the administrator as just this type of strategic investment for the library. Appropriate emphasis in the library's mission statement may be required to ensure that research is not invariably sacrificed to short-term goals and the pressures of the moment.

EXERCISE INFLUENCE ON LIBRARY ORGANIZATIONS CONDUCTING RESEARCH

Just as the library administrator can act directly to improve the quality of in-house "information gathering," "status inquiries," and other research-like investigation, he or she can often exercise a direct influence—through service on boards, committees, and advisory councils—on the research activities of organizations, such as national and regional networks, professional organizations, state library agencies, library consortia, the Association of Research Libraries (ARL) and the Council on Library Resources (CLR). For example, these organizations sometimes show a tendency to initiate surveys "at the drop of a hat" with little assessment of information already available or regard for the time of their member libraries or potential respondents. The design and instrumentation of surveys from these organizations are not always of the quality expected from such auspices.

When placed in a position of organizational influence, the library administrator should insist that specific research and planning projects meet the highest reasonable standards of quality. When serving on boards at the governing level, the administrator could initiate consideration of policies relating to the organization's research activities. For example, should organizations of significant size and resources have research specialists on the staff? Is there a need for formal mechanisms of board authorization and outside review of staff-initiated projects? Under what conditions should paid consultants or independent research firms be utilized? At the very least, library administrators serving on governing boards should require that the executive accountable directly to the board take full responsibility for the quality and usefulness of the research performed under the organization's auspices.

A similar opportunity for the library administrator to improve LIS research exists through service as reviewer for Federal agencies and foundations which offer grants to support library programs. Although funds are usually being sought to support library projects and programs of various types rather than research *per se*, the project evaluation plan is often a grading criterion of these proposals. In all too many cases, applicants and reviewers alike treat evaluation plans in a perfunctory manner. The library administrator, whether applicant for funds or reviewer of proposals, is in a position to insist that the statement of an evaluation strategy be treated as more than a proforma criterion. More serious treatment of this aspect of funded programs in libraries could greatly improve the status of developmental/evaluative LIS research.

ARTICULATE THE RESEARCH NEEDS AND CONCERNS OF THE PRACTITIONER COMMUNITY

Library administrators should assume, individually and in concert, a central role in articulating research needs and concerns on behalf of libraries as organizations. "Research," as a topic of discussion in the committees of professional organizations, and in programs and workshops of various types, is for the most part the province of individual professionals representing their personal views and interests. Even the items that are incorporated into the "research agendas" promulgated by various organizations are usually a collection of individual interests, sometimes considered and negotiated, but rarely embodying statements of need developed by persons empowered to represent a given constituency or position. In articulating the research needs of the practitioner community, the library administrator needs to assume an obligation to represent the assessed needs of library organizations as identified by some deliberative process within the library. In doing so, it may be necessary for the administrator to de-emphasize his or her personal research interests.

An interest in research is the ultimate expression of an individual's professional curiosity. In a modestly funded discipline such as LIS, the great bulk of research results from the drive and initiative of individual researchers. Within the library, in fact, much research is conducted by librarians pursuing personal professional interests. Given the fact that the research effort in LIS is so centered on the individual, it is only natural that a corporate position on research has been slow to emerge in libraries. On the other hand, if research agendas, proposals to bolster the research infrastructure, and programs to engage research more directly in practice are to be effective, they must reflect the needs of library organizations as represented by persons empowered to commit them to participation and support. It is the role of administrators to develop such positions and articulate them in appropriate venues.[5] In expressing the research concerns of the library organization, the administrator needs especially to articulate those needs for applied research that could actually be used in the operation of libraries and perhaps extended through developmental/evaluative research conducted in libraries.

SUPPORT ONGOING TRAINING IN RESEARCH SKILLS

The lack of training in research skills is frequently cited as a cause for low quality and volume of research from the practitioners community and for the fact that research does not play a prominent role in the management of libraries. Although this is no doubt the case, it represents only part of the picture. It is perhaps equally true that the content of introductory research methods courses to which the library professional has been exposed is not highly relevant to the situations of practice.

In terms of needs for research skills for professional staff, the administrator should, in particular, concentrate on those skills which are needed by the organization and which the librarian would employ in professional practice in service to

---

[5] An example of such an effort may be seen in the Ad Hoc Committee on Future Online Library Information Systems. The Committee, a group of seven ARL library directors organized by Paula Kaufman of the University of Tennessee, is seeking to define desirable characteristics for future generations of online library systems and strategies for attaining them (see Kaufman, 1990).

the institution. At some point, if the integration of research into practice is to progress, there must be greater discrimination of those academic research methodologies which research-oriented librarians should master on their own, perhaps through Ph.D. programs, and those which are actually required in the situations of professional practice.

As a result of the emphasis of some of the academic LIS research community on scientific research (i.e., hypothesis testing) and the use of inferential statistics as the basis for all legitimate research, research workshops for practitioners often represent little more than watered down versions of introductory content of a Ph.D. research methods course. The library administrator needs to take a strong stand in support of training for descriptive analytical methods, case study methods, analysis of documentary records, qualitative methods, and evaluation methodologies which the professional staffs of libraries are most likely to need in the fulfillment of assigned responsibilities in the library. This is not to imply that the administrator should not also support training in other methodologies, but these are likely to find forceful advocates in other quarters. In articulating the research needs of practice, the library administrator is uniquely qualified to play a role in advancing those applied methodologies that the academic research community may neglect.

PROVIDE INTELLECTUAL LEADERSHIP IN THE LIBRARY

The administrator occupies a position of leadership in terms of the organization of the library and, therefore, leads the library staff in the fulfillment of the library's mission of service. This in itself is a challenging responsibility. Yet, if research as well as other intellectual underpinnings of the profession are to be advanced, the administrator must also assume a role of intellectual leadership within the library.

Styles of intellectual leadership are highly individualistic, thus "recommendations" on how to pursue this ambiguous objective can only be suggestive and illustrative. Following are several examples of areas in which intellectual leadership might be exercised within the operational context of a library. Specific situations in libraries could provide numerous other examples.

- Professional staff members in libraries sometimes explain their lack of research productivity by the fact that they do not have good "ideas" for research projects. In many cases, this results from the fact that staff deeply involved in their own specializations and specific assignments are not in a position to discern the broader implications of their work. The library administrator is more strategically placed within the library and institution, and generally in the profession as well, to appreciate the significance of issues exemplified by specific local conditions and projects. An important aspect of intellectual

leadership is to constantly provide context, a comparative base, and perspective in a way that stimulates awareness of the research potential of the work in which staff are involved.
- In academic research libraries, high-level research competence that is not being fully utilized to serve the interests of LIS research may exist among the staff. This is especially the case with staff holding doctorates in humanistic disciplines who serve as bibliographers, curators, reference librarians, branch librarians, or specialized catalogers. Profession-wide, the failure to engage persons with the MLS and a subject Ph.D. in the LIS research effort on a broad scale represents a tremendous loss. This failure may be due in part to the fact that persons with these qualifications are not sufficiently excited by the intellectual challenges of LIS. The administrator in libraries where professional staff of this caliber are to be found should make a special effort to stimulate them to make a contribution to LIS research.
- A commonly observed phenomenon is that of young professionals losing their intellectual enthusiasm for the profession following the shock of the real world. The resource constraints of most libraries, the bureaucracy of large organizations, institutional politics, and the routine nature of some beginning professional positions often stand in stark contrast to the idealistic expectations instilled in programs of LIS education. No amount of "intellectual leadership" can prevent the deadening of fresh idealism and curiosity in all cases, but those who would exercise intellectual leadership within the library must attempt to do so. This can be done in part by orientation programs that give the beginning professional a perspective on the library as a whole and by assigning the most stimulating and creative senior professionals the role of training and mentoring new librarians. The real key, however, in keeping intellectual curiosity alive among beginning professionals is to attempt to transfer their interests to the intellectual dimensions of the real-world situations they face. Having mastered the contrived and sanitized intellectual puzzles of LIS education, they may be overwhelmed and discouraged by the complexities of interaction in organizational life, the competition of values, the discipline of closure without conclusive evidence, the art of practical compromise without abandoning principle, and so on.

The administrator exercises "intellectual leadership" when the staff, and in particular the new professionals, are stimulated to understand the world of practice at a deeper level and perhaps to learn better how to influence it through methods developed by research, even if they are frustrated in applying their findings. The administrator must attempt to prevent staff from being discouraged about the ultimate benefits of research, even though organizational context may dictate that it is not the determining factor in most decisions. The key is to provide an environment for a serious intellectual engagement in the profession, while at the same time effectively pursuing the practical ends of the library.

In the broadest sense, "intellectual leadership" may come closest to describing what is needed generally in LIS for the advancement of research, not only from library administrators, but from all sectors represented in this collection. This need not be as daunting a goal as it may appear. We are accustomed to thinking of intellectual leadership in terms of the Jesse Shera's and other true giants of the profession, but the emergence of intellectual leadership of this stature is a matter of pure chance. A more critical need, in fact, is for a larger number of individuals to begin exercising intellectual leadership within their libraries, and otherwise, within the scope of their professional activity, however circumscribed it may be, if the general caliber of research in LIS is to be improved.

CONCLUSION

There may appear to be a fundamental conflict between the introductory segment of this chapter, which concentrates on the barriers to research playing a vital role in the practice of the profession, and the description of the 11 measures (expressed in rather optimistic terms) which the library administrator can take to promote the integration of research into practice. It is hoped that the two views are not taken as contradictory.

On the one hand, research may never become the controlling factor in the majority of important, value-laden, politically conscious decisions which must be made in libraries. On the other hand, it is important that research become a more prominent element in decision making, taking over some areas now controlled by subjective elements of professional judgment, if LIS is to maintain its credibility as a knowledge-based profession and gain a greater measure of predictability and control over its actions and their outcomes. This is presented as a balanced and, one hopes, realistic position which in itself could help to promote LIS research. By actively supporting research in appropriate arenas of practice, while not aggressively asserting its hegemony in areas of high sensitivity to practitioners, research can gain adherents from those who would otherwise feel threatened.

The 11 suggested measures by which administrators can act to improve LIS research may appear to involve a heavy commitment of energy and attention, even for those who are active supporters of research. But improvement can occur even if action is taken only in a few of these areas. The key is for these strategies to become as habitual and self-perpetuating as those which they replace.

REFERENCES

Glass, Gene V. "Educational Knowledge Use," *The Educational Forum*, 36 (November 1971): 21–29.

Heron, David W. "More on the Production and Distribution of Knowledge in the United States," *AAUP Bulletin*, 63 (November 1977): 289–291.

Kaufman, Paula T. *Future Library Information System: An Exploration of Needs and Strategies*. Unpublished report distributed to directors of ARL member libraries, February 1990.

Machlup, Fritz. *Knowledge, Its Creation, Distribution, and Economic Significance*. Volumes 1–3. Princeton, NJ, Princeton University Press, 1980–1984.

———. "My Short Shoelaces and the Shortage of Library Data," *AAUP Bulletin*, 63 (November 1977): 291–293.

———. "Our Libraries: Can We Measure Their Holdings and Acquisitions?," *AAUP Bulletin*, 62 (October 1976): 303–307.

———. *The Production and Distribution of Knowledge in the United States*. Princeton, NJ, Princeton University Press, 1962.

Mintzberg, Henry. *The Nature of Managerial Work*. New York: Harper & Row, 1973.

Schön, Donald A. *The Reflective Practitioner: How Professionals Think in Action*. New York: Basic Books, 1982.

Strategic Plan. Chapel Hill, NC: Health Sciences Library, University of North Carolina, August 1988 (Draft).

chapter thirteen

The Role of Practicing LIS Professionals

Irene B. Hoadley

The definition of library roles must be broadened to include a research component. Research has value because it affords an opportunity to influence the profession and to more fully integrate libraries with the goals of the institution. Research also provides recognition. Research efforts must be supported with time, money, and institutional support. The greatest inhibiting factor is the ability and expertise to do research. Strategies can be implemented to bring the need for research to reality.

When one thinks of libraries, it is usually of books and services. These are the traditional roles of libraries, but the concept of a library includes much more, especially in areas such as technology transfer. However, another component of the library should be included in a broadened definition, and that component is research. Research is part of the fabric of librarianship just as it is for other disciplines. In fact, according to the "Joint Statement on Faculty Status of College and University Librarians" (1988, p.5),

> Librarians perform a teaching and research role inasmuch as they instruct students formally and informally and advise and assist faculty in their scholarly pursuits. Librarians are also themselves involved in the research function; many conduct research in their own professional interests and in the discharge of their duties.

In making the assumption that research should be integral to librarianship, there should be an opportunity for research to influence the profession and to be integrated into the academic goals of the institution. Research can also afford recognition to librarians. On the other hand, librarians face constraints, such as time, financial and institutional support, research abilities, and laboratory opportunities.

No one questions the need for research in librarianship, but there are questions about the quality and quantity of that research. Perhaps Engle (1987) made the most appropriate statement of the need for research when he noted that librarians must participate in the process of research to really be a part of the endeavor of creating knowledge. Research should not be an external process but a part of our professional responsibility.

If the conduct of research is a professional responsibility, it falls to each segment of the profession to contribute to the totality. Over the years, there have been many efforts to create a research agenda for the profession, all of which have achieved very little (see Chapter 3). A top-down dictum is likely to never get substantial support from the profession. A bottom-up approach that integrates research into every aspect of the profession has a much better chance for success.

ISSUES AFFECTING RESEARCH

A number of studies have shown that practicing librarians contribute significantly to research in library and information science (LIS) (see, for example, McClure and Bishop, 1989, pp. 130–131; Feehan, Gragg, Havener, and Kester, 1987, p. 180; Olsgaard and Olsgaard, 1980, p. 51; and Adamson and Zamora, 1981, pp. 237, 239). However, the number of individuals who get published is actually limited. Clearly, a small proportion of people do a large percentage of the writing and research, especially on an ongoing basis.

Influencing the Profession

The opportunity to influence the profession should be an issue. Librarians can use research efforts to determine the feasibility of introducing new services. They can undertake research to determine if a new product is better than an existing one, to compare several products, or to decide how best to provide a particular service. For example, when end-user searching first became feasible, it was possible to test a few alternatives and see how best to schedule users and the most appropriate type of instructional materials. The conduct of research affords an opportunity for libraries to improve the quality of the environment in which they provide services and complete operations. Librarians can examine operations with the intent of improving library efficiency, effectiveness, and accountability. They can demonstrate how they can utilize existing and new technologies to enhance or extend library operations.

Integration in Institutional Goals

Involvement in the research process enables academic libraries to meet the teaching, research, and service goals of the institution. If research is a part of the library's ethic, it is more in sync with the goals of the institution. Research integrates the library into the structure of the organization. In a public or special library environment, the completion of research endeavors can help establish credibility.

Recognition

Librarians and libraries gain recognition from the completion of research efforts. A library that has an active research program will be known for those efforts. Research is a means of legitimizing the role of librarians and adding to our professional credibility. Recognition can be enhanced by something as simple as having librarians' publications, service involvement, and presentations included in a campus newsletter. Librarians need to be nominated for campus awards. These are all little things, but over time they might make a difference. In libraries where the professional staff have faculty status, usually individuals must meet criteria equivalent to other faculty members. One of those requirements may be the conduct of research. In any event, it makes good sense for stakeholders to be participants in the process.

Librarians should share in any campus funding for research, such as mini-grant funding or institutional research funds. Sharing in the receipt of these funds also opens the door to participation in the distribution of those funds when decision making takes place through a faculty process. It is better to influence our future than to have someone else determine it for us.

A number of librarians claim that there is a lack of topics to research. In fact, one only needs to look around a library to identify a myriad of possible research topics. There is always a need for statistics, information, and data comparing libraries. Most statistics deal with extensiveness and size, but often these statistics are not very current. Where are the statistics on access measures or on services? Where are the statistics that promote quality and effectiveness, rather than quantity? What happens to service levels when budgets are stable and materials' prices escalate? There is little comparative information on services. Is one CD-ROM product more useful than another? What measures are useful in comparing computerized services? What factors should be used to determine when to use a CD-ROM database or when to load that database as a part of the online catalog?

Librarians and users benefit from assessments of existing services and operations. How can routine operations, such as shelving books, become more efficient? Or, what is an acceptable standard for moving a book from receipt to the shelf? There should be studies of use patterns of libraries (and not only catalogs). Studies can examine the organization of library functions based on use patterns. Studies correlating use and grades, or publication rate, would be beneficial. How do libraries determine which items will be used and build more relevant collections? The list of topics can go on and on.

CONSTRAINTS AND OPPORTUNITIES

The key issues, constraints, and opportunities effecting the role of practicing LIS professionals and research overlap. All center around time, money, and institutional support.

Time

Time is a precious commodity in any organization. All libraries must prioritize the need to acquire, process, and service their collections, as well as to offer an array of other access services ranging from providing microcomputer laboratories to instructing faculty in how to search an automated database. Many academic librarians also have service, research, and publication commitments. When these multilayered responsibilities are combined with limited staff, it is often easier to forgo secondary responsibilities. It may be easier, but it is not always beneficial or economical. It takes time to evaluate new services and procedures, but in the end it may be less time-consuming than continuing an unproductive or even wasteful procedure.

Financial Support

Financial support is also an issue when it comes to research. It takes money to carry out a research project even though in library and information science the money may be modest in comparison to other disciplines. Hundred of dollars may be adequate to conduct a survey or to hire students to work on a complex project. Without the availability of some funds, there may be little incentive to conduct a study.

The amount of financial resources available in libraries is always limited. Some libraries have funds provided by the institution, or they share in general institutional support for research. Some libraries have secured external funding for the conduct of research endeavors. A broader array of agencies have the potential to provide funding to libraries, although little of this money goes to the completion of research efforts. Some funds come from release time and operating budgets, but this type of funding allows only for a very modest research program.

Institutional Support

Institutional support is defined as commitment since financial support has already been mentioned. The first and most important commitment is from the library administration. Commitment in this situation is both belief and support. If the library's upper-level administrators do not believe in the value and importance of research, their viewpoint will be evident to the other library staff. The administrators must identify a value and benefit that can result from research efforts. The value can be improved salary or position, or more simply it can be the opportunity to continue to improve the operations of the organization.

Institutional support also includes the provision of tools to carry out research. Computer time for data analysis, access to word processing equipment, or the freedom to use the library as a laboratory are a few examples. Without these and other tools, the ability of staff to do research can be very limited.

Research Abilities

One constraint that practicing LIS professionals face is limited ability, expertise, and knowledge to conduct research. Because many library education programs do not require a research course, graduates come into the profession without basic research skills unless they had obtained them in another educational program, or in some other way. Research must be viewed as part of the ethic of the profession, required of all students in library education programs, and integrated into all library education courses.

In addition, local-level initiatives can supplement formal educational programs in developing research skills. A library or perhaps a consortium of libraries can provide in-house courses on research methodologies. This would require bringing in a librarian, library educator/researcher, or someone from another discipline to provide the necessary instruction. At this level, a course can be aimed at the particular needs of individuals rather than trying to provide a generic program that may only benefit a small number of participants. This is, then, a bottom-up process which involves those with an interest and the capabilities for the conduct of research.

Laboratory Opportunities

The library is a laboratory for identifying research opportunities. Every service or procedure is a ready-made research project. Libraries can analyze what they are doing, and, with any kind of luck, become more efficient and effective organizations.

Accountability has never been a major concern of most librarians. Librarians tend to view the library as an integral part of the parent organization. This is an attitude whose time has passed. One only need look at library budgets and the library's place in the organization to know this is no longer true. By using research to show, in an analytical way, that libraries are improving their operations and obtaining better insight into what needs to be done to meet the information needs of their users, the library strengthens its position in terms of accountability.

Planning

Research is a mechanism to improve planning in libraries. It provides a means of examining what the library does well and what it should be doing.

External Funding

Another opportunity centers around an expanded group of external sources for funding. With an enlarged view of the academic library as an information node for the campus and for its external constituencies, there is an increasing willingness on the part of nontraditional sources to provide funding that libraries can use to support research initiatives. However, librarians will have to be aggressive in seeking such funding. Libraries are a tremendous showplace for new products and equipment because of the multiplicity of users and the disciplines they represent. What better place to showcase new equipment to a large numbers of individuals who will soon be a part of the corporate or public sector world and be in a position to make decisions about acquiring equipment or systems.

WHERE WE SHOULD GO FROM HERE

A number of strategies should be implemented during the next three to five years. At the outset it must be recognized that what should happen will not occur if leadership or a stated impetus is lacking. Six strategies can be pursued.

Proposed Strategies

Research Interaction. There should be more interaction among practicing librarians, LIS faculty, and other faculty in the conduct of research. An examination of the literature will show that there is only limited interaction among these three groups regarding research. Much of the interaction has been stimulated by the Council on Library Resources through its Cooperative Research Grants program. Such interaction could strengthen research in librarianship by bringing together the laboratory, the practitioner, and the theoretician; and by focusing some research on helping libraries to fulfill their role in a more meaningful way.

Interaction also brings an expertise to the process which may be missing. For example, involving a statistician in drawing a sample or implementing a use assessment project, or consulting someone with expertise in survey instrument development, provides more opportunity for a study to have reliable and valid results. If a project explores how different segments of the university community utilize information, that project could be strengthened by involving scholars in various disciplines.

Continuing Education. There should be additional opportunities for continuing education related to the use of different research methodologies. Few continuing education courses center on research, although the Association of College and Research Libraries (ACRL) does have one available continuing education course. When ACRL had a preconference several years ago on research, that program was over subscribed. Another indication of interest is the proliferation of research committees within ALA. Research previously centered within two groups, but now every division and some sections have initiated their own research efforts.

A library education program recently established a new research institute, but its primary flaw is that the institute's programs and services are directed at library educators. The Office of Library Programs, Office of Education Research and Improvement, U.S. Department of Education, recently undertook an initiative to build a library research infrastructure ("Workshop on Building a Library Research Infrastructive," 1988). So far, these efforts have touched only a selected group of professionals who consider themselves primarily researchers. Through continued activities, a larger number of individuals will be involved. The pyramid must continue to be expanded if research is to be integrated into ongoing library initiatives at every level.

Funding Opportunities. There should be more involvement in research funding opportunities. Even though the specific funding sources for LIS research are limited, an embarrassingly small number of people apply for these grants. The Baber Award sponsored by ALA is a good example. On the other hand, there are large numbers of applications for the demonstration programs funded by the Federal government. Libraries need to find a way to move from the demonstration to the research mode. It must be recognized that funding levels are also a part of this picture since the funds for most awards are quite limited.

Some initiatives could be undertaken to increase interest in pursuing funding opportunities. First, there needs to be a better recognition in the profession of individuals who receive funding. Particularly for novice researchers, this is an added impetus for the effort made. Second, individuals need to be made aware that funding benefits both the institution and the individual. Awards create visibility for an individual which, in turn, creates more opportunities for that individual. The winning of awards is also a positive reinforcement factor in career development.

State Organizations. Research units should be incorporated into state organizations. Most state library organizations do not have a research initiative or, if they do, it is a very modest one. There needs to be an effort to encourage such initiatives to foster more base-level support for the initiation of research activities.

Library Research Committees. There is a need to incorporate research committees/units into libraries. A few libraries have had such initiatives for a long period; however, such initiatives are not a common occurrence. Such activities provide a training ground for many professionals in gaining the skills and expertise to move up to another level of accomplishment. This recommendation is also tied to the need for continuing education opportunities. Programs should exist not only on the national level, but also on the state and local level since only a small percentage of librarians travel to national meetings/programs. Either a prepackaged program, or perhaps a listing of speakers on program possibilities that could be provided to those at the state or local level, could be an added impetus for moving forward in encouraging more and better research.

The creation of such tools could be accomplished in one of several ways. The most plausible organization would be the American Library Association (ALA), and more explicitly the Library Research Round Table or the Committee on Research because of the diversity of their memberships. Another alternative would be to draw members from the division research committees to form a task force to prepare a listing of possible speakers that would include all types of libraries. The creation of a prepackaged program could be accomplished by an ALA unit or perhaps more appropriately by a library education program or faculty members in such a program, or through the auspices of the Association of Library and Information Science Education (ALISE). If all else fails, get a volunteer who would be willing to take on one or both tasks.

Research in Librarianship. Research should be an integral part of the fabric of librarianship. Achieving this aspiration is neither a simple nor easy task, and it does not pertain only to practicing LIS professionals. It will take all of the above strategies, plus the leadership of both individuals and library organizations, to achieve this long-range aspiration.

THE NEXT STEP

If these strategies could be implemented before the end of the decade, librarianship will have made a great stride forward. If LIS is to be both a profession and a discipline, it must move away from debate and take action.

Beginning at the base level, libraries must create research initiatives and support for LIS professionals. Specific actions which can be taken include establishing research committees which will promote research activities and foster the development of research expertise. Expertise can be enhanced by offering an onsite workshop on research methodologies, by having experienced researchers who can mentor beginning researchers, or by contracting with experienced researchers to assist those who are inexperienced. This should not be a one-time activity, but must be a part of an ongoing program so that LIS professionals can continue to develop their research skills over time and so that new professionals can begin to assimilate research skills just as they assimilate other skills.

An identified leadership component must make change materialize. Already established organizations, such as ALA and ALISE, could take on such a role, but this will not happen unless there is an impetus to make it happen.

Another important strategy is to impact library education programs. Over time, there has been a "yo-yo posture" on the place of a research course in the curriculum of some library education programs. This must be changed. Library education programs must educate our future librarians about the value and mechanics of research. This can be done through a specific research course, but it could also be done by incorporating a research component throughout the curriculum. In a reference course, for instance, a component might introduce appropriate methodologies for measuring or evaluating reference service. An integrated approach would have more relevance in bringing research and library functions together in a way that would encourage evaluation at all levels of activity.

Priorities often arise from crisis, but it will be difficult to show that librarianship is in a crisis because of the limited amount of research now being conducted and reported. Perhaps it is time for the profession to work to avert a crisis by taking the offensive. The problem has long been recognized and touted in the professional literature, but few corrective measures have been implemented. Once again, the profession seems to be choosing the path of least resistance; that path will end up taking us everywhere and nowhere. The preferred path would be to make something happen and let research achieve its proper role within the profession.

REFERENCES

Adamson, Martha C. and Gloria J. Zamora. "Publishing in Library Science Journals: A Test of the Olsgaard Profile," *College & Research Libraries*, 42 (May 1981):235–241.

Engle, Michael. "Creativity and the Research Process in Academic Libraries," *College & Research Libraries News*, 10 (November 1987):629–631.

Feehan, Patricia E., W. Lee Gragg II, W. Michael Havener, and Diane D. Kester. "Information Science Research: An Analysis of the 1984 Journal Literature," *Library & Information Science Research*, 9 (July 1987):173–185.

"Joint Statement on Faculty Status of College and University Librarians," in *Academic Status: Statements and Resources*. Chicago, IL: Academic Status Committee, Association of College and Research Libraries, American Library Association, 1988.

McClure, Charles R. and Ann Bishop. "The Status of Research in Library/Information Science: Guarded Optimism," *College & Research Libraries*, 50 (March 1989): 127–143.

Olsgaard, John N. and Jane Kinch Olsgaard. "Authorship in Five Library Periodicals," *College & Research Libraries*, 41 (January 1980):49–53.

"Workshop on Building a Library Research Infrastructure." Washington, D.C.: Office of Library Programs, Office of Education Research and Improvement, U.S. Department of Education, October 31 and November 1, 1988.

chapter fourteen

The Role of Professional Associations

Julie A. C. Virgo

Professional associations play a critical role in fostering research through accreditation standards, stimulating research capabilities by conducting continuing education courses, recognizing outstanding research through awards programs, disseminating the results of research through publications and conferences, and providing a forum for the exchange of ideas on likely avenues of research. Thus, the appropriate role for an association is to stimulate, coordinate, and disseminate the research of its members, but not usually to actually conduct the research which would serve to put the association in competition with its own membership.

Webster's Third New International Dictionary (1968, pp. 132–133) defines an association as "a formal or social group expressly organized to satisfy the specific intents and purposes of its members." A professional association is generally characterized as having:

- A volunteer membership;
- Access to a large number of people in the profession;
- A body of people who collectively have a tremendous wealth of experiences to draw upon in a common field;
- Access to pooled funds (from membership dues and other revenue sources) to attack problems that are industry-wide and which may be too expensive for any one institution to deal with;
- Many competing interests and priorities within its membership;
- Influence on entry into the profession, and the education of those in the profession because of the association's concern with professional practice;
- General standards for the performance of its members, by the promotion of statements, such as "Codes of Professional Ethics," and the expectation of continuing professional development;

- Journals and other literature for disseminating research developments and reports;
- The ability to attract a significant mass of the profession whenever it holds meetings, be they national, regional, or local;
- The numbers to speak on behalf of the profession, in presenting a unified voice on issues affecting the profession; and
- The perception by outside groups as a voice of legitimacy and authority about issues and matters relating to that profession.

SOME REALITIES

In considering the role of professional associations in improving library and information science research, it is useful to consider the realities in which professional associations exist, the things that associations do well that can support research efforts, and those areas where they are less effective. A recent task force (Virgo et al., 1989, pp. 19–31) addressed the role of associations in supporting library and information science research. Building on arguments by Jeffrey Katzer (1987, 1989) and Robert Wedgeworth (1987), it concluded that while it is possible for associations to promote a better understanding of library research and to disseminate the results to a wider audience, several factors tend to limit the role of library and information science associations. By recognizing these factors explicitly, we may be able to determine appropriate roles that will "step around" these realities.

Priorities

Associations reflect the interest of their members. Only a very small percentage of the library and information science (LIS) community has an interest in research. As an example, the American Library Association's membership is dominated by practitioners and institutions. Less than two percent of ALA's members belong to its Library Research Round Table (Katzer, 1987, 1989). Association priorities are dictated by the concerns of either a large group of members or a small, highly vocal minority. The majority of library and information science association members place a low priority on research. People appear to be more concerned with day-to-day issues of funding, staffing, technology, and services. There is an emphasis on short-term thinking rather than long-term learning and development. Even when research is addressed, it is often of the statistics-gathering or most basic applied type. One of the major causes for the current state of research is that too much falls under the heading of consulting, demonstration projects, or other activities that are designed to assist information professionals with their immediate problems (Katzer, 1987, 1989).

It is doubtful that a significant portion of membership dues will ever be used to support research activities. Institutional resources for associations—income from membership dues, publications, and conferences—are heavily committed to the defined objectives of the associations, and for those in the field of library and information science, research has not been a priority concern.

Because of these factors, the priority given to research depends on the undependable ingredients of attitude and leadership, both of which in a volunteer membership organization can change from year to year.

Autonomy

At the heart of the integrity of the research process is the autonomy or independence of the researcher in making judgments with regard to the design, methodology, and other aspects of the work. When a library association is the sponsor of the research, the collective judgment of the association—usually represented by a committee—must be reconciled with that of the researcher. Under the circumstances, the critical research judgments are at best a sound compromise. If the association seeks to promote its own research priorities, either the priorities will not be accepted or they will unduly influence the selection of research questions. Both outcomes represent a challenge to research autonomy and diminish the potential contribution that independently conceived research can make to the field.

Competition for Funding

Library associations can promote research by using their influence to obtain funding for worthy research projects; however, this places the association in competition with its members for scarce research funds. From time to time this situation arises when government agencies announce competitive research grants in the areas deemed to be of national significance to the field. For the most part, associations have resisted the temptation to compete with member researchers, but they have been unsuccessful when the temptation has been overwhelming. On several occasions associations have sought advisory status with the successful research grantee. This practice seems questionable at best, since reputable researchers are already open to competent advice from associations. Further, it would be difficult for an official advisor to claim any significant degree of objectivity in reviewing the results of the research.

Motivation

The desire to elevate the importance of research, while understandable, clearly relates to the politics of research. In examining this factor, the question of which research is to be elevated is an important one. The motive for elevating the importance of research relates to the political objectives of the association in relation to the external world rather than the intrinsic merits of research. The process of selecting one or more types of research for promotion over others is much more difficult for an association to justify than for a government agency, and the potential rewards are dubious.

Research Competence

The competence to carry out a research project differs greatly from the competence to administer, coordinate, or otherwise assure its successful outcome. Competence for an association involves financial stability of the organization, administrative continuity of its leadership, and the commitment of a cadre of members knowledgeable about research. Few library associations are capable of meeting the requirements for carrying out (as opposed to administering) an extended research program beyond that of serving as a forum for the presentation of results.

Authority

The authority of an association with respect to its field is not automatically transferrable to the field of research. The authority of an individual researcher stems from experience and the cumulative judgment of peers as to the quality of his or her work. Therefore, the ability of an association to influence the work of a reputable researcher is limited by the kinds of rewards that can be provided as inducements. Since the authority of the association is more diffuse than that of the researcher, the inducements must take the form of public recognition, as distinct from peer recognition or financial rewards. Here again, the selection process runs the risk of alienating some members of the research community if the process is not administered by or for researchers on the basis of the intrinsic merits of the research rather than the political objectives of the association.

DRIVING FORCES

Given the reality that a very small percentage of the library and information science community places a priority on research, and that associations' priorities are usually a reflection of their membership, at first glance it may seem surprising that our professional associations do, in fact, support the research element of the profession. The reasons for this have been cogently summarized by Robert Hayes (1989, p. 12) and are quoted here:

- Associations gain value for both themselves, as organizations, and especially for their members;
- The associations and their members gain visibility by publicizing research efforts;

- By collaborating on activities that one institution cannot do as readily (e.g., gathering profession-wide statistics), the associations gain in effectiveness;
- The associations can add to their image of having more clout than any one individual institution;
- The associations can draw on the tremendous range of talents of their members; and
- The associations can increase their impact on the educational process.

In addition, a strong driving force for associations is the realization, not necessarily in conscious awareness, but there nevertheless, of the underlying premise of being a "profession." As defined by *Webster's Third New International Dictionary* (1968, p. 1811), a profession is "a calling requiring specialized knowledge and often long and intensive preparation including instruction in skills and methods as well as in the scientific, historical, or scholarly principles underlying such skills and methods." If the association does not embrace responsibility for promoting and improving research, how then can it justify its existence as a *professional* association?

ROLES FOR ASSOCIATIONS

Building on the characteristics of associations, there are activities that associations can pursue with best effect and, in some instances, are the only organizations that can undertake these initiatives.

Accreditation

To the extent that an association is involved in the accreditation process, it has an impact on the skills and competencies that will be required as entry to the profession, on the curricula and objectives of the school, and on the qualification and activities of those who educate these students. Ideally, the accreditation process can be used to stimulate the development of a "research ethic" in the schools, to instill a value strong enough to make the quality of faculty research the norm rather than the exception, and to ensure the training of practitioners, all of whom are competent consumers of research and some of whom are trained in the rudiments of the research process.

Critical Mass

Within the profession, library and information science researchers are usually a geographically scattered group. Even within the largest LIS schools or libraries there is rarely a critical mass of researchers working on closely related topics. Associations, through their conferences and publications, provide the opportunity for informal discussion, the exchange of ideas, and the mentoring of younger researchers in the profession. These occasions provide nurturing support, reinforcement, and new ideas that are critical for a researcher working in relative isolation.

At the other end of the spectrum, when desirable, an association can bring together with relative ease a *broad* range of members to identify issues and expertise.

Conferences

Along with opportunities for informal discussion, association conferences provide opportunities for the formal communication and dissemination of the results of research. Additionally, at meetings such as these there is the possibility of the identification of emerging research issues and the setting of priorities for future research directions.

Research Committees

Associations can establish structures, within their organizations, whose purpose is to promote and stimulate research. Such committees can plan activities that serve to foster research and conduct clearinghouse functions that might otherwise be handled by paid staff in the larger associations.

Clearinghouse Functions

Activities that go beyond the limits of any one institution are well-suited for associations. Associations can serve as clearinghouses for:

- Research in progress;
- Information from a broad number of individuals and institutions;
- Referrals and advice;
- Expertise about trends, issues, and methodologies; and
- Information on potential funding sources.

Joint Projects

In a similar vein, associations can coordinate the collection of data from their members, such data forming the basis for subsequent research activity. Some research projects require the imprimatur of an impartial association to free some members to contribute data and other information.

A recent survey across professions indicates a number of vehicles associations use to encourage and improve research (Virgo et al., 1989, p. 30). These activities include: Conducting workshops or clinics on research methodologies, evaluating research, and getting published; offering awards, such as the "best" paper published in the association's scholarly journals, or a panel or award for the most outstanding doctoral dissertations; providing small grants or scholarships to help defray out-of-pocket expenses for members to conduct research projects; compiling and publicizing guides to funding sources or research opportunities; and, providing competitions or special conferences for students, aimed solely to encourage research and the dissemination of the results.

Publications

A primary mark of a profession is the development of a scholarly body of knowledge which continues to grow and be furthered. Hence, an important role for an association is the dissemination of its scholarly literature through the publication of refereed journals, monographs, and other formal communication media.

Focal Point

Associations can serve as the focal point for government agencies or other bodies wanting to explore specific issues or topics. Similarly, an association can spearhead drives for funding and focus when topics of national or of a "very large size" become apparent. Potentially, an association can serve as a means for influencing political policies relating to research agendas.

RECOMMENDATIONS

Research is critical for the survival and growth of information science and librarianship as a profession. Our researchers are relatively few in number and geographically scattered. Some of our most respected schools with strong Ph.D. programs (e.g., Case Western Reserve, the University of Chicago, and now Columbia University) are or have been closed in recent years. Our associations, both individually and collaboratively, must consciously take the lead to instill an understanding and appreciation of the centrality of research to the professions, and to provide opportunities to foster research and the dissemination of its results.

Recognizing that associations respond to the majority or a highly vocal minority, research groups within associations must plan to be highly vocal and visible.

Possible avenues for individual association efforts have been spelled out previously. Collaborative efforts can include: developing and exchanging research agendas, and publicizing these as a way to stimulate specific research projects; sponsoring joint programs at conferences either with other associations or with institutions that conduct research, such as OCLC or the National Library of Medicine; coordinating and publicizing information across associations about research related to libraries and information science; and engaging in cooperative efforts to support Federal and other forms of funding for research in librarianship and information science.

No one association has responsibility for research. Yet, all associations share that responsibility. Each must contribute by promoting research and by disseminating results or, as a profession, we will die.

REFERENCES

Hayes, Robert. "Overview of Position Papers and Discussion," in *Rethinking the Library in the Information Age*. Vol. 3. Prepared by the Department of Education. Washington, D.C.: GPO, 1989, pp. 1–17.

Katzer, Jeffrey. "A Look at Library/Information Science Research and Methods." Paper presented at the Library Research Roundtable Forum III. San Francisco, CA: American Library Association, June 30, 1987.

———. "ALA and the Status of Research in Library/Information Science," *Library & Information Science Research,* 11(1989): 83–87.

Virgo, Julie, A.C., Miriam Drake, Jeffrey Katzer, Mary Jo Lynch, Ann Prentice, and Robert Wedgeworth. "The Role of Professional Library Associations in Creating an Infrastructure for Research in Library and Information Science," in *Rethinking the Library in the Information Age*. Vol. 3. Prepared by Department of Education. Washington, D.C.: GPO, 1989, pp. 19–31.

Webster's Third New International Dictionary. Springfield, MA: Merriam Co., 1968.

Wedgeworth, Robert. "Promoting Research through Library Associations." Paper presented at IFLA Conference, Brighton, England, 1987.

chapter fifteen

The Role of Editors and Editorial Boards in Journal Publishing*

Dorothy L. Steffens
Jane B. Robbins

This chapter discusses the role that editors and editorial boards play in the dissemination of research. Researchers and practioners of library and information science must have an understanding of the publication process. A discussion of editorial board selection, the referee process, and guidelines for publishing is supported by a review of the literature and input from a poll of editors of seven scholarly journals in library and information studies/science. Suggestions for improvement include better communication among authors, editors, and publishers, and active solicitation of research from members of the research and practitioner communities.

Every day of the week a myriad of researchers in library and information studies submit their work to journal editors. Few of these researchers fully understand the publication process or know what journal editors do. This chapter addresses the role that editors and editorial board members play in the research enterprise. The chapter focuses on *the dissemination process* and *assumes working editorial boards* as opposed to *cosmetic boards*, the latter formed primarily to legitimize the authority of a journal rather than to participate in the process of selecting material for publication. The chapter is based upon a review of the literature regarding the publication process, peer reviews, and the role of editors. In addition, editors of seven of the field's scholarly journals (*College & Resarch Libraries, Journal of Academic Librarianship, Journal of Education for Library and Information Science, Journal of the American Society of Information Science, Library Quarterly, Library Trends* and *RQ*) were contacted in order to

---

* The authors wish to thank Deena Karadsheh, a doctoral student at the University of Wisconsin-Madison, School of Library and Information Studies, for aid in the initial work in the development of this chapter.

obtain their views concerning editorial policies and procedures; six of the seven editors responded.

RESEARCH PRODUCTION AND THE ROLE OF EDITORS

As the library and information community has become more sophisticated, the researcher and practitioner communities have come closer to a shared understanding of the importance of research for the field. In the past only the very small researcher community had been interested in the systematic search for foundations in library and information science. But now, as the field matures into its second century, a growing number of practitioners have become interested in the field's research base. Additionally, information as a concept has become a vital interest to other disciplines, making applicable research more available. Because practitioners are acutely aware of serious service effectiveness problems and information agency managers confront critical economic questions, they look to this growing body of research to aid them in making informed decisions.

Editors play a critical role in the communication of the growing body of knowledge in library and information science. Because the need to communicate research methods and findings with peers is virtually second nature for library researchers, they have tended to develop communication channels that grow insular. Editors should take responsibility for identifying research that has practical applications and, if necessary, encourage researchers to make available their results in a format and style useful to practitioners. If the researchers are not so inclined to do so themselves, then the editors can encourage them to solicit participation by others who will prepare articles for practitioner audiences.

THE ROLE OF THE EDITORIAL BOARD

The purpose of an editorial board is to work with the editor in:

- Determining the development of and changes to the scope and policies of the journal; and
- Developing the review process of both submitted and solicited manuscripts.

It is important that editorial board members agree to support editorial decisions of the editor regarding the dispensation (rejection or selection) of articles. They also should be fully informed about editorial responsibilities, such as bibliographic style, editorial column inclusion, and policies. This helps them encourage contributions to and use of the journal's contents.

Duties of typical board members are as follows:

- Maintaining active contact with members of the profession;
- Reviewing or writing editorials;
- Serving as the "first choice" for refereeing manuscripts;
- Functioning as tie-breakers in split decisions between other referees; and
- Soliciting manuscripts.

Editors typically try to schedule a meeting with the publisher and board members at least once a year in order to formulate new policy, discuss any changes in the direction and scope of the journal, and debate the quality of submissions to the journal in the previous year. Most importantly, this meeting develops and maintains ties among the editor, board, and publisher, all of whom are usually geographically dispersed.

CRITERIA FOR SELECTING EDITORIAL BOARD MEMBERS

Editorial boards are chosen by the editor, occasionally with the required approval of the publisher. Members are selected on the basis of their individual subject or methodological expertise, institutional focus, individual interests, and perhaps geographic distribution. Personal style attributes, such as timeliness and attention to detail, are also considered in making selections. The editors responding to a short questionnaire for this chapter reported that in most cases the editor selected the members. Some editors mentioned they encountered self-nominated or other solicitations for prospective members, but such solicitation produced limited results. Editors attempt to select an editorial board representative of the audience targeted by the journal.

THE REFEREEING PROCESS

Refereeing has been defined as "review of solicited or submitted manuscripts by external reviewers" (Robbins, 1988, p. a8). This process is carried out for fewer than half of the journals published in the profession. The *Authors Guide to Journals in Library and Information Science* (Stevens and Stevens, 1982) notes that only 38 percent of the 140 journals in library and information science include a review process using external referees. Some journal editors do not use external referees (those people not on the editorial board), either because the journal does not referee manuscripts, or the depth of subject coverage and expertise encompassed by members of an editorial board satisfies the need for referees. As examples of the variety of "refereeing" practices, manuscripts submitted to *Library Journal* are generally only reviewed by the editorial staff of that journal; *Library & Information Science Research* makes use of both its editorial board members and external referees. The *Journal of Academic Librarianship* uses principally its editorial board.

Of the suggestions posed for improving the quality of manuscripts selected for publication, improved refereeing is the one cited most often. Assuming that editors have access to and select knowledgeable referees, then it is hoped that referees will use their knowledge to make valid judgments regarding the gestalt of appropriate methods, contribution to knowledge, and clarity of expression of the manuscript. In making recommendations, referees have several options:

- To accept the manuscript without comment;
- To accept pending revisions as outlined in their response;
- To reject the manuscript with suggestions for revision that may include a recommendation for submission to another journal; or
- To reject without comment (Garrison, 1980).

Referee comments may include: Questions pertaining to how a sample was drawn, appropriateness of statistical methods, validity and reliability of results, as well as organizational comments.

Glogoff's (1988) survey of referees of library journals included a question pertaining to the number of referees who should evaluate a manuscript. Ninety-five of the 105 responses (approximately 90%) indicated a minimum of two referees. When the results of the refereeing are returned, the editor makes the final decision regarding rejection or selection for publication. If there is agreement among the referees then the editor normally accepts their recommendation; however, if they do not agree, then the manuscript and comments are used by the editor alone to reach a final decision. Occasionally, the editor may solicit an additional referee for arbitration; that referee may well be an editorial board member. It is generally preferred that arbitrators not be informed that they are playing such a role. Editors have often recognized articles that they have rejected in other journals, now substantially improved. Occasionally, the improvement is so significant that they wished they had worked with the author themselves. More often, however, their original decision is corroborated.

Double-blind refereeing is seen as an unbiased means of evaluation. "Practicing a double-blind refereeing process where the author's name is not revealed as well as the referee remaining anonymous to the author seems the most objective method" (Glogoff, 1988, pp. 404–405). This procedure works well unless the content area of the manuscript has only been studied by a small group, for example, the case of the economics of libraries. It is then virtually impossible for qualified referees to be unaware of their colleagues' approaches, techniques, and writing styles.

When refereeing a manuscript, certain criteria are kept in mind, the most important of which is the scope of the journal to which the manuscript has been submitted. Examples of some scope statements follow. In a recent issue of the

Bulletin of the American Society for Information Science, Kraft (1990, p. 2) listed five areas in which the *Journal of the American Society for Information Science* was seeking articles, "theory of information science, communications, management economics and marketing, applied information science, and social and legal aspects of information." The *Journal of Education for Library and Information Science* (*JELIS*) ("Guidelines for Authors," 1990) accepts major articles which include:

> Scholarly papers relevant to library and information science education, papers with quantitative evaluation of teaching methods, state-of-the-art reviews in the field, reports of studies pertaining to library and information science education, highlighting results and implications.

The editors of *College & Research Libraries* ("About *College & Research Libraries,*" 1990, p. 84) solicit manuscripts of a subject content which includes "articles in all fields of interest and concern to academic and research librarians—for example library collections, their acquisition and organization, services to readers and bibliographic instruction; and library history."

Finally, it is important that editors of research journals become attentive to research that is submitted to popular journals that do not use a refereeing process. *Library Journal,* and to a lesser extent *American Libraries,* have unfortunately published poorly conceived and executed research. By publication, such research gains a level of legitimization that damages the belief that research contributes to practical decision making.

THE ROLE OF EDITORS AND EDITORIAL BOARD MEMBERS IN IMPROVING THE QUALITY OF RESEARCH IN LIBRARY AND INFORMATION STUDIES

In response to this study's survey, one respondent noted that editors and editorial board members could not aid in the improvement of the quality of research in the profession, but the others held that they could. Editors can aid in the improvement of quality by encouraging the already evident inclination of researchers to replicate quality library research. For example, they can encourage replication of successful studies in public librarianship for academic librarianship or in a large academic library for small academic libraries. Additionally, editors believe that their responsibility is to provide a forum for quality scholarly research in terms of style, content, and timeliness. Timeliness is defined as selecting specific referees and obtaining results within an appropriate time frame, which most agree is within six to eight weeks from initial receipt of a manuscript to the publication decision. When manuscripts require revision, the time required to final acceptance increases. While editors realize the importance of getting new research published as soon as possible, increases in the amount of material being submitted to journals has resulted in large backlogs in publication schedules. Kraft (1990) addressed this in a recent editorial; in order to relieve backlog at *JASIS*, the editorial board and publisher agreed to increase publication from a previous six issues to ten per year, beginning with Volume 42 in 1990. *Library & Information Science Research* in 1988 negotiated an increase in the number of printed pages per year while maintaining its quarterly status.

As stated previously, the key role that could lead to improvement of the quality of research is the continued careful review by referees and editors of the manuscripts that are submitted. The review covers subject content, hypotheses construction, experimental design, mathematical calculations, tables and figures, as well as spelling, paragraph construction, and other organizational issues. Journal articles should state all components of the research process, for example, the purpose of research, the question(s) raised or the problem(s) addressed, and the data collected. There should be a clear explication of the analysis of the data followed by a separate interpretation of the meaning of the results. It is important for authors to consult "instructions to authors" which are published in every issue of some journals, such as *Library & Information Science Research, Journal of Education for Library and Information Science,* and *Journal of the American Society of Information Science,* and at least once per year by others. This insures a submission that meets the guidelines for publishing set by the publisher and editor, and greatly reduces the amount of time required for the review process.

CONCLUSION

It is realistic to expect that "major improvements in the dissemination and exploitation of information will come when the entire communication cycle—from the composition of a document to its distribution and use—is automated" (Lancaster, 1989). Microcomputers and word processors have allowed information to be organized and prepared more efficiently. Authors can submit their work on computer disks. Submitting disk copy allows for easier copyediting by the publisher. Improved technology has enabled editors and publishers to process manuscripts more rapidly. As the level of sophistication of research in the field increases, so do the pools from which editors can select editorial board members who play the important role in assuring the quality of published research.

Editors and referees must keep in mind the need for timely review and publication of results. Care must be taken to avoid conflict of interest concerns with regard to the solicitation, review, and eventual acceptance of manuscripts. Serebnick and Harter (1990) reported the results of a major survey pertaining to ethics in journal publishing dealing with these areas. Publishers, editors, referees, authors, and the professionals who read the literature need to pay attention to the critical components which form quality research in order to assure that research

The Role of Editors and Editorial Boards in Journal Publishing

in library and information science meets the standards the profession must expect from itself.

REFERENCES

"About *College & Research Libraries*," *College & Research Libraries*, 51 (January 1990): 83–84.

Garrison, L.P. "Computer-Aided Selection of Reviewers and Manuscript Control," *Scholarly Publishing*, 12 (1980): 65–74.

Glogoff, Stuart. "Reviewing the Gatekeepers: A Survey of Referees of Library Journals," *Journal of the American Society for Information Science*, 39(1988): 400–407.

"Guidelines for Authors," *Journal of Education for Library and Information Science*, 30 (Winter 1990), verso of the table of contents.

Kraft, Donald. "Letters," *Bulletin of the American Society for Information Science*, 16 (1990): 2.

Lancaster, F. Wilfred. "Whither Libraries? or, Wither Libraries," *College & Research Libraries*, 50 (1989): 406–419.

Robbins, Jane. "Communicating Research in the Information Profession: An Essay," in *Current Research for the Information Profession, 1987/88*, edited by Elliott Pirrko. London, England: The Library Association, 1988, p. a8.

Serebnick, Judith and Stephen P. Harter. "Ethical Practices in Journal Publishing: A Study of Library and Information Science Periodicals," *Library Quarterly*, 60 (1990): 91–119.

Stevens, Norman and Nora D. Stevens, Eds. *Author's Guide to Journals in Library and Information Science*. New York: Haworth, 1982.

chapter sixteen

The Secret Science: The Role of Consulting and LIS Research

Douglas L. Zweizig

The research process is characterized as an ongoing conversation that requires communication in order to function. Consulting activities are seen as rarely resulting in contributions to the research literature and therefore as silent in the conversation. The research process and consulting can be contrasted in terms of such questions as: Who is the client? How is the problem conceived? Are there attempts to falsify findings? Is external validity addressed? Is cumulation a concern? How is the product evaluated? How is the product communicated? The introduction of peer review is suggested as one strategy for involving consultants in the research process.

DEFINING LIS RESEARCH

A discussion of library/information science research begs for clarification of what is meant by *research*. The term can be used to describe any systematic investigation, but when research that is intended to contribute to the knowledge base of a professional arena such as library and information science is involved, then what is implied is *scientific research*, and the characteristics of that research can be more clearly specified.

The prestige attributed to research activities results in the term being attributed to a wide range of activities. For example, it is in the interest of many academic librarians to label what is written as research so that it will apply to the record for tenure. Consulting firms can add credibility to their activities when they are labeled as research. Clients of consulting firms can more easily justify the expenditures they make for management advice or for contracted products when they can label them as research.

The model for this confusion of research and other activities is provided at the Federal level. The only funding through the U. S. Department of Education for research is under a program for research and demonstration, and that program makes no distinction between those two activities and, in fact, has used the same criteria for evaluating proposals for both research and demonstration. Yet, these are different terms. Research is a process of investigation to determine the state of the objective world with as little intervention from the researcher as possible. The product of research is a report of findings. Demonstration is an activity intended to develop and try out solutions to problems or improvements in service that can be applied by other libraries. The product of a demonstration project may be a description of the solution or improvement, instruction on how to apply the results, or a tool for use by other libraries. Thus, the term *research* comes to refer to a variety of activities with a variety of purposes.

But the issue of library/information science research refers to a more limited meaning, to the issue of how a field of endeavor learns—how it accumulates knowledge about the phenomena of interest. There are some conditions that need to be met if these ends are to be achieved. This chapter will enumerate a number of those conditions and will assess the place of consulting activities in that learning process.

The basic steps of a research investigation are well established:

- Definition of the research problem;
- Formation of hypotheses for testing;
- Development of a research plan or design;
- Collection of data appropriate to the hypotheses;
- Analysis of the data and interpretation of the findings; and
- Communication of the results.

In addition, when the purpose is scientific research, these characteristics should be present:

- *Emphasis on the explicit identification of assumptions:* It is widely believed that it is impossible to initiate an investigation without some starting points of belief, without accepting some aspects as given for the purposes of the study. Scientific research makes an effort to spell these out since they are not subjected to testing
- *Precise definition of concepts and terms:* It is important that the words used refer to clearly identified phenomena. Concepts are discussed in terms of the literature from which they are obtained; variables are defined in terms of the operations used to observe them
- *Skepticism toward results:* The tests of evidence used are probabilistic; there is some probability that findings of any study may be in error. Therefore the results of any investigation are to be used with caution. Subsequent researchers are obligated to treat the results of a study with skepticism
- *Valid and reliable evidence:* It is never possible to obtain evidence that per-

fectly addresses the intended question and that is absolutely stable or repeatable. The challenge for the researcher is to devise a way of making observations that will produce data that are sufficiently on point and under sufficient control so that conclusions can be drawn from them. Serious research investigations will discuss how this was achieved in the particular study
- *Explicit use of a systematic approach:* In order for the researcher to be sure of not contaminating data and for subsequent researchers to verify findings, it is important that the approach to obtaining data and reaching conclusions be planned in advance, followed in the investigation, and reported fully enough to allow replication.

The theme of communication is found throughout the research steps listed and the characteristics of scientific research. In order for the research process to work, researchers must communicate with each other. A researcher needs to know what work has preceded a planned investigation in order to be able to build on that work. The evaluation of research requires "full disclosure" of the definitions and procedures used so that the research findings can be independently verified. In the absence of such communication, no learning can occur—the research process stops.

CONSULTING

For the purposes of this discussion, consulting firms will be understood to include a wide range of organizations that are conducting investigations under contract. For example, from 1980 to 1987, the Library Research and Demonstration Program (Title II-B of the Higher Education Act) funded only contracts. (Only in 1987 were field-initiated projects again sought or funded.) Of the 16 contracts awarded in fiscal years 1981 through 1986, six were to for-profit agencies and nine were to nonprofit agencies, but the nature of the contracting process causes all 16 of the investigators to behave like consulting firms.

Rethinking the Library in the Information Age (1989, p. 6) gave the following summary of the role of consulting firms in library and information science research:

> A direct role of the commercial sector is in mission-oriented research, especially under contract to the Federal government, to address information problems in agencies as diverse as the Patent Office and the U.S. Army. The rationale is that companies are able to assemble staff, resources, and facilities and risk the capital necessary to carry out major research projects, and that the necessity to provide a return on investment will assure that work will be efficiently done. Indeed, for these reasons, the commercial sector has been the predominant means for conducting organized research in library and information science during the past several

years. There is every reason to expect that most contract mission-oriented research will continue to be carried out in this way in the future.

This description provides a beneficent view of research for hire provided by consulting firms, but obscures or neglects a number of aspects of this means of conducting research. These aspects severely limit the contribution that might be made to the research base of library and information science. It also, in the case of research contracted for through the Library Research and Demonstration Program, underestimates the amount of consulting activity in the noncommercial sector. Over half of the projects contracted for in the years 1981–1986 were performed by nonprofit agencies, although the greater share of the dollar amount (64% of the approximately $1.7 million spent) went to for-profit organizations (*The Bowker Annual of Library and Book Trade Information*, 1981–1986).

CONTRASTS BETWEEN RESEARCH AND CONSULTING

The research perspective taken in this chapter is that of social science research. This method of inquiry is characterized by its process, not by its techniques. Failure to make this distinction has lead to confusing any investigation that uses research techniques, such as statistics, with scientific research. The services provided by consulting firms and the contributions that are made by research may be contrasted on the following aspects:

- Who is the client?
- How is the problem conceived?
- Are there attempts to falsify findings?
- Is external validity addressed?
- Is cumulation a concern?
- How is the product evaluated?
- How is the product communicated?

Who Is the Client?

On whose behalf is research conducted? That question quickly produces the answer that scientific research is conducted to add to general knowledge. Specifically, library/information science research is conducted in order to add to our knowledge of library/information science phenomena. Therefore, the client for LIS research is first the information professions and indirectly those who fund and who benefit from information services.

However, the client for consulting activities is much more limited. That client is the person contracting for services. It is that client to whom the consulting activities are addressed. The term "mission-oriented research" implies a much more limited purpose than increasing the overall knowledge of the field; it implies addressing an individual problem in isolation from other questions.

Identifying the client is not always easy; sometimes there is no clearly identified client for government-funded studies. In a recent study funded by the U.S. Department of Education, the project officers and the consultants were asked repeatedly for an identification of the client or the purpose for a $250,000 study. No definition of the client could ever be provided, and when some suggestions of who might be the client were made, these suggestions were rejected by the putative clients themselves.

How Is the Problem Conceived?

The formulation of a research problem is a critical step in an investigation. The researcher needs to consider what formulation will yield the maximum insight on the area to be studied, to review the ways in which related studies have formulated their problems, to relate the formulation to a theoretical perspective, and to consider how the formulation affects the approach taken by the question.

Contract research is often performed on a problem formulated by the contracting agency. Not only is the problem often specified as part of the request for proposal, the RFP may also specify the kind of solution to be produced. But the contracting agency is most probably not aware of the literature that might be brought to bear on the area for investigation, not deliberate in the choice of a theoretical perspective, and not skilled in the diagnosis of problems. The consultant, however, must attempt to propose to address the problem as formulated by the client. (As one Federal project officer stated, "If the government says that it wants to buy something, someone out there is going to say that they're able to sell it to them.") The presentation of the proposal is not the occasion for the consultant to attempt to reshape the client's conceptualization of the problem. Such an attempt would make the proposal nonresponsive and noncompetitive. This situation results in the pursuit of investigations that have limited utility and limited informativeness.

Are There Attempts to Falsify Findings?

As stated earlier, skepticism is an important perspective for the conduct of research. The eye or the mind can be fooled too easily, and therefore the researcher uses research designs and statistical tests that attempt to remove the contamination of the researcher's perceptions or preconceptions. Hypotheses are phrased in a form that can be falsified, and statistical tests are constructed in such a way as to make it difficult to find relationships or differences. Strenuous efforts are bent to test the validity of the findings.

The investigations performed under consulting agreements rarely employ the falsification approaches that are central to research investigations. The attempt in contract research is to describe the state of affairs, not to contradict our perceptions of it. Contracts need to be brought to completion in a timely manner and with demonstrable results. Skepticism can result in the doubting of results, repetition of observations, and delays in completion. Such delays are in the interest of neither the client nor the contractor, so skepticism and challenges to results are frequently set aside in the interests of completion of studies on time.

Is External Validity Addressed?

LIS research is conducted on particular cases for the purpose of generalization to other, comparable situations—for the purpose of gaining understanding of cases not studied. For example, a study conducted of a systematic sample of members of the community is not for the purpose of understanding only those persons who ended up in the sample, but in order to generalize from the observations made on the sample to all members of the community. Likewise, scientific research is not conducted for the purpose of solving isolated problems, but in order to generalize from the situation studied to others not studied. In order to be able to generalize the results of a study, a number of stringent guidelines must be followed, particularly in the manner in which cases are selected for study.

Clients for consulting investigations are often requesting that their agency be the object of study, or that they will control the selection of cases for study. Solution of the local problem or creation of the needed product is the concern. Development of generalizable solutions, products, or understanding is not seen as the goal. Further, in contrast to research, the rules for arriving at a solution are unspecified, and since the development of a solution requires judgment, experience, and artistry, the process of arriving at a solution is inherently nonreplicable. Thus, the results of an investigation of a specific organization with recommendations to be applied to that organization is probably of local interest only, and even the process used may not be explicit or explicable enough to be used by a subsequent investigator.

In short, the distinction between LIS consulting and LIS research may be roughly analogous to the difference between the practice of medicine and medical research. The client for medical practice is the individual patient, just as the client for consulting is a specific agency or organization. The questions of the patient are: "What is happening to me?," and "What is the best course of action in my case?" The client for medical research is the profession of medicine and indirectly the general public. Medical research will focus on what accounts for the differences of results across cases rather than attempting to affect the outcome of a particular case. Although these two activities, medical practice and medical research, both address the general topic of health and may use similar analytical tools, they do so from distinct perspectives and with quite different purposes. In spite of some points of similarity, they could not be expected to work toward the same ends.

Is Cumulation a Concern?

The intent of scientific research is to progress to increased understanding and perhaps control of the phenomena being studied. This progress requires that studies are designed with an awareness of what research has preceded and that the results are communicated so that other researchers may be able to use the findings in their subsequent research designs.

This awareness of continuity is innate in the scientific enterprise, but is often missing from research conducted under contract because the client does not require it and because the client has often formulated the problem without any reference to previous work on the question. Contractors may want to repeat the same study for a succession of clients, but cumulation of findings from one study to another is unlikely to occur. Each study is treated as a unique service for each client. And the general observations from a number of studies are not reported in the general research literature.

How Is the Product Evaluated?

Often a consulting contract provides for withholding a portion of the payment until acceptance of the final report by the client. In effect then, the final evaluation of a consultant's work is in the final payment from the client. A second, more subtle evaluation of a consultant's work is testimony from former clients. Whatever the mechanism, the criteria for evaluation are the degree to which the questions of the contracting agency have been answered or the degree to which the solutions fit the requirements of the client.

This kind of evaluation is in strong contrast to the process of evaluation used for social science research, and therefore for LIS research. The product of a research effort is publication of an account of that research. The proposed publication is evaluated by peer researchers in advance of publication to ensure that the conduct of the research meets standard criteria for the conduct of research. Proposed publications that fall short of the standard are rejected for publication or are returned to the author for revision. After publication, the research study is evaluated by subsequent researchers with interest in the same area, and errors may be identified at any time.

In the absence of such a review process, errors in the research are unlikely to be caught by the consultant conducting the study or by the client, who in most cases may not be competent to judge the rigor of the process of inquiry used.

How Is the Product Communicated?

Communication of results is a necessary step in the research process. Science has been characterized as an ongoing conversation. Each new finding is a new contribution to that conversation and, if it is pertinent, should result in a response from other researchers. It is in this ongoing conversation that error is identified and weeded out and that what is known is questioned and confirmed or rejected.

But the results of consulting firms' efforts are rarely communicated to other researchers. The reports produced by consultants are delivered to the client and become the property of the client. In the case of individual libraries or library agencies as clients, consulting reports are rarely distributed beyond the contracting organization. Therefore, other researchers are unable to learn from the findings of the investigation and may not even be aware that an investigation has been conducted. Even in the case of the "mission-oriented research" conducted for the Federal government, too little attention is paid to dissemination of results. From the consultant's point of view, dissemination of results may require revealing proprietary methods of investigation or analysis and will generally require time spent preparing a publication for which there is no compensation. Publication for a consultant is then either a gratuitous contribution to the welfare of the profession or a form of advertisement for the consulting firm.

The silence of the consulting science was demonstrated in a recent review of the projects funded through the U.S. Department of Education's Library Research and Demonstration Program between the years 1965 and 1980. These projects were a mixture of types as noted before, but the conclusion is nevertheless serious for LIS research: "Approximately half of the projects funded by the Library Research and Demonstration Branch, from 1965 through 1980, made no impact in the literature. No later author found it necessary to cite studies, at least in the major serials in the discipline" (Altman and Antieau, 1988, p. 53). The neglect of these studies in the literature is an indication that they could not have been conceived of as contributors to the larger LIS research enterprise.

Editors of five major research journals publishing LIS research were asked about the number of submissions they had received that could have resulted from consulting activities. The editors were prompted to think of articles that might have been "spin-offs" from consulting efforts in addition to straight publication of consulting reports. The editors were uniform in their observation that consulting efforts rarely resulted in submissions for publication. One of the editors estimated that of 350 manuscript submissions received, fewer than 10 could be characterized as resulting from consulting activities. In the absence of publications of results from consulting activities, those investigations (to the extent that they can be characterized as research investigations) are silent in the conversation of LIS research.

SUMMARY

Research involves the pursuit of a *method* of investigation in order to test statements about the natural world by making a deliberate attempt to falsify the statements. When a rigorous attempt to disprove the statement fails, then confidence is increased in the correctness of the statement that survives such a test. Consulting involves the application of research *techniques* to the study of LIS questions or the solution of LIS problems. Typically, essential steps of the research process are not followed. This is not to say that consulting activities are not useful, they are, but they are not research, for they do not advance the knowledge base.

To call these activities research and to fund them as part of the meager LIS research enterprise is the LIS research equivalent of releasing sterile Mediterranean fruit flies. That is, the falsely labeled research activities absorb resources that otherwise might be used to fund needed LIS research, and delude the profession into thinking that it might anticipate the rewards of supporting and conducting research while instead only a number of disconnected and *secret* study reports result.

Some recommendations may be offered to increase the contribution from consulting:

- Require in the criteria for the evaluation of federally funded projects that the proposal include a thorough review of previous research and indicate the place of the proposed project in that research stream. Require that previous methods have systematically been reviewed and incorporated into the proposed design
- Use peer researchers as reviewers for funded projects. Altman and Antieau (1988, p. 55) proposed using peer researchers as reviewers of proposals for government contracts and grants. Peer reviewers could also be used to evaluate the products of contracted investigations before acceptance of the final report by the government
- Enroll consultants in the LIS research process by requiring dissemination in core research journals as a condition for acceptance of the final report. Again, peer evaluation would be provided by the review process required for the acceptance of journal articles. This requirement would necessitate a delay of some months while the writing and reviewing processes are completed, but the cost would be balanced by the increased utility of the research products
- Educate clients that their formulation of the problem should be tentative only, that they should encourage alternative formulations of the problem in their requests for proposal or should devote considerably more attention to the request for proposal. The recommendation would introduce ambiguity into the contracting process, since the process as it now operates has been modeled on government procurements of manufactured products, not consulting services. However, experience with the inappropriateness of that model for research investigations requires that alternate models be developed that will result in the needed flexibility and profession-wide accountability.

The research enterprise requires open communication in order to function. Those who conduct consulting activities have little motivation to communicate results of their investigations. Consultants are strongly interested in efficiency (because budgets and time are always too limited), in protecting proprietary information (and so may seek to limit disclosure), in maintaining access to potential clients (where confidentiality may be an issue), and in not placing a firm's reputation at risk (when work done to meet contract deadlines may not sustain the scrutiny provided by peer review).

If this description fairly identifies the interests of consultants and if these remain their interests, consulting activities will continue to make little contribution to the knowledge base of LIS research.

REFERENCES

Altman, Ellen and Kim Antieau. "Dissemination and Impact of U.S. Department of Education's Library Research and Demonstration Projects: A Citation Analysis," *Government Information Quarterly*, 5 (1988): 45–56.

The Bowker Annual of Library and Book Trade Information. New York: R.R. Bowker, 1981–1986.

Rethinking the Library in the Information Age. Prepared by the Department of Education. Vol. 3. Washington, D.C.: GPO, 1989.

chapter seventeen

The Role of Private Funding Agencies

Peter R. Young

This chapter provides an overview of the current function and condition of private funding agency support for library and information science (LIS) research. Key issues, constraints, and opportunities related to private LIS research support are examined within the context of national science and technology research investments. In addition, specific feasible strategies for implementation during the next three to five years are developed to increase private support of LIS research. These strategies are designed to improve the quality and usefulness of basic research in LIS by private agency investment.

Lack of an existing structural base of well-established private support has limited progress and advancement in the library profession, information science, and in those allied knowledge industries concerned with publishing and information/communication technologies. Insufficient resources allocated to LIS basic research have impeded advances in the understanding of natural and social phenomena related to the creation and use of information. This has prevented the development of informed and innovative national LIS policies.

As vigorous scientific research and technological development in other disciplines has fostered new knowledge and critical thinking in recent years, much of LIS research has not kept pace. Attraction of private source support for LIS research presents a strategic approach for improving the current state of information-related knowledge and for revitalizing LIS by strengthening the research infrastructure.

STATEMENT OF THE ISSUES

The Nature of the Research Process

The research process involves the formal pursuit of systematic and rigorous inquiry or investigation resulting in the discovery of new knowledge (McClure and Bishop, 1989, p. 128). Researchers often challenge accepted theories or laws in light of new facts, data, and discoveries. As the central component of scientific inquiry, fundamental research nurtures the development of new ideas for subsequent technological transference into innovative processes and products. In recent years, national investments in research and development have served as indicators of public policy priorities and international competitiveness. LIS research can be viewed in relation to this global research context to provide a comparative perspective.

Research Program Support and Incentives

Research requires support from a variety of sponsoring sources. At the same time, however, research demands freedom from external constraint and stipulation. Tangible incentives for performing difficult and complex research must encourage the application of intellectual energies in an environment dedicated to the open pursuit of new knowledge. At the same time, however, determination of research topics for investigation, especially for projects receiving private agency support, involve funding source policy interests and program support goals. There is a need for LIS research funding strategies which attract the support of those private agencies capable of supplying the resources required to undertake and maintain quality LIS research.

Research incentives are often cited as nonmonetary in nature, more related to academic status and professional standing than to direct monetary rewards to individual researchers. Individual economic incentive rewards in the LIS research field, however, do not compare with rewards commonly found in other professional research environments, especially in the sciences and engineering. Opportunities for improving this situation by the attraction of private agency LIS research support will only occur when the LIS profession develops a marketing program for relating specific LIS research topic areas to the priorities of private funding agencies and foundations.

Funding from Public Agencies

New strategies for increased support of LIS research are required that take into account the differences between funding from public and private sources. Public funding from Federal, state, and local agencies usually involves program support under statutory authority, regulated through a highly structured formalized process involving deadlines and standard procedures for proposal submission and award. Public support is usually provided for research which has a specific problem or topic of concern related to a clearly defined social, natural, or technical issue, problem, or condition. Public agency research funding support is primarily directed toward finding a specific solution to a problem by applied research techniques. Publicly funded research is often renewable and involves research project accountability through bureaucratic procedures involving oversight review of proposals and project milestones. Researchers contracting to perform publicly funded research are engaged in a process which is ultimately accountable to taxpayers.

Funding from Private Agencies

Private sources of support for research are available from the following types of foundations:

- Independent foundations organized to aid social, educational, or other charitable activities through grants made from endowments generally derived from a single source, such as a family or individual;
- Company-sponsored independent foundations with close ties to the profit-making corporation providing funds for grants from endowment and annual contributions. Grants tend to be in fields related to corporate activities or in communities where the company operates;
- Operating foundations which use resources to conduct research or provide a direct service through grants made from endowments usually provided from a single source for activities generally related to the foundation's program; and
- Community foundations which are publicly supported organizations making grants for social, educational, religious, or other charitable purposes in a specific community or region based on contributions received from many donors for grants in local communities.

Foundations provide different types of support for research and other activities through general support awards, endowment awards, project or program grants, fellowships, capital grants, and program-related investment grants. More than public research funding sources, private agencies are likely to focus on emerging issues, new needs, and populations not yet organized into large "special interest groups." Private agency funding sources, in general, follow less formal application procedures than public agency funding sources and respond to research topics addressing a broad range of issues affecting society. Private funding agencies, however, often change program funding priorities rapidly and do not always provide for renewal funding. These funding sources also require more lead time for development and research. In general, private funding from company-sponsored independent foundations and operating foundations are a source of start-up or experimental funds for pure research topics.

Value and Research Investments

Inherent in the research investigative process is the perceived value of the research endeavor to produce outcomes which provide a return on the investment.

This return or outcome may take the form of a solution to a social problem or the development of useful new products or processes. Whatever the intended research outcome, the performance of sponsored research involves the adherence to direct or indirect values central to the policies and program objectives of the funding source.

Value-laden stipulations can potentially impose significant conditions and constraints on research protocols and influence research findings. Thus, for example, research results reflecting adversely on the public image of a corporate sponsor are not likely to be published openly. Private support for research from company-sponsored independent foundations and from operating foundations involve value questions relating to possible conflicts between program goals of the funding source and research project methodology. Research sponsorship involves matching the interests of the funding parties with the ability and qualifications of the researcher to perform the required work in a manner consistent with the standards and methodologies appropriate to the field.

Pure and Applied Research

Pure or fundamental research can be contrasted with applied research, although, in reality, it is often difficult to differentiate clearly the pure and applied aspects of any research project. Applied research usually investigates specific issues or practical problems. Thus, applied research focuses on developing solutions to problems following a fixed schedule in a well-defined subject area. Pure research, on the other hand, is characterized by a comparatively long-term investment of resources with less well-defined objective results. Pure research has a theoretical orientation rather than a purely practical application, concentrating on the development of theories and basic knowledge about a field. Pure research findings are more likely to challenge conventional presuppositions in a field and to cause practitioners to question application of conventional methods and applications on a broad front.

Basic and applied research occur in both academic and industrial environments. The results of academic research are generally published in the open literature, thereby adding to the store of publicly accessible knowledge. On the other hand, information science research and development sponsored by industry, nonprofit institutions, and government laboratories is frequently directed to specific, practical results rather than to overall growth in the knowledge and theory of a discipline. The results and findings of industry-supported basic and applied research may not, however, be publicly available in the general literature for competitive reasons. Research resulting from private industry support is motivated by profit incentives and is not likely to result in contributions to overall LIS theory development.

LIS Research Investment

A combination of both pure and applied research is critical to the progress and advancement of LIS-related fields. From both a practitioner and researcher perspective, the health and viability of libraries, information science, and the information/communication industry is directly related to the quality, effectiveness, and application of LIS research. The ideal annual research investment in LIS is not easily determined, but an estimate of the investment required to perform research in the field can be obtained by comparing the total national annual investment in research and development for science and technology with the estimated annual LIS research investment. This measurement, employing the annual U.S. science and technology research investment as a scale, will provide a basis for estimating the LIS research support required to improve the current state of the field.

In 1987, the United States devoted 2.76 percent of the Gross National Product to research and development in the sciences and technology, with Federal spending on national defense related research and development the biggest component of recent growth. In the period from 1980 to 1987, *industry support* for academic research and development grew from $276 million to $568 million, representing an increase from 3.9 percent to 6 percent of the total annual science and technology research and development investment of almost nine and one-half billion dollars (National Science Board, 1987, p. 244).

These total national science and technology annual research investments can serve as the basis for judging the adequacy of the total national LIS research investment. The total national research and development investment from Federal, industrial, and private foundation sources for science and technology-related research account for almost 3 percent of the nation's total annual productive output in 1987. In order for LIS to match this total research investment, an annual investment of $285 million is required. This level of LIS research investment is based on a conservative estimate of $9.5 billion as the total annual library expenditure nationwide based on total operating expenditures of $2.9 billion for academic libraries (Department of Education, 1990), $3.6 billion for public libraries (Department of Education, 1989), $2 billion estimated for special libraries, and $1 billion for school libraries.

If a total annual LIS research investment of $285 million is required to provide a level of support comparable to the nation's annual support of science and technology-related research, then it is useful to estimate contributions to LIS-research funding from industrial, Federal, and foundation sources. Such an estimate will enable us to determine if current levels of LIS research support are meeting the estimated annual requirement.

LIS-related research expenditures by private information industry companies are one component of total estimated annual LIS research support. As noted above, industrial support of academic science and technology research and development, in 1987, was around 6 percent of the total annual national investment. Using this percentage as the basis for comparison, the annual industrial investment for LIS research and development should be approximately $14.4 million. It is difficult to estimate accurately the actual information industry's annual research and development investment since many of the research results are translated into corporate products and services offered to customers. This estimated annual investment represents less than 2 percent of the total estimated annual revenue of $85 billion attributed to the information industry (*Information Industry/Factbook*, 1990, p. 3).

Federal support of research and development in LIS-related fields has averaged $1 million annually since 1967, under the Higher Education Act, Title II-B program administered by the Department of Education. Even factoring in HEA Title II-D for 1988 and 1989, as presented in Chapter 4, this total annual average is only $1.16 million. In addition, National Science Foundation support for LIS-related research has averaged $300,000 annually, according to Ellen Altman (see Chapter 9). National Library of Medicine has averaged $90,000 annually for LIS research according to this same study. The total HEA Title II-B and D, NSF, and NLM annual investment in LIS research is $1.55 million. Thus, the total estimated current industrial ($14.4 million) and Federal ($1.55 million) support for LIS research annually is $15.9 million. In order for LIS research to receive a level of national support comparable to that provided to science and technology research, an additional annual investment of $269.1 million is required.

If the Council on Library Resources (CLR) is assumed to be the chief private foundation source of LIS-related research funding, then the Council's *estimated* average annual investment of $300,000 constitutes a significant proportion of foundation support for LIS research which totaled $3.7 million in 1986 according to the Foundation Center.[1] Even if the entire $3.7 million CLR contribution were devoted entirely to LIS research, an additional $81.9 million annual investment is required to provide LIS research with support comparable to the annual 3 percent national science and technology research investment. The conclusion of this analysis is to be expected: Our current national annual investment for support of pure and applied LIS research is not currently comparable to the level of national investment in science and technology research.

IMPORTANCE OF PRIVATE AGENCY FUNDING FOR LIS RESEARCH

Foundation investment activity in LIS actually amounted to more than $89 million in 1986 according to the Foundation Center, but the majority of these funds

---

[1] The $300,000 is an average for the years 1977 through 1983, as based on the data reported in Fitzgibbons (1984).

Table 17–1. 1985 R&D Expenditures by Sector and Character of Work (in hundred thousands).*

	Basic Research	Applied Research	Development
Universities and colleges	6,377	2,572	555
Nonprofit institutions	1,063	869	633
Federal government	1,961	3,148	7,889
Industry	2,600	14,958	58,776
Totals (%)	12,001 (12%)	21,547 (21%)	67,853 (67%)

*Source: National Science Board (1987, p. 241).

were provided to libraries for capital support and program development rather than for research and development in LIS. This level of private foundation support of libraries presents opportunities for attracting a larger base of funding support for LIS research from private foundation sources in the future.

Funding Support for Pure and Applied LIS Research and Development

Patterns of research investment from different component sources in the science and technology fields provide a useful context for comparing current levels of support for both pure and applied LIS research. In general, the nature of the Federal science and technology investment in research and development differs from investments made by private institutions including nonprofits, universities and colleges, and industry. Each component funding sector has specific research objectives and program goals which determine varying levels of investment in pure and applied research activities. Table 17-1 illustrates these differences.

Federal support of science and technology research and development in 1985 was almost six times greater than Federal support for basic research, while the nonprofit, college, and university investment in basic research was almost twice the amount these institutions devoted to applied research and development expenditures. Clearly, the investment made by the Federal sector, as well as research and development investments made by industry, are primarily in the applied research and development area, while pure research support funding is largely through private foundation (and academic) sources. Overall, in 1985, science and technology-related research and development funding for pure research was 12 percent of the total, compared to 88 percent for applied research and development.

Comparable LIS research investment by Federal, industrial, and foundation sources of support generally appear to follow this same pattern. Industrial research investments in LIS similarly are directed toward applied research and development activities which have specific product and service potential for the parent corporation.

Table 17-2. The Role of Private Funding Agencies (in billions).*

	1980	1990	% Δ
Nonprofit's Share of U.S. GNP	5.5%	6.4%	+.9%
Total Corporate Contributions	$2.3	$4.8	+109%
Total Charitable Giving	$48.7	$104.3	+114%
Total Foundation Giving	$3.4	$6.3	+85%

*Source: "How the Non-Profit World Grew and Changed in the 80's" (1990, p. 12).

The missing element in the component LIS research support area is private foundation support for pure research of a theoretical nature. Increased funding support for LIS pure research from other component sectors, including the Federal government and industry, is unlikely given the traditional objectives and program priorities for these sources of research support.

Private Foundation Support for LIS Research

Private agency funding for all fields of research from corporate, charitable, and foundation sources in general has increased significantly in the past decade (see Table 17-2). Growing 85 percent since 1980 to a total of $115.4 billion in 1990, private funding agency general support for all activities does not seem to have been reflected in foundation support for LIS research activities in the same period.

It is doubtful that data for LIS from similar periods would demonstrate that LIS is comparable. LIS research support, especially for those theoretical areas involved in fundamental or pure research, must increase in order for the profession and industry to keep pace with the rapid and pervasive changes brought on by advances in technology and by changing socioeconomic information structures. Traditionally, the primary source for pure research support has been the private independent foundations. For improvement to be achieved, strategies are required to present LIS research needs successfully to these nonprofit independent foundations.

STRATEGIES FOR PRIVATE LIS RESEARCH FUNDING

Strategies for increasing private foundation support of LIS research involve the development, identification, and marketing of innovative action plans and fundamental research agendas which build upon historically important foundation-supported LIS research and which relate pure LIS research to the changing program goals and objectives of these foundations. Two organizations which provide potential channels for increased LIS research funding from the private foundation sector are the Council on Library Resources and the Faxon Institute.

Council on Library Resources

Since its formation in 1956, as an independent, nonprofit organization for addressing library problems, the Council on Library Resources (CLR) has devoted the past three decades to aiding in finding the solutions to the problems of libraries generally and of research libraries in particular; to conducting research in, developing and demonstrating new techniques and methods, and disseminating through any medium the results thereof; for making grants to other institutions and persons for such purposes; and for providing leadership, and, whatever appropriate, coordination of efforts. This single agency provides the most significant percentage of private philanthropy funding support to research in the LIS field. Established with an initial grant of $5 million from the Ford Foundation in 1956, CLR has averaged $1,454,000 a year in grants, contracts, and Council-administered projects primarily focusing on management, automation, networks, national library services, standardization, libraries and their users, microforms and preservation, professional development, and international library development (see Council on Library Resources, 1956–1989).

The Faxon Institute

The newly created Faxon Institute for Advanced Studies in Scholarly and Scientific Communications represents a new approach towards support of LIS-related basic research. Created initially by the Faxon Company, The Faxon Institute performs research, policy analysis, continuing learning, and professional development programs from a global perspective. The current issues which form the focus of the Faxon Institute include the increasingly desperate response from the research library community to the escalation of scholarly journal prices, reduced confidence in the peer review process, rising litigation and confusion over intellectual property rights, acquisition of U.S. publishers by global communications conglomerates, well-publicized examples of fraud and ethical misconduct in published research, and the growing concern about the future competitiveness of the U.S. research establishment within the emerging global economy.

Private LIS Research Funding Strategies and Action Plan

This chapter identifies the need for additional support of basic LIS research. Basic LIS research explores and develops new theories relevant to understanding natural and social phenomena related to the generation, selection, dissemination, access, and use of information as well as the evolving role of libraries in these activities. In order to provide sufficient resources to foster a broad-based program of basic LIS research, strategies to accomplish the attraction or redirection of foundation support for LIS-related activities must relate LIS basic research to issues of national or international importance. Along with this, concrete representations of LIS basic research needs must be communicated to those private support foundations and industries with sufficient resources and related program priorities to support a program for increasing LIS research at the fundamental, theoretical level.

The task of attracting private funding agency interest and investment in basic LIS research is complex and demanding, especially in a practice-oriented discipline where the majority of professional practitioners are concerned with improving current collections and services within institutional library environments. Successful strategies for increasing private agency LIS research support require a shift in emphasis from library-owned collection resources to research which emphasizes the accessibility of information resources and the policies associated with knowledge transmission and dissemination. LIS research topics need reformulation into the research concerns of other related disciplines, such as education, law, communications, international relations, economics, and information technology, in order to provide an LIS component to the research programs currently supported by private agency support.

The key to attracting additional support for LIS basic research is to redefine the LIS agenda to emphasize recent shifts towards a world knowledge economy. Signs of this shift are evident from a seven-fold increase in world trade since 1970 and recent improvements in world-wide industrial and commercial transportation and communications capabilities. Similarly, knowledge has become a critical economic commodity through the rise of industries based primarily on knowledge-products, such as computers, semiconductors, synthesized materials, and biotechnology. A redefined LIS research agenda incorporating these trends involves cooperatively funded, multidisciplinary, international projects, performing research into theoretical issues related to the fundamental nature of information, including the value, ownership, creation, dissemination, and consumption of information resources within a global knowledge economy.

The following plan is suggested as the basis for redefining the LIS research agenda toward intensive study of areas related to major private foundation program emphases. The LIS research agenda should focus on:

- The effectiveness and efficiency of knowledge transfer and diffusion. Given the rapid pace of technological and social change, together with the need to be competitive in international markets, traditional methods of publishing, dissemination, and information service are rapidly being challenged;
- Studying the changing role of libraries in society, especially in relation to the need to articulate a systematic foundation for identifying impact measurement criteria which indicate library performance effectiveness. The development of such a systematic measurement process for the functional evaluation of libraries based on the needs and expectations of constituent user communities will address the need for library performance effectiveness measurement on a

national scale similar to the current program for identifying national educational goals and outcomes;
- Studying the differences between public and private information resources in order to identify barriers which impede communication among educators, researchers, scholars, and other information users. The availability of public- and private-sponsored research results, along with the cost of access, constitutes an important area for investigation, especially with increased international ownership of private commercial publishers;
- Studying measures of research effectiveness in order to contribute to efforts to develop new systems for measurement of research contribution. Research into new systems for evaluating and measuring scholarly output need to go beyond the existing quantity-based determinations which employ published output regardless of the quality or value of such research;
- Studying intellectual property rights balancing, especially in light of efforts to initiate new forms of publishing through electronic technology and high-speed national digital networks. Legal structures for information ownership rights need to be reexamined in light of new developments;
- Studying the changes in publication and dissemination of research results brought on by the changing economics of research funding in scholarly and scientific programs. With public funding proposals for developing a national network for research and education, new forms of communication will evolve which will have a significant impact on future patterns of research investment; and
- Studying the changing economics of scholarly access and communications. This research concentrates on defining the value of research communication products in terms of the support required for those engaged in producing knowledge products.

ENHANCING RESEARCH SUPPORT

In reviewing the current function and condition of LIS research support from private sources two points emerge: (1) current LIS research support levels from private funding agencies are not comparable to research and development investments made by private agencies to science and technology, when support is measured as a percentage of estimated total annual national expenditures in these fields; and (2) pure LIS research support from private funding agencies is far less than the annual contribution made by these sources for library facilities and resources.

The lack of strong private agency support for basic LIS research is especially critical, since private foundations traditionally provide major pure research funding in the engineering and scientific fields. Limited support for pure LIS research has constrained progress and development. An effective case must be made for investment in pure LIS research from private foundation sources to adjust the LIS research balance from applied to pure. Pure LIS research can provide the basis for understanding recent fundamental changes in the creation, communication, and use of knowledge, and is critical for strategic progress and development.

Recent emphasis on knowledge as a central component of global economic competitiveness provides an opportunity for repositioning LIS research. Policy officials are discovering the importance of knowledge creation, transmission, and diffusion to industrial innovation and economic competitiveness. New electronic network technologies are awakening this discovery by radically altering information and communication infrastructures. These new technologies are forcing structural changes in libraries and other information-based institutions that call for research into the social and economic effects of changing knowledge technology structures. Support for basic LIS research into these changes can come from new sources, including publishers, vendors, and other companies in the private sector.

Achieving enhanced support for pure LIS research from private foundation sources requires a coordinated effort among multiple LIS constituencies. Successful planning requires development of a national strategic LIS agenda along with a plan for gaining sufficient private support for implementation. Opportunities for collective research program planning should be made to build on professional relationships with foundations. Coordinated efforts between the various LIS research organizations can result in a planning process which encourages agreement and consensus about research priorities and defining the problems.

Priority investment in LIS research support, at the expense of private agency support for facilities and resources, is required. Effective translation of LIS research into national and international economic, educational, and industrial agendas can demonstrate the linkage between the future of LIS research and the effectiveness of the infrastructure of knowledge. If this process is not successful, the opportunity afforded by new electronic technologies for providing greatly expanded access to a wider variety of information resources to the greatest number of users will not be realized. New basic research strategies are needed as libraries move from concentration on collection ownership toward an emphasis on access. The LIS community requires new visions to allow the profession to move to a new knowledge service paradigm.

REFERENCES

Council on Library Resources. *Annual Reports*. Washington, D.C.: Council on Library Resources, 1956–1989.
Department of Education. Office of Educational Research and Improvement. National Center for Education Statistics. Integrated Postsecondary Education Data System

(IPEDS). *Academic Libraries: 1988*. Unpublished internal review copy, March, 1990.

Department of Education. Office of Educational Research and Improvement. National Center for Education Statistics. Federal-State Cooperative System for Public Library Data. *FSCS: An NCES Working Paper: Public Libraries in Forty-Four States and the District of Columbia: 1988*. Washington, D.C.: National Center for Education Statistics, 1989.

Fitzgibbons, Shirley Grinnell. "Funding of Research in Librarianship," *Library Trends*, 32 (Spring 1984): 537–556.

"How the Non-Profit World Grew and Changed in the 80's," *The Chronicle of Philanthropy* (January 9, 1990), p. 12.

Information Industry/Factbook: The Information Industry's Annual Report. Stamford, CT: Digital Information Group, 1990.

McClure, Charles R. and Ann Bishop. "The Status of Research in Library/Information Science: Guarded Optimism," *College & Research Libraries*, 50 (March 1989): 127–143.

National Science Board. *Science & Engineering Indicators—1987*. Washington, D.C.: GPO, 1987.

chapter eighteen

The Role of Networks and Consortia in Library Research

Michael Koenig

In the last quarter century, networks have been at the center of developments in library and information service. This trend will accelerate. It is argued that we are now moving from a second stage of information system development to a third stage, where communications capability will join computational capability and storage capability in growing at a Moore's law rate. This trend has major ramifications for information systems development, and it has ramifications both for the need for research and for the conduct of research.

In terms of research needs, major areas needing research include: the economics and politics of networks and network governance and structure (both technical and organizational) in general; the economics of information; and the effect of networks and network-provided services upon knowledge worker productivity. A major set of concerns, in particular, are those surrounding the economics of network membership, and the potential for new technology to create an environment in which it is economically attractive in the near term for networks members to opt out, a situation that in the long run has the potential to be disastrous to the larger community. In terms of conducting research, networks will have major effects in terms of internationalizing research in particular and in facilitating research in general.

RESEARCH ABOUT NETWORKS AND THEIR ROLE

Much of the development in the field of library and information science in the last decade has either centered on or has been directly linked to the growth of networks, bibliographic utilities, and regional and local networks. This chapter cannot review that extensive literature, but the reader should at least be quickly referred to the recent report prepared for the congressional Office of Technology

Assessment (McClure, Bishop, and Doty, 1990), relatively recent chapters in the *Annual Review of Information Science and Technology* (ARIST) (Shaw and Culkin, 1987; Segal 1985; and Evans, 1981), and the section each year in the *Bowker Annual* (now called the *Library and Book Trade Almanac*) (Segal, 1989, 1988, 1987,1986; Evans, 1985). The reader is also referred to several articles and a book by Martin (1984, 1986, 1989), and to the articles by Hildreth (1987a, 1987b) for analyses of some of the issues that are emerging as technology changes.

A particularly interesting collection of papers was put together by Sugnet (1988) for *Library Hi Tech*; the contributors included Henrietta Avram, Rowland Brown, Clifford Lynch, Susan Martin, Ron Miller, Jim Schmidt, Lou Wetherbee, and Bruce Ziegman. Finally, of particular interest is the Molholt (1988) study paper prepared for the U.S. Department of Education.

Underway at present, but much broader in scope, is a concerted effort to develop an NREN (National Research and Education Network). Starting in 1988, EDUCOM, in particular, began promoting such a network (Segal, 1989). Legislation has been introduced in both the House of Representatives (H.R. 3131) and the Senate (S.1067) under the title of the "National High Performance Computer Technology Act of 1989." NREN would be a major component and would link educational and R & D facilities (McClure et al., 1990). There appears to be a broad consensus forming that such a system is very much in the national interest in order to maintain and enhance a competitive position in R & D. There are numerous stakeholders and interest groups with vested interests, various technical issues which must be resolved, and, of course, the question of who subsidizes and who pays. (See Ibid. for a good review of the complex issues that are involved in the NREN concept.) The resolution of these issues will, of course, take some time, but the creation of NREN looks extremely promising. The intent of this chapter is to examine some of the issues that the likelihood of NREN raises.

The role of networks and consortia in research falls naturally into two major subthemes—research about networks and the topics of vital interest to them, and the role of networks in research. While the latter is indeed important, the former is certainly the more intriguing, particularly at this juncture. As will be argued in this chapter, information system development is at a major transition point, entering a new stage of vastly increased interdependency in which networks and consortial arrangement will play an increasingly important role. Research is needed to guide the decisions that we will have to make in this new era.

The most obvious consequence of changing information technology is the convergence of information services, a phenomenon whose aspects have been variously described as "the deinstitutionalization of the library," the "library without walls," or "access based rather than collection based services." One very clear corollary of the convergence phenomenon is that those mechanisms or networks by which libraries and services interconnect will and must increasingly be the subject of research. For that reason, research about networks will inevitably be of increasing importance.

Another, and perhaps more rigorous, framework in which to approach those changes is in terms of the stage hypotheses that have been proposed with the hope that they will help illuminate the implementation and the management of information technology. These stage hypotheses, which posit that information systems develop in a succession of relatively clear and predictable stages, bear directly on the question of research about networks.

As pointed out by Broadbent and Koenig (1988), the major stage hypotheses of information systems converge on essentially the same conclusion, that in this period of the late 1980s and early 1990s we are moving from a second stage of information systems development to a third stage. What is particularly intriguing, and more than a little convincing, is that the results of these stage hypotheses have converged from very different starting points: Marchand (1983) from Information Resources Management in the government sector; Rockart and Scott (1984), and Gibson and Jackson (1987), from corporate information management; and Koenig (1986, 1987) from an analysis of the components of technology particularly as related to library-like operations. Figure 18-1, reproduced from (Broadbent and Koenig, 1988), displays the surprising degree of congruence.

Given this chapter's emphasis on networks, the Koenig stage hypothesis seems the most obviously salient. The hypothesis derives from a pair of fundamental observations:

- The doubling periods of the components of information technology tend to become very brief, on the order of a year or two, a phenomenon known as *Moores'* Law; and
- There are three fundamental components of information systems: computation, storage, and communication.

An analysis of those components in terms of their growth rates, argues Koenig, leads neatly to three stages: Stage 1 (pre-1971) characterized by exponential *Moores'* Law growth of computational capability, and relative stasis in storage and communication; Stage II (1971–1989?) characterized by exponential growth of computation and storage, and relative stasis in communication; and Stage III (post-1989?) characterized by exponential growth of all three components.

In retrospect, the beginning of Stage II can be characterized by the appearance of real-time online access to large (millions of records) online databases, such as those produced by the National Library of Medicine and Chemical Abstracts Service. Looking back in a few years it may well be that the emergence of facsimile transmission, after two decades of being the technology that continually and frustratingly stayed just ahead of us like a water mirage on a hot dry road, was the event that characterized the beginning of Stage III.

Koenig has extended his stage hypotheses, in this case adding a fourth stage

Figure 18-1. Comparison of Developmental Stage Hypotheses for Information Management.

(◄─────► = Roughly the Present Time)

Marchand Stages (1983)	Rockart Eras (1984)	Gibson & Jackson Domains (1987)	Koenig Stages (1985)	
Stage 1 Management of Automated Technology	First Era Clerical & Accounting	First Domain Efficiency and Effectiveness of Unit Operations	Stage I Exponential Growth of Computation Stasis in Storage & Communication	**T**
Stage 2 Information Resources Management	Second Era Operational	Second Domain Efficiency and Effectiveness of Individual Operations	Stage II Exponential Growth of Computation & Storage Stasis in Communication	**I** **M** **E**
Stage 3 Knowledge Management	Third Era Managerial	Third Domain Efficiency and Effectiveness of the Organization & Transformation	Stage III Exponential Growth of Computation & Storage & Communcation	
			Stage IV Exponential Growth of Computation & Storage & Communication plus Continuous Speech Recognition	↓

Note: We have taken the liberty of excluding Marchants' first stage (Physical Control, 1900–1950s) as out of scope—pre-computer—and renumbering the other three stages.

derived from *Moores'* Law. *Moores'* Law is the now classic observation that an information system will be used only when it is more trouble not to use the system than it is to use it. This fourth stage will be ushered in by the achievement of continuous speech recognition: When we can talk to our devices rather than being a slave to the keyboard.

The consequences for networks and for research about networks in moving from Stage II to Stage III are immense. One obvious corollary is that in Stage III communication becomes increasingly substitutable for storage and there is a mushrooming of the concept of "access-based" rather than "collection-based" library service. Library and network systems will become increasingly interdependent.

Some of the obvious topics for research that emerge from our entry into Stage III will now be discussed.

The Economics of Networking

One of the major topics of that research will need to be the economics of networking. A major concern among networks, indeed a concern among the library community at large is that some of the recent developments in information technology have created a climate that encourages suboptimal decisions on the part of libraries in regard to network membership.

The specific major concern is that in the era of centralized online databases it was very much in the libraries' interest to join networks and to participate in the creation of the data files that those networks created and maintained. The networks were the only effective source of current cataloging information, and their pricing policy rewarded input and data creation (Martin 1984, 1989). Now the concern is that with the emergence of CD-ROM (Compact Disc-Read Only Memory), libraries will be tempted to get their cataloging data direct from vendors on CD-ROM, and use the networks only for locating and borrowing purposes and for cataloging only for the occasional items too exotic or too current to be on CD-ROM. Such a decision could, in the short term, be very much in the self-interest of the individual library. However, if a significant number of libraries make that decision, then the amount of material input to the networks would decline, as would their utility; a vicious spiral would set in with the remaining network members having to spread fixed costs among fewer member libraries, thus causing more members to elect to drop out, until the golden egg producing goose was destroyed. The great irony is that CD-ROM, almost the perfect embodiment of that long hoped for vision of a fast and efficient Library of Congress card distribution service, is now seen as a threat, a clear and present danger to the networks which grew up as substitutes for the long venerated but less than optimal Library of Congress card distribution scheme.

Martin (1987, p.135) very succinctly phrased the problem thusly:

> To be specific, we may all think that system or network is a good idea; but if individually we turn away from network services to commercial services or local systems, we will ultimately destroy the very system we created to suit our need.

This problem of the "peril of sub-optimization" as it was phrased at the recent Network Management Institute supported by the U.S. Department of Education and held at the Rosary College's Graduate School of Library and Information Science is a major concern.[1] It quite specifically was one of the reasons the Department of Education funded the Institute, and it is also a major concern of the Council on Library Resources, which is actively soliciting research aimed at how to avoid or eliminate the problem.

Two obvious issues arise from this concern. If networks, because of changing technology, are taking on the aspects of a public good, that is, a good which like street lighting cannot be adequately supported by voluntary membership in a street lighting association, since one can receive the benefits without paying the dues, and there is thus no motivation to join or maintain membership, then:

- How can we reconfigure networks and their structure to avoid the problem?
- How can we document and quantify the benefits of network membership, both to the individual institutions and to the community at large, so that individual libraries can justify to their administrations their continued network membership?

The assumptions here are twofold. First unlike the street lighting example, there are benefits that directly accrue to libraries from network membership that would not be available to those libraries were they to cancel their membership. However, we do not know how to articulate and quantify those benefits in a convincing fashion. Second, in any case, the culture of the academic community and of librarianship, in particular, is such that there is a willingness to join the street lighting association as it were, and not succumb to the temptation to profit at the expense of one's peer institutions.

The Technological Ramifications of Systems Design

One of the beneficial aspects of Stage III is that systems design should be more robust over time, because the three components of information systems technology will be growing roughly apace in capability (see Figure 18-2). In Stage III, any system that made heavy use of both storage and communications capabilities

---

[1] The Institute, supported by U.S. Dept. of Education Grant #R036A90020, was held May 15–19, 1989.

Figure 18-2. Ratios of Information Technology Capabilities.

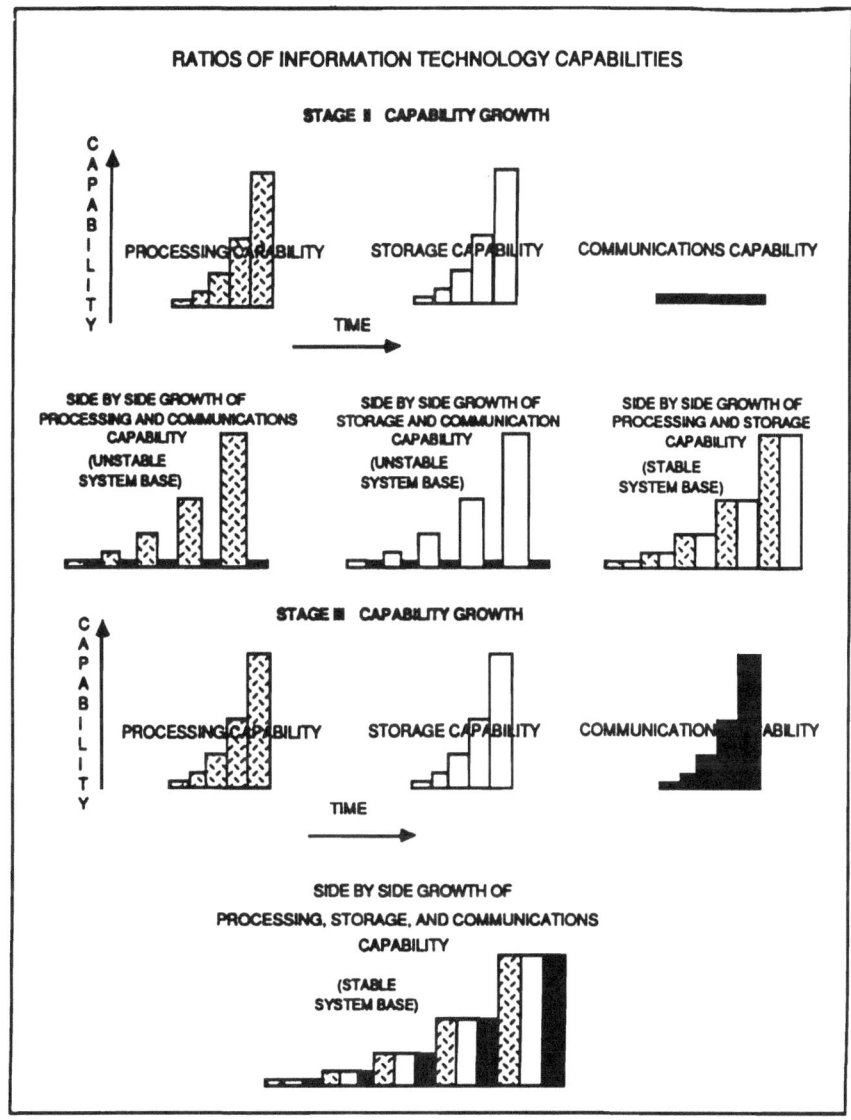

was built on an unstable base where the comparative capabilities of storage and communications grew rapidly more divergent. That should not happen in Stage III, but reality will, of course, not be quite so simple. In the first case, the introduction of communication technology is not so straightforward as that of computation and storage technology; numerous bureaucratic and regulatory hurdles must be cleared. Additionally, there will be numerous technological alternatives to pursue, not all of which will be equally fruitful.

A related issue is what functions are best accomplished by networks and which ones by the member institutions? In the mid-1980s, a spate of articles suggested that the pendulum had swung back from system development at the network level to local systems development (Martin, 1984). This was a clear Stage II phenomenon, a development driven by the ratio of storage costs to communication costs becoming increasingly more attractive on the storage side. Institutions were driven to invest in storage and minimize communications. An obvious ramification of Stage III is that with the storage and communications technologies growing apace, such technologically driven swings of the pendulum should be much less marked. What the increasing communication capability is likely to mean is an increased emphasis upon resource sharing. In other words, instead of a period, like the late 1970s and 1980s where the increasingly divergent storage and communications capabilities of network systems drove much of the decision making about networks, we are now entering a period where what will drive decision making is the overall potential of electronic data storage and communication technology in comparison to print on paper technology.

Another related issue is that of where the logical delimitations between networks occur. Hoadley (1987) discusses, in particular, the relations between OCLC and the regional brokering networks. Another long festering issue is that of the proper relationships between national networks, such as OCLC and RLIN. The concept of linked systems linking OCLC and RLIN (and other systems) has been extensively treated in the literature (see Hildreth 1987b; Martin 1987; and Segal, 1986, 1987, 1988, 1989).

Standards

Research and development of standards will be particularly important for networks. The need for the development of standards is obvious, but much more subtle is the question of research about standards, and when they are useful and when they should or should not be expedited. The current problem with the lack of standardization, or more accurately, the partial standardization of CD-ROM products, is a case in point. How we should have done it better is not quite so clear. A bad standard may well be worse than having no standard. The world was well on its way to standardizing letter-size paper at 8 1/2 x 11, had no attempt to formally introduce a standard taken place. The consequence of the ISO standardization attempt is that we now and probably always will have two office size standards, 8 1/2 x 11 "letter size," and "A4." The intention was good, and the mechanism not implausible—submit a new standard which belongs to nobody and to which nobody can object because it is someone else's standard. With many competing standards such an approach would have worked, but with 8 1/2 x 11 already a near de facto standard and too widely used to be displaced, the result was two standards. The problems of developing standards is discussed in some length by McClure et al. (1990).

Networks must be vitally interested in developing standards in a timely fashion and in promoting research that can help to illuminate the appropriate timing and content of those standards.

Organization of Information

One major consequence of the increasing digitalization of information and the potentiation of networks is that we still have a great deal to do to develop:

- Navigational tools for negotiating those networks; and
- Adequate structuring methodologies for the data and information they carry.

This topic is beyond the scope of this chapter, but it is imperative that it not be ignored.

We take the constraints of the print on paper world for granted, but when we study the history of printing and of the book, it is apparent that it took centuries for consensus to emerge, not only for such things as tables of contents and indexes, but also for basic notions like chapters and pagination. Similar constructs must be developed for the network environment, but it must be done quickly for a far more complex environment.

There is much discussion at the moment regarding hypertext and the problems of navigating in any large corpus of hypertext; how will we avoid "spaghetti code"[2] as it were. We do not yet know how to establish navigational structures for large bodies of hypertext, but yet in an ideal world they are only the tip of the iceberg. The research that is needed here seems far greater than the resources we have to expend. Inevitably much of that research will have to come from outside the field that we now traditionally call library and information science. We must respond quickly if we and not others are to have a major impact.

THE ROLE OF NETWORKS IN UNDERTAKING AND PROMOTING RESEARCH

A major role of networks is, of course, the undertaking of research. OCLC, in particular, has been energetic in this regard, conducting extensive in-house pro-

---

[2] The colorful jargon term for a computer program, the lines of code of which are as complexly intertwined as a bowl of spaghetti, and consequently extremely difficult to navigate or to reconstruct what connects with what.

jects (e.g., "Applying Neural Networks to Classification Problems" and "Cataloging Time and Workflow Studies"), supporting a large number of external research projects by means of grants (e.g., "Knowledge-Based Descriptive Cataloging of Cartographic Publications" and "A Systematic Approach to Automatic Book Indexing"), and collaborating on other projects (e.g., the "Mercury Electronic Library" project at Carnegie Mellon University) (OCLC, 1988 and 1989). The Research Library Group has also undertaken research, but on a much smaller scale.

Networks are, of course, not simply funding research for purely altruistic reasons or merely for good public relations. There are a number of reasons why networks need to be involved in research. First, they need research for all of the reasons discussed above; they need help in charting their own way. Second, because they must coordinate the needs and desires of their constituent members, they must, if they are to continue to be successful, have a vision of the forest and not merely the trees. It is easy for the constituent library or information center to focus on a tree or a very restricted area of the forest, but the network must attempt to view the whole forest. Third, the network, even if not seeing more clearly than its members, benefits from their aggregated views. Armstrong (1978) argues cogently that the quality of prediction rapidly plateaus as expertise increases, and then little if any more as expertise continues to increase. Furthermore, the consensus, the aggregate of prediction of a number of parties, is substantially more apt to be correct than the prediction of any one party, however expert. The network, with its typically elaborate governance and consultative structure is ideally situated to assemble and recognize that consensus. Fourth, networks can take advantage of scale economies and fund research that would be beyond the scope of most of their constituents.

Collaboration

Obviously one of the great consequences of networks will be to facilitate collaborative research. On phoning a colleague recently in South America after two letters had gone unanswered and apparently undelivered, the response was that the colleague would be pleased to work on a project and what was my Bitnet number? On the day this paragraph was penned, the author sent facsimile messages to Israel, Pakistan, and Botswana, one purely administrative, but one regarding an ARIST chapter, and another regarding an article for a new journal, *Third World Libraries*. Data compiled by the National Science Board (1987) for its Science and Engineering Indicators series shows an increase from 12 percent in 1973 to 19 percent in 1984, both in multiple authorship of articles in general, and internationally coauthored scientific articles in particular. This trend will almost certainly be accelerated by the development of more effective networks.

CONCLUSION

The impact of improved networks upon research will be dramatic. The most obvious impact will simply be in the availability and accessibility of data, and of software. Better research will be done in a more timely fashion because researchers will be able to get at more information and more data more quickly, as well as the software with which to manipulate both the information and data. One ramification of this is that a great deal of work still needs to be done quickly on how to link, structure, and organize that data.

A more subtle but perhaps ultimately more dramatic effect will be the increase in cooperation, particularly internationally, among researchers. The desire of researchers to stake their claim and to use the most effective means of achieving that end is very difficult to contain within national boundaries. One can plausibly argue that much of the cause of the collapse of the Soviet bloc political systems was a direct function of information technology. Information technology revealed the alternatives. It is not unrealistic to expect the growth of networks to have equally dramatic effects on scientific and scholarly cooperation. He or she who holds the purse strings will still have considerable power, but inevitably scholarship will become more international and cooperative, and science policy, trade terms, etc., will have to change to reflect those realities.

Exciting times lie ahead. Networks are major new research tools, but they are themselves a fascinating and fruitful area for research.

REFERENCES

Armstrong, J. Scott. *Long-Range Forecasting, from Crystal Ball to Computer.* New York: Wiley-Interscience, 1978.

Broadbent, Marianne and Michael E. D. Koenig. "Information and Information Technology Management," in *Annual Review of Information Science and Technology.* Vol. 23, edited by Martha E. Williams. New York: Elsevier, 1988, pp. 237–270.

Evans, Glyn T. "Library Networks," in *Annual Review of Information Science and Technology.* Vol. 16, edited by Martha E. Wiliams. White Plains, NY: Knowledge Industry Publications, 1981, pp. 211–245.

———. "Networking in 1984," in *The Bowker Annual of Library & Book Trade Information.* 30th Edition. New York: Bowker, 1985, pp. 49–63.

Gibson, Cyrus F. and Barbara Bund Jackson. *The Information Imperative: Managing the Impact of Information Technology on Business and People.* Lexington, MA.: D.C. Heath, 1987.

Hildreth, Charles R. "Library Networking in North America in the 1980s. Part 1: The Dreams, the Realities," *The Electronic Library.* 5, (August 1987a): 222–228.

———. "Library Networking in North American in the 1980s. Part 2: The Response of the Bibliographic Utilities to Local Integrated Systems," *The Electronic Library,* 5 (October 1987b): 270–275.

Hoadley, Irene Braden. "The Future of Networks and OCLC," *Journal of Library Administration,* 8 (Fall–Winter 1987):85–91.

Koenig, Michael E.D. "The Convergence of Computers and Telecommunications: Information Management Implications," *Information Management Review.* 1 (September 1987): 23–33.

———. "Information Services and Downstream Productivity," in *Annual Review of Information Science and Technology.* Vol. 25, edited by Martha E. Williams. Amsterdam: Elsevier, 1990, forthcoming.

———. "Stage III of Information Systems Technology," in *Intelligent Information Systems for the Information Society,* edited by B. C. Brookes. Amsterdam: Elsevier Science Publishers, 1986, pp. 11–33. (A collection of papers presented at the Sixth International Research Forum on Information Science held at Frascati, Italy, Sept. 1985).

Marchand, Donald A. "Strategies and Tools in Transition?," *Business and Economic Review,* 29 (May 1983): 4–8.

Martin, Susan K. "Information Technology and Libraries: Toward the Year 2000," *College and Research Libraries,* 50 (1989): 387–405.

———. *Library Networks, 1986–87; Libraries in Partnership.* White Plains, NY: Knowledge Industry Publications, 1986.

———. "Library Networks: Trends and Issues," *Journal of Library Administration,* 8 (Summer 1987): 27–33.

———. "The New Technologies and Library Networks," *Library Journal,* 109 (June 15, 1984): 1194–1196.

McClure, Charles R, Ann Bishop, and Philip Doty. *Electronic Networks, the Research Process, and Scholarly Communications: An Empirical Study with Policy Recommendations for the National Research and Education Network.* Syracuse, NY: School of Information Studies, Syracuse University, 1990.

Molholt, Pat. *Library Networking, the Interface of Ideas and Actions.* Washington D.C.: Department of Education, 1988.

National Science Board. *Science and Engineering Indicators–1987.* Washington D.C.: The National Science Foundation, 1987.

OCLC. *Annual Review of OCLC Research July 1987–June 1988.* Dublin, OH: OCLC, 1988.

———. *Annual Review of OCLC Research July 1988–June 1989.* Dublin, OH: OCLC, 1989.

Rockart, John F. and Michael Morton Scott. "Implications of Changes in Information Technology for Corporate Strategy," *Interfaces,* 14 (1984): 84–95.

Segal, Jo An S. "Library Networking and Resource Sharing in 1985," in *The Bowker Annual of Library & Book Trade Information.* 31st Edition. New York: Bowker, 1986, pp. 50–67.

———. "Library Networking in 1988," in *The Bowker Annual of Library & Book Trade Almanac.* 34 Edition. New York: Bowker, 1989, pp. 26–49.

———. "Library Networks, Coorperation and Resources Sharing in 1987," in *The Bowker Annual of Library and Book Trade Information.* 33rd Edition. New York: Bowker, 1989, pp. 22–43.

———. "Networking and Decentralization," in *Annual Review of Information Science and Technology*. Vol. 20, edited by Martha E. Williams. White Plains, NY: Knowledge Industry Publications, 1987, pp. 203–231.

———. "Networking and Resource Sharing in 1986: Facilitating Access to Information," in *The Bowker Annual of Library and Book Trade Information*. 32nd Edition. New York: Bowker, 1987, pp. 42–59.

Shaw, Ward and Patricia B. Culkin. "Systems That Inform: Emerging Trends in Library Automation and Network Development," in *Annual Review of Information Science and Technology*. Vol. 22, edited by Martha E. Williams. Amsterdam: Elsevier, 1987, pp. 265–292.

Sugnet, Chris. "Networking in Transition; Current and Future Issues" (a forum of 8 papers), *Library Hi Tech*, 6 (1988): 101–119.

chapter nineteen

The Role of the Information Industry

Candy Schwartz

> The information industry provides funding and other support for library and information science research in a variety of ways. However, the motives which drive industry and the academic research community are sufficiently at odds that a number of unresolved problems have arisen from the relationship between the two. In particular, the need for collaborative and long-range projects has not been addressed. Solutions exist, but will demand strong leadership.

The interests of the information industry (or industries, as some would have it) are closely intertwined with those of library and information science (LIS) research. The relationship is sometimes a fruitful one, but is often difficult. Both sides need each other in order to thrive, but may often find themselves at odds. The role of the information industry in library and information science research has obvious aspects and also more subtle ones, and this chapter will attempt to explore the current state and suggest future directions.

THE INFORMATION INDUSTRY

The Information Industry Association (IIA) defines its membership as "companies interested in the business opportunities associated with the creation, dissemination, and use of information" (Van Gorder, 1988, pp. ii). A glance through the IIA directory reveals that this includes indexing and abstracting services (print and online), information consultants, electronic publishers, telecommunications hardware and software producers, library automation services, document delivery companies, entrepreneurs, expert systems and artificial intelligence consultants, optical and video media production and distribution services, data con-

The Role of the Information Industry 241

version companies, and so on. The cover of the directory shows a map identifying the major segments of the industry (Figure 19-1). Of these, library and information science research is assumed to be most directly concerned with those grouped under "Content Services," "Content Packages," and "Information Technologies."

The National Federation of Abstracting and Information Services (NFAIS), another organization closely associated with the information industry, seeks to address "all segments of the information processing and dissemination community, including primary publishers, libraries, commercial and industrial abstracting and indexing services, data analysis centers, information dissemination centers" (Burek, Koek, and Novallo, 1989, p. 674). Since other chapters in this volume cover agencies and institutions which are included in the broadest definitions of "information industry," this chapter will concentrate on those companies, both profit and nonprofit, which provide information products and services such as libraries might purchase, subscribe to, or otherwise acquire in the pursuit of normal operations. Sales and advertising revenues for these types of companies approached $85 billion in 1988 (Fleming, Rosenbaum, Elwell, and Silverstein, 1989).

That the information industry plays a significant role in everyday library life cannot be denied. In terms of machine-readable files alone, there are currently over 4,000 online databases published by close to 2,000 producers and available from 645 service providers (Barg, 1990a). To this *embarras de richesses* has recently been added well over 500 portable files, 80 percent of them on CD-ROM (Barg, 1990b), with estimates that by 1991 over one million CD-ROM drives will be in use in the United States (Emard, 1988).

The information industry has effectively changed the environment in which libraries exist, especially in the past decade. From the library community's point of view, the result of the drive to capture markets has led to proliferation of an immense and confusing array of products and services. The need to make purchase decisions or provide "quick fix" responses to user needs, coupled with a lack of research training and limited financial resource, has the inevitable result that "too much of what has been called [LIS] research falls under the heading of consulting or demonstration products" (Katzer, 1989, pp. 83–84). Small wonder that "librarians tend to be more interested in explaining their immediate environment than in contributing to the longitudinal development of theory" (Enger, Quirk, and Stewart, 1989, pp. 44).

CURRENT SUPPORT FOR LIS RESEARCH

Figure 19-2 lists direct and indirect support for LIS research provided by the information industry, and this section takes each up separately.

Figure 19-1. The Information Industries.*

Broadcast Channels	Communications Channels
	Physical Delivery
	U.S. Post Office
	Telephone
Radio Networks	Telegraph
Multipoint Distribution Services	Satellite Carriers
TV Networks	International Record Carriers
Teletext	Cable TV
	Mobile Services
	Value-Added Carriers
	Paging Services

Content Services	Content Packages
	Newspapers
News Services	Magazines
	Newsletters
Electronic Database Providers	Books
Non-Electronic Database Providers	Directories
	Loose Leaf
Indexes	Films
Libraries	Video Discs
Information Brokers	Reports
Database Distributors	Records
Videotex	Tapes
	Micropublishing

Communications Technologies	Integrating Technologies
Radios	
Televisions	Packet Switchers
Video Disc Players	Modems
Telephones	Digital Switches
Transmission Systems	Facsimile
Switchboards	
Mail Equipment	

Facilitation Services	Information Technologies
Banks	
Time Sharing	
Electronic Funds Transfer	Computers
Ad Agencies	Terminals
Software Services	Office Equipment
Systems Design	Optical Media
Conference Management Consultants	Microforms
Market & Business Research	Laser Disc
Facilities Management	Printing/Graphic Equipment
Service Bureaus	Business Forms

*The Information Industry Association (adapted from *Information Sources*, 1988, cover).

Figure 19-2. Information Industry Support for LIS Research.

Direct Support of LIS Research
Equipment and Dataset Support
Research and Visiting Fellowships
Funding of Externally Conducted Research
Support of Internal (i.e., In-house) Research
Research Center Support

Indirect Support of LIS Research
Academic Scholarship and Fellowship Programs
Recognition of Research (i.e., Awards)
Conference and Association Support
Involvement with the LIS Academic Community

Direct Support

Equipment and Dataset Support. It is quite common for information service providers to give grants of free or greatly reduced cost online time to investigators of some online phenomenon. Alternatively, database producers frequently give large machine-readable data files directly to researchers for their further in-house manipulation. Hardware and software equipment grants have come from companies as diverse as Apple Computers and OCLC, usually in connection with a specific research agenda and a request for proposals.

Research and Visiting Fellowships. Many information service companies have regular programs whereby scholars are encouraged to spend a year on site, working on a specific research project. These scholars may be well-known in the field, or they may be graduate students or recent doctorates. While the specific project will, of course, be under the domain (and possibly ownership) of the company, the advantage to the scholar is that of having a wealth of resources at hand. One of the best examples of this support can be seen in the visiting scholar, postdoctoral fellowship, and research assistant programs at OCLC.

Funding of Externally Conducted Research. Some information industry members do fund research projects performed externally to the company, typically at academic institutions. Unfortunately, the proportion of direct financial support for LIS research which emanates from the information industry is a very small proportion of total research funding. An informal examination of six refereed research journals, two refereed proceedings of conferences which tend to have a high number of LIS research presentations, and the "Current Research" subfile of *Library and Information Science Abstracts* (1969-) revealed a dearth of funding source acknowledgment at all, much less support from the information industries.

The *Journal of the American Society for Information Science* for 1989 showed the highest frequency of acknowledged funding from information industry sources of any of the journals examined, but over half of these were accounted for by a "Perspectives" collection of solicited papers on hypertext. That same year, *Information Processing and Management* identified five or six industrial support sources. In the case of the four other journals (*Journal of Documentation*, latter half of 1988 and first half of 1989; *Library & Information Science Research*, 1989; *Library Quarterly*, 1989; and *College & Research Libraries*, 1989), very little mention was made of funding for research, and where sources were acknowledged they were principally academic institutions or government funding agencies.

The two proceedings (Belkin & van Rijsbergen, 1989; Katzer and Newby, 1989) together represent about 60 published papers. Information industry support was mentioned some dozen times, not only for equipment or datasets, but also for grants or other material aid. Some 115 of the most recent 150 "Current Research" reports in *Library and Information Science Abstracts* acknowledge financial support, but only eight of those could be construed as emanating from the information industry (and two of these eight are research projects involving the funder's own publications).

The companies and institutions which are mentioned in these various sources include OCLC, DIALOG, Bellcore, Eastman Kodak, Hughes Aircraft, Martin Marietta, AT&T, Logica (Cambridge), Lockheed-Georgia, General Electric, Chemical Abstracts Service, Texas Instruments, Apple, Digital Equipment Corporation, Mead Data Central, Bibliographic Retrieval Services, Apple Computers, TRW, and the Information Access Corporation. With many of these, it is hard to tell whether the support is for a direct grant of funds, equipment, data, or online time.

Support of Internal (i.e., In-house) Research. Using the same sources as in the preceding section, it is revealing to examine the affiliations of the authors. While not a direct indicator of the nature of research activity in information industry settings, this at least reveals the extent to which industrial LIS research may be shared in the professional literature. As before, the largest amount of information industry research authorship was found in the two conference proceedings. Of approximately 130 authors of papers (with some overlap between the two conferences), about nine information industry affiliations are listed, including Thinking Machines Corporation, Lotus Development Corporation, IBM, Sun MicroSystems Inc., Bellcore, AT&T, Engineering Information, EBSCO, Microelectronics and Computer Technology Corporation, Xerox, and a few consulting firms.

Research Center Support. The *Computer Industry Almanac* (Juliussen and Juliussen, 1988) lists a number of U.S. research centers that conduct LIS-related research (Figure 19-3). Some of these are for-profit, some are not. The fruits of their labors are shared with the outside world to some degree (as discussed above), but in many cases research results will only be evidenced in the form of products and services. Also of interest in this category are the supercomputer

Figure 19-3. Research Centers Involved in LIS-Related Research.

Research Centers
AT&T Bell Laboratories
Arthur D. Little, Inc.
Battelle Memorial Institute
Bell Communications Research (Bellcore)
IBM Thomas J. Watson Research Center
Microelectronics & Computer Technology Corp (MCC)
Rand Corporation
SRI International
Xerox Palo Alto Research Center (PARC)

Supercomputer Centers
Center for Theory and Simulation, Cornell University
John von Neumann National Supercomputer Center, Princeton, NJ
National Center for Supercomputing Applications, Champaign, IL
Pittsburgh Supercomputing Center, Mellon Institute
San Diego Supercomputer Center

centers established by the National Science Foundation, but usually funded by some conglomeration of government, academic, and industrial support.

Indirect Support

While more difficult to observe, there is considerable indirect support on the part of the information industry for research and research-related activities.

Academic Scholarship and Fellowship Programs. Funding to individuals for professional education may not contribute directly to research, but it certainly enables the development of future generations of scholars. The American Library Association (ALA) publishes an annual listing of financial assistance opportunities for library education (American Library Association, 1989). The printing of the 1990/1991 edition was supported by a grant from the H.W. Wilson Foundation, and of the over 500 awards of various kinds, about 15 percent are granted by private industry, including publishers, binderies, local corporations, research laboratories, and H. W. Wilson.

Recognition of Research (i.e., Awards). Many professional associations present annual awards for distinguished achievement in research and education. A number of these awards are funded in full or in part by information service companies. For instance, the Institute for Scientific Information (ISI) funds the "Outstanding Information Science Teacher Award" and the "ISI Information Science Doctoral Dissertation Award" presented by the American Society for Information Science (ASIS). While the dollar amounts associated with recognition are never very large, they are at least a tangible acknowledgment of excellence.

Conference and Association Support. Conference sessions often serve as the first public forum for dissemination of research activities. There are a few annual conferences (especially in the realm of online searching) which are entirely administered by publishing companies. More commonly, professional associations seek corporate funding in support of national (and regional) meetings. The Association for Computing Machinery (ACM) SIGIR '89 meeting was partially supported by several corporate donations. The conference program for ASIS '89 lists eight sponsors, seven of whom represent information industry businesses. In addition, any LIS association accepting exhibitor fees or soliciting corporate memberships hopes to gain some profit over expenses.

The information industry contributes leaders to professional associations. AT&T Bell Laboratories has been particularly well represented in ASIS and ACM at leadership levels, and all LIS associations can point to committee chairs, local chapter officers, and other active participants who are employees in online services, publishing houses, and so on. These associations, especially the large national bodies, affect the general LIS research agenda through their contributions to such activities as accreditation, representation to government, publishing, continuing education, and (to some degree) award granting.

Involvement with the LIS Academic Community. Many LIS schools enjoy close relationships with their local information service companies, and engage in such mutually beneficial activities as student internships, "day on the job" opportunities, fund-raising, consulting, and adjunct or guest lecture programs. The information industry market endorses LIS schools and ensures their continuance (and the continuance of research conducted in these institutions) by consuming the product (i.e., graduates).

Those research activities which are conducted in graduate programs of library and information science benefit from the availability of up-to-date information resources and tools. Much of the hardware and software used in support of LIS curricula is the result of direct corporate gifts or special instructional discounts (with, of course, future customers in mind). Recent examples of this can be seen in the flourishing of subsidized CD-ROM databases and workstations in the libraries and laboratories of LIS programs.

REMAINING PROBLEMS

Even with the support detailed above, the state of LIS research is usually described by adjectives which are rarely more encouraging than "guardedly optimistic." To what degree does the information industry offer possible solutions? What improvements in LIS research could be brought about by increased support from the information industry, and how can the LIS research community make persuasive arguments for that support?

"Better" LIS research requires four interrelated elements:

- Resources;
- Training;
- Collaboration; and
- Cumulation.

In the arena of *resources*, information businesses seem to have been willing and able to provide assistance (if approached with the appropriate hat in hand and with a reminder of the tax advantages of gift giving). In fact, in the case of data-handling resources, the information industry has been indirectly supportive by dramatically increasing capabilities at affordable levels of computing. Adequate academic *and* office computing resources play an important role in recruiting new LIS faculty.

With respect to the human component of *training* and education, however, academic institutions may suffer. With the current economic state of the nation being what it is, the information industry has become a rewarding career path for new LIS doctoral graduates, who take substantial research training with them to the workplace and away from the creation of future scholars. Since most LIS schools cannot compete in salary with private industry, some other method must be found of making the academic life desirable to new generations of scholars. The opportunity to contribute to substantial and important ongoing research efforts is an attractive benefit, although it may be difficult for deans and directors to balance appropriate course load reductions against fiscal realities.

The opportunity for *collaboration* among researchers (both within LIS, and between LIS and other fields) presents a related problem. Few LIS schools are sufficiently well-endowed to support significant research efforts without substantial outside funding, and few faculty or doctoral students have the leisure of being able to focus solely on a specific project without distraction.

The development of a continuing and *cumulative* body of research is probably the most difficult issue. Information utilities are concerned primarily with product development and testing, and with market research. These activities are driven by short-term profit motives, and are usually related to very specific market segments. Online service suppliers which are planning a product innovation rarely do more than study markets and test prototypes, and they do not appear to monitor transactions or study user behavior on a regular basis at all (Smit and Kochen, 1988). What little research that is conducted is rarely shared in the form of publication. Even for those companies which do support other forms of research and which do publish, any contribution to overall theory development is indirect. LIS graduates who might be capable of developing a cumulative body of research are faced with choosing between limited resource and reward if they remain in academia, or directing their efforts to special and proprietary interests if they go into industry.

CONCLUSION

There are no easy answers. It is unrealistic to expect the information industry to be altruistic, and it is equally unrealistic to expect the LIS academic research community to muster larger financial resources. In this society, the case has to be made that improved LIS research contributes directly to improved profit, whether by providing better-trained workers or a richer understanding of users.

In the interests of maintaining high standards of LIS education, IIA and/or NFAIS could take examples from the Council on Library Resources, and offer grants to cooperative research projects carried out by LIS faculty and members of industry. The argument on behalf of such a program would be that the faculty member would impart research skills and a broad-based knowledge of user behavior. These elements, brought to bear in a specific setting, would presumably contribute to improvements in product or service and hence to improvement in profit. In a similar vein, sabbatical (or more frequent) exchanges between industry and academia would benefit both sides of the partnership.

McClure and Bishop (1989) suggest establishing "centers of excellence" in leading LIS schools. While this may offer the best avenue to a cumulated body of research, it has some possibly undesirable side effects in drawing a wide line between "research" programs and "professional" programs. Schools with centers of excellence would draw the best scholars and funding, while the remaining schools would inevitably find it difficult to support research programs of any substance, or to attract good faculty and students. Perhaps the final result would be fewer graduate programs, and an increase in undergraduate LIS specializations (both of these trends are already in evidence). This is not inherently bad, but it does imply some major changes in the LIS educational infrastructure.

An alternative way to bring together critical numbers of researchers would be to use the success of fellowship and internship programs at locations such as OCLC to persuade other businesses as to the desirability of providing temporary homes for intensive research efforts which are not *product* directed, but which are sufficiently *problem* oriented for the findings to be of benefit. This would have the effect of bringing together scholars with different backgrounds and orientations, and would also send those same scholars back to their own programs armed with fresh viewpoints and a sense of accomplishment.

If these or other programs are to be adopted to further a symbiosis between research and industry, the effort has to be made with a concerted and coordinated voice at a leadership level. If leadership is not forthcoming from the Federal government and/or individual or amalgamated professional associations, then we can expect a continuation of isolated support, increased competition for fewer resources, and rapid deterioration in our institutions of professional education.

REFERENCES

American Library Association, Standing Committee on Library Education. *Financial Assistance for Library Education: Academic Year 1990-1991*. Chicago: ALA, 1989.

Barg, Jeffrey, Ed. *Directory of Online Databases*. Vol. 11, No. 1. New York: Cuadra/Elsevier, January 1990a.

――――. *Directory of Portable Databases*. Vol. 1, No. 1. New York: Cuadra/Elsevier, January 1990b.

Belkin, N.J. and C.J. van Rijsbergen, Eds. *SIGIR '89*: Proceedings of the Twelfth Annual International ACMSIGIR Conference on Research and Development in Information Retrieval, Cambridge, Massachusetts, USA, June 25-28, 1989. New York: Association for Computing Machinery, 1989 (Special issue of SIGIR Forum).

Burek, Deborah M., Karin E. Koek, and Annette Novallo, Eds. *Encyclopedia of Associations*. Vol. 1: National Organizations of the U.S. 24th ed. Detroit, MI: Gale Research Inc., 1989.

Emard, Jean-Paul, Ed. *CD-ROMs in Print, 1988-1989: An International Guide*. Westport, CT: Meckler, 1988.

Enger, Kathy B., Georgia Quirk, and Andrew J. Stewart. "Statistical Methods Used by Authors of Library and Information Science Journal Articles," *Library & Information Science Research*, 11 (1989): 37-46.

Fleming, Maureen, Melanie Rosenbaum, Chris Elwell, and Jeff Silverstein. *Information Industry Factbook, 1989/90 Edition*. Stamford, CT: Digital Information Group, 1989.

Juliussen, Egil and Karen Juliussen. *The Computer Industry Almanac, 1989*. New York: Simon & Schuster, 1988.

Katzer, Jeffrey. "ALA and the Status of Research in Library/Information Science," *Library & Information Science Research*, 11 (1989): 83-87.

―――― and Gregory B. Newby, Eds. *Managing Information and Technology*: Proceedings of the 52nd ASIS Annual Meeting of the American Society for Information Science, October 30- November 2, 1989, Washington D.C. Medford, NJ: Learned Information, 1989.

LISA (Library and Information Science Abstracts). London, England: Library Association Publishing, 1969- (Dialog File 61).

McClure, Charles R. and Ann Bishop. "The Status of Research in Library/Information Science: Guarded Optimism," *College & Research Libraries*, 50 (March 1989): 127-143.

Smit, Peter H. and Manfred Kochen. "Information Impediments to Innovation of On-Line Database Vendors," *Information Processing & Management*, 24 (1988): 229-241.

Van Gorder, Barbara E., Ed. *Information Sources 1988: The Annual Directory of the Information Industry Association*. Washington, D.C.: Information Industry Association, 1988.

part iii
Issues and Concerns Related to Research in Library and Information Science

chapter twenty

Communicating Applied Library/Information Science Research to Decision Makers: Some Methodological Considerations

Charles R. McClure

> LIS researchers must take greater responsibility for increasing the effectiveness with which research is communicated to the LIS profession, especially those in decision-making positions. Improving the effectiveness of this communication, however, entails recognizing a number of issues and factors *prior* to and *during* the conduct of the study. These issues and factors are at least as important, and possibly more important, than improving report writing and oral communication skills. This chapter offers a number of strategies and recommendations to address these factors and improve the effectiveness with which LIS research is communicated.

If communication is an interactive process of disseminating, receiving, and discussing/reviewing information, then the communication of library/information science (LIS) research is a topic which clearly requires closer scrutiny as part of the overall LIS research process. Unfortunately, the effective communication of LIS research is oftentimes not considered as part of the research process.

Improving the effectiveness with which LIS researchers communicate their research to the profession, and the effectiveness with which members of the LIS profession obtain, understand, and use LIS research, are not new topics. Indeed, DeProspo (1972, p. 1) wrote:

> The library researcher must learn to communicate with the library policymaker on some equal basis. If he continues to talk only to himself or to other researchers, research efforts are not likely to contribute toward the solutions of some of the pressing and growing problems confronting the library today and in the foreseeable future.

DeProspo's assessment of the situation is as valid today as it was when originally written—almost two decades ago. In fact, his admonition to LIS researchers takes on increased importance as the range of issues and unknowns confronting library decision makers continues to expand.

Of special interest to this chapter are LIS researchers who conduct inquiry that has potential applications for addressing a range of issues broadly related to acquiring, managing, and using information. Since the vast majority of LIS research is applied or action research in nature, as opposed to basic research (McClure and Bishop, 1989), LIS researchers should be especially concerned about the degree to which their research is communicated effectively to LIS decision makers.

Attention to conducting more and better basic research in library/information science is needed. The sense of this chapter is that those researchers conducting applied or action research have a responsibility to communicate their research effectively to library decision makers. Moreover, such communication is essential if applied and action research is to have an impact on the way in which libraries are managed.

The term, LIS decision makers, is important because it suggests a broad range of stakeholders who may have an interest in LIS research. Virtually all professional librarians and information specialists are decision makers and managers as they go about the business of converting information into decisions and taking action on a day-to-day basis. Other stakeholders may include library and information center administrators, government officials, or policy makers whose actions may affect library and information centers.

The purpose of this chapter is to discuss selected key issues and factors, and to offer strategies related to communicating LIS research from the researcher to the decision maker. There is a large body of literature on the general topic of better communicating research and increasing the usefulness of research. Because Rothman (1980) and Lawler (1985) discuss that literature, a similar introduction will not be repeated here.

A key theme of this chapter is that improving the communication of LIS research requires LIS researchers to consider a number of issues and factors *prior* to and *during* the conduct of the study. While there are additional issues related to LIS researchers that better communicate research to other LIS researchers and to the broader research community, this chapter will not address those issues here. Rather, the chapter focuses on key issues and strategies that may be of use to LIS researchers in more effectively communicating their research to LIS decision makers.

CONFLICTING PERSPECTIVES

One can argue that LIS researchers and decision makers are of two different worlds and have sharply differing frames of reference in their views toward research. Any "we-them" adversarial relationship between the two groups must be minimized. As a first step in improving the communication of LIS research, both groups should recognize these conflicts. This section discusses some of the most important ones.

Research That Is "Good Enough"

Researchers are trained to conduct research that meets the scientific community's standards of inquiry, that demonstrate acceptable levels of reliability and validity, and addresses a topic deemed to be "important." Appropriateness of method, data collection, and precision of findings are additional criteria that must be met. But decision makers are often less interested in method and precision than they are in the degree to which the research either identifies a managerial problem or helps to improve a particular activity or service in the library/information center.

For example, a researcher might be concerned that the method used to compute a performance measure (i.e., a quantitative assessment of the quality of library services or activities), for example, "percentage of books cataloged that circulated in their first year of availability," has a confidence interval of plus or minus 4 percent. But for the library decision maker it is much less important to know the error within the measure than it is to know if the percentage of books cataloged that circulated in their first year of availability is 35 percent or 65 percent. "Good enough" research and findings for decision makers are typically seen as not "good enough" for LIS researchers.

Power, Politics, and Personality

The three P's of organizational reality are power relationships between and among key positions, the politics and brokering of that power, and idiosyncratic personality characteristics and behavior of organizational members. Researchers rarely ever take these factors into consideration as they conduct research, unless they rely primarily on case-site study designs.

Yet, in organizational settings, power, politics, and personality are key considerations affecting the decision-making process. In many instances, the best research can be stymied by the three P's, perhaps for reasons having nothing to do with the research itself. For example, the head of cataloging might resist *any* research-based recommendations simply because they are supported by the head of public services—a person who has designs on the director's job and might then dismiss the head of cataloging.

Thus, almost by definition, LIS research usually fails to consider the three P's in designing research and making recommendations. LIS decision makers bemoan the fact that the research fails to consider organizational realities. The result is that the research has limited impact.

Generalization

For years, the holy grail for social science research is external validity, that is, the degree to which research can be generalized to the larger population. But LIS decision makers have less interest in the degree to which findings can be generalized to other settings than they do the degree to which findings are useful in *their* particular setting. Due, in part, to the problems related to the three P's of organizational reality, and despite the best efforts of many researchers, much of the LIS research cannot be generalized beyond a particular setting.

Yet, LIS researchers continue to design studies in such a way that they hope generalization will be possible. Further, the scientific community sometimes holds in low esteem case-study methods and qualitative techniques, thereby limiting their use by researchers. As a result, researchers strive for generalized findings and give less attention to studies that produce specific implications for particular library/information centers.

Timeliness

LIS decision makers live in real-time situations and under a broad range of decision-making constraints. LIS researchers live in virtual time situations where the primary time constraint imposed on them is their own. This situation allows researchers the luxury of determining how much time they wish to spend on a particular study and when they should complete it.

LIS decision makers need research at specific points in the organizational decision-making process, at specific "crises" or exceptions in daily operations, or when called upon to make immediate determinations on particular situations. Such a context may be difficult for researchers to consider in their study designs.

Reward Structures

LIS researchers receive little tangible reward for conducting applied or action research that has been well-communicated to LIS decision makers and has a demonstrated impact on LIS decision making. The reward structure for most academic LIS researchers is geared toward two basic criteria:

- Obtaining external funding in support of the research; and
- Publishing research studies in nationally prominent peer reviewed journals.

The results and impact of that research on LIS decision making are of secondary or no importance to the majority of research institutions where the research is conducted. In short, there are limited rewards provided in the scholarly community for those wishing to spend the time and energy on communicating research effectively to LIS decision makers.

Problems versus Messes

One of the most useful insights into understanding the context of decision makers and the problem of communicating research to managers has been offered by Russell Ackoff (as cited in Schön, 1983, p. 16):

> Managers are not confronted with problems that are independent of each other, but with dynamic situations that consist of complex systems of changing problems that interact with each other. I call such situations messes. Problems are abstractions extracted from messes by analysis. . . . Managers do not solve problems, they manage messes.

For researchers, developing problem statements, objectives, research questions, and hypotheses form the framework of the study. But for LIS decision makers, these "problems" are already an abstraction that fail to recognize the dynamic and fluid nature of the "messes" they manage. Indeed, the process of "conceptualizing" the problems in order to study them may only increase the distance between the "real" problem and that which the researcher studies.

A Difficult Relationship

The conflicting perspectives outlined above are not a comprehensive listing of all the possible conflicts. Clearly, others can be added to this list. But they do point out that there are very real reasons for why communicating research to LIS decision makers effectively, and increasing the impact of LIS research in the decision-making process, are difficult propositions. This context between researcher and decision maker has to be understood if communication between the two groups is to be improved.

COMPETING FRAMES OF REFERENCE

The previous discussion identified a number of factors that contribute to conflicts between LIS researchers and decision makers regarding the research process. These conflicts, however, can be better understood in the context of "frames of reference." A frame of reference is the set of assumptions, values, perspectives, and needs that a particular group of people bring to bear on a topic or issue. Shrivastava and Mitroff (1984) provide an excellent discussion of the competing frames of reference between researchers and decision makers, and this section of the chapter summarizes their work.

Shrivastava and Mitroff (Ibid.) propose six basic factors that comprise researchers' and decision makers' frames of reference. They define these factors as follows (pp. 20–22):

- *Cognitive Elements:* These are bits of data that are taken for granted or regarded as so basic that they are beyond doubt; they are the fundamental units of information that support a person's inquiring system or concept of the world
- *Cognitive Operators:* These are the methods by which individuals order and rearrange information and make meaning out of large amounts of data; they can include classification schemes, models, analytical devices, or common sense theories with which individuals approach inquiry
- *Reality Tests:* These guarantee or validate the "realness" of cognitive elements, cognitive operators, and information itself; they validate the process of inquiry by expressing their connection with critical, shared social and cultural experiences—collective social and cultural experiences form the basis of these reality tests
- *Domain of Inquiry:* This includes the individual's assumptions about the scope of the inquiry and the nature of its boundaries; the domain of inquiry limits the inquirer's access to alternative frames of reference
- *Degree of Articulation:* This factor refers to the degree to which the assumptions embodied in the other four elements have been articulated and codified; it also reflects the degree to which the individual's frame of reference will be and can be shared by others
- *Metaphors:* These permit the symbolic reconstruction of the organizational world in meaningful ways; they describe unidentifiable characteristics of an individual's frame of reference by drawing implicit analogies with known objects and experiences—thereby clarifying and explaining obscure and nebulous aspects of one's frame of reference.

Understanding these six factors and their implications can assist LIS researchers to better communicate research to LIS decision makers.

Figure 20-1 provides specific examples of each of these factors. The figure clearly suggests that researchers and managers have quite different frames of reference. Indeed, the difference among these cognitive elements may comprise significant barriers for the researcher hoping to communicate research effectively to decision makers. But perhaps more importantly, the figure also suggests possible strategies that can be developed to better communicate research as well as increase the likelihood that the research impacts decision making. The next section discusses these and other strategies.

Figure 20-1. Researchers' and Decision Makers' Frames of Reference (FOR).*

Elements of FOR	Researchers' FOR	Decision Makers' FOR
1. Cognitive Elements	Preference for objective, measurable, verifiable data.	Preference for subjective, experiential data. Intellectual commitment to (a) organizational and personal goals, (b) incremental improvement of practice, (c) problem solving.
2. Cognitive Operators	Preference for impersonal analytical models, well structured categorical schemes, scientific theories. "Problems" defined as a lack of theoretical knowledge, or paradoxes in need of explanation. "Solutions" involve creation of theoretical structures consistent with data. Rules of inquiry are formal, structured, and standard across the discipline.	Preference for intuitive images of the problem, personal statement of problems. Narrow definition of problems focused on specific performance indicators. Solutions consist of improvement in predefined performance indicators. Inquiry is conducted through informal, personal, non-standard procedures.
3. Reality Tests	Empirically observable and experimentally verifiable proofs. Consensus among experts. Conceptual adequacy and theoretical consistency.	Pragmatic value or workability. Issues are "real" if they can influence situation. Reality is embedded in personal experience.
4. Domain of Inquiry	Discipline or field of research. Preferred research tradition or paradigm. Relevance to the problem.	Department, division, field organization, or the economy as the boundary for inquiry.
5. Degree of Articulation	Implicit articulation of FOR through institutional means such as professional bodies' regulations, editorial policies. Explicit articulation in specific research reports through a description of methodological assumptions	Low degree of articulation, FORs are implicit in decisions. Explicit articulation via organizational policies, norms, and decision making practices.
6. Metaphors	Scientific vocabulary, technical jargon. Theories as metaphors.	Professional jargon. Metaphors used for personal "sense-making" and explication of FOR.

*Reprinted with permission of the Academy of Management, from Paul Shrivastava and Ian I. Mitroff, "Enhancing Organizational Research Utilization: The Role of Decision Makers' Assumptions," *Academy of Management Review,* 9 (January, 1984): 20.

STRATEGIES AND TECHNIQUES

While it is unlikely that problems associated with the effective communication of LIS research will be resolved quickly or easily, a number of strategies and techniques can improve the present situation. The following approaches might improve both the usefulness of LIS research for decision makers as well as comprise a means for increasing the effectiveness of researchers' communication of their studies and results.

Frame of Reference Assessment

Perhaps most importantly, researchers must better understand the different frames of reference they, versus the decision makers, have with regard to research. Examples depicting the researchers' and decision makers' frame of reference, as shown in Figure 20-1, suggest that researchers will need to design, implement, and communicate their research to better accommodate the decision makers' frame of reference.

One implication of this figure is to determine who the audiences of the research are *prior* to designing the study. The broader the intended audience, the more difficult it will be to target the study to a particular frame of reference. For example, it is quite likely that the decision makers' frame of reference will vary from target audience to target audience, e.g., the metaphors used by government officials making decisions about appropriate LIS research topics might be quite different than the metaphors used by academic librarians. Thus, the metaphors that a researcher might use in conducting and reporting the study vary from audience to audience.

A useful strategy for LIS researchers, then, is to consider the implications of each of the six factors comprising the frame of reference for the specific target audience to whom the research is directed. The researcher should make certain that the "reality tests," for example, incorporated in the study and in the report are congruent with the reality tests used by the target audience. A similar procedure should be followed for each of the criteria and examples shown in Figure 20-1.

Redesign Study Methodologies

A key theme throughout this chapter has been that communication of LIS research must be considered *before* and *during* the implementation of the study. While it is necessary to produce well-written reports and offer coherent oral presentations (see discussion below), this alone is not sufficient for improving the effective communication of LIS research.

LIS researchers must move toward research designs that accomplish the following:

- Establish mechanisms for direct involvement by LIS decision maker;
- Reduce the time between initiation and completion of the study;
- Produce *both* scientific results and management results;
- Recognize organizational constraints and limitations (strive for internal validity rather than external validity); and
- Incorporate qualitative (rather than or in addition to quantitative) research designs and data collection techniques into LIS research.

While all of these recommendations for LIS study designs improve the effective communication of LIS research, the last one—using qualitative research designs and data collection techniques—is especially important.

A number of useful texts (Marshal and Rossman, 1989; Patton, 1990) describe qualitative research techniques. One by Mellon (1990) is targeted specifically at the library/information science community. Other works describe specific qualitative data collection strategies, e.g., Weimer and Vining (1989) present policy analysis, and Krueger (1988) discusses focus group interviewing.

The premise behind qualitative research designs is that the direct involvement of the researcher with the study participants is likely to provide more accurate findings and insights than traditional techniques. "The data for qualitative analysis typically come from fieldwork . . . [;] the researcher spends time in the setting under study" (Patton, 1990, p. 10). For example, a focus group interview of the library's department heads, which allows probing, follow-up, and the opportunity for the participants to direct the discussion to topics *they* think important, will provide much better and more useful data than simply administering them a questionnaire.

There is a large body of literature on the failure of traditional (positivist) research techniques to produce useful results in the social sciences (Harris, 1986). While that debate will not be summarized here, some useful introductory sources to the discussion are Argyris, Putnam, and Smith (1985), Schön (1983 and 1987), and Krathwohl (1985). The main point here, however, is that LIS researchers should carefully consider alternative research epistemologies to traditional scientific inquiry. Qualitative research methods, including policy analysis, offer much potential for both improving the usefulness of LIS research and better communicating the results of that research to LIS decision makers.

A Client Perspective

LIS researchers can greatly improve the communication of their research to LIS decision makers by developing a client perspective. This client perspective is one where the researcher constantly considers the client for whom the research is intended. Indeed, considering the perspective of the client, and identifying a particular client or target group to receive the research is an important first step in increasing the effective communication of LIS research to LIS decision makers.

Figure 20-2 summarizes a set of propositions, which based on the experience of the author, appear to have significant importance in increasing the usefulness of LIS research for LIS decision makers. McClure (1989, pp. 285–288) discusses these propositions in greater detail.

Some of these propositions reinforce suggestions offered earlier in this chapter. Nonetheless, they suggest possible strategies that will serve as discussion points for improving the effectiveness with which LIS research is communicated. Overall, the propositions suggest that the research should be initiated and supported by the primary clients of such research; designed to encourage ongoing communication during the study between the researcher(s) and the clients; and translated into practical procedures that can be easily understood by LIS decision makers. Furthermore, converting the propositions into strategies should take into consideration specific organizational constraints, personalities, and politics unique to a client and his or her organization.

Written, Electronic, and Oral Presentations

After LIS researchers have considered the issues and factors previously discussed, they should give careful thought to the preparation of reports and presentations. Bradley and Bradley (1988) provide an excellent guide for improving writing skills, and Hernon and McClure (1990, pp. 199–213) discuss how specifically to communicate, in writing and orally, research findings. McCabe and Bender (1976) suggest a number of practical techniques to improve oral presentations.

In all of these discussions, however, it is important to recognize that the manner, content, and format in which one reports research depends on the intended audience and the objectives of the reporting. For example, the typical dissertation, while successfully communicating its results to the academy, is unlikely to be a successful communication device for library decision makers.

Researchers should also consider that communication of studies is no longer limited to written and oral formats. With the advent of electronic networks, bulletin boards, e-mail, and electronic conferences, additional opportunities to disseminate research results are present. The American Library Association's ALANET and the various networks linked through the INTERNET (Quarterman, 1990) provide a range of options and opportunities to make available research findings and discuss study implications with various target audiences.

Regardless of the technique (written, electronic, or oral), key questions to address *before* the product is developed are:

Communicating Applied Library/Information Science Research

- Who is the target audience for the message, and what are the needs and expectations of that audience?
- What specific message or objective does the researcher wish to accomplish with the dissemination?
- How can the study be translated into *actionable* recommendations for LIS decision makers?
- Are the message and presentation credible and understandable to the target audience?
- What mechanisms can be put in place to allow feedback and follow-up between the researcher and the LIS decision maker?

Considering these questions *prior* to actually writing a report or making a presentation about the study will improve the effectiveness with which the study is communicated to LIS decision makers.

In report writing, LIS researchers should consider producing at least two, and possibly three, different versions of the study. The first might be intended for the funder of the study, the second for publication in an appropriate scholarly journal or as a monograph, and a third for LIS decision makers. Minimally, the report should have a section that specifically addresses the findings and implications for LIS decision making—with specific recommendations for how the findings might be used in particular LIS organizations or settings.

Figure 20-2. Propositions for Improving the Communication of Research to Decision Makers.*

- Research NOT initiated or at least agreed upon by those libraries or librarians most affected is unlikely to have much impact.
- The greater the ongoing communication during the research project between the researcher and the primary stakeholders, the greater the impact of the research for decision making.
- Research results which do not include carefully designed, practical, step-by-step guidelines, for implementing results in a specific context are likely to have little impact.
- The greater the effort researchers make to produce broadly generalizable findings, the less likely the research will have impact on practice in a particular library.
- Research designs and implementation strategies must consider politics and personality characteristics in individual organizational settings for impact to occur.
- The greater the practical library experience of the researcher, or the greater the research skills and knowledge of the library director, the greater the likelihood that a research study will affect library practice.
- For research efforts to affect library decision making or otherwise have impact on library management, long time-lines and specific attention to implementation are required.
- The degree to which a key stakeholder funds the projects or commits other direct resources to the research project tends to encourage greater impact of study findings.
- When researchers serve as consultants, they greatly increase the likelihood that research findings will have an impact on library decision making.

*Charles R. McClure, "Increasing the Usefulness of Research for Library Managers: Propositions, Issues, and Strategies," *Library Trends*, 38 (Fall 1989): 280–294.

Research that is intended for consumption and use by decision makers should give less attention to the literature review, study design, and method, and more to graphics, summary figures, specific recommendations, and implementation strategies. Use of research jargon must be minimized and the overall writing style must be concise and to the point. Indeed, the literature review and method might best be summarized in a short appendix. Moreover, the recommendations and implementation strategies should take into consideration typical organizational variables and constraints. In short, successful reporting of research to decision makers requires an entirely different strategy and approach than reporting research in a refereed journal.

Oral presentations to specific target groups of LIS decision makers are an excellent means to communicate research studies, obtain feedback from particular target audiences on their views of the study, and offer a mechanism where target audiences can suggest possible follow-ups to the study and probe more deeply into findings or implications for their particular setting. Generally, LIS researchers inadequately provide opportunities to LIS decision makers for direct and real-time feedback and assessment of their research.

The American National Standards Institute (1990) provides a guide, "Preparation of Scientific Papers for Written or Oral Presentation," for improving research communication. This guide offers a number of technical suggestions and approaches for improving research presentations in both written and oral formats *to the scientific community*. It does not, however, recognize the factors and issues discussed earlier in this chapter that also have a direct bearing on the effectiveness with which research is communicated to decision makers.

MAKING ADJUSTMENTS

Ultimately, *both* the researcher and the decision maker have responsibilities for improving the communication of research, but this chapter has focused primarily on strategies that the researcher might use. As DeProspo (1972, pp. 20–21) pointed out:

> The fact is that those who accept the label of "researcher" must be more willing than they have been to find better ways of selling their products; more willing to reduce the mystique of the research process; more willing to report their failures; and more willing to appraise the library policymaker of some of the risks involved in the policymaker's efforts to put the findings into practice.

In short, if researchers want their research to have greater impact on LIS decision makers, then it is the responsibility of researchers to initiate strategies to better communicate their studies and findings.

Improving the communication of research requires researchers to consider, *from the initiation of the study*, a range of factors that ultimately contribute to more effective communication. Improved communication of research goes beyond better report writing and oral presentations of the research. Successful strategies will require a better understanding of the competing frames of reference held by the two groups, a clearer picture of the information needs and preferences of decision makers, redesigning research methods, and describing the results of research in actionable terms, that is, how exactly decision makers might use the results.

REFERENCES

American National Standards Institute. "American National Standard for the Preparation of Scientific Papers for Written or Oral Presentation." New York: the Institute, 1990 [1430 Broadway, New York, NY, 10018].

Argyris, Chris, Robert Putnam, and Diana McLain Smith. *Action Science*. San Francisco, CA: Jossey-Bass, 1985.

Bradley, Jana and Larry Bradley. *Improving Written Communication in Libraries*. Chicago, IL: American Library Association, 1988.

DeProspo, Ernest R. *The Library Researcher and Policymaker—An Observation Here and a Speculation There*. New Brunswick, NJ: Rutgers University, 1972 [available from ERIC Clearinghouse as 004-460].

Harris, Michael. "The Dialectic of Defeat: Antinomies in Research in Library and Information Science," *Library Trends*, 34 (1986): 515-534.

Hernon, Peter and Charles R. McClure. *Evaluation and Library Decision Making*. Norwood, NJ: Ablex Publishing Corp., 1990.

Krathwohl, David R. *Social and Behavioral Science Research*. San Francisco, CA: Jossey Bass, 1985.

Krueger, Richard A. *Focus Groups: A Practical Guide for Applied Research*. Newbury Park, CA: Sage, 1988.

Lawler, Edward E. III. *Doing Research That Is Useful for Theory and Practice*. San Francisco, CA: Jossey Bass, 1985.

McCabe, Bernard P., Jr., and Coleman C. Bender. *Speaking as a Practical Matter*. 3rd Edition. Boston, MA: Holbrook Press, 1976.

McClure, Charles R. "Increasing the Usefulness of Research for Library Managers: Propositions, Issues and Strategies," *Library Trends*, 38 (Fall, 1989): 280-294.

———. and Ann Bishop. "The Status of Research in Library/Information Science: Guarded Optimism," *College & Research Libraries*, 50 (March, 1989): 127-143.

Marshal, Catherine and Gretchen B. Rossman. *Designing Qualitative Research*. Newbury Park, CA: Sage, 1989.

Mellon, Constance Ann. *Naturalistic Inquiry for Library Science and Applications for Research, Evaluation, and Teaching*. Westwood, CT: Greenwood Press, 1990.

Patton, Michael Quinn. *Qualitative Evaluation as Research Methods*. Newbury Park, CA: Sage, 1990.

Quarterman, J. *The Matrix: Computer Networks and Conferencing Systems Worldwide*. Boston, MA: Digital Press, 1990.

Rothman, Jack. *Using Research in Organizations: A Guide to Successful Application*. Beverly Hills, CA: Sage, 1980.

Schön, Donald A. *The Reflective Practitioner*. New York: Basic Books, Inc., 1983.

──── . *Educating the Reflective Practitioner*. San Francisco, CA: Jossey Bass, 1987.

Shrivastava, Paul and Ian I. Mitroff. "Enhancing Organizational Research Utilization: The Role of Decision Makers' Assumptions," *Academy of Management Review*, 9 (January 1984): 18–26.

Weimer, David L. and Aidan R. Vining. *Policy Analysis: Concepts and Practice*. Englewood Cliffs, NJ: Prentice-Hall, 1989.

chapter twenty-one

Opportunities and Challenges for LIS Research in Academic Libraries: Elements of Strategy

Charles T. Townley

Academic librarians undertake LIS research to improve their practice and to contribute to the knowledge base of librarianship. As professionals working in an intellectual environment, academic librarians enjoy unique opportunities and must meet several challenges in undertaking research. Components that strengthen research include leadership, education for research, collegial support, and research organization support. By building strategies with these components, academic librarians can improve themselves and their profession.

RATIONALE FOR LIS RESEARCH IN ACADEMIC LIBRARIES

By definition, research is one characteristic of a profession (Shera, 1972, pp. 66–74). Through research, professionals contribute to the knowledge base of their profession in ways that inform and guide practice and that develop the theoretical structure of the profession. While not every professional person is constantly engaged in research, all recognize it as a characteristic of a professional occupation and most will make periodic contributions to research throughout their career (Freeman, 1985, pp. 27–29; McClure and Bishop, 1989, p. 127; Odi, 1982, p. 313).

In human services professions, like academic librarianship, sustained research activity contributes to the quality of a client centered professional practice. Recent LIS research on the "goodness" of reference service, for example, is intended to improve the quality and responsiveness of library services (Van House and Childers, 1984). Librarians who participate in this research possess a better understanding of user needs and behavior and, thus, can design more responsive services. Librarians engaged in research can also establish priorities for their time and demonstrate the effectiveness of their efforts (McClure and Bishop, 1989).

As professional organizations, academic libraries should find it useful and practical to support LIS research. Research is first and foremost an opportunity for the development of professional personnel. Librarians can grow as professionals through research projects directed to library concerns. Research also enables an academic library to maintain its currency and demonstrate its organizational effectiveness to academic administrators and trustees. LIS research can generate support for new initiatives and assure support for existing services. Innovative research enables the academic library to deal with change and contributes to the professional reputation of the library and its personnel. This, in turn, makes it easier to attract strong personnel capable of enriching library services (Montanelli and Stenstrom, 1986, pp. 482–485; Townley, 1989, pp. 16–20).

Academic librarianship is establishing its theoretical structure and common principles of practice in ways that will assure its future role and function in an information age having a global economy. LIS research contributes to the attainment of both efforts and must, therefore, be supported by academic librarians, library organizations, library schools, academic administrators, funders, and others (Heilprin, 1980, pp. 392–393).

LIS RESEARCH OPPORTUNITIES IN ACADEMIC LIBRARIES

Academic librarians enjoy unique opportunities in undertaking LIS research. Organizationally, academic libraries are part of intellectual organizations committed to valuing research. Professionals working in an academic environment are routinely expected to use and apply the findings of research in their work. Academic librarians can readily justify undertaking LIS research on the basis of its ability to create new knowledge (Lynch, 1984, pp. 377–381).

An active program of LIS research by librarians in an academic library can reduce tensions between instructional and library personnel by confirming the collegial roles of librarians and instructors (Biggs, 1981, pp. 182–201). It gives the library an opportunity to place its agenda in the arena of public policy debate (*Rethinking the Library in the Information Age,* 1989, p. 35). LIS research contributes to the academic reputation of the institution. Some research topics confirm and support the teaching role of librarians (Sewell, 1983, pp. 213–214; Werrell and Sullivan, 1987, pp. 96–97).

LIS research also reinforces the concept of academic freedom in the library. A librarian who is engaged in research must be free to follow where the research leads. This carries over to the practice of academic librarianship when research is used to guide library practice. Research helps assure professional autonomy for all the professionals in an academic library (Sewell, 1983, pp. 214–216; Montanelli and Stenstrom, 1986, p. 484).

Reward systems in academic libraries can recognize research as an integral part of professional assignments. Almost 75 percent of academic librarians are faculty members (Jenkins, Cook, and Fox, 1981, p. 83). Most colleges and universities consider research productivity as one factor in determining faculty salary adjustments (Montanelli and Stenstrom, 1986, p. 483). A growing number of institutions insist that all members of the faculty demonstrate successful records of research for retention and advancement (Werrell and Sullivan 1987, pp. 96–97).

Intrinsic rewards, such as leaves and released time, can be contingent on LIS research. Office space, travel funds, and computers are increasingly distributed on the basis of research activity. Recognition too, such as an annual research award, is used in a growing number of academic libraries to support research (Healey, 1982, pp. 286–288; Townley, 1989, pp. 17–19).

Academic librarianship demonstrates a tendency to differentiate LIS research specialties by institutional size and type. Large universities and consortia are more likely to carry on large-scale research capable of making major additions to the LIS theory base (*Rethinking the Library in the Information Age,* 1989, pp. 43–44). Research in smaller institutions is more likely to create new information that will guide professional practice. Librarians working in community colleges have shown a marked ability to incorporate new media and methods in their practice. College librarians demonstrate particular strengths in bibliographic instruction and consortial relationships, while universities seem to lead the way in automation and telecommunications.

There does appear to be a growing number of librarians regularly contributing LIS research related to academic libraries (McClure and Bishop, 1989, p. 134). LIS research is organizationally and politically useful in an academic environment. It offers intrinsic and extrinsic rewards to the librarians who participate. LIS research can respond to local information needs and contribute to the development of the professional knowledge base in academic libraries.

RESEARCH CHALLENGES IN ACADEMIC LIBRARIANSHIP

Academic librarianship also faces challenges in undertaking LIS research. Some of these challenges arise from the nature of research issues in academic librarianship. Some arise from the focus of research. And, some challenges come from the needs of the librarians involved. For the profession to advance, these challenges must be identified and addressed.

Academic librarianship supports a sizeable literature. Like other professions, much of this literature is generated by practitioners working in academic libraries. However, most of this literature is descriptive and does not report research. In a study of papers submitted to ACRL national conferences, Coughlin and Snelson (1983, p. 23) find that only 33 percent of the papers submitted are based on research. Also, some of what purports to be research fails to meet the key tests of testing hypotheses and being reproducible. One challenge then is to increase the proportion of publications using research methodologies appearing in the literature.

A second challenge to LIS research in academic libraries is its focus. The profession tends to address research topics that cannot be generalized or which do not address real needs. While LIS research is applied, it must use rigorous research designs, provide indicators of reliability and validity, and be capable of being generalized to basic issues confronting academic library practice and theory (Hernon, 1989). To accomplish this, it is necessary to develop a researchable question and apply a rigorous research process to address that question. By doing so a librarian can address a local problem and contribute to the further development of the profession and its theory (Metz, 1985, pp. 390–394).

Much of the existing body of LIS research has been criticized for not responding to real user needs or to developments in the use (planned and actual) of technology in academic libraries. Research questions should respond to substantive user needs. While it would be possible to design research on how scholars use the *National Union Catalog*, it might be more realistic and responsive to the broad majority of library users to study how a principle of artificial intelligence can be successfully incorporated in an online public access catalog.

As important a challenge as any other is the need for most academic librarians to either obtain or upgrade their education in research design and methodology. It is unreasonable to expect librarians to become competent consumers, let alone producers of research, after only one research methods course in their professional curriculum. While library schools are trying to increase the research skills of new academic librarians, it will be an unacceptably long time before this source provides a critical mass of researchers able to address the research needs of academic librarianship.

Current practitioners working in all types of academic libraries must acquire research skills. One method to obtain these skills is to participate in social science or humanities research courses at the local institution. But most librarians prefer courses especially designed to cover the types of problems facing LIS. Robbins (1989) reports a recent effort to provide such course work which did not meet with great success. Fewer students completed the course and met program objectives than expected. Those who did complete the course and who retained an interest in continuing their research activities tended to enroll in doctoral programs. Alternative delivery methods involving proven distance education techniques need to be applied.

Inertia, both organizational and personal, is one of the principal challenges to academic library research. While academic libraries ought to encourage research, the plain fact is that many do not. Often this is the result of omission rather than commission. Research is not done because it has never been done at the particular library. The library has developed no infrastructure to support LIS research activity. All academic libraries should view LIS research as an opportunity to improve human resources and organizational competitiveness (see Allen, 1986, pp. 157–159). Until then, the librarian or librarians who begin the research process must be prepared to overcome organizational inertia with a sound rationale and a willingness to pay a price for innovation.

Personal inertia is also a challenge. Some academic librarians indicate they are attracted to library work because it does not require teaching or research. Others state that their institution is a teaching organization that does not require research. The point is that research is one activity that a professional person undertakes to improve the quality of his or her practice and to contribute to the profession. To fail to use or carry out research is to condemn academic librarianship to a collection of clerical and technical tasks susceptible to trivialization and replacement (Montanelli and Stenstrom, 1986, pp. 482–485), as well as to undervalue the MLS, as a graduate degree.

The final challenge to LIS research in academic libraries is motivation. Academic librarians must develop strong motivations to use and undertake research. Individual librarians must feel strongly enough about research to master and apply research methods. Academic library managers must support research activities of personnel by offering training, guidance, and support. Professional organizations, such as the Association of College and Research Libraries, must work to encourage the extension of LIS research skills to more academic libraries.

COMPONENTS FOR STRENGTHENING ACADEMIC LIBRARY RESEARCH

Strengthening library research should be a concern for the whole profession. Different strategic components can help academic librarians obtain appropriate support for LIS research. This chapter proposes four sets of components that can enhance the quantity and quality of LIS research in academic libraries: leadership, education for research, collegial support, and professional organization support.

Leadership

Leadership in academic libraries should undertake five initiatives to encourage LIS research. First, leadership must assert the value of research to the library and the parent organization. This includes making positive statements in strategic plans, budget hearings, and other public forums. It also includes leading by example. Leaders should evaluate and apply research findings in their day-to-day practice of academic librarianship. Further, leaders must undertake at least some

LIS research on a regular basis to maintain professional knowledge as well as to demonstrate a commitment to the research process (Allen, 1986, pp. 159–162). Involvement in research will also help leaders in asking the right questions of personnel planning and conducting research. Leaders will also be able to judge the quality of final research products.

Leadership must also enable others to undertake LIS research by providing time and money as part of regular library activity (Varlejs, 1987, p. 359). Research activity should be routinely expected and supported in the organizational culture. Librarians should be encouraged to make time for research, either through a responsive system of released time or through appropriate language in contracts or work assignments. Funds to support the costs of appropriate and well-designed research should be readily available. Computer time, printing and mailing costs, appropriate travel, and other support should be available. Dialogues established as part of each funding process should be used to strengthen research proposals. Leaders should support research proposals that have value beyond the immediate library, even if this requires some additional support in terms of organizational resources.

Leaders must also work with library personnel to establish a collegial atmosphere that supports LIS research. Colleagues should be encouraged to read, evaluate, and apply research in their practice of academic librarianship. Leaders should help library personnel encourage research as a means to improve the effectiveness and efficiency of academic library programs, services, and operations. Academic leadership should foster understanding and flexibility on the part of all library personnel to accommodate the demands of current LIS research projects. Librarians engaged in research must have the opportunity to follow their muse from time to time with the assurance that essential library services are being provided.

Clarifying the rewards structure is essential so that practitioners will perceive worthwhile rewards emerging from research efforts. As explained earlier, rewards can be both intrinsic and extrinsic. Surely, salary increases and promotions are important, but much can also be done with time, awards and perquisites, such as travel, speaking, equipment, and working conditions.

The final component of any leadership strategy must be to communicate the results of LIS research to librarians and colleagues on a regular and sustained basis. LIS research initiated, grants received, and publications are all important milestones that should be appropriately recognized. Discussion and application of others' research represents an opportunity to communicate the usefulness of research.

Training for Research

Academic librarians will undertake significant amounts of education and training for the foreseeable future to maintain currency and to incorporate change in their practice (Moran, 1984, pp. 56–57). The increasing pace of programmatic and technological change makes it necessary for every academic librarian to update periodically and learn new skills and knowledge. Such retraining and education should include significant content on research methods. Librarians as part of a profession should consider how best to assure that training programs cover the research process. When professional organizations or government authorities adopt continuing education requirements, they should indicate how research skills will be acquired and used.

Academic librarians should be encouraged to enroll in or audit formal courses on research design, methodology, and statistics at their own institutions. Research courses in humanities, social science, and many professional curricula, can often be directly applied to academic libraries. A course in public administration research, for example, might be useful in learning how to run focus groups, or analyze inferential statistics on user needs. In cases where librarians express some reluctance to undertake research courses at the local institution, teams of two or more might enroll or a reciprocal arrangement might be arranged with a nearby institution.

Opportunities also exist to deliver library school instruction addressing research using consortia and distance education techniques. Many academic library consortia provide a regular program of continuing education for their members. Some of this instruction could address research design and methodology. Distance education, using two-way telecommunications or computer-assisted instruction, also offers some exciting opportunities to deliver research courses to practicing librarians.

Mutually Responsible and Interdependent Collegial Support

For LIS research to flourish in any academic library, librarians must work with each other and often with colleagues outside the library to create a critical mass of scholars capable of continuously encouraging each others' research activities. The purpose of this critical mass is to provide an opportunity to practice the designing of research proposals, apply knowledge gained in formal instruction to LIS problems, and support research in progress.

Colleagues should become coaches, consultants, and teammates in the conduct of research. Skills learned in formal instruction can be practiced in a supportive environment. Suggestions and criticism intended to strengthen research proposals and analysis can be offered without threatening careers. Individuals with similar interests can form cooperative alliances—brownbags and other informal meetings where they can discuss alternative methodologies and analysis techniques. In larger libraries, a research committee in the library can help in organizing research (Jenkins, Cook, and Fox, 1981).

Professional Organization Support

Professional organizations have long had a role in academic LIS research in academic libraries. The Association of College and Research Libraries regularly reports research through its journal, *College & Research Libraries*, at the American Library Association Annual Conference program meetings, and at its National Conferences. The ACRL Continuing Education Committee regularly sponsors a continuing education course for the beginning researcher. Several LIS professional organizations recognize outstanding research with awards as a means of encouragement. It would also be useful to recognize academic libraries that are striving to encourage and use worthwhile research.

In 1986, ACRL established a Research Committee to encourage LIS research in academic libraries. In January 1990, the Committee approved a research agenda intended to identify broad areas needing research and to suggest a few representative researchable topics in each area (see Appendix). During 1990, the Committee intends to develop conference programs on appropriate research methods for academic librarians. Within two years, these programs will be linked to ongoing e-mail conferences intended to encourage communication among small groups of experienced and inexperienced researchers with similar interests. The intent is to reinforce practitioners actively engaged in planning or executing LIS research.

Academic librarians should also work closely with private, state, and Federal agencies looking to improve the effectiveness and role of academic libraries. Organizations such as the Association of Research Libraries and the U. S. Department of Education can provide information, guidance, and support. Experienced research personnel should be funded by these organizations to undertake theoretical research considered important by the profession. This should include buying an individual's time as well as providing support for research. Intermediate researchers should be encouraged to undertake applied research in well-defined and limited target areas through limited funding and networking among peers. New researchers should be encouraged and led to undertake confirming studies that will extend good research and permit promising individuals to gain research skills.

BUILDING YOUR STRATEGY

Academic librarians are professionally obliged to participate in research. Colleagues who read this chapter have already taken the first step in undertaking research. The remainder of this chapter deals with how to create and implement a research strategy.

First, find a topic you find interesting and would like to learn more about. Read recent research in the area to get a sense of the research skills you will need, the current authors, and topics needing further study. If the topic does not wear well, change it.

Once you feel you have some general ideas, try to develop a research proposal including a problem statement, hypotheses, and research methods. If your research skills are rusty, negotiate an agreement with management to improve your research skills. They should do as best they can with extrinsic and intrinsic rewards to support your research initiative.

Try to identify some colleagues to help. If your library has a research committee, discuss your thoughts with its members. Call, write, and meet those writers you respect. Many will give you a great deal of help. Revise your ideas and incorporate what you have learned in an updated research proposal that targets a small area of research that you can do well. Ask your library and institution for the support you need to complete the research.

Begin the research process, perhaps with a part of your research. Involve your colleagues and supervisors and give them periodic updates.

Analyze the results using your newly acquired research skills. If you need help, ask your colleagues for help. Inevitably some things come up that need outside help to solve.

Write up your research and share it—even if it is a failure. Contact your new friends and share it. Revise and publish in the most appropriate journal or data file. It will give you satisfaction, even if the first editor rejects it.

Take what you have learned and apply it in your own practice. Develop new issues and start all over again. In time research becomes habit-forming to the benefit of the individual and the profession. If a hundred academic librarians undertake continuing research as the result of this book, it will make a significant positive impact on the quality of our profession.

Research should be an integral part of academic librarianship. Through rigorous study of major issues arising during a period of profound change, academic libraries will enhance their role as information providers. Academic libraries can use LIS research to improve and justify their activities to their publics and administrations. Academic librarians can use research to build theory and guide practice. Strategies can be developed and applied to strengthen LIS research and academic libraries. By undertaking LIS research, librarians can assure for the future of being a vital and socially responsible profession.

REFERENCES

Allen, G. G. "Management and the Conduct of In-House Library Research," *Library & Information Science Research*, 8 (April-June 1986): 155–162.

Biggs, Mary. "Sources of Tension and Conflict between Librarians and Faculty," *Journal of Higher Education*, 52 (March/April 1981): 182–201.

Coughlin, Caroline and Pamela Snelson. "Searching for Research in ACRL Conference Papers," *Journal of Academic Librarianship*, 9 (March 1983): 21–26.

Freeman, Michael S. "The Simplicity of His Pragmatism: Librarians and Research," *Library Journal*, 110 (May 15, 1985): 27-29.
Healey, James S. "Developing Human Resources: An Administrative View," in *Strategies for Library Administration: Concepts and Approaches*. edited by Charles R. McClure and Alan R. Samuels. Littleton, CO.: Libraries Unlimited, 1982, pp. 277-288.
Heilprin, Laurence. "The Library Community at a Technological and Philosophical Crossroads: Necessary and Sufficient Conditions for Survival," *Journal of the American Society for Information Science*, 31 (November 1980): 389-395.
Hernon, Peter. "Research and the Use of Statistics for Library Decision Making," *Library Administration & Management*, 3 (Fall 1989): 176-180.
Jenkins, Darrell L., M. Kathy Cook, and Mary Anne Fox. "Research Development of Academic Librarians: One University's Approach," *Journal of Academic Librarianship*, 7 (May 1981): 83-86.
Lynch, Mary Jo, Ed. "Research and Librarianship: An Uneasy Connection," *Library Trends*, 32 (Spring 1984): 367-383.
McClure, Charles R. and Ann Bishop. "The Status of Research in Library Information Science: Guarded Optimism," *College & Research Libraries*, 50 (March 1989): 127-143.
Metz, Paul. "Thinking Big: A Commentary on the Research Agenda in Librarianship," *College & Research Libraries*, 46 (September 1985): 390-394.
Montanelli, Dale S. and Patricia F. Stenstrom. "The Benefits of Research for Academic Librarians and the Institutions They Serve," *College & Research Libraries*, 47 (September 1986): 482-485.
Moran, Barbara B. *Academic Libraries: The Changing Knowledge Centers of Colleges and Universities*. Washington, D.C.: Association for the Study of Higher Education, 1984.
Odi, Amus. "Creative Research and Theory Building in Library and Information Sciences," *College & Research Libraries*, 43 (July 1982): 312-319.
Rethinking the Library in the Information Age. Vol. 3. Prepared by the U.S. Department of Education, Office of Educational Research and Improvement, Washington, D.C.: GPO, 1989.
Robbins, Jane. "Research Skills for Research Librarians," *Journal of Academic Librarianship*, 15 (March 1989): 4-6.
Sewell, Robert G. "Faculty Status and Librarians: The Rationale and the Case of Illinois," *College & Research Libraries*, 44 (May 1983): 211-222.
Shera, Jesse H. *The Foundations of Education for Librarianship*. New York: Wiley, 1972.
Townley, Charles T. "Nurturing Library Effectiveness: Leadership for Professional Development," *Library Administration & Management*, 3 (Winter 1989): 16-20.
Van House, Nancy A. and Thomas Childers. "Unobtrusive Evaluation of a Reference Referral Network: The California Experience," *Library & Information Science Research*, 6 (July-September 1984): 305-319.
Varlejs, Jana. "Cost Models for Staff Development," *Journal of Academic Librarianship*, 12 (January 1987): 359-364.
Werrell, Emily and Laura Sullivan. "Faculty Status for Academic Librarians: A Review of the Literature," *College & Research Libraries*, 48 (March 1987): 95-103.

APPENDIX. ACRL RESEARCH AGENDA*

Prepared by the ACRL Research Committee

The Association of College and Research Libraries' Research Committee has three major goals: (1) to explore, develop, and promote a research agenda which focuses on the current research needs of academic/research libraries and the association; (2) to develop programs and other activities which will assist in the accomplishment of the needed research; and (3) to develop activities and programs to encourage improvement in research skills among academic/research librarians.

For the past four years, the ACRL Research Committee has sought to fulfill this first goal by developing a research agenda with particular application to current needs. More than 300 articles have been culled for relevant research concerns. A set of over 360 research questions was edited to 80 questions then distributed to more than 110 academic and research librarians for their suggestions.

Using the responses from that survey, the committee has focused the general areas of research need down to seven topics. In the following research agenda, seven general topics are described in broad terms then followed by a short list of exemplary research questions.

The intent of the research agenda is to identify general areas where research is needed and to provide examples of researchable questions. It is not intended to be in any way either comprehensive or prescriptive.

The ACRL Research Committee hopes that this research agenda will be of use to academic and research librarians as they consider issues related to practice and research.

ACRL research agenda

The intent of this research agenda is to identify general areas where research is needed and to provide examples of researchable questions. It is not intended to be in any way either comprehensive or prescriptive.

1. Library Education

There is a need for research on the analytical, cognitive, and affective skills likely to be needed by information professionals in the future. Work should be conducted also on how those skills are germinated and nurtured.

1.1 What aspects of library and information science curricula teach and foster the knowledge, skills, and competencies needed by future information professionals?

1.2 What kinds of continuing education programs would improve the performance of veteran librarians?

1.3 Is there institutional support for training, continuing education, and institutional change?

2. Library Administration

Research is needed on those characteristics of planning, organizing, budgeting, staffing, and directing which are particularly critical to academic and research libraries. Historical and philosophical orientations should be recognized.

2.1. What are the leadership styles and tools of successful academic library managers?

2.2. How do academic library managers successfully compete for institutional support?

2.3. How can academic library managers create an environment that encourages innovation, creativity, and efficiency?

2.4. How do academic administrators perceive libraries and their role?

3. Public Services

There is a need for research on how to improve client-centered services provided in academic and research libraries particularly in light of the changing nature and context of those needs.

---

*Reprinted with permission of American Library Association. Source: *College & Research Libraries News*, 51 (April 1990): 317–319.

3.1. How has information technology changed the behavior of academic library users?

3.2. What impact does the increasingly diverse academic library clientele have on information services?

3.3. What is the impact of user education programs on students and faculty?

3.4. What is the impact of the commercialization of access to information on the operation of academic libraries?

4. Library Collections and Organization

Research should identify alternative ways of selecting, collecting, organizing, and retaining information to enhance its use by scholars.

4.1. What is the relationship between the knowledge base and the development of academic library collections?

4.2. What are the components of various collection development models, and how do they relate to collections that are actually developed?

4.3. How effective are alternative methods of preservation (e.g. deacidification, microfilming, and storage on optical disks)?

4.4. What are the critical aspects in organizing collections of machine readable data?

5. External Relations

Research should examine the relationships among and impact of campus computer centers, media services, networking and resource sharing, international relationships and cooperation, and bibliographic utilities with academic and research libraries.

5.1. What conditions in a library or university support or hinder interorganizational cooperation?

5.2. What is the impact of rising telecommunications costs?

5.3. What languages and specialized materials would best be cataloged by national centers for specialized cataloging and how might such centers operate?

5.4. What practices in academic libraries abroad can be successfully used to enrich American libraries?

6. Information Technology and Communications

Research should examine the relationships between intellectual access and physical access. It should determine the extent to which technology in libraries supports resources and enhances learning.

6.1. To what extent do training and awareness affect the acceptance of new technology among both staff and library users?

6.2. What factors would help library administrators predict the impact of changing information technology on library services and buildings?

6.3. Do varying research methods in individual disciplines pose specific requirements for information system performance?

7. Library and Information Science Research

Research should examine the attitudes, mechanisms, and tools with which academic and research librarians analyze the entire spectrum of their profession.

7.1. What forms of evaluation and measurement are the most realistic and meaningful when analyzing library and information services?

7.2. What is the impact of new technology on the way in which academic and research librarians conduct and communicate their research?

7.3. What are the attitudes toward research in various parts of the profession?

chapter twenty-two

Research Needs in Public Librarianship

Joan C. Durrance

The public library operates within a model created to respond to 19th-century societal needs. Research is needed to strengthen this institution so that it can more effectively meet the needs of society in the 21st century. Researchers have begun to effectively address information needs; however, research has had little impact on the ways that public libraries do business due to the lack of a well-developed research culture in public librarianship. This article addresses that gap. It discusses barriers to the creation and consumption of research, examines research which has the potential for helping librarians develop and evaluate services which can more effectively meet societal needs, and presents what can be done to create and nurture a research culture in public librarianship.

CONTEXT FOR NEEDED RESEARCH IN PUBLIC LIBRARIANSHIP

The American public library is a creature of the 19th century, and there is some question as to whether "the 110 year old model of public library service, which is still in use" can meet the needs of late 20th-century society (*Rethinking the Library in the Information Age*, 1988, vol. 1, p. 23). The research needs of public libraries must be examined within a societal context. Academic, special, and school libraries operate within the context of their parent organization. Public libraries, on the other hand, are institutions responsible to society in general and to the citizens of their communities in particular. Because the roles public libraries play in society are not well understood, they are underused and undervalued by the public.

At the same time that this nation is undergoing a revolution in the development and use of information technologies, it is experiencing major demographic changes. By the year 2000 the minority populations will become the majority in many communities. According to Vagianos and Lesser (1988, p. 9), "in today's climate of technology-driven change in the information marketplace, the library—society's traditional institution for gathering, organizing, and transferring information on behalf of the general public—stands in a tenuous position."

Research is needed to strengthen the public library so that it can more effectively meet the needs of society in the 21st century. *Rethinking the Library in the Information Age* (1988–1989) details a number of areas in which research is needed. These were distilled into four categories—access to information, information needs and uses, library funding and economics, and libraries and education. All of these are crucial to helping public librarians as they prepare for the next century; the first two set the framework for response to societal needs, and the latter two provide the means for public libraries to respond.

Research has played a relatively small role in changing the way public librarians do business. Butler (1933) noticed almost 60 years ago that librarians were pragmatic professionals who had little need to be introspective about their practice. Ten years ago Garrison (1980) blamed both researchers and librarians for the problems related to public library research; researchers do not disseminate their research well and librarians do not consume it. This creates a major gap which limits the application of research findings to the problems faced by the nation's public libraries. This article addresses that gap. It discusses barriers to the creation and consumption of research, examines research which has the potential for helping librarians develop and evaluate services which can more effectively meet societal needs, and considers steps necessary to create and nurture a research culture in public librarianship.

BARRIERS TO THE CREATION OF A PUBLIC LIBRARY RESEARCH CULTURE

Lack of Adequate Mechanisms

Most library education programs prepare librarians neither to consume nor to conduct research. Although no more prepared to do research than public librarians, increasing numbers of academic librarians, seeking status in a system which does reward scholarly publication, have chosen to "publish or perish" along with faculty. By publishing, these librarians transmit their work which is sometimes research based. Academic librarians have both institutional support and institutional reward structures to encourage research; public librarians have neither. Furthermore, the primary instruments for change in public libraries—professional associations, the Federal government, and state library agencies—dominated as they are by practitioners, have not fostered interest in public library research and, thus, there is a poor climate both for production and consumption of public library research.

Academic librarians have had within their professional association, the Association of College and Research Libraries (ACRL), a journal whose purpose from its beginning in 1939 included "stimulating research and experimentation" (Moffett, 1989, p. 609). On the other hand, until recently, the official publication of the Public Library Association (PLA) has functioned primarily as a newsletter with a minimum of articles. This journal has no mandate to communicate research. It is too soon to speculate whether a major change in *Public Libraries*, begun in 1989, will bring some research closer to public librarians. Finally, far too little relevant research is produced by public library researchers (most of whom are library school faculty).

Researchers are relatively new to librarianship. Wilson (1979) suggested that a lack of faculty productivity might be attributed to inadequate socialization to research. Heim (1986) noted that the percentage of faculty with Ph.D.s rose from 32.1 percent in 1960 to 65.9 percent in 1979 to 77.9 percent by the mid-1980s. Although faculty with Ph.D.s are more likely to produce research, there is not yet adequate research on major problems which face public libraries. The future looks bleak for the production of a critical mass of researchers in the future because of a lack of funding for doctoral fellowships.

Faulty Assumptions

If public libraries are creatures of society and responsible to citizens, what roles should they play? Librarians are not in agreement about what roles the public library should assume in a community. Most present practice is built on the assumption that libraries are in the reading business. Most librarians have accepted the monolithic assumption that they serve "the public"—more specifically, "the reading public." That assumption has focused primary attention on reading and, more recently, on viewing the library's products. By focusing on reading, public librarians have identified circulation, a surrogate measure for reading, as the primary measure of library output. Circulation was incorporated into both editions of PLA's manual for output measures, as the first measure of output (Zweizig and Rodger, 1982; Van House, Lynch, McClure, Zweizig, and Rodger, 1987). Circulation as a primary indicator may lead to the development of what a disgruntled wit recently labeled "McLibraries" (Akey, 1990, p. 12).

The monolithic approach combined with the use of marketing data can result in superficial treatment of public library users (readers) as consumers (only). Marketing research entered public librarianship some time ago (Madden, 1979; Bolton, 1982). During the 1980s, the ability to computerize detailed demographic data and combine them with market research data has provided marketers with extraordinarily powerful tools to more effectively reach the consumer most likely to buy a specific product. Weiss (1989) has presented these sophisticated techniques to public librarians. These tools lend themselves to perpetuating the assumption that public libraries serve readers and in particular those readers whose reading tastes, like their tastes for alcohol and tobacco, automobiles, food products, popular magazines, and TV shows, can be characterized by marketers. Public librarians who use these techniques will market the business they think they are in.

PUBLIC LIBRARY LEADERS AND RESEARCH

Durrance and Van Fleet (1990) examined research from the perspective of public library leaders within the context of change and transmission of ideas. They found that although public library leaders see major concerns facing the profession, they lack an awareness of research which is being done in public librarianship and, by and large, do not believe that most published research is relevant to changes facing the institution.[1]

Public library leaders and researchers operate largely in separate networks which reduces effective communication (Durrance and Van Fleet, 1990). Not surprisingly, public library leaders exchange ideas and discuss problems and their solutions with colleagues with whom they interact on the national level and locally. This is the primary method of gaining new information about practice. Nearly every one of the leaders mentioned colleagues as the most important influence on their thinking about the profession. They communicate with other public library directors and professional colleagues through the American Library Association (ALA) or the Public Library Association (PLA), and the state agency.

Public library leaders are not likely to read public library research-based articles. In general, these articles are seen as not readily available, too long, esoteric, impractical, difficult to understand, and lacking in relevance. On the other hand, the reward structures in academia encourage researchers to publish in scholarly journals which are read by other scholars; these reward structures breed the type of articles which are eschewed by practitioners.

Although not hostile to relevant research, public library leaders knew of little potential use in their situations except the current planning and evaluation literature and some work being done on reference effectiveness. Indeed, Durrance and Van Fleet (Ibid.) found that some public library leaders had involved their libraries in community surveys as well as management and evaluation, and marketing

---

[1] Durrance and Van Fleet, in February and March 1990, conducted telephone interviews with 24 perceived public library leaders. The top 24 public library leaders were selected from several different lists including: (1) PLA Board members and Committee chairs 1988–89 and 1989–90; (2) public librarians who attended the OCLC Future of the Public Library Conference; and (3) library leaders indicated by Gerzog (1989), and Crismond and Leisner (1988).

studies, and had implemented management systems and accountability mechanisms.

The field's journals scanned by these busy public library leaders are not those whose mainstay is the scholarly, research-based article, but the more popular journals: *Library Journal, Library Hotline, American Libraries, Wilson Library Bulletin,* and *Public Libraries.* Several leaders indicated that if they were not told about research by a colleague or at a meeting, or, if it did not appear in something they regularly looked at, they were not likely to find out about it. By and large, they seek research only on a "need-to-know" basis.

However, these public library leaders are concerned with a wide variety of issues which lend themselves to research, including the effect of a lack of adequate funding for changing roles, resource allocation, changing information technologies and the need to revamp the aging library infrastructure to incorporate them, rapidly changing demographics in their communities, and the increased need for accountability. Most want library services to better meet the needs of citizens, including specific groups, such as multicultural constituencies and the aging. They are concerned about how to change public perceptions of the role of the library and librarians; most predict that in the next decade there will be a range of concerns regarding staffing, including skills and salaries, training for changing roles, and the need to emphasize librarians and services more. Their concerns are not unlike many of those identified by the U. S. Department of Education in volume 3 of *Rethinking the Library in the Information Age* (1989).

There is a wide range of researchable problems in the nation's public libraries, but most leaders tend not to bring them to public library researchers or only to a select few. One director said, "I can't communicate with most researchers." Leaders indicated that there are far too few public library researchers willing to work with the problems with which they are concerned. In one leader's words (Durrance and Van Fleet, 1990),

> There is a gap between the library research community and public libraries. The few people doing public library research have very good relationships with the libraries that they work with. However, the real problem is that library schools either are not doing the kind of research that's useful or they don't know how to network with us. I am eternally frustrated with library schools that don't invite public libraries in at the conceptualization stage and don't use us as raw material for research.

INFORMATION NEEDS RESEARCH—A KEY TO UNDERSTANDING SOCIETAL NEEDS

Reading, Buckland (1989, p. 393) cautions, "is only a means to the more important ends of learning, discovering, and writing." Buckland's learning, discovering, and writing are three broadly stated examples of processes which result in activities (ends) which require information. Other, more specific, activities include: Writing a term paper (Kuhlthau, 1988), attempting to influence public policy decisions (Durrance, 1984), or looking for a better job (Durrance and Nelson, 1987). Information needs researchers whose work has, for years, examined ends and means, have shown that what people *do* drives their need for information. This work has the potential of moving librarians past limiting assumptions which have focused on books and reading toward effectively meeting societal information needs.

McClure and Bishop (1989, p. 136) report that a group of active library researchers agree that "user information needs" have become better understood in the last decade. This research has shown that the public library, perceived by the public as a book-centered institution, is not high on the list of places people go to get information which is important to their lives. Nearly 20 years ago, Warner, Murray, and Palmour (1973) found that the public library was not an important source of everyday information for the average citizen. Zweizig (1973), Dervin (1976), Zweizig and Dervin (1977), and, later, Chen and Hernon (1982) came to similar conclusions. Chatman (1985, 1987a, 1987b), in more recent studies of the information needs of low-income individuals, commented that her findings supported what other researchers had found—that the library is not a central resource for many people.

Researchers have shown that people get their information from other people. Learning about situations and activities that people engage in and how people look for information is a key to knowing how to meet information needs and to plan services which effectively meet information needs (Durrance, 1988). Durrance and Van Fleet (1990) found that a major concern of several public library leaders is how to identify ways to better meet the needs of a multicultural constituency and how to serve the increasing numbers of illiterates. The concerns of these leaders may increase consumption by librarians of information needs research, since most leaders indicated that they only look for research on a "need-to-know basis."

Since the 1960s the Federal government, through LSCA funds, has encouraged the development of library services designed to increase public library access for the disadvantaged, but most of these programs have lacked an adequate research basis and evaluation mechanisms. There are, therefore, not yet data "that will make more visible the magnitude of the public library's contribution to our society" (Turock, 1990a, p. 67). Information needs research has the potential to facilitate moving public librarians conceptually into a greater understanding of problems or situations which require information and thus enable them to more effectively respond to actual societal needs. MacMullin and Taylor (1984, pp. 94–95) recommend that librarians focus on problems, rather than questions, "since the problem represents the information use environment more completely than the question."

Problems and situations require contextual understanding. Chatman (1987a, pp. 279–280), speaking of situations in which low-skilled workers find themselves, sees "a real need for librarians to become more knowledgeable generally about what information means in every day content and use [and] become more aware of barriers to information." Research into problems undertaken by citizen groups showed that they actively seek information in order to influence decisions on local public policy issues (Durrance, 1984). These leaders who represent citizens in all parts of the community encountered a number of problems in getting information, some of which could have been alleviated if they had seen their public library as a source of relevant information for the community problems they tried to solve.

Zweizig, Robbins, and Johnson (1988) in a federally funded examination of literacy programs in libraries found that these programs are largely carried out by volunteers; most often they are special services with outside funding; and they tend not to be institutionalized. These researchers note that evaluation focused on numbers rather than impact; that evaluation approach is inadequate to determine the value of these services to the community. Turock (1987, p. 168) in a nationwide study of services to older adults found that "public libraries have a long way to go before they become a significant part of the growing national movement to recognize and encourage the potential of older adults."

Librarians who work with adults engaged in the job-seeking process find that they must understand the situation better before they can adequately meet these needs. Durrance (1990) conducted a study of the training needs of librarians who were starting Education Information Centers funded by the W. K. Kellogg Foundation. It showed that these librarians felt that they needed to: (1) gain specific skills in the use of computer career advising software, such as SIGI Plus and Discover; (2) better understand how to interact with adults who were seeking job, career, and education information; (3) develop referral and networking skills; (4) obtain a greater understanding of the job-seeking process; and (5) develop a far wider knowledge of the local, state, and national employment and educational picture—including demographics, projections, the extent of need, and the processes involved. These educational needs center on gaining a better understanding of the problems their clients are attempting to solve and the contexts of their problems. Impact measures are being developed to evaluate these programs.

ADVANCES IN PLANNING AND EVALUATION OF PUBLIC LIBRARY SERVICES: TOWARD MORE EFFECTIVE LIBRARY SERVICES

PLA's Recent Planning and Evaluation Manuals

The planning, measurement, and evaluation work of PLA over the past few years, under Public Library Development Program (PLDP) and previous work of

PLA's Goals, Guidelines, and Standards Committee, have been a radical departure from past planning for public library excellence, which had been standards based for the better part of this century.[2] Both the *Planning and Role Setting for Public Libraries* (McClure, Owen, Zweizig, Lynch, and Van House, 1987) and *Output Measures for Public Libraries* (Van House et al., 1987) were developed on the premise that no longer would national standards be adequate to help local public libraries develop goals based on community needs.

The adoption of the planning process, output measures, and computerization were the most frequently mentioned changes in practice in the past decade by the public library leaders (Durrance and Van Fleet, 1990). Apparently PLDP and its predecessors have placed the idea of planning to meet the community's needs prominently in the minds of a number of public library managers. Pungitore (1989, p. 119) notes that PLA leaders, through their experience with the development of these planning and evaluation manuals, "seem to have gained an appreciation of the role of the researcher in advancing the practice of the profession" and in the process reduced the mistrust in

> the ability of the scholar/researcher to understand and relate the "real world" problems of the practitioner. PLA's innovation provided an opportunity for the two groups to interact and to forge linkages that should extend beyond this project to future endeavors (Ibid.).

A weakness of the planning and goal-setting process may be its implied assumption that libraries have considered and included all possible roles. This is a problem for an institution which is not sure what business it is in. The manual's recommendation for library staff to select only one or two primary roles and only one or two secondary ones compounds the problem (McClure et al., 1987, p. 42). An examination of the *Public Library Data Service Statistical Report '88* (Public Library Association, 1988) showed that most libraries which limited their selection to four or fewer roles are likely to have selected the most traditional roles: "Popular Library," "Reference," and "Preschooler's Door to Learning" (likely modified to "Children's Door to Learning").

D'Elia (1988; D'Elia and Rodger, 1987) has been an outspoken critic of the PLA output measures. In Turock (1990a, p. 32) he indicates that while output measures are "managerially necessary, politically useful and socially valuable, the measures proposed and operationalized in *Output Measures for Public Libraries* have serious limitations" since they address only "the document/ infor-

---

[2] Work done in the development of community-centered planning manuals began with Ernie DeProspo's *A Program Planning and Evaluation Training Manual* (1973), and included those manuals developed by the PLA Goals, Guidelines and Standards Committee: *A Planning Process for Public Libraries* (Palmour, Bellassai, and DeWath, 1980) and *Output Measures for Public Libraries* (Zweizig and Rodger, 1982). PLDP manuals include: *Planning and Role Setting for Public Libraries* (McClure et al., 1987), and *Output Measures for Public Libraries* (Van House et al., 1987).

mation retrieval system." Output measures have been a step forward for evaluating some functions of public libraries, but Turock (1990a, p. 67) notes that there is clear "evidence that they may make difficult the fair assessment of nontraditional library programs in non-traditional settings."

In spite of warnings from its developers (see McClure in Turock, 1990a, p. 42) that output measures "were developed *primarily* for individual library use and not as a vehicle for [state library agencies] to promote statewide measurement of public library services," several states have begun requiring the use of output measures and, in addition, have begun to tie state aid to output measure scores. This is a problem due to their lack of comparability and their inability to examine the quality of library services (Turock, 1990b, n.p.). If output measures are misused by public librarians and state agencies, they may impede moving toward more problem-centered or client-centered services.

A Convergence of Approaches—Toward Impact Measures

One of the principal authors of the output measures, Van House, seems to express reservations about the assumptions behind the output measures in co-authored articles with Childers (Childers and Van House, 1989a, 1989b). These authors note that, in spite of the flood of library literature which points to library service outputs as the primary valid measure of effectiveness, there is no single model of evaluating library services. They note that the output measures were based on only one of several possible approaches to evaluation, the goal model.

Cameron (1981, p. 27), a management researcher whose constructs are heavily cited by Van House and Childers, indicates that the "goal model" is "most appropriate when organizational domains are narrowly defined, goals are consensual, or when outcomes are easily identifiable," a situation which does not describe most public libraries. Other evaluation models—process, open systems, and multiple constituencies—have also been identified (see Childers and Van House, 1989a, 1989b). A multiple constituencies approach to evaluation appears to be particularly suited to public libraries. Cameron (1981, p. 27) indicates that the approach is most applicable when it is necessary "to respond to a diverse group of constituency demands."

If public librarians were to adopt a multiple constituencies approach, they would more readily be equipped to adopt knowledge gained from information needs research. This would likely lead to the development and promulgation of a client-centered context in evaluation and the development of impact measures which would provide evaluation from the perspective of the value of the service to the client. A new manual developed by Turock (1990b) for evaluating Federal library programs is a positive move in this direction. The manual represents a convergence of approaches which focus more effectively on individuals with divergent needs. These approaches have much to commend them to public librarians who must serve communities with diverse needs. They will build on the philosophy behind PLDP, if not from some of the methods espoused. They will be client- or user-centered and will focus on the impact of library services on a particular constituent group; they may bridge the longstanding gap between information needs researchers and librarians.

Researchers must continue to develop additional methods of evaluation designed to move the profession toward impact measurement. Public librarians in an era of accountability will want to know how effectively they are meeting the needs of, for example, government and business leaders who are concerned with economic development in these communities, local elected officials who prepare to make public policy decisions for their communities, and citizen group leaders who seek to influence those decisions. They will want to know how well they have met the literacy challenge or the extent to which they have helped people prepare themselves for more appropriate careers. Researchers need to build on the multiple constituencies approach and—equally important—span the gap between public librarians who need to have a logical framework for constituent-based services and researchers who can help develop it.

PROMISING RESEARCH IN REFERENCE EFFECTIVENESS

Durrance and Van Fleet (1990) found that public library leaders felt that they needed to know more about reference effectiveness, for a number of reasons, not the least of which is that staffing constitutes a major part of most public library budgets. In recent years there have been a number of fine articles on reference effectiveness, some of which have appeared in the popular journals (see Hernon and McClure, 1987, pp. 6–14, for a discussion of reference effectiveness). It is quite likely that many of these articles were stimulated by the major work which has been done on unobtrusive testing of reference effectiveness, first by Crowley and Childers (1971), and more recently primarily by McClure and Hernon (1983) and Hernon and McClure (1986, 1987). Through these works, researchers have presented a great challenge to librarians. Concern over low levels of accuracy has prodded some state library agencies toward developing programs aimed at increasing the effectiveness of reference librarians (see, for example, Dervin and Clark, 1987; and *A Skill Building Workshop towards Better Reference Service*, 1988).

Researchers have only begun to unlock the secrets of reference effectiveness. However, recent work on effectiveness has strengthened the basis for understanding the phenomenon. Robinson (1989) has contributed to the development of a conceptual framework of question handling. Researchers have examined factors such as interpersonal and interviewing skills which, in combination, contribute to increasing reference effectiveness (Nielsen, 1988; Gers and Seward, 1985;

Dervin and Dewdney, 1986; Durrance, 1989; Bunge, 1990). Dervin and Dewdney (1986) developed neutral questioning techniques to elicit responses which help librarians discretely determine why information is needed without appearing to pry. They note that public librarians who had experienced difficult interviews "almost always found a description of the user's situation and objectives to be extremely useful for understanding the kind of information and material needed" (Ibid., p. 508).

Whitlach (1989) and Durrance (1989) have questioned accuracy as a key indicator of reference performance. Whitlatch (1989, p. 184) postulates that accuracy is probably not "a key indicator of reference performance." Durrance (1983, 1988, 1989) posits that librarians have created an environment which fosters anonymity; that environment produces professionals who are not known to their clients. This situation places often unnecessary demands on librarians, such as the need to provide an accurate answer to each question, since the environment discourages returning to the professional at a later time for clarification. Durrance (1989) examined a number of variables, including accuracy, using willingness to return to the same librarian at another time as a key measure of success.

DEVELOPMENT OF A RESEARCH INFRASTRUCTURE WHICH WILL FOSTER PUBLIC LIBRARY RESEARCH PRODUCTION AND CONSUMPTION

Successful Approaches to Diffusion of Research

Since public librarianship has not yet developed a culture which fosters the consumption of research, public library researchers are limited in the ways that they can influence change in practice. However, recent research by Pungitore (1989), using a diffusion framework, indicates that PLA's planning and evaluation manuals have, indeed, influenced change. She shows that the process of creating and disseminating these manuals involved extensive interaction among "the government sector, the education and research communities, and practicing public librarians during the origination and development stages, as well as [during] the dissemination [period]" (Ibid, p. iv). Dissemination included extensive workshops, involvement of public library opinion leaders who endorsed the process, test libraries, and state agency mandates. Articles were written in popular journals, and speeches were made at national, state, and local conferences. The past president of PLA recalls having done over 40 speeches and workshops herself (Durrance and Van Fleet, 1990). Given the success of this model, consideration must be given to partnership approaches and using a variety of methods to put research before public librarians.

The Need for More and Better Research

Public library leaders and others have identified a myriad of problems that face public libraries in the next decade. They recognize the paucity of relevant research. Federal fellowships in the late 1960s and early 1970s began to create a generation of researchers with the skills to attack these problems. This support has greatly diminished in the past decade. In the 1990s, there will be a crisis in relevant public library research unless there is an infusion of researchers with adequate skills and inclination.

Development of Collaborative Mechanisms

The U.S. Department of Education, Office of Library Programs (OLP), has begun to create a better framework for understanding the role of research as a foundation for practice through its extensive project which resulted in *Rethinking the Library in the Information Age* (1988–1989). Much professional guidance and deliberation went into this examination of the key players and approaches needed to develop a research infrastructure for the future. However, public librarians (except for a representative of New York Public Library as a research library) and state library agency staff are conspicuously absent from the deliberations of the individuals which led to the third volume focusing on building an infrastructure for research. The result is that the discussions of an infrastructure fail to realize the potential role for the state library agency in the development of an infrastructure (Ibid., vol.3).

At about the same time that the research establishment omitted public librarians and state agency representatives from their conclave, OCLC sponsored a conference on the future of the public library (OCLC, Online Computer Library Center, 1988). This conference included only token representation from library educators, and active public library researchers were not in attendance. Therefore, the recommendations of that conference are, likewise, limited. The lack of public library presence at the Federal conclave and the similar lack of research presence at the public library director dominated OCLC conference, coupled with the relative unimportance of research to public library leaders, illustrates the gulf that separates public librarians and public library researchers. That gap contributes to the failure to develop a public library research culture.

If research is to contribute to an understanding of the problems faced by public librarians in the next decade, mechanisms must be developed to bridge the gap between research and practice. *Rethinking the Library* (vol. 3, 1989) recommends broad participation by a variety of players to create a "Research Roundtable." The key players in creating a research culture for public libraries include leaders drawn from public librarianship, state agency staff members, and public library researchers.

Indeed, coalitions can be built on the mechanisms which are already in place. The state library agency is a major player in the development of the culture of public librarianship and could be a much more powerful vehicle for the development and dissemination of research. Within individual states, the state library agency can be an important contributor to change as well as being a funder and disseminator of research and data to public librarians. Although they are not used, state agencies have within their existing powers the ability to create incentives (mandates) for the production and consumption of research; if the argument were sufficiently strong, mandated research might well aid in library development efforts. The power of collaborative efforts among the states to stimulate research, operating through the Chief Officers of State Library Agencies (COSLA), could greatly increase the production and dissemination of research relevant to public libraries.

Several states have taken steps toward creating a culture for the consumption of research. For example, state library agencies in California and Maryland have underwritten programs designed to increase reference effectiveness based on the current work of researchers (Dervin and Clark, 1987; *A Skill Building Workshop towards Better Reference Service*, 1988). The Minnesota state library agency has identified competencies of children's services. (See Ptacek and Van Fleet, 1990, for a summary of a survey of state library agency research projects conducted in 1989 by the Public Library Association Research Committee.)

Much stronger bonds between library school researchers and state library agencies should be forged. A notable example of collaboration is seen in the state of Illinois. There the State Library and the Library Research Center at the University of Illinois Graduate School of Library and Information Science have developed several cooperative research projects. For example, the Library Research Center conducts research and statistical analysis for the state agency and public libraries under contract with the state. In addition, the School develops and distributes a State library-funded white paper series summarizing selected research. (It also undertakes other research projects under contract with selected public libraries throughout the nation.) Considerably more collaboration between state agencies and library schools using models similar to that forged in Illinois needs to be developed.

Contact between researchers and librarians needs to be fostered. A natural mechanism can be found in the Public Library Association and other divisions of the American Library Association. PLA's Research Committee attempts to inform members of relevant research. It regularly sponsors research-based programs and periodically has space in *Public Libraries* (see, for example, Ptacek and Van Fleet, 1990). However, a committee of this sort has limited visibility. PLA could contribute to the development of a research culture by actively promoting research through its publishing program, conferences, and continuing education activities; conducting environmental scans for relevant research; and developing mechanisms that foster interaction between researchers and public library directors. Researchers will need to participate more fully in practitioner organizations such as PLA. Selected research-based library development projects should follow the pattern described by Pungitore (1989).

The Federal conclave suggested the creation of a think tank which would be devoted to sustained research on the problems and issues facing the nation's libraries. Both a think tank and individual researchers who seek to conduct research relevant to public libraries should address such global questions as how can librarians better meet the information needs of citizens and other concerns raised in *Rethinking the Library in the Information Age* (1988–1989), and by public library leaders (Durrance and Van Fleet, 1990). Equally important are the far more difficult questions which need to be addressed both from a researcher's perspective and as an implementation concern: "What roles can the public library best play to meet societal needs in the next century?" and "Is the 19th-century model adequate to meet the information needs of the 21st century?"

Researchers need to look at how the 19th-century model contributes to the undervaluing of this institution by the public. Researchers and librarians alike need to assess the impact of the undervaluing of libraries on the public's ability to get and use information and on the ability of public libraries and librarians to provide it. Researchers need to look at new ways to assess the value of the public library to society. Once adequate assessments have been made, researchers and librarians need to examine how best that value can be transmitted to citizens. Whether libraries will benefit from such research, however, will depend on the strength and viability of a public library research culture.

REFERENCES

Akey, Stephen. "Mclibraries," *New Republic*, 202 (February 26, 1990): 12–13.
Bolton, W. Theodore. "Life Style Research," *Library Journal*, 107 (May 15, 1982): 963–968.
Buckland, Michael K. "Foundations of Academic Librarianship," *College & Research Libraries*, 50 (July 1989): 389–396.
Bunge, Charles A. "Factors Related to Output Measures for Reference Services in Public Libraries: Data from Thirty-six Libraries," *Public Libraries*, 29 (January-February 1990): 42–48.
Butler, Pierce. *An Introduction to Library Science*. Chicago, IL: University of Chicago Press, 1933.
Cameron, Kim S. "Domains of Organizational Effectiveness in Colleges and Universities," *Academy of Management Journal*, 24 (1981): 25–47.
Chatman, Elfreda A. "Information, Mass Media Use and the Working Poor," *Library & Information Science Research*, 7 (1985): 97–113.
―――. "The Information World of Low-Skilled Workers," *Library & Information Science Research*, 9 (1987a): 265–283.
―――. "Opinion Leadership, Poverty, and Information Sharing," *RQ*, 28 (Spring 1987b): 341–353.

Chen, Ching-Chih and Peter Hernon. *Information Seeking; Assessing and Anticipating User Needs.* New York: Neal-Schuman, 1982.

Childers, Thomas and Nancy R. Van House. "The Grail of Goodness: The Effective Public Library," *Library Journal*, 114 (October 1, 1989a): 44–49.

──────. "Dimensions of Public Library Effectiveness," *Library & Information Science Research*, 11 (1989b): 273–301.

Crismond, Linda F. and Anthony B. Leisner. "The Top Ten Public Library Leaders: A Survey," *Public Libraries*, 27 (Fall 1988): 122–124.

Crowley, Terry and Thomas Childers. *Information Service in Public Libraries: Two Studies.* Metuchen, NJ: Scarecrow, 1971.

D'Elia, George. "Materials Availability Fill Rates: Additional Data Addressing the Question of the Usefulness of the Measures," *Public Libraries*, 27 (Spring 1988): 15–23.

──────ー and Eleanor Jo Rodger. "Comparative Assessment of Patrons' Uses and Evaluations across Public Libraries within a System: A Replication," *Library & Information Science Research*, 9 (January-March 1987): 5–20.

DeProspo, Ernest R. *A Program Planning and Evaluation Training Manual.* New York: College Entrance Examination Board, 1973.

Dervin, Brenda. "The Development of Strategies for Dealing with the Information Needs of Urban Residents: Phase I—Citizens Study." Final Report on Project No. L0035JA, Grant No. OEG-0-74-7308 to the Office of Education, U.S. Department of Health Education and Welfare, April 1976.

──────ー and Kathleen Clark. *ASQ: Asking Significant Questions, Alternative Tools for Information Need and Accountability Assessments by Libraries.* Belmont, CA: Peninsula Library System for California State Library, 1987.

──────ー and Patricia Dewdney. "Neutral Questioning: A New Approach to the Reference Interview," *RQ*, 25 (Summer 1986): 506–513.

Durrance, Joan C. "The Generic Librarian: Anonymity vs. Accountability." *RQ*, 22 (Spring, 1983): 278–283.

──────. *Armed for Action: Library Response to Citizen Information Needs.* New York: Neal-Schuman, 1984.

──────. "Information Needs: Old Song, New Tune," in *Rethinking the Library in the Information Age: Issues in Library Research, Proposals for the 1990s.* Prepared by U.S. Department of Education. Washington, D.C.: GPO, 1988, pp. 159–178.

──────. "Does the 55% Rule Tell the Whole Story?," *Library Journal*, 114 (April 15, 1989): 31–36.

──────. "Serving Adults in Transition: Insights from Kellogg Sponsored Education Information Centers in Public Libraries," *Public Libraries*, November-December, 1990), forthcoming.

──────ー and James Nelson. "Education Information Centers Invest in People," *Public Libraries*, 26 (Winter 1987): 153–156.

──────ー and Connie Van Fleet. "Change, Diffusion, and Research: A Survey of Public Library Leaders," Unpublished research project, 1990.

Garrison, Guy. "A Look at Research on Public Library Problems in the 70's," *Public Libraries*, 19 (Spring 1980): 4–8.

Gers, Ralph and Lillie J. Seward. "Improving Reference Performance," *Library Journal*, 110 (November 1985): 32–35.

Gerzog, Alice. *An Investigation into the Relationship between the Structure of Leadership and the Social Structure of the Library Profession.* Unpublished Ph.D. dissertation, Rutgers University, 1989.

Heim, Kathleen. "The Changing Faculty Mandate," *Library Trends*, 34 (Winter 1986): 581–606.

Hernon, Peter and Charles R. McClure. "Unobtrusive Reference Testing: The 55 Percent Rule," *Library Journal*, 111 (April 15,1986): 37–41.

———. *Unobtrusive Testing and Library Reference Service.* Norwood, NJ: Ablex, 1987.

Kuhlthau, Carol Collier. "Developing a Model of the Library Search Process: Cognitive and Affective Aspect," *RQ*, 27 (Winter 1988): 232–242.

McClure, Charles R. and Ann Bishop. "The Status of Research in Library/Information Science: Guarded Optimism," *College & Research Libraries*, 50 (March 1989): 127–143.

McClure, Charles R. and Peter Hernon. *Improving the Quality of Reference Service for Government Publications.* Chicago, IL: American Library Association, 1983.

McClure, Charles, R., Amy Owen, Douglas L. Zweizig, Mary Jo Lynch, and Nancy A. Van House. *Planning and Role Setting for Public Libraries: A Manual of Options and Procedures.* Chicago, IL: American Library Association, 1987.

MacMullin, Susan E. & Robert S. Taylor. "Problem Dimensions and Information Traits," *The Information Society*, 3 (1984): 91–111.

Madden, Michael. "Life Styles of Library Users and Non-Users." Occasional Paper No. 137. Urbana, IL: University of Illinois, Graduate School of Library and Information Science, 1979.

Moffett, William A. "Guest Editorial," *College & Research Libraries*, 50 (November 1989): 609–610.

Nielsen, Brian. "The Role of The Public Services Librarian: The New Revolution," in *Rethinking the Library in the Information Age: Issues in Library Research, Proposals for the 1990s.* Prepared by U.S. Department of Education. Washington, D.C.: GPO, 1988, pp. 179–200.

OCLC Online Computer Library Center. *The Future of the Public Library. Conference Proceedings.* Dublin, OH, OCLC, 1988.

Palmour, Vernon E., Marcia C. Bellassai, and Nancy V. DeWath. *A Planning Process for Public Libraries.* Chicago, IL: American Library Association, 1980.

Ptacek, William and Connie Van Fleet. "Public Library Research: The State Agency Connection," *Public Libraries*, (Summer 1990), forthcoming.

Public Library Association. *Public Library Data Service Statistical Report '88.* Chicago, IL: American Library Association, 1988.

Pungitore, Verna L. *A Study of the Development and Diffusion of the Public Library Association's Planning and Evaluation Manuals.* Report to U.S. Department of Education, Project No. R039A80012. Bloomington, IN, December 1989.

Rethinking the Library in the Information Age: Issues in Library Research, Proposals for the 1990s. 3 volumes. Prepared by Department of Education. Office of Educational Research and Improvement. Washington, D.C.: GPO, 1988–1989.

Robinson, Barbara. "Reference Services: A Model of Question Handling," *RQ*, 28 (Fall 1989): 48–61.

A Skill Building Workshop towards Better Reference Service. Baltimore, MD: Maryland

State Department of Education, Division of Library Development and Services, 1988.
Turock, Betty J. "Public Library Service for Older Adults: Update 1984," *Library Quarterly*, 57 (April 1987): 137-70.
_____. *Evaluating Federally Funded Public Library Programs*, U.S. Department of Education, Office of Education Research and Improvement. Washington, D.C.: GPO, 1990a.
_____. "Evaluation in Context," Unpublished draft, U.S. Department of Education, Office of Education Research and Improvement, 1990b.
Vagianos, Louis and Barry Lesser. "Information Policy Issues: Putting Library Policy in Context," in *Rethinking the Library in the Information Age: Issues in Library Research, Proposals for the 1990s*. Vol. 2. Prepared by U.S. Department of Education. Washington, D.C.: GPO, 1988, pp. 9-41.
Van House, Nancy A., Mary Jo Lynch, Charles R. McClure, Douglas Zweizig, and Eleanor Jo Rodger. *Output Measures for Public Libraries: A Manual of Standardized Procedures*. 2nd ed. Chicago, IL: American Library Association, 1987.
Warner, Edward S., Ann D. Murray, and Vernon E. Palmour. *Information Needs of Urban Residents*. Final Report. by Regional Planning Council and Westat, Baltimore, MD. U.S. Department of Health, Education, and Welfare. Bureau of Library Programs, 1973 (ED 088 464).
Weiss, Michael J. "Clustered America: The Communities We Serve," *Public Libraries*, 28 (May-June 1989): 161-165.
Whitlatch, Jo Bell. "Unobtrusive Studies and the Quality of Academic Library Reference Services," *College & Research Libraries*, 50 (March 1989): 181-194.
Wilson, Pauline. "Factors Effecting Research Productivity," *Journal of Education for Librarianship*, 20 (Summer 1979): 3-24.
Zweizig, Douglas. "Predicting the Amount of Library Use: An Empirical Study of the Role of the Public Library in the Life of the Adult Public," Ph.D. Dissertation, Syracuse University, 1973.
_____ and Brenda Dervin. "Public Library Use, Users, and Uses—Advances in Knowledge of Characteristics and Needs of the Adult Clientele of American Public Libraries," in *Advances in Librarianship*. Vol. 7, edited by Melvin J. Voigt. New York: Seminar Press, 1977, pp. 231-255.
_____, Jane Robbins, and Debra Wilcox Johnson. *Libraries and Literacy Education: Comprehensive Survey Report*. Washington, D. C.: GPO, 1988.
_____ and Eleanor Jo Rodger. *Output Measures for Public Libraries: A Manual of Standardized Procedures*. Chicago, IL: American Library Association, 1982.

chapter twenty-three

Research Needs and Issues in School Librarianship*

Shirley Fitzgibbons
Daniel Callison

This chapter assesses the status of research in school librarianship through an analysis of characteristics of research, such as quantity, methodologies, subjects, and publication formats. The major previous reviews, as well as a comprehensive review of all dissertations in the area from 1927 through 1988 related to school librarianship, are presented.

Descriptive surveys have been the primary methodology used in the research. Only a small number of the research documents have appeared in journal articles up to 1980 with one journal (*School Library Media Quarterly*) including most of the studies. There has been a steady increase in dissertations related to school librarianship since 1960. The dominant theme of the dissertations has been a description of the field through role perception and competency studies as well as an emphasis on ascertaining the curricular role. One half of the dissertations since 1970 have been written at doctoral programs in universities without accredited MLS programs.

Specific recommendations are suggested for action including: Identification of a major funding source, the establishment of a research center, promoting interdisciplinary research projects, focusing on a research agenda of the most critical issues, more attention to theory building, implementing a greater diversity of inquiry methods, and the need for better-trained researchers.

Whether practitioners in school library media centers do in fact make themselves aware of, and implement into practice, the new insights, evaluative measures, and challenges to accepted assumptions which are resulting from current research will determine in the near future, not only the professional competence of school library personnel themselves, but also the effectiveness and the significance for children's educational growth, of the resources which they administer. (Gaver, 1969, p. 771)

---

*The authors acknowledge Mary Jackson, current doctoral student in library and information science at Indiana University, for her assistance in compiling the materials for this review.

This prediction offered over 20 years ago by Mary Gaver, a pioneer in school library media research, is still true today. Since the release of *A Nation at Risk* (National Commission on Excellence in Education, 1982) and other reports on the success (failure) of public schools, it is evident that school library media centers continue to receive little recognition as being essential to good schools and effective teaching/learning processes. Even the report, *National Goals for Education* (1990), does not mention school libraries.

The changing profession and current educational crises have intensified an accountability/evaluation need within school librarianship. Research techniques, especially evaluation and action research, can answer some of these accountability questions and assess the impact of school library media programs. The current national and state movements to improve public school education, the literacy movement, and the changes in the teaching of reading at the elementary school level to include children's literature, make the 1990s and the 21st century an opportune time to establish a newly defined role for school librarians. There should be careful assessment of the impact of specific programs on students and teachers in the teaching/learning process.

The purpose of this chapter is to describe historical patterns and the current status of research relating to school librarianship, and to recommend future action to move the field of practice into the next century based on research results.

BACKGROUND

The late 1950s and early 1960s were years of major development for school libraries in the United States. This was mainly a result of Federal support for library materials through both the National Defense Education Act and the Elementary and Secondary Education Act. Trends in education also influenced school library development in the 1960s. Research in school librarianship was sporadic in the 1930s and 1940s, increased by 1950, and continued to show growth in the 1960s and 1970s. Major Federal funds were provided for school library model and demonstration projects. Evaluations of these projects accounted for a major portion of the significant research of the 1960s and 1970s. There was an increasing number of doctoral programs in both graduate library education and educational media programs. Research remained practical and field-based to support the development of elementary school library programs.

Influences on Research Productivity

Aaron (1983), a principal author of several research review articles, has identified some of the factors which have led to increased interest and a greater quantity of research studies in the area of school librarianship. The profession exemplified by the American Library Association's (ALA's) American Association of School Librarians (AASL), and specific leaders, has continued to bring research in focus to practitioners and scholars. For the past 20 years, AASL has had an active research committee which has sponsored annual research forums and research programs at conferences, and the division's journal, *School Library Media Quarterly* (*SLMQ*), has included a research column. Its predecessor, *School Libraries*, began to have a Current Research section as early as 1959. There are more research articles in *SLMQ* in the 1980s though the journal still tries to be both a professional organ and a source of research studies.

A New Research Agenda

The most recent agenda for review of the research in school librarianship was established through the gathering of approximately 50 researchers and practicing school library media specialists at Park City, Utah in October 1989 (Woolls, 1990). Although the papers developed for the retreat represent some traditional areas of study, such as "collection development," "intellectual freedom," and "facility design," the emphasis was clearly on the curricular role of the school library media specialist. A majority of the retreat papers concentrated on such areas as "critical thinking," "enriching the curriculum," "the information search process," "educational computing research," "information skills instruction," and "the instructional consulting role of the school library media specialist." Additional reviews were presented on the impact of technology related to accessing materials. These reviews included such topics as "access to information and the effect of automation," and "studies of multitype library networking."

Research Funding

Funding of research is a problem for the whole field of library and information science, but it is even more critical in the area of school librarianship. Several major funding agencies do not include school libraries as a target research area. There are no funding organizations for school librarianship which have the structure to support a research agenda such as the Council on Library Resources is able to do for the Association for Research Libraries. There has been little funded research from the U.S. Office of Education in the area of school libraries in the last decade.

CURRENT STUDY

Questions

The following questions guide this analysis of the research in the school library field:

- What is the status of research in school librarianship?
- What are the characteristics of the research including: quantity, methodologies, subjects, and publication formats?
- What are the problems and key issues relevant to research in school librarianship?
- What recommendations can be made to move the field forward in its research base and dissemination of findings?

Methodology

Two approaches were used to address the questions listed above. First, an analysis was undertaken of the major reviews of the research including the research sections of the seven annual publications of the *School Library Media Annual* (*SMLA*) (Aaron, 1983, 1985, 1986, 1987; Didier, 1984; Bracy, 1988, 1989). Second, a complete search of all dissertations from 1927–1989 which focus on school librarianship was undertaken through *Dissertation Abstracts International*.

The earlier reviews of the research were compared and contrasted concerning the characteristics of the research and each reviewers' conclusions and recommendations. Two other earlier reviews of dissertations which cover a much shorter period, part of the 1960s and the 1970s, provide a framework of analysis and comparison for the current study of dissertations. Though the study includes all dissertations in the database, a more in-depth examination is given to the dissertations completed in the 1980s.

WHAT THE REVIEWS OF RESEARCH TELL US

Throughout the 1950s and 1960s, Mary Gaver influenced others to recognize the need for research and the importance of the dissemination and use of research findings. She wrote two of the first three reviews of research published in the 1960s and was the editor of the "Current Research" column in *School Libraries* beginning in 1959.

In a review essay, Fedder (1953, p. 388) noted two patterns of research concerning school libraries in major library schools from 1927 to 1952:

- A group of closely related theses within a particular library school; and
- The investigation of major problems in a particular period.

In a general article on "School Libraries" in the *Encyclopedia of Educational Research*, Hurley (1960, p.1203) concluded that "the period of systematic research started around 1927, . . . [and felt this was understandable] since the school library movement did not get underway until 1900 and since its main impetus has come since 1920."

Table 23–1. Reviews of Research in School Librarianship.

Reviewer	Time Period	No. of Studies
Gaver (1962)	1940–1960	41
Gaver (1969)	1950–1960	14
Lowrie (1968)	1950–1966	80
Aaron (1972a)	1967–1971	58 dissertations
Aaron (1972b)	1967–1971	23 other studies
Barron (1977)	1972–1976	96
Aaron (1982)	1972–1980	151 dissertations
Stroud (1982)	1976–1981	89 dissertations
Aaron (1983)	1972–1981	283

Eight major reviews of research were published between 1962 and 1983. These reviews which vary in time spans, in inclusivity, and in types of research, reflect different perspectives. Several of the annual review articles focus on research relating to a particular subject, such as microcomputers or student learning achievement. Aaron (1972a, 1982) and Stroud (1982) only reviewed dissertations. The time period covered is not always clear as in the Gaver reviews. The quantity of studies could be misleading if one were to aggregate the totals because some of the reviews include many of the same studies and many of the reviews overlap in their coverage of publication years. The list of reviews, the period covered, and the number of studies are listed in Table 23-1.

The following section compares the studies in the reviews first, by type of publication; second, by methodology; and third, by subject category; followed by a brief discussion section.

Type of Publication

Table 23-2 indicates the quantity of studies being reviewed with breakdowns by the following type of publication: doctoral dissertations, ERIC documents, reports, journal articles, monographs, and other (including pamphlets, yearbook articles, etc.). The most general, inclusive review by Aaron (1983), which covers approximately a ten-year period, 1972–1981, included 283 studies with the following type of publication:

- 236 (83%) dissertations;
- 20 (7%) journal articles;
- 16 (6%) reports;
- 8 (3%) ERIC documents; and
- 3 (1%) monographs.

Table 23-2. Type of Research Publication Included in Research Reviews.

Review	Percentage of Studies					
	Dissertation	ERIC	Report	Journal	Monograph	Other
Gaver (1962) n = 41	27	—	29	5	7	7
Gaver (1969) n = 14	43	—	14	21	21	—
Lowrie (1968) n = 80	7	—	5	3	6	15*
Aaron (1972a,b) n = 81	72	—	10	11	6	1
Barron (1977) n = 96	73	23	1	—	3	
Aaron (1982) n = 151	100					
Stroud (1982) n = 89	100					
Aaron (1983) n = 283	83	3	6	7	1	
Didier (1984) n = 36	64	3	8	17	3	5
Aaron (1987) n = 33	21	15	6	58		
Bracy (1989) n = 58	31	41	5	22		
Callison/ Fitzgibbons (this chapter) n = 357	100					

*Masters' Theses

Journal articles have not been the major mode of communicating research results in this field throughout the total time period under examination; this is unlike research dissemination in most fields of study.

Of the research reviewed in these major reviews, only *School Library Media Quarterly* (formerly *School Libraries* and *School Media Quarterly*) has published a major number of the studies. Twenty-four research reports published in this journal since 1960 are included in the research reviews. Six reports have been included in *School Library Journal*; four in *Library Journal*; three in *Library Trends*; and two in each of the following: *Library & Information Science Research*, *Wilson Library Bulletin*, *School Library Media Monthly*, and the

International Journal of Instructional Media. Sixteen journals have included one article each for the research included in these major reviews.

Methodologies Used in the Research

It is apparent that the descriptive survey has been the primary method used in school librarianship research. A limited, early review of research between 1936 and 1938 concluded that the survey technique was used in more than 90 percent of the studies (Heaps, 1940). Hurley (1960, p. 1203) commented that surveys of school library facilities constituted almost 40 percent of the school library studies up to the late 1950s.

Lowrie (1968) characterized a majority of the research as survey studies often of only local significance as compared to the few studies which presented hypotheses followed by a controlled experiment. She called for more experiments following the "scientific" method. Gaver (1969), Aaron (1972a, 1972b), and Barron (1977) found that throughout the period, the survey method was used most frequently. Of the 16 studies listed as "in progress" in the 1989 *SLMA*, nine were surveys (Bracy, 1989); the 1989 ERIC document review included 12 surveys out of 24 studies (Minor, 1989).

Subject Categories

This was a most difficult type of analysis to perform due to the various categories used by each reviewer. In some cases, it was evident that the time period, and the development and changes in school libraries, influenced the topics under study. The categories give some indication of trends in research topics. However, it appears that some reviewers may have forced studies into a particular category. This analysis must rely on the reviewers' categories. The analysis by categories of the dissertations in the later section is a much more solid analysis because it is based on a review of each abstract.

Aaron (1972a, 1972b) felt that the research indicated an increasing acceptance of the instructional media center concept by educators in general and that Federal funds had made a great impact on school libraries. She found that researchers had given increased attention to wider areas of service, such as district or system level services, and to examining the job competencies, values, attitudes, and roles of media specialists. There were also continued investigations of the effects of Federal legislation on school libraries and their users. Aaron found several evaluations of major funded model and demonstration programs, such as the Knapp Projects, JIMS (Jobs in Instructional Media Services), and the Philadelphia Project.

The early reviews used the following categories:

- Descriptive surveys/status quo studies;
- Resources;
- Personnel;
- Perception/role studies;
- Services; and
- Impact on students.

Barron (1977) found a somewhat wider range of topics even though the field was still trying to define the role of the school library media program and its personnel. Barron's review revealed new studies in the following areas:

- Projected needs of the profession;
- Critical issues which are related to school library media programs, such as:
  — Recent educational technology;
  — Need for greater cooperation between types of libraries; and
- Need for specially trained professionals.

More recently in the *SLMA* reviews, research studies exploring technology, networking, collection development, and issues in intellectual freedom and censorship appear, while personnel areas especially role/perception studies persist.

Discussion of the Reviews

Reviews of research of the 1950s and 1960s relied on research findings of national educational studies and statistical surveys which had direct implications for school libraries as Gaver (1962, 1969) so aptly pointed out in her first two reviews. In addition, Gaver included several doctoral studies, some master's theses, and many state, regional, and city surveys of school libraries. According to the Gaver reviews, few dissertations until the 1960s had direct emphasis on school libraries. A small number of researchers were or became library educators, including pioneers like Gaver and Lowrie.

Gaver (1962) concluded that much of the research was part of overall investigations of education in general (and felt this was appropriate) and that there were few studies; the studies were uneven in scope and depth. Yet, she still felt they were beginning to justify certain generalizations. She (Ibid., p. 122) recognized that "one of the basic needs of school librarianship is for advanced students to enter doctoral programs so that they can be equipped to carry out research." Gaver recommended coordinated investigations between graduate schools of education and librarianship and for funded sponsorship of students. She advocated the regular collection of statistics of school libraries at the state and national levels. She also recognized the need for research that requires considerable financial support and greater cooperative projects.

Gaver (1969) questioned how to implement research into practice. She tried to identify a small number of highly significant research studies which would help with current problems in school libraries.

Lowrie (1968) identified the need to establish a core of professional researchers who recognize the importance of indirect approaches, the experimental method, and the testing of theories to establish guidelines for practice. Her review identified a very small number of studies (57) over a 20-year period, which were mostly doctoral studies, and were mainly completed in schools or departments of education.

Aaron (1972a) also found that of the 58 dissertations completed between 1967 and 1971, 40 were done outside schools of library science, chiefly in education departments.

This reevaluation of research between 1950 and 1970 reveals a heyday of funded model projects, Federal funding for school library resources, and an intense attempt to evaluate both programs and personnel.

In the Aaron (Ibid.) review, several studies were sponsored and/or funded by professional associations. Both the Gaver and Aaron reviews highlighted several major studies relating to school libraries funded by the U.S. Office of Education. Though the difference between research and demonstration or modeling projects has been unclear in some of these reviews, several demonstration projects resulted in separate evaluation projects which were sometimes funded but also often dissertation topics.

Recently, Kuhlthau (1989) in a review of her own research, called attention to research in school library media as being mostly fragmented and piecemeal rather than building on prior research findings. Her series of five studies try to use and test theory from three separate fields: education, psychology, and information/communication.

Didier's reviews (1984, 1985) have synthesized several related research studies. For example, Didier (1984) reviewed studies which explore the relationship between school library media programs and student achievement including her own dissertation, subsequent studies, and previous research. She recommended that further research in this area use a series of case studies of selected school systems which illustrate differences in program and personnel which can be related to differential impact on student performance. She also recognized the need for alternative tests and measurements of student achievement. Her review in *SLMA* is an example of a cohesive review of research in an important area, the impact of school library media programs.

One improvement noted in several recent reviews has been the addition of regular statistical reports on school libraries, including the national surveys of school libraries by the U.S. Department of Education and the biannual surveys on expenditures in *School Library Journal* (Miller and Moran, 1983, 1985, 1987; Miller and Shontz, 1989).

DISSERTATION STUDIES RELATED TO SCHOOL LIBRARIANSHIP (1927–1988)

Stroud's Baseline Report

Stroud (1982) reported a comprehensive review of school library-related dissertations. Her study examined studies listed in *Dissertation Abstracts International*, 1976–1981. From the 89 dissertations she identified, Stroud established several baseline structures against which comparisons can be made both on a longevity basis and in relationship to dissertation works in general from library and information science.

Stroud categorized the school library dissertations according to the following areas: (a) research methods; (b) type of doctoral degree; (c) granting institutions; (d) sex of author; and (e) subject areas covered. A search of *Dissertation Abstracts International* (*DAI*), 1861–1989, on CD-ROM, completed in March 1990, resulted in identification of 357 studies, defended from 1927 to 1988, directly related to school library media center programs. The initial search identified 423 dissertations, but 65 were eliminated from the group because the search terms also matched to studies which emphasized one of the following areas: (a) library schools; (b) medical school libraries; and (c) reading program or children's literature studies which referred only in a brief manner to the use of school library services.

These 357 dissertations, although not a complete population of all dissertations related in some manner to school library media programs, provide a substantial sample of the studies completed over a 62-year period and allow for a review of the characteristics of such studies to date in this century. The dissertations identified for this review include studies written for graduate programs in library and information science and graduate programs in education. The 1990 search was conducted too early to include studies completed in 1989. The most recent set of dissertations in the *DAI* database included 16 dissertations defended during 1988. The earliest study listed in the CD-ROM search was authored by Frank Hermann Koos (1927) and defended at Columbia University. His study concerned the state's participation in public school library service.

One test of completeness of the CD-ROM search would be a numerical comparison to the studies identified by Stroud. She found 89 dissertations in her manual search of *DAI* from the search of only two categories, "Library Science" and "Information Science." The 1990 CD-ROM search included all of the categories offered by the *DAI* database. For the same time period searched by Stroud, 1976–1981, the 1990 search generated 96 studies directly related to school library programs. The additional studies may have resulted from the increased field search, or the fact that additional studies did not enter the database for the Stroud time period until after she had reported her findings. The

357 studies examined for this descriptive review is the most comprehensive coverage of dissertations in school library programs to date.

Sorting by Research Method

A vast majority of the dissertations completed in library and information science are descriptive or historical studies (see Table 23-3). Since 1927, the dominant method employed has been the survey instrument mailed to a selected population. In more recent years, the descriptive method continues with several different approaches for data collection employed: Personal interview, objective observation, in-depth case studies, content analysis, and citation analysis.

Dissertations which target the school library area are more frequently based on the survey approach than dissertations from the library science discipline in general. Stroud reported that school library-related dissertations were even more frequently based on the survey approach if the doctorate was granted from a school of education (88%) compared to the doctor of philosophy granted from a

Table 23–3. Various Research Methods Used in Dissertations Related to Library Science in General or School Libraries in Specific.

	Percentage of Studies Employing Such Method				
Review	Survey	Historical	Citation or Content Analysis	Experimental	Theory
Schlacter and Thomison (1974), (all library science areas, 1925–1972)	44	30	10	4	2
Grotzinger (1981), (all library science areas, 1977–1978)	42	17	—	—	—
Stroud (1982), (school libraries, 1976–1981) n = 89	56	8	15	6	—
Callison/Fitzgibbons, (school libraries 1980–1988) n = 145	77	10	5	8	—

Table 23-4. Comparison of Research Methods in Ed.D. to Ph.D. Dissertations with Emphasis on School Libraries, 1980-1988* (Percentages).

	Survey	Interview	Citation Analysis	Content Analysis	Case Study	Historical	Experimental
Ph.D. (n = 80)	63	5	9	0	3	12	9
Ed.D. (n = 58)	81	3	2	2	0	5	7

*Two percent of the studies could not be classified in the above categories because insufficient information was available.

graduate school (50%). Table 23-4 shows similar frequencies; it compares Ed.D. and Ph.D. dissertations examined from the current investigation.

Stroud reported that 78 percent of the 89 dissertations in her study were completed for the doctorate in philosophy, while 18 percent were completed for the doctorate in education and 4 percent for doctorates in library science (D.L.S.) at Columbia University. Stroud's cluster of dissertations probably reflects a high percentage of Ph.D. studies because she did not also examine studies listed under the category "Education." Consistently, except for the 1960 decade, the Ph.D. degree is the dominant degree awarded for dissertations in school librarianship. The dissertations, included in this latest review, were 65 percent Ph.D. degrees to 35 percent Ed.D. degrees. The exception is where there is a reverse of this division; a majority of the degrees were granted as Ed.D.'s or D.L.S.'s in the 1960s (see Table 23-5).

Table 23-5. Percentage by Types of Doctoral Degrees Granted for Dissertations Related to School Libraries, 1927-1988 (N = 357).

	Education (Ed.D.)	Philosophy (Ph.D.)	Library Science (D.L.S.)
1927-1959 (n = 38)	32	68	0
1960-1969 (n = 45)	60	31	9
1970-1979 (n = 129)	33	65	2
Callison/Fitzgibbons 1976-1981 (n = 96)	34	64	2
Stroud 1976-1981 (n = 89)	18	78	4
Callison/Fitzgibbons 1980-1988 (n = 145)	41	56	3

308 Fitzgibbons and Callison

Sorting by Granting Institutions

Many of the current Ph.D. programs in library and information science were established in the 1970s. In all cases, these schools also supported a master's program accredited by the American Library Association. A sorting of the dissertations completed over the past two decades shows that half of the doctorates granted since 1970 related to school librarianship came from a doctoral program which did not have an accredited MLS program on the same campus (see Table 23-6).

The average number of dissertations defended each year in school librarianship has increased dramatically since the 1950s. Prior to 1959, one dissertation on average was defended each year. In the 1960s the average increased to 5 per year; 13 per year in the 1970s; and, in the 1980s, an average of 16 dissertations have been completed per year.

While Columbia University granted the largest number of doctorates related to school librarianship until 1969, the University of Pittsburgh with at least 26 dissertations completed in the school library area and Florida State University with 15 have clearly taken the lead since 1970 (see Table 23-7).

Stroud reported that for the 89 dissertations (1976–1981) from her sample, the programs granting doctorates most frequently were: University of Pittsburgh (11), Florida State University (7), Indiana University (6), University of Michigan (5), Southern Illinois University (5), and Rutgers (5).

The current search generated seven dissertations completed by international students since 1970. Three of these were completed at the University of Pittsburgh as evaluations of school library media services in Saudi Arabia, Nigeria, and Iran.

Dispersion of Dissertations among Institutions

Stroud reported that the 89 dissertations from her sample emanated from 41 different institutions. The ratio of dissertations to institutions, or 2.17 dissertations for each institution, suggest that there were many institutions responsible for granting only a few doctorates in the school library area. Over the 62 years examined through the current search, this ratio has changed.

The 38 dissertations written before 1960 originated from 22 different institutions (1.73:1 ratio); 45 written between 1960 and 1969 came from 33 different institutions (1.36:1 ratio); and 129 written between 1970 and 1979 originated from 64 institutions (2.01:1 ratio). In the 1980s, the ratio moves beyond the two dissertations on average written per institution as 61 institutions were responsible for 145 dissertations (2.4:1 ratio). This also reflects what seems to be a slightly greater concentration of activity in a group of 13 most productive institutions reported for 1980–1988 (see Table 23-7).

Table 23-6. Percentage of School Library-Related Doctorates Granted by Institutions Associated with ALA Accredited Master's Degree Programs.

	1970-1979 (n = 129)	1980-1989 (n = 145)
Doctorate granted by institution which has both a doctoral program in library science and ALA accredited MLS program.	38	40
Doctorate granted by institution which has an ALA accredited MLS program, but doctorate is granted from some school other than library science.	12	10
Doctorate granted by institution which does not also house an ALA accredited MLS program.	50	50

Sorting by Sex of Author

Stroud reported that three of every four dissertations from her sample were written by a female. Figures from the current search clearly show that this ratio is

Table 23-7. Institutions Most Frequently Granting Doctorates Related to School Librarianship, 1927-1988.

	Institutions with ALA Accredited MLS Program (Ph.D. in Library Science)	Institutions without ALA Accredited MLS Program (Graduate School of Education)
Pre-1960	Columbia (4) U. of Chicago (3)	Stanford (3)
1960-1969	Columbia (5) U. of Michigan (4)	New York University (4) Wayne State (3)
1970-1979	U. of Pittsburgh (11) Florida State (7) Southern Illinois (5) Indiana U. (4) U. of Illinois (4) U. of Michigan (4)	U. of Alabama (4)* U. of Oregon (4) Boston U. (3) U. of Colorado (3)
1980-1988	U. of Pittsburgh (15) Florida State (10) Texas Women's (5) U. of Michigan (4) SUNY at Buffalo (3) U. of North Texas (3)	G. Peabody Teacher's (5)* Boston U. (4) Georgia State (4) Kansas State (4) Temple (4) U. of Virginia (4) U. of Colorado (3)

*ALA accredited MLS program on campus, but doctoral degree granted through the School of Education.

Table 23-8. Level of Library Programs Emphasized in Dissertations Concerning School Libraries, 1927–1988 (N = 357) (Percentages).

	Elementary Programs	Secondary Programs	Unable to Identify
Pre-1960 (n = 38)	26	26	48
1960–1969 (n = 45)	21	25	53
1970–1979 (n = 129)	19	21	60
1980–1988 (n = 145)	18	24	58

present through the end of the 1980s, but was not the case before 1970. Only 45 percent of the dissertations related to school librarianship written prior to 1960 were authored by females. Between 1960 and 1969, 57 percent were written by females. Between 1970 and 1979, the percentage jumps to 74 percent and remains at that level for the 145 dissertations completed between 1980 and 1988. There was no evidence to support the statement that "women earned more Ph.D. degrees and men earned more Ed.D. degrees or visa versa."

Sorting by Subject Content

The 357 dissertations pulled from the current search were sorted through two paths in order to determine trends in context over the past 62 years. The first sort was to determine if there has been any shift in the population of patrons of school libraries examined in the dissertations. The second was to determine if any subject areas tended to dominate the studies either over the entire time period or during a specific time period.

Table 23-8 supports the statement that the frequency of the level of school library examined in the dissertations has not changed over the past four decades. Under half of the 357 dissertations, from title or abstract, gave enough information to classify the study in this way. Of those which could be classified, the split has clearly remained equally divided between elementary and secondary school libraries.

If there has been any dominant theme in the dissertation studies in school librarianship from 1927 to 1988, it must be the persistent attempt to describe the field through definition of services, professional competencies, and basic standards. Since 1960, nearly one-third of the dissertations have attempted through the use of surveys, perception ratings and comparisons, and evaluation methods to describe either the functions of the school library media center and competencies of those who manage it. Before 1960, most of the studies defined the library services which should be introduced to elementary schools in every school district. These studies, along with examinations of the use of resources and information books to enhance the secondary school curriculum, accounted for nearly half of the dissertations.

Between 1960 and 1969, five of the 34 dissertations gathered from the current search examined national standards for school library programs and the extent of change toward the media concept. Five researchers examined definitions for the specific role of the school librarian, and three surveyed the reasons that practicing school librarians decided to select school librarianship as a career.

In the 1970s, the dominant theme for dissertations in school librarianship continued to be perceptions of the role of the school library media specialist. At least 11 role perception studies were completed in this decade or about 13 percent of the total studies. At least 10 studies measured the effectiveness of teaching library skills, how such skills should be presented and how they might be related to the standard school curriculum. Collection development, information access, and program evaluation also received major attention in at least five doctoral studies.

1980s

During the 1980s, more dissertations related to school librarianship have been completed than in any other previous decade. Furthermore, the greatest number of institutions have granted the doctorate in either education or library science. Perception studies continue to be the major focus. Most of the early (1970s) role perception studies originated from doctoral programs in library science which were also associated with an ALA accredited program. The majority of the role perception studies in the 1980s were conducted at programs based at institutions without library science doctoral programs and without any association with the ALA accredited masters-level program. One could assume that these later role perception studies were based on those completed in the 1960s and 1970s, but further investigation is necessary in order to determine any linkage or relationships.

Coupled with the 21 perception studies completed in the 1980s are at least nine other studies which attempted to define the competencies of the school library media specialist. This obsession with "defining who we are, what we do, and testing if others agree or not" accounts for over 20 percent of the dissertations completed since 1980 in school librarianship.

At least nine dissertations centered on further testing of methods for teaching library skills or, using the new terminology, information skills. At least seven studies investigated intellectual freedom and censorship, and at least six studies investigated services to special patrons (minority, gifted, and disabled) in the school library.

Historical studies accounted for at least 11 percent of the dissertations in the 1970s, and for at least 8 percent of the studies in the 1980s. The history of national or state organizations was documented; important early national leaders in school librarianship were examined; and the history of Federal funding to school library programs was traced.

CONCLUSION AND RECOMMENDATIONS

Findings of This Review

Generally, research related to school librarianship over the past 40 years can be characterized in the following manner:
- Reports of studies tend to be limited to the dissertation format. Although research articles regularly appear in professional journals, the vast majority of completed studies in the school library area do not get disseminated beyond the dissertation format as either journal articles or as monographs. Further investigation should be conducted to determine the cause of this lack of dissemination in publication. One might assume that the dissertation, in school librarianship, for most researchers, is the only research project. The reasons for this could include: A lack of commitment to contribute to the knowledge base, the lack of financial or promotional rewards, or a lack of interest or demand for research from practitioners.
- Most research in the school librarianship area is survey-based and descriptive. Even though there are examples of different methodologies being used (citation analysis, content analysis, observation, and interviewing), over 90 percent of the studies employ some methodology other than experimental. Few studies propose hypotheses or explore cause and effect relationships.
- Although clusters of subject areas represent a large number of related studies, there is little evidence that attention has been given to building specifically on the findings of previous studies. There is a tremendous need for more reviews of the research in a broad area which attempt to consolidate findings and recommendations from several related studies.
  It appears that research is not cumulative; however, a few attempts in the 1980s to undertake these major reviews of research in a specific area present some contradictory evidence. Craver (1986) has provided one model for such an approach in her review of the research on the instructional role of the school library media specialist.
- Dissertations on school librarians originate fairly equally from graduate programs of education and graduate programs in library and information science. Investigations should be conducted concerning the differences and similarities between the studies completed from these different educational environments and the differences in patterns of research productivity of each researcher.
- Research studies in school librarianship have covered a wide variety of subject areas. There is evidence that new studies have explored the potential for technological applications, new budgeting approaches, and greater instructional involvement of school libraries. However, the driving theme has consistently been the attempt "to define the field" over the past 30 years. Through evaluation of programs, role perception surveys, library

education reviews, and exploration of characteristics of exemplary programs through checklists, researchers continue to seek to answer the question: What is a school library media program and who should manage such programs?

Recommendations for Action

It is necessary to locate and institutionalize a major funding source for research focused on school librarianship which will either serve itself or establish an intermediary organization for funding research, similar to the pattern of the Council on Library Resources with its focus on academic librarianship.

A research center should be established which will concentrate on school librarianship, similar to the centers established and funded by the U.S. Department of Education on reading and other content areas of public school curriculum. The center concept would allow identification and investigations of important questions related to school librarianship. Research teams could be brought together to pursue their own research agenda through sabbatical leaves or funded research fellowships or by contract with the center for specified time periods or projects.

Teams of researchers which represent both library and information science as well as related fields, such as reading and literacy, special education, and computers in education, would be able to collectively approach major questions and to bring to the process both individual content specializations and research methodological expertise. Many questions concerning school librarianship would benefit from cross-disciplinary, cooperative research. An example in point is the following set of questions:

- What programs or interventions improve or impact on children and adolescent reading attitudes, behaviors, and skills?
- What is the role of the school library program in the process?

A research agenda should be formulated, identifying the important problems which need exploration to add to both theoretical and practical knowledge in the field. The work at the 1989 Treasure Mountain retreat is a beginning effort, but there should be a series of meetings to continue this effort with participation from a broader group of people and with time for interaction and reaction to each other's views.

More attention needs to be given to theory building in the research process. Both hypothesis testing of significant relationships (deductive process) and theory building through grounded theory (inductive process) need to be given credence. The multioperational approach to methods and techniques should be encouraged. The new research paradigm of naturalistic inquiry should be accepted as another tool in the process of asking questions and seeking answers in a systematic way.

Advanced educational opportunities for current faculty at schools of library and information science and education need to be created by professional organizations as well as deans and directors to allow faculty to develop their research expertise. This will help to improve the quality of their individual research, encourage them to incorporate research findings and methods in their teaching, and help them in directing the research of doctoral students. The cycle of inadequate research skills on the part of current and prospective faculty needs to be broken. The research perspective will only be included in courses in school librarianship when the faculty are active researchers and users of the research completed by colleagues.

This study has attempted to assess patterns in research in school librarianship and has offered recommendations for the future in order to improve the quality, quantity, and dissemination of research. It has not tried to assess the impact of past research. Additional investigations should assess whether today's school library practitioner uses the findings of these studies. Are research findings and the critical sense of assessing research a part of the university programs preparing school librarians? As Gaver (1969) so astutely asked, "Is anyone listening?"

REFERENCES

Aaron, Shirley L. "A Review of Selected Research Studies in School Librarianship, 1967–1971: Part 1," *School Libraries*, 21 (1972a): 29–46.

———. "A Review of Selected Research Studies in School Librarianship, 1967–1971: Part II," *School Media Quarterly*, 1 (1972b): 41–48.

———. "A Review of Selected Doctoral Dissertations about School Library Media Programs and Resources, January 1972–December 1980," *School Library Media Quarterly*, 10 (1982): 210–245.

———. "A Review of Selected Research Studies about School Library Media Programs, Resources, and Personnel: January 1972–June 1981," *School Library Media Annual*, 1 (1983): 303–385.

———. "Selected Research Studies about School Library Media Program, Resources and Personnel: January 1983–January 1984," *School Library Media Annual*, 3 (1985): 372-379.

———. "Selected Research Studies about School Library Media Programs, Resources, and Personnel," *School Library Media Annual*, 4 (1986): 409–417.

———. "Selected Research Studies about School Library Media Programs, Resources, and Personnel," *School Library Media Annual*, 5 (1987): 309–321.

Barron, Daniel. "A Review of Selected Research in School Librarianship: 1972–1976," *School Media Quarterly*, 5 (1977): 271–276.

Bracy, Pauletta. "Research of Interest," *School Library Media Annual*, 6 (1988): 94–127.

———. "Research of Interest," *School Library Media Annual*, 7 (1989): 96–123.

Craver, Kathleen W. *The Changing Instructional Role of the High School Librarian*. Champaign, IL: University of Illinois, Graduate School of Library and Information Science, 1986.

Didier, Elaine K. "Research on the Impact of School Library Media Programs on Student Achievement—Implications for School Media Professionals," *School Library Media Annual*, 2 (1984): 343–361.

———. "Microcomputers in School Library Media Centers: Utilization and Research," *School Library Media Annual*, 3 (1985): 336–347.

Fedder, Alice N. "Research in the School Library Field," *Library Trends*, 1 (1953): 386–401.

Gaver, Mary V. "Research on Elementary School Libraries," *ALA Bulletin*, 56 (1962): 117–124.

———. "Is Anyone Listening? Significant Research Studies for Practicing Librarians," *Wilson Library Bulletin*, 43 (1969): 764–772.

Grotzinger, Laurel. "Methodology of Library Science Inquiry—Past and Present," in *A Library Research Reader and Bibliographic Guide*, edited by Charles H. Busha. Littleton, CO: Libraries Unlimited, 1981, pp. 38–50.

Heaps, Willard A. "School-Library Studies and Research, 1936–38: A Survey, Critique, and Bibliography," *Library Quarterly*, 10 (1940): 366–392.

Hurley, Richard J. "School Libraries," *Encyclopedia of Educational Research* (Rev. ed.). New York: Macmillan, 1960, pp. 1203–1210.

Koos, Frank Herman. *State Participation in Public School Library Service*. Doctoral dissertation, Columbia University, 1927.

Kuhlthau, Carol C. "Information Search Process: A Summary of Research and Implications for School Library Media Programs," *School Library Media Quarterly*, 18 (1989): 19–25.

Lowrie, Jean E. "A Review of Research in School Librarianship," in *Research Methods in Librarianship: Measurement and Evaluation*, edited by H. Goldhor. Urbana, IL: University of Illinois Graduate School of Library Science, 1968.

Miller, Marilyn L. and Moran, Barbara. "Expenditures for Resources in School Library Media Centers," *School Library Journal*, 30 (1983): 105–114; 31 (1985): 19–31; 33 (1987): 37–45.

Miller, Marilyn L. and Marilyn L. Shontz. "Expenditures for Resources in School Library Media Centers," *School Library Journal*, 35 (1989): 31–40.

Minor, Barbara. "ERIC Research Studies Dealing with School Library Media Programs: June 1981–June 1984," *School Library Media Annual*, 3 (1985): 348–371. Updates in *SLMA*, 4 (1986): 394–408; 5 (1987): 294–308; 6 (1988): 101–115; 7 (1989): 103–119.

National Commission on Excellence in Education. *A Nation at Risk: The Imperative for Educational Reform*. Prepared for U.S. Department of Education. Washington, D.C.: GPO, 1982.

National Goals for Education. Office of the Press Secretary, The White House, Washington, D.C., February 26, 1990 (Press release).

Schlacter, Gail A. and Dennis Thomison. *Library Science Dissertations, 1925–1972*. Littleton, CO: Libraries Unlimited, 1974.

Stroud, Janet. "Research Methodology Use in School Library Dissertations," *School Library Media Quarterly*, 10 (1982): 124–134.

Woolls, Blanche, Ed. *The Research of School Library Media Centers: Papers of the Treasure Mountain Research Retreat, October 17–18, 1989*. Englewood, CO: Hi Willow Research and Publishing, 1990.

chapter twenty-four

Research Needs and Issues in Special Librarianship

James M. Matarazzo

> This chapter traces the resurgence of interest in research by the Special Libraries Association, the lack of library school faculty involvement in this Association, and the subsequent lack of contributions to research on special libraries by faculty members. This chapter presents an argument that either SLA join with other organizations in the profession to complete its research agenda or it vastly increase funding to attract practitioners and/or faculty to the topics which require the research.

With a membership of 12,500, the Special Libraries Association (SLA) surely plays a major role in shaping and defining research needs and issues for its members in the United States, Canada, and Europe. It would be difficult to discuss the research needs and issues in special librarianship without due consideration of the role of the second largest association in library and information science in North America.

This chapter will discuss the role of SLA, the involvement of library school faculty in research on special libraries, and SLA's research agenda. SLA's research agenda must be seen as appealing to a wider audience, and this chapter will explore suggestions for increased funding for research as well as a sharing of the costs of research. This author is of the opinion that SLA ought to join with other organizations in the library and information professions if this research agenda is ever to be completed or if there is to be a vast increase in the funding for research in areas contained in its agenda.

SPECIAL LIBRARIES ASSOCIATION

A renewed interest in research began in the Special Libraries Association (SLA) in 1986 with the appointment of a Special Committee on Research. This committee was charged to determine the need for a research program and, if such a need were established, to outline a research scheme as well as identify research opportunities of possible interest to SLA members. Based on the report of the Special Committee, SLA's Board of Directors authorized the position of Director of Research and Information Resources in the association office in Washington, D.C. and established a standing Research Committee.

By June of 1989, SLA approved a research agenda. Drake (1989, p. 266) described the specific reasons for the format and priorities of the agenda as follows:

> The Research Committee decided the research agenda should be formulated in terms of researchable questions rather than general statements of interest. Priorities for the research agenda focus on what special librarians don't know but need to know in order to improve the performance of libraries, information centers, and information professionals.

With a research agenda, an association staff member to conduct research and assist SLA members, as well as the Standing Committee on Research, SLA has demonstrated that research is certainly one of its priorities. These actions are further reinforced by the funds provided on an annual basis through the association's Special Programs Grants and Research Awards.

These research-related advances by SLA are sufficient to make one agree with Drake (1989, p. 268) who states, "SLA has made a solid commitment to research." Indeed, many of the just-described activities have been impressive. It is hoped this interest and enthusiasm for research will follow for many years to come. Since all of these initiatives for research have taken place in the past few years, one is forced to raise questions of the past and to search for evidence of the association's not so recent record.

A past president of SLA, Tees (1989, p. 302), notes that the association's "commitment to research has been at best, uneven." She found that the funds made available through SLA's grant programs are minimal. More important, perhaps, than the amount of funding is her suggestion that the reports funded by these grant programs are either not available or not taken seriously. Tees (Ibid.) also recalls that SLA had a long-standing research committee which it dissolved in 1981.

Thus, the progress made by SLA from 1986 through 1990 must be seen in the context of the past which appears to suggest a cyclical interest in and support for research. These comments should not diminish in any way the splendid accomplishments made by the association in this area in the recent past. It does, however, suggest that this heightened activity around and desire for research may also pass as quickly as it reappeared.

FACULTY INVOLVEMENT WITH SLA

A glance around the annual conference at SLA to see who is in attendance will reveal a notable lack of faculty from schools of library and information science. This comes as little surprise to this author who has attended the annual conferences for over two decades, but the record as recently revealed (Tees, 1989, p. 300) is actually worse than one might expect. Her study finds that 0.5 percent of faculty have held offices in any of the 50-plus chapters of SLA, 4.1 percent have served on an SLA committee, and, in the five years covered by her study, a total of 58 library school faculty have contributed in some way to the principal association of special librarians and special libraries.

One might speculate that faculty might make the greatest contribution by presenting the results of their research in the quarterly journal of SLA, *Special Libraries*. Tees (Ibid.), in her review of faculty involvement from 1983–1984 to 1987–1988, sets the record straight when she notes:

> Of 136 full-scale articles, only 26 were contributed by faculty. Of these, four appeared in a special issue on library education and two others in a special issue on continuing education for information professionals. Three others dealt with education, six with management topics, and four with new technology. A very small number reported on research projects. . . . Many of the articles were didactic or opinion pieces.

If library school faculty are not active at the local chapter level, on committees, or as authors, one might conclude that they are sharing research results by speaking at SLA conferences. Tees (Ibid.) notes that in the years covered by her survey, there were 1,185 speaking opportunities at these annual events. Unfortunately, only 52 faculty spoke during this five year period. Thus, she could easily conclude, "It seems clear that SLA has not been blessed with a close relationship with library school faculty" (Tees, Ibid.).

SLA's Research Agenda: Research Needs

The Research Agenda was approved by the SLA Board of Directors in June of 1989 (Drake, 1989, p. 266), and is reproduced in Figure 24-1.

Research agendas have not been well received by the library and information community in general (see Chapter 3). Robbins (1987, pp. 141–142) notes that the research process and research agendas do not mix well at all. Two years later, Hurt (1989, p. 1) termed one research agenda a political document for a funding agency and speculated that research would continue with or without an agenda.

The promulgation of a research agenda is, however, one way in which library school faculty can determine which topics would be of research interest to SLA

Figure 24-1. SLA Research Agenda.*

1.0 *Futures*
1.1 What is the impact of the projections of futurists (as identified in the literature) on the special library?
1.2 What technologies currently in the development stage will impact special libraries? How will these technologies impact?

2.0 *Current/User Issues*
2.1 How do people decide what they need to know? How do they learn or find what they need to know?
2.2 How can artificial intelligence applications and expert systems facilitate access to source and content information?
2.3 How will artificial intelligence applications and expert systems change user access and interaction with computerized databases?
2.4 What are information seeking and using behaviors of people in different professions or fields of work?
2.5 What are the design considerations for question-answering or fact-providing online systems?
2.6 What consumer behavior models can be adapted for use by librarians?

3.0 *Measures of Productivity and Value*
3.1 What are existing measures of productivity and value resulting from information access and use? How can these measures be used by special libraries?
3.2 How do clients/users value information?
3.3 To what extent is there a difference between the cost of information and its perceived value?
3.4 What is the relationship between library/information services and corporate or institutional success?
3.5 How can existing cost/benefit methodologies be used by the special librarian?

4.0 *Client/User Satisfaction Measures*
4.1 How can existing consumer satisfaction measurement methods be adapted to the needs of special libraries? What additional measures are needed?
4.2 What is the role of client/user expectations in measuring quality and value of service?
4.3 What are client/user perceptions about the quality of information services?
4.4 What techniques can be used to measure the potential value of new services?
4.5 What can librarians learn from other service businesses, e.g., airlines, hotels, and hospitals?
4.6 What corporate marketing strategies can be adapted to marketing the services of special libraries?

5.0 *Staffing*
5.1 What measures and methods are available to assess optimum size of staff and organizational structures in special libraries?
5.2 What data and criteria are needed to optimize library staffing?

*Reprinted with permission of Special Libraries Association.

members. Since so few full-time library educators have been actively involved in SLA, this *could* open the door to increased faculty involvement in the activities of the association. The research agenda does not guarantee participation. It does, however, provide a focus for faculty and for others interested in the research topics of most value to the members of SLA. The suggested topics are an excellent summary of the research needs of special librarians and special libraries. It would be a serious mistake, however, to conclude that the topics listed in the agenda are the only ones of interest or of value to the special library community.

TASK FORCE ON THE VALUE OF THE INFORMATION PROFESSIONAL

In June of 1985, Frank H. Spaulding, the President-Elect of SLA, issued a challenge to the membership and the profession to define the value of the information professional. As a result, he appointed a Presidential Task Force to conduct the research on this topic. On June 10, 1987, the Task Force (Matarazzo, 1987) presented a report to then President Spaulding and the results of its yearlong efforts. The six member task force's efforts are summarized by Veaner (1987, p. 8):

> The Task Force members identified and addressed three basic approaches to measuring the value of the information professional:
> - Measuring the amount of clients' time—and its monetary equivalent—saved by using the information professional's products and services. Possible tools for this method of valuation include:
>   —In-plant measurements
>   —Magnitude estimation
> - Determining significant instances of real-dollar cost savings, financial gains, or liability avoidance directly attributable to the utilization of a professional's information services
> - Assessing the worth of "testimonials" and other anecdotal evidence from scientists or corporate officers as opposed to "hard data."

Several thousand copies of the task force report were distributed to SLA members and other interested individuals until supplies were exhausted. It is estimated that over 10,000 copies were requested and received by individuals who thought the topic of enough importance to at least read the report. The task force (Matarazzo 1987, p. 4) recommended continued research on this topic since "the future of information professionals depends on their ability to clearly and persuasively justify their positions in the corporation." And, yet, this topic is not among those enumerated in the SLA Research Agenda.

VALUING CORPORATE LIBRARIES

New research which is based on the SLA President's Task Force on the Value of Information has been published (Matarazzo and Prusak, 1990). The task force report recommended a study of the value placed by senior executives on both the corporate library and the information professional. *Valuing Corporate Libraries* (Ibid.) is a survey of 164 companies, and how those firms value special libraries and special librarians, and the emerging trends for special libraries. This research, however, also raised other questions which should be investigated.

In the preface to this new study, David R. Bender, Executive Director of Special Libraries Association, observes (Ibid):

> Like all good research, the investigation raises questions that call for additional research, suggests new explorations, and proposes possible solutions to some of the problems identified. For example, the study notes that only three of the librarians at these 164 library/information centers report to an individual who has some background in library and information science. The finding thus raises questions about the career paths of information managers. Similarly, the senior-level managers interviewed heaped praise on librarians and the roles libraries play, yet we know the salaries paid to librarians lag those paid to other types of information specialists in corporations. Why this occurs should be the focus for future research, as should other topics raised by the findings reported.

Valuing Corporate Libraries was conducted in response to a recommendation made for further research in the *President's Task Force on the Value of the Information Professional.* In his prefatory remarks on the sequel to the President's Task Force report, Bender (Ibid.) has suggested still further research on the questions raised by the new study, as well as its findings. Will these suggested studies be done or will a more familiar scenario take over where these two research efforts will stand alone and be labeled just two more research reports—never replicated, never challenged, and never used?

Drake (1989, p. 265) reported the Special Committee on Research concluded in part:

> From the practicing librarian's viewpoint, research is like planning; it is an activity postponed until tomorrow, because one is too busy with the demands of today's clients to plan, let alone conduct research.

If the report of the Special Committee is an accurate reflection of the reality for the special library community, the burden on the new Research Committee will be enormous. For the many thousands of SLA members, research appears to be the responsibility of a single staff member in the Association Office and a volunteer committee of five SLA members. No matter how gifted this six-person team of staff and members may be, they cannot carry the load for special libraries and special librarians. They can lead, encourage, cheer, provide opportunities for research, and recommend rewards for successfully completed and significant research.

With a documented lack of faculty involvement with special libraries and a group of practitioners too busy to even plan a research project, the prospects for a significant research effort appear most unlikely.

ISSUES

Faculty

It is a simple fact that those who teach courses in special libraries at the majority of schools of library and information science are part-time faculty and full-time special librarians. This situation developed, in my judgment, not out of any plan to systematically exclude faculty with strong ties to SLA or because of a rift between faculty and special library practitioners. It is a fact that the Association of Library and Information Science Educators (ALISE) usually meets in conjunction with, and proximity to, the meetings of the American Library Association (ALA). From a simple economic standpoint, if a faculty member attends the ALISE conference, he or she can just stay on for the ALA conference. At the ALA meetings, the specialty divisions meet and are often representative of areas of their primary teaching responsibility, e.g., reference, cataloging, management, and technology. One could point out also that library school faculty have been elected to ALA's highest offices at a rate disproportionate to their absolute numbers in the association. The exact opposite is true for library school faculty members in SLA.

However, SLA has one clear advantage which can offset the current situation, and that is, very visible local chapters. Library school faculty can become involved in SLA and, thereby, special libraries, by becoming active in these local units. In light of tight travel budgets, faculty involvement with SLA at the local level is a reasonable recommendation and one which ought to be encouraged if faculty are to be expected to contribute to any research effort.

The current scenario of practitioners in special libraries too busy to even plan, let alone execute research projects, and a group of faculty isolated from both practitioners and their places of business, does not bode well for any menu of needed research. If nothing changes, two lifetimes will pass before this agenda is completed.

The Research Agenda of SLA

This wish list of topics which requires research certainly focuses on the articulated needs of the special library community. A careful review of the research questions poised in the agenda will reveal them as important to this community of practitioners within library and information science. With such a specific list, those interested in the welfare of special libraries will be the only ones likely to attempt the necessary effort to carry out these projects. But, who will attempt one or several of the 20-plus researchable questions?

Practicing librarians were earlier described as fully involved, just meeting the demands of their clients and unlikely to have time for research. On the other hand, faculty have been described as less than fully involved in the affairs of SLA and thus less informed of the needs of its members. While the agenda may pinpoint the areas where investigation may profitably take place, it does not ensure that the projects will find a welcome home in the heart of a researcher looking for a new project. It has been my experience that research projects attempted have often been in areas of interest which coincide with the researcher's specialization.

There are several issues presented by the above description of the potential cast who may wish to engage in any of these research projects. For the special library practitioner, the rewards at his or her place of employment may not lie with research and publication. Since half of SLA members work in the for-profit sector, such lack of recognition may eliminate many who might otherwise wish to and be capable of undertaking this research. Many of those in the not-for-profit special library community may also find little professional reward for the conduct and publication of research.

If the Special Libraries Association were a new association, one might suggest that full-time faculty might be teaching in this area in time. However, SLA is over 80 years old. And the shift of members of the full-time faculty to this specialization by those in charge of library/information science education programs does not appear likely at this time.

Thus, the Research Agenda is just that—an agenda without a core of researchers at hand at this time or in the near future. Certainly, one major issue for the special libraries area is who will carry out the needed research. Perhaps, the research agenda of SLA must be made known to a wider audience in the library/information community than just the special library community if there is a real desire to see progress on these topics. These research questions are significant to the special library community; however, many would be of wider interest to the library/information community. One task is to make this research agenda more widely known.

Many past research projects on special libraries contain suggestions for research. In this chapter the *President's Task Force* Report and *Valuing Corporate*

Libraries studies were used as examples. These suggestions for further research, while not part of the research agenda, ought to be pursued by interested researchers as well.

The Research Record and Use of Research

Both the *President's Task Force on the Value of the Information Professional* (Matarazzo, 1987) and *Valuing Corporate Libraries* (Matarazzo and Prusak, 1990) contain recommendations for further research. It seems important that these proposed areas of research be pursued. As noted before, the second title grew out of a recommendation made by the task force. By completing the second study, the investigators hoped to add to the understandings made in the task force report. If the second study had not been done, then the task force report would have stood alone—another example of a fragment of research. It was the investigator's intention to continue to add to the base of understanding of just which services are the most highly valued in the corporate sector and to specify which services are the most highly regarded. With two studies related to one another, an accumulation of research results is possible and these data lead to greater understanding of our worth and our most valuable contributions.

Research agendas and research committees do not, in my opinion, mean that special librarians are suddenly research-oriented or committed to research over the long term. This recent, new beginning must be sustained and nurtured. Perhaps the key role to be played by a research committee will be not in carrying out the research, but in sustaining member interest in and curiosity about the latest research findings. One possible method of sustaining that interest is to present a program at the annual conference of SLA on research results.

SLA's research agenda is really of interest to the profession as a whole. The topics in the agenda are broad and most clearly transcend special libraries as a type of library. Since the topics are so broad, the dollars available through SLA are not sufficient to fund most of the projects. For example, *Valuing Corporate Libraries* received an SLA Special Programs Grant Award which was matched by Temple, Barker & Sloane, Inc., a Lexington, Massachusetts-based management consulting firm. Two subsequent grants, one from CLSI and the other from the Emily Hollowell Fund of the Graduate School of Library and Information Science at Simmons College brought the total available for this study to slightly less than $8,000. The study, in fact, cost 25,000 dollars to complete, including the printing of the report, but excluding any payment to the authors. Clearly, if the topics in the agenda are to be completed, a serious expansion of the funding available will have to be budgeted each year by SLA. If the association and its members are really interested in research, the money for research will have to follow if the agenda is to be completed.

It is possible that the importance of special libraries reached a high point 20 years ago when members of SLA were on the frontiers of the application of computers to library functions. As the technology spread to other libraries, special libraries may be of less interest to the profession as a whole than in the past. It may very well be the time to test that thought by joining with other associations and types of libraries to jointly fund some of these projects on an interassociation basis. The topics in SLA's research agenda are broad enough to interest all types of libraries and librarians.

Finally, there appears to be a continued plea for more research with precious little evidence that what is currently produced is of any interest and/or use to those to whom the results are addressed. We certainly need to know more about the application, lack of application, or even consideration of what is currently produced. If we fail to at least look at the issue, those who conduct research will continue to produce studies and those whose primary responsibility it is to deliver services will also continue. And, like ships in the night, we will pass each other unaware of the other's presence. Clearly, the greatest benefit would be for those who conduct research and those who can use the results of research to work together to gain a greater understanding of the nature of our work and needs of our clients.

REFERENCES

Drake, Miriam A. "Research and Special Libraries," *Special Libraries*, 80 (Fall 1989): 264–268.

Hurt, C.D. "Research Agendas and Ghosts of the Past," *Library & Information Science Research*, 11 (1989): 1.

Matarazzo, James M., Ed. *President's Task Force on the Value of the Information Professional.* Washington, D.C.: Special Libraries Association, 1987.

———— and Laurence Prusak. *Valuing Corporate Libraries: A Survey of Senior Managers.* Washington, D.C.: Special Libraries Association, 1990.

Robbins, Jane. "Another! Research Agenda," *Library & Information Science Research*, 9 (1987): 141–142.

Tees, Miriam H. "Faculty Involvement in the Special Libraries Association," *Journal of Education for Library and Information Science*, 29 (Spring 1989): 297–304.

Veaner, Allan. "Introduction," in *President's Task Force on the Value of the Information Professional*, edited by James M. Matarazzo. Washington, D.C.: Special Libraries Association, 1987.

chapter twenty-five

Research Needs and Issues in State Librarianship

Robert E. Dugan
Jane Ouderkirk

This chapter identifies three roles of state libraries in research. The importance of research in, by, and about state libraries is emphasized. Factors contributing to the limited body of research are discussed. Specific recommendations for enhancing research are made based upon existing survey data, recent NCES projects, and strengthening the cooperative effort among state and national library and research agencies.

State libraries have three identifiable research-related roles. There is the research conducted by (or through) state libraries, usually focused on the status and use of libraries in the state and/or in the development and extension of library services. There is the research about the state library and its operations and services, as in the decision-making processes employed during planning and policy development. And, the state library supports research projects through its resources and services.

Although most state libraries are involved in at least one of the three aspect of research, research is seldom a primary activity conducted by state libraries. In many instances, that research activity which does exist is not particularly scholarly or complex. This may be caused by the need for state libraries to be "general" in nature due to multiple responsibilities of their mission reflected in legislation or practice, and a lack of valid and reliable data collection and analysis, both internally and externally. A minimal amount of surveying and discussion among state libraries to determine common and/or unique needs has produced a deficiency in the identification of the research needed by state libraries.

IMPORTANCE OF RESEARCH

Despite the relatively low priority assigned to research, state libraries have their roles in these pursuits. Perhaps the most visible are those efforts to gather data about library activity at the local level and information about related library development issues.

Most state libraries are responsible for promoting local library development. In a few states this responsibility has been assigned to a state library administrative agency that is a separate agency rather than a division of the state library. Local assistance is provided through the allocation of state and/or Federal funds, and the provision of technical advice on library services, programs, operations, and other functions. State libraries or other library agencies with this responsibility usually collect annual data about local library programs. These data may include resource information describing financial support, staffing and collection growth, and usage measures, such as annual circulation of materials and number of reference inquiries. The information compiled is usually disseminated with descriptive statistics.

The state library may assist local libraries in the design and analysis of user/nonuser surveys and evaluations to gather perceptions about needs and usage, or other types of studies. The state library may also conduct its own similar studies, surveys, and evaluations for use in statewide planning and program development. State libraries and agencies distributing state and/or Federal funds may conduct evaluations on program implementation and the subsequent impact on services.

The current edition of *Standards for Library Functions at the State Level* (Association of Specialized and Cooperative Library Agencies, 1985, p. 3) includes:

7. The state library agency shall initiate and encourage research, planning, and evaluation relating to the library service and information needs of citizens and to alternatives to meeting these needs.

The language of this current standard emphasizes needs assessment and needs fulfillment.

The importance and impact of library development research assisted or conducted by the state library should not be understated. Information about library use, local user needs and perceptions, resource allocation and related or tangential effects, and other data from a wide range of studies concerning libraries are used in decision making, development and examination of public policy, and in the political/financial processes of every level of government. The allocation of hundreds of millions of dollars, and the services offered or denied the residents of the states, are in part based upon the information collected, analyzed, and presented.

The dilemma of this economic environment is that state libraries are forced to demonstrate success in meeting identified user and library needs with funds allocated, while simultaneously proving to funders the need for additional allocations which infers less than complete success (McClure, 1990). Because of these contradictory needs in research results and reports, researchers planning to engage in the study of state libraries "must be much more knowledgeable about public policy, the policy making process, and the political context within which power, position, and persuasion are used. . . . Research findings must be presented in this context if they are to have an impact on decision making" (McClure, 1989, p. 289).

The state library has related research needs. For example, state library staff need research assistance in the design of survey instruments, analysis of data, and development and/or application of evaluation methodologies to the programs the state library provides directly or sponsors through other library agencies.

Another aspect of research involves the state library's analysis of internal operations. As with libraries of all types, state libraries compile information about their own resources and usage. In addition, state libraries may collect information about the practices, procedures, and guidelines related to development, implementation, and revision of policies which may affect other libraries and their activities in the state. For example, state libraries which allocate state and/or Federal funds usually maintain a file system including statistical and other information on libraries applying for, and receiving, financial assistance. Internal working documents used in deliberations while developing and implementing policies related to providing and evaluating financial assistance becomes part of the file for later referral. Information collected about state library resources and activities and the files related to the development of program practices become invaluable for public accountability when used by auditors, politicians, library advocates, and others, such as researchers of state library policy and decision making in quantifying and qualifying program administration. Research needs related to this specific area include records management methodologies, data compilation and analysis, evaluation, and presentation strategies.

A third important role and need is the support provided to researchers through the development, maintenance, and accessibility of a collection of materials, and related services provided by state library staff. Many state libraries began as law libraries to support the specific research needs of the state legislature and executive officials. Later, collections were developed to support other needs, primarily broader governmental research needs, and still later to support public and other libraries' reference needs. Many state libraries include extensive holdings of Federal and state documents, law materials, and state history and genealogy. Others include more general materials to supplement local library collections and for direct public use. In most cases, state library collections have been developed to support the reference and research needs of specific government-related professions and individuals, and in some cases, the general public (Monypenny, 1975).

A state library's need for research to support other researchers may include identification of users and potential users, needs assessment, collection development and management, and analysis of operations and functions.

ISSUES AND CONSTRAINTS

Among the constraints which impede the use of any research are: Limited resources, particularly staff; competency of staff; inability of library managers to accept new findings; and management style and philosophy (McClure, 1989, p. 287). As stated earlier, the key issue concerning research in state libraries is that it is rarely a primary activity, although its importance is acknowledged. The most obvious constraints to the ascendancy of research to a primary activity status are:

- The multiple responsibilities of the state library;
- The lack of a valid and reliable body of collected and analyzed data related to libraries, state libraries, users and their needs, and other library development related areas of study; and
- A lack of surveying and discussion among state libraries identifying and evolving methodologies concerning their research needs.

All state libraries and state library administrative agencies have mission statements delineating functional responsibilities. Only a few of these mission statements refer to specifically research activities (Association of Specialized and Cooperative Library Agencies, 1989). As a result, the state library (or agency) may find it necessary to divide its limited resources to support both library user services (collections and staff) and library development (technical assistance and allocation of funds to the local level) in order to meet legislated, ascribed, or assumed multiple responsibilities and roles. Internal specialization is limited, except for the two or three largest state libraries (Monypenny, 1975, p. 277). One result of this diversification of responsibilities and roles is a general limitation of scope and depth in the approach to research.

Another constraint involves the lack of a valid and reliable body of data and research concerning library services, user needs assessment, evaluation, and other library functions and services, both internal and external to the state library. Until the recent establishment of the Public Library Association's PLDS (Public Library Data Service) and the U.S. National Center for Education Statistics' (NCES) FSCS (Federal State Cooperative System) program, public library statistics were not collected consistently nationwide. Although state libraries have collected public library statistics for decades, there were no "national" standardized definitions applied to every state and every local public library. Furthermore, there was no consistent methodology applied towards collecting the data.

NCES, in the past, has collected statistics from academic, school, and public libraries, but the data were often published years after collection. This constraint is being addressed through the more recent efforts of NCES as it begins a more systematic collection of public, school, and academic library data.[1] Because public library data are available only from 1988, longitudinal studies are years away. Furthermore, the first nationwide collection of the public library data revealed problems in data survey forms, definitions, and reporting consistency. State libraries will undoubtedly continue to be very involved in the public library FSCS program.

Although many state and local libraries conduct studies and surveys, this body of data is not easily available or accessible, and may not be of general value except to the specific local situation. Information includes local library and user needs assessments, perception surveys, cost-benefit analyses, accuracy of reference services, program evaluation, and other topics.

In addition to the general lack of access to these data, the validity and reliability of the data may also be suspect. Questions about reliability and validity could be raised concerning the development of the survey instrument and its application, and the subsequent analysis of the data gathered. The same could be stated about needs assessments related to local and state library services, and the program evaluations conducted and analyzed. Very few state libraries have staff specifically trained in survey and research methodologies, data analysis, or development and application of evaluation methodologies. In some instances the state library may contract with consultants to assist them and/or the local libraries in these research and survey efforts.

Related to this constraint is the problem state libraries, and all libraries, in fact, are facing—the format of information gathered and stored. As library information and records are more frequently stored in electronic formats, it will become increasingly important to consider means of accessing that information at a later time. If state library and/or other public records are stored in a particular format which is not translated to new formats as original storage and retrieval devices become obsolete, the data become inaccessible and useless.

A third constraint involves the lack of identification and discussion of common and unique research roles and needs among the state libraries and state library administrative agencies. This may be because no two state libraries are identical in mission, responsibilities, roles, governance structure, or other identifiers. Therefore, state libraries have difficulty in comparing themselves with other state libraries. Furthermore, state libraries are not comparable with other

---

[1] Public Law 100-297, the Hawkins-Stafford Elementary and Secondary School Improvement Amendments of 1988. This law specifically mandates NCES to collect library statistics.

types of libraries—no other type of library agency in the information services community has similar responsibilities and roles.

Other factors contribute to this lack of discussion concerning research needs and roles. It appears that there is little or no survey information about research efforts of all the states. For example, there have been eight editions to date of *The State Library Agencies, A Survey Project Report* (Association of Specialized and Cooperative Library Agencies, 1989). The latest survey instrument (8th edition) requested information specifically on research responsibilities only as it relates to whether or not research is considered to function under statewide library development. Responses to that item are not included in the report's appendices. To learn about research at the state libraries and agencies, one must read the mission statement for each state, and peruse the activities and lists of publications. The narrative descriptions of major functions and notable activities indicate that 11 state libraries identify research activity as an administrative function of their organization.

Each edition of *The Book of the States* (Council of State Governments) includes responses to a question concerning "research" in a table labeled "Functions and Responsibilities of State Library Agencies." The survey question refers to the aforementioned *Standards* #7 which involves research concerning the planning and evaluation of user needs, which could be referred to as a component of library development. The latest edition of *The Book of the States* (1988, p. 323) finds that 23 states report having a primary role in research, 25 share it with libraries on the local level, and two have no responsibility. However, the table does not indicate the types of research conducted or supported, or needs identified.

The scope and emphasis of research in state libraries may have changed during the past two decades. It is important to note that the language of the current 1985 state library standard has been revised since the last edition. The 1970 standard stated:

8. It is the responsibilty and obligation of the state library agency to initiate and encourage research. A position including the duties of research and planning should appear in each state library position roster.

Although both standards are under the statewide library development section, the current standard certainly deemphasizes the research intent of the former standard.

There are few references to studies or reports concerning research roles and needs of state libraries in the professional literature. For example, a DIALOG search of *Dissertations Abstracts*, using the terms STATE(W)LIBRARY AND RESEARCH, extracted only 12 titles. Of the 12, only four indicate by title and other descriptors that they are studies about state library services. In addition, although it has been suggested in the past and present that state libraries collect information about their services, resources, and activities more frequently and comprehensively than the ASCLA surveys, COSLA (the Chief Officers of State Library Agencies) has done little to implement such an effort. Discussions of research activities, needs, and roles do not appear regularly on the COSLA meeting agendas.

This absence of discussion among and between state libraries concerning research is further indication that research is not a primary activity of the state library, and may indicate that it is not likely to become a primary activity in the very near future.

OPPORTUNITIES AND STRATEGIES

Despite existing constraints, there are several opportunities and strategies whereby the role of research in the state libraries can be strengthened. As the public library and other library data compiled by NCES improves in reliability and validity, the body of information concerning library activities will dramatically increase. State libraries should continue their cooperation with NCES in this important national statistical program, and analytically apply the federally compiled information within the context of their state's activities.

Information and data about the resources, operations, and activities of state libraries are scarce and could be expanded through more frequent surveys. This effort would require identification of information and data to be collected, standardization of commonly applied definitions, and consistency in reporting. In the early 1980s, there were at least three different surveys conducted about state libraries: The ASCLA survey on operations and activities of state library agencies; the biennial Council of State Governments' survey concerning functions and responsibilities; and the ASCLA surveys on library cooperation which indicate the involvement of the state library in interlibrary activity. In 1988, NCES proposed a survey of state library operations similar to the current survey of public libraries which has, to the middle of 1990, yet to be implemented.

COSLA should request that NCES propose a survey instrument designed to compile the "best of" the information from the three aforementioned surveys. After consideration and approval of the instrument, COSLA could turn the administration, collection, and compilation of the data over to NCES. Analysis could be a joint effort of the American Library Association's Office for Research and COSLA, with the compilation and analysis published and disseminated by the U.S. Department of Education (NCES or Library Programs), Council of State Governments, the American Library Association, or a cooperative among these three. A coordinator role, if desirable, could be provided by the U.S. National Commission on Libraries and Information Science (NCLIS).

Rethinking the Library in the Information Age: Issues in Library Research in the 1990s (U.S. Department of Education, 1988-1989) did not specifically identify or discuss research issues and the needs of state libraries. This deficiency, however, does not mean that there are no research needs for state libraries.

State libraries, through COSLA, should consider establishing a consortium in a serious effort to increase discussion to identify common and unique research issues and needs. Other members of this endeavor would include members of the research and library community, such as the American Library Association's Office for Research and Library Research Round Table (LRRT); the U.S. Department of Education's NCES and Library Programs; and possibly others, such as NCLIS. Funded through grants or membership subscriptions, the consortium could develop an agenda, investigate and recommend study methodologies, and implement strategies to collect, compile, analyze, interpret, and disseminate information and data specifically intended to aid in research conducted by, and about, state libraries (McClure, 1989, p. 291).

An alternative to the research consortium, or even in concert with that particular strategy, would have COSLA establishing a program of "visiting researcher" positions (McClure, 1989, p. 291). Working independently of the consortium, or as its principal investigator, the researcher(s) would undertake a substantial project including design, implementation, compilation, and analysis resulting in a usable product which furthers the research concerning state libraries.

Implementation of these three activities would increase the body of knowledge about libraries in general and state libraries in particular. Executed appropriately, the data can be reliable and valid.

In addition to the information and data which could be produced by these strategies, it is essential that state libraries have appropriately trained staff to develop research methodologies, to design and apply survey instruments, and to collect, analyze, and interpret the resultant data so that they will be used as well as useful. However, state libraries must recognize the serious deficiencies and limitations of the ability of most library science schools to produce professional librarians who can conduct and understand research in only 36 credit hours (McClure, 1989). Therefore, COSLA should work with the U.S. Department of Education to provide opportunities for workshops and/or scholarships so that appropriate staff may develop and improve research skills. Furthermore, because of the emphasis at the state and Federal levels on "accountability," state library staff must also be trained in program evaluation methodologies. Few state libraries have carefully developed programs for collecting, organizing, and reporting internal and/or external evaluation data. State libraries need to look at the broader evaluation issues, methods, and approaches rather than focusing exclusively on extensiveness measures, and progress towards efficiency, effectiveness, and impact measures. COSLA could assume a leadership role to develop or sponsor evaluation training programs. It may even consider proposing a model evaluation process which could be applied in most, if not all, of the other states. It is essential that policy making and research by testimony and opinion does not replace policy analysis and evaluation research by empirical data (McClure, 1990).

Although each state library is unique, there is a need to develop a paradigm of the "whole" of state libraries, and paradigms of the common functions, organizational structures, and services shared by state libraries. Several paradigms are required based upon the multiplicity of responsibilities and activities among the state libraries. Preliminary extensiveness measures could be the basis of developing the organizational, functional, and service paradigms.

Paradigm development will require considerable information gathering about state libraries which does not now exist in any centralized place. State library staff currently communicate with each other seeking such resource, organizational, functional, and service information. However, because of the importance of the state libraries in the library community, especially the public library community, and the need to explain to the information services community at large, citizens, and policy makers, what it is that state libraries do, it is necessary to begin to describe state libraries in terms other than purely descriptive, i.e., "there are fifty state libraries which do a variety of functions and activities." Information from the last two ASCLA *Project Survey Reports* would provide the basic information for structuring expanded state library data collection projects.

In addition to the information concerning themselves, each state library should be encouraged to centralize and publicize research studies about and for libraries in order to facilitate access to them. There are many library and user studies, reports, and other research activities undertaken and completed each year that should be made widely available for scrutiny. This effort would also contribute to the body of information concerning library and information services.

A final strategy would suggest that state libraries need to adapt other models of research, such as public administration and market or even clinical research, in order to improve their own research methodologies. Methodologies now in place rely upon standard techniques applied primarily to libraries. This effort would require state library staff, contracted consultant assistance or scholars, to identify, explore, test, and recommend other research models.

A COMMITMENT TO RESEARCH

This chapter has discussed the importance of improving research by and about state libraries. To improve research, two things must occur. State libraries need to work together and with other members of the research and library community to address and resolve research issues. That will mean that state libraries must allow "outsiders" access to their information and data concerning internal and external activities.

Second, state libraries must make a commitment towards improving research. It cannot do so with words alone—this commitment must be backed by the allocation of time, access to the information and data held, and recognition that the level of research by and about state libraries is not as high as it could be. Only when state libraries work cooperatively and become more committed to exploring and dealing with the needs for and issues surrounding research will real improvements in the body of knowledge be real. And, research can then be considered a primary activity of the state library community.

REFERENCES

Association of Specialized and Cooperative Library Agencies. *The State Library Agencies, A Survey Project Report: 1987*. 8th Edition. Chicago, IL: American Library Association, 1989.

———. Subcommittee for Library Functions at the State Level, *Standards for Library Functions at the State Level*. 3rd Edition. Chicago, IL: American Library Association, 1985.

The Book of the States, 1988–89 edition, Lexington, KY: The Council of State Governments, 1988.

McClure, Charles R. "Increasing the Usefulness of Research for Library Managers: Propositions, Issues, and Strategies," *Library Trends*, 38 (Fall 1989): 280–294.

———. "The State Library and Evaluating Federal Aid to Libraries: Suggestions for Improving the Process," in *Evaluating Federal Aid to Libraries*, edited by Betty Turock. Washington, D.C.: Department of Education, 1990, pp. 39–53.

Monypenny, Phillip. "Library Functions of the State," in *Encyclopedia of Library and Information Science*. Vol. 15. New York: Marcel Dekker, 1975, pp. 264–281.

Rethinking the Library in the Information Age. 3 volumes. Prepared by the U.S. Department of Education, Office of Educational Research and Improvement. Washington, D.C.: GPO, 1988–1989.

chapter twenty-six

Paradigmatic Shift in Library and Information Science

Martha L. Hale

Is library and information science (LIS) research experiencing a shift in methodology, content, and values? This chapter explores the question in light of the characteristics of disciplines and current changes in society that constitute a new paradigm. The implications of the paradigmatic changes on research, practice, and education are introduced.

Scientific investigation involves problem and puzzle solving. Most researchers who conduct such investigations practice their craft within a discipline, an artificial but convenient division of the immense arena available for investigation. Within disciplines, researchers investigate phenomena that are considered to be that discipline's area of responsibility. Researchers in any discipline see the phenomena under investigation with the lens or paradigm which dominated their own learning. But, according to Kuhn (1962), there comes a time when the puzzles about phenomena under study can no longer be explained using the methods or ways of thinking that have brought the science to that point. New discoveries, new methods, and new values seep into disciplines and influence how phenomena are viewed, how they are studied, and how the findings are interpreted.

Such a paradigmatic shift with its new knowledge, new methods, and new values eventually becomes the normal lens and in time it, too, is replaced by an emerging paradigm. The shift is not instantaneous, and does not occur simultaneously in all disciplines or in all the research questions considered within a discipline. The roots of a dominant paradigm are in a former lens, while the clues of the emerging paradigm will, with hindsight, be seen in the existing paradigm.

In the 1970s, Schwartz and Ogilvy (1979), two researchers at Stanford Research Institute, studied 13 disciplines or discipline-like areas and discovered sufficient similarities to declare a paradigmatic shift.[1] Lincoln (1989) extended their study and discovered parallel development in 13 additional academic areas.[2]

The purpose of this chapter is to examine if library and information science (LIS) is experiencing a similar shift in methodology, content, and values. Methodological shifts do not emerge independent of the phenomena being studied. No one sits down to develop a new methodology; methodologies shift when the phenomenon under investigation cannot be examined using current techniques. Therefore, after a summary discussion of research and a review of Schwartz and Ogilvy's (1979) findings, this chapter asks "Is research experiencing a similar paradigmatic shift?" and "Are the methodologies likewise developing?"

KEY QUESTIONS FOR A DISCIPLINE

Researchers investigate *what* a phenomenon is, *why* it is like that, how the *anomalies* can be explained, what is *predictable* about the unknown, and *how* the answers are found. This oversimplified summary of research should be expanded by a series of questions:

- *What* is in the domain of each discipline? What is the piece of the reality being studied? What has been assigned or chosen for investigation? What are the parameters of research and why? What are the influencing values within the discipline? What images are used to describe the phenomenon. Thus, the question that will emerge is, what is library and information science? What is included in it? How does the world look from LIS point of view?
- *Why* are the phenomena as they are found to be? What *causes* the world to be as it is perceived to be? How did the world under study get to be as it is now seen? In other words, what causes what within the domain of the discipline? A few years ago the question what causes truth in a discipline might have been raised, now we are truly asking what causes the people in a discipline to view the world as they do
- How does a discipline put its domain in order? How is order put into the world and why? Researchers seek to make sense or make order out of the unknown, i.e., that which is not understood. Most researchers and practitioners try to bring order out of disorder, or clarity to erase an ignorance

---

[1] Schwartz and Ogilvy (1979) studied physics, chemistry, brain theory, ecology, evolution, mathematics, philosophy, politics, psychology, linguistics, religion, consciousness, and arts.

[2] Lincoln (1989) dealt with business administration and organization theory, social welfare, business communications, history, theater and drama, psychology, economics, sociology, occupational therapy, nursing, medicine and family practice, women's studies, and education.

- How is change handled? How is change accommodated in the domain? The effort of researchers to predict the unknown is an effort to deal with change
- How is research conducted? What evidence is considered legitimate and why? What are the methodological issues confronting the discipline?

CHANGE AND SHIFT FROM THE OLD PARADIGM

Clearer evidence of a paradigmatic shift emerges from the contrast of the answers given under the old paradigm to the current responses within these same basic areas of investigation. While the old paradigm defined the domain as simple, the emerging definitions of the various fields studied by Schwartz and Ogilvy (1979) and Lincoln (1989) are complex. "Diversity" and "interaction" are terms used to define the emerging realities within most disciplines. Entities are no longer being studied apart from the environment in which they exist; systems are no longer viewed as the "sum of the parts," but rather the whole is unique from the characteristics of the individual parts.

This means that the metaphors used to define the domains are no longer simple, machine-like, mechanistic images (Morgan, 1986). Rather, images like a hologram, where pieces of the whole are evident throughout the parts of the image, are being used more widely to describe the domain being studied.

There is also a shift from seeing simple, linear cause/effect relations among events in a domain to a view of mutual causality. The distinction between cause and effect is now meaningless. The new paradigm includes discussions of positive feedback and feed-forward.

The old notion of order was based on the concept of hierarchy. Influenced by the image of God as the Prime Mover, there was a divine right of kings, the father as the head of the household, a bureaucratic organization—all hierarchical systems of order. The emerging concept is that there may be no single natural order, but that multiple orders exist simultaneously.

Change is no longer viewed as a planned assembly of events that can be predicted or controlled. Change occurs unpredictably, morphogenetically, and constantly. A complex domain that functions under conditions of openness and diversity, mutual causality, and indeterminacy would logically change unpredictably and uncontrollably. Moving from a view that the future can be determined toward an acceptance that the future is indeterminate is seen in Heisenberg's Indeterminacy Principle,[3] as well as the evidence that the form of a flower cannot be accounted for solely by the form of its cells; not all roses are identical but they are recognizable as roses (Schwartz and Ogilvy, 1979).

---

[3] Heisenberg's Indeterminacy Principle calls into question the idea of the neutral observer. This principle states that at the submicroscopic level any act of measurement is determined by the relationship between the observer and the observed.

Finally, there is a growing acceptance that perceptions, instruments, disciplines, and researchers are not neutral. Indeed, in the mere process of conducting a study researchers often influence the phenomena. The perspective of the researchers influences not only what they see, but what they choose to study and the methods considered legitimate to be used. Furthermore, as Schwartz and Ogilvy (1979, p. 15) wrote, "we see a shift from the 'absolute' truth discovered by the 'right' method toward a plurality of kinds of knowledge explored by a multiplicity of methods."

LIBRARY SCIENCE

In using this framework to examine recent changes in the practice and research of library science, it is important not to condemn the old and praise the new. A paradigmatic change is not a good/bad shift, it is a change in lens that could not have occurred at another time.

What Is the Domain of Library Science? Has It Shifted from Simple To Complex? Are We Imaging the Domain of Library/Information Science in More Complex Ways?

Even the words used in the first question sound simplistic. The field is rarely called "library science;" even the name is more complex, more diverse. The field is at least library and information science, information science, information studies, information transfer, all of the above, or none of the above ("MLS Accreditation Standards Revision Will Be Difficult," 1990).

As shown below, the increased awareness of the complexity of the domain can also be seen in the contrast between library science and information science, in the product of the profession, and in our image of the product, in the growth of that product, and in the shift in curricular emphasis to the complex human patterns of transferring information.

Karande (1986, p. 83) contrasted the shift in research in library science to information science as a difference in scope and a shift from a study of "methods for the acquisition, cataloguing, storage and dissemination" to an interest in how information is "created, used and communicated." While there will continue to be attempts to solve the puzzles or provide the recipes for solutions to questions within a specific aspect of library science (see, e.g., Schmidt, 1986), simple solutions that do not respond to the issue from multiple perspectives are no longer realistic. The pejorative definition of "ivory tower" is now hurled if responses are too simplistic to be used in the complex organizations of small libraries or large information centers.

Furthermore, there has been a major change in the perception of the product supplied by information studies. We have moved from thinking that we deal in warehousing books to identifying our business as the dissemination of information. The dominant image in the field of the book as an object in all of its beauty and the influence of this image on the available items in a card catalog, such as definitions of size in cm., illustrations, author birthdates, and two subject headings, now seems limiting and insufficient.

Authors, such as Cleveland (1982) and Wurman (1989), have attempted to define information. In so doing, some have merely substituted terms, but others have realized the need for greater complexity in the newer terms. Cronin and Gudim (1986, p. 87) subdivide the term *information* into three categories, "information, information technology, and intellectual technology." They advocate that all three, the interaction among the three categories, and the interaction of the three categories with productivity concepts must be an arena of research in the information professions. Their article is an example of an attempt to change from research about a simple concept to investigation of very complex phenomena.

The increased complexity of the domain of LIS is also evident from the fact that the quantity of available information has expanded the domain of research. Information is expandable, that is, it expands as it is used. For example, an author locates the answer to a question and uses it to make a point in several articles, a recording, or a speech. There are now so many industries involved in the process of adding value to information that librarians must also investigate the business of compressing it (Saracevic, 1986). Research and practice have expanded to include repackaging information in order to customize it for particular users.

The shift in research from a concentration on the book to human information use patterns is also evident in the practice of librarianship. The shift of assisting people to access what is *in* those books and all other media in a manner that fits with their use patterns is far more complex than pointing to the card catalog. The research of LIS faculty has shifted from creating bibliographies of all that has been written on a given subject to studying how information is transferred in various subsocieties, disciplines, and professions (Grover and Hale, 1988).

One final example of a more complex domain is evident in a curricular approach suggested by Greer (1987). The shift from courses such as "Bibliography of the Social Sciences" or "Children's Literature" to "Information Transfer in the Social Sciences" and "Information Transfer among Children" is not merely a cosmetic change. The information transfer approach centers on how information is created, diffused, and used among the people in a subset of society plus the utility of the available resources (all media) for the people carrying out different roles within that sector of society. This is obviously more complex than the show and tell of best sources.

How Does LIS Answer the "Why" Questions? Is the Issue of Cause-and-Effect within the More Complex Domain of LIS Also Reflected in the Research in the Discipline?

A strong area of research in library and information science has been the attempts to understand why some people use libraries and others do not, commonly called user studies. Early research centered only on the demographics of users and nonusers (Berelson, 1949). As the design of studies and the use of statistics became more sophisticated, and the ability to manipulate datasets in computers increased so that researchers could easily move from the use of chi-square to factor analysis, researchers began to realize that a nice, tidy, simple linear cause that effected library use was elusive. It could not be found. Now the aim of user and use studies is to examine interactions among many variables and to explain patterns of information use among people within a given social role.

How Do We Make Order Out of the Chaos of the Complex Domain of Information Studies? Have We Moved from a "One Best Way" of Doing Library Science and of Researching Issues to an Acceptance of Multiple and Heterarchical Systems?

Remember struggling to learn the Dewey Decimal system in high school only to discover the college library used something called "LC" to catalog its books! Each of these systems is an excellent example of a hierarchical system of putting an order into a domain. The past disputes among librarians about which is the superior system is an even greater indication of the search for a single, simple, orderly domain.

The way librarians have put order into the world of books has frustrated users in recent years. The system separates disciplines from each other rather than promotes the multidisciplinary access needed for the study of complex phenomena. As computerized catalogs are introduced, users want access to the information within the books. They are not satisfied with access to the address of the resource on the shelf. Public librarians report that people have been seen struggling over the use of automated catalogs and finally admit, "I can't make it work to tell me who won the World Series in 1948," or some such question not answerable in a traditional card catalog, but solvable from the books identified in the catalog. There is now talk about alternative means of ordering information in order to provide access from many different perspectives. In fact, some full-text databases can be searched from any major term therein. In short, the users want to access the information as well as the resources in the collections, and the information professionals are accepting that complex need.

Furthermore, librarians have shifted their thinking from wanting single organizations that possess all the materials users might ever want to use one day to organizations that help people access information electronically from around the globe. We must continue to move from private ownership to shared access (Hendrick, 1986), that is, multiple owners and multiple sources. Libraries and information centers will put new money into interlibrary loan and databases rather than in book and serial budgets. Practical research centers on how to transmit documents or answers most efficiently rather than on determining what items each library needs to have in its collection, or on how to share resources rather than on deciding what to purchase. As we accept the reality of shared resources, we will accept the challenge of international access.

Another interesting set of changes is emerging in the area of ordering the domain of library/information science. The organizational structure of libraries cannot remain hierarchical; it is no longer feasible to think of the expert at the head of the organization who knows it all. The move is toward heterarchical systems of organization, valuing and using the expertise of the student worker as well as the person with the advanced degree (Peters, 1987). The research related to the management of organizations is reflected in LIS literature. Practice is also shifting from "the one best way" of running libraries to alternative organizational configurations where power is indeed shared (Glesecke, forthcoming). There is a growing awareness that system-wide policies are counterproductive to individual outlets designed to customize services to a specific audience.

How Is Change Accommodated in the More Complex Domain?
Are We Still Explaining Anomalies in Our Domain Using
Simple Cause and Effect Methods and Answers?

In the 1950s, Downes (1954) articulated the four phases of bibliographic control: (1) identify records as they are created (national bibliography); (2) acquire these records in libraries; (3) list the location of these items; and (4) produce subject bibliographies so that libraries could exercise control over their resources. A significant amount of effort has been expended on the second, third, and fourth elements of bibliographic control, while achievement of the first one not only remains elusive, but is falling further behind because of the proliferation of publishing modes, for example, desktop and electronic publishing are among those being ignored or difficult to bring under effective control.

"Xerox advertises that 72 billion pieces of new information are created annually and that the amount of available information doubles every ten years" (Brinberg, 1981, p. 10). The changes in technology, in demands from users, in the publishing industry, and in the speed of distribution over fiber optics are so astounding and comprise a moving target for investigation. The excitement of hypermedia has just begun to affect research in fields from Shakespeare to geology. This multimedia change in the dissemination of research findings will strongly affect the LIS approach to resources and information technology.

As investigators change methods of research because of greater access to greater amounts and types of information from many more sources, the tasks of information professionals and the research about how information is used will change dramatically and become increasingly more complex.

Have Research Methods Shifted to Accommodate the Investigation of a More Complex Domain of Multiple Causality, Heterarchical Orders, and Morphogenetic Change?

Positivistic research methods do not always lead to truth; such methods are not always useful when studying a complex domain. Qualitative methods are more appropriate for some issues under study, and are no longer considered as "sloppy" dissertation research.

Dervin's (1977) early work urging that the context of reference questions influences what the user will accept as satisfactory is an example of a more complex approach to a LIS problem. As dissatisfaction with traditional methods increases, evaluation of services and programs might follow Lincoln and Guba's (1989) fourth generation evaluation model to ascertain and improve program effectiveness. The use of triangulation, or multiple methods, is evident in other fields and will undoubtedly gain greater acceptance in LIS as the realization that multiple perspectives yield greater insights into complex problems increases.

CONCLUSION

This chapter began with a reminder that a paradigm is the lens through which members of a discipline observe the phenomena in their areas of responsibility. Changing the lens shifts the methods chosen to accomplish the practice or research, redefines the values that influence practice and research, and alters the view of what is included in the domain of the discipline.

After a review of Schwartz and Ogilvy's (1979) definition of the emerging paradigm, a discussion of changes in LIS led to the conclusion that like other disciplines, a new lens is evident in library and information science. The shift in LIS is not as complete as in physics, but a shift is emerging. The changes in methodologies of study may be slower than alterations in discussions about the nature of the domain or the values of discipline.

What Are the Consequences and Implications of the Paradigmatic Shift Described in This Chapter for Researchers, Practitioners, and Educators in Library and Information Science?

First, researchers feel the most direct impact from the methodological changes of a paradigmatic shift. As the research puzzles within the discipline are defined as increasingly complex and less determinate, as the relation between cause and effect comes to be viewed as a mutual rather than a linear one, the research methodologies must account for multiple perspectives. Furthermore, less mechanical, more holographic metaphors will be needed to describe the patterns found during research. The use of multiple methodologies that respect perspective and search for patterns will, in turn, lead to new discoveries about the more complex domain.

As in other disciplines, the methodologies used by researchers in LIS have begun to shift from a positivistic commitment to neutrality to an inclusion of perspectives as a legitimate part of a study. The greater acceptance of quality ethnographic research will lead to further development of research techniques that address both the practical and theoretical needs of the discipline.

While it is now common for LIS students to enroll in a research methods course, and many such courses include a unit on qualitative methods, qualitative researchers are seldom identified as outstanding investigators in LIS. Many researchers will avoid the either/or debate encouraging students to use the methods that match the phenomena under study.

For the researcher, the implication of the shift will be the challenge of investigating more complex puzzles from multiple perspectives. Changes in what researchers define as legitimate problems and methods they use for study will probably cause a decrease in research productivity as new patterns are developed.

What are the implications of the paradigmatic shift in the practice of librarianship? The shift in values is more directly evident in practice than in research and education. The development of electronic networking has placed access to the world's recorded resources at any point in the world where there is a terminal and modem. The prestige of possessing the largest collection with the largest building, largest staff, and largest budget is diminishing in favor of a concern for users and their success in the use of information. This shift in value from a preoccupation with collections to a preoccupation with user needs is at the core of the paradigmatic shift. It influences all aspects of practice, education, research, policy, and perspective. It is a shift of perspective from standardization to customization, from large to small, from possession to utility, and from general to specific.

Customizing services to match the needs and interests of neighbors at the branch library service areas, creating individualized databases for a scholar or a community, repackaging information for administrators, integrating literature into the school teacher's lessons, and enabling people to search the literature themselves are all examples of developments in the practice of librarianship that reflect the paradigmatic shift.

Finally, the alteration in the definition of the domain of LIS most directly affects those who practice and research within the context of library education. The challenge of preparing students to work in more complex, less predictable environments demands wholesale revisions. The struggle is not to choose between simple alternatives (library science vs. information science), but rather to encourage heterarchical, integrated patterns of study. The impact of more complicated research methodologies and a reflection of value changes in the new paradigm of practice must be incorporated into curricula, courses, and educational structures if LIS educators are to keep pace with the paradigmatic shift in library and information science.

REFERENCES

Berelson, Bernard. *The Library's Public*. New York: Columbia University Press, 1949.
Brinberg, Herbert R. "Content, Not Quantity...," *Management Review* (1981), p. 10.
Cleveland, Harlan. "Information as a Resource," *The Futurist*, (December 1982), pp. 34–39.
Cronin, B. and M. Gudim. "Information and Productivity: A Review of Research," *International Journal of Information Management*, 6 (1986): 85–101.
Dervin, Brenda, "Useful Theory for Librarianship: Communication, Not Information," *Drexel Library Quarterly*, 13 (1977): 16–32.
Downes, Robert. "Bibliographic Control," *Library Trends*, 2 (April 1954): 498–508.
Glesecke, Joan. "Creativity and Innovation in an Organized Anarchy," *Journal of Library Administration*, forthcoming.
Greer, Roger C. "A Model for the Discipline of Information Science," in *Intellectual Foundations for Information Professionals*, edited by Herbert K. Achleitner. New York: Social Science Monographs, 1987 (dist. by Columbia University Press), pp. 3–25.
Grover, R. and M. Hale. "The Role of the Librarian in Faculty Research," *College & Research Libraries*, 49 (1988): 9–15.
Hendrick, Clyde. "The University Library in the Twenty-first Century," *College & Research Libraries*, 47 (1986): 127–131.
Karande, A.G. "A Review of Research in Library and Information Science," *Lucknow Librarian*, 18 (1986): 83–89.
Kuhn, Thomas. *The Structure of Scientific Revolutions*. Chicago, IL: University of Chicago, 1962.
Lincoln, Yvonna S. "Trouble in the Land: The Paradigm Revolution in the Academic Disciplines," in *Higher Education: Handbook of Theory and Research*. Vol. V, edited by John C. Smart. New York: Agathon Press, 1989, pp. 57–133.
_____ and Egon G. Guba. *Fourth Generation Evaluation*. Newbury Park, CA: Sage, 1989.
"MLS Accreditation Standards Revision Will Be Difficult," *American Libraries*, 21 (March 1990): 256–257.
Morgan, Gareth. *Images of Organization*. Newbury Park, CA.: Sage, 1986.
Peters, Tom. *Thriving on Chaos*. New York: Alfred A. Knopf, 1987.
Saracevic, Tefko. "Processes and Problems in Information Consolidation," *Information Processing and Management*, 22 (1986): 45–60.
Schmidt, Karen A. "Buying Good Pennyworths? A Review of the Literature of Acquisi-

tions in the Eighties," *Library Resources and Technical Services*, 30 (1986): 333–339.

Schwartz, Peter and James Ogilvy. *The Emergent Paradigm: Changing Patterns of Thought and Belief*. Menlo Park, CA.: Values and Lifestyles Program, 1979.

Wurman, Richard Saul. *Information Anxiety*. New York: Doubleday, 1989.

chapter twenty-seven

Becoming Critical: For a Theory of Purpose and Necessity in American Librarianship

Michael H. Harris
Masaru Itoga

After arguing that librarianship must be considered a mediating profession and not a separate discipline, the authors suggest that the most productive route to a theoretical foundation for research in library and information science is the critical and opportunistic utilization of promising paradigm candidates in the social, or human, sciences. Then the authors proceed to outline what they feel to be the most promising of these paradigm candidates, and point to the implications of the new research on "cultural production" for research in library and information science. Finally, the authors present a case for a qualified methodological pluralism in the prosecution of research in library and information science.

The editors of this volume charged us with the responsibility of reflecting on options, alternatives, and strategies for exploiting various methods and designs in a range of epistemological contexts as a basis of extending and improving library and information science (LIS) research. And since, unlike several other contributors to this volume, we do not think that librarianship can or should think of itself as a discipline, we intend to proceed by presenting what might be considered a theoretical intervention designed to exploit paradigm candidates (drawn mostly from social or, as they are now commonly called, the "human sciences") that have the potential for framing research problems in a way that will allow us to develop a critical theoretical understanding of library service in the United States.

This choice of approach reflects our conviction that *library science* does not represent a separate discipline, but rather a mediating profession dependent upon knowledge intelligently and opportunistically drawn from the acknowledged disciplines, especially the social sciences (Harris, 1986a, 1986b, 1986c). Library research will continue its mindless and incestuous wanderings within the close confines of *library science,* until we become alert to, and prepared to draw upon, theoretical and methodological developments in the social sciences which promise to contribute to the solution of problems specific to librarianship in the United States. "The skilled problem-solver," Barnes (1982, p. 50) points out, "sees the themes of solved problems in those he seeks to solve." We believe that research on American librarianship will advance only to the extent that librarians broaden their knowledge of the social sciences so that they might proceed analogically from concrete problem solutions in the social sciences to unsolved problems in library science. This project assumes, somewhat hesitantly, that the library community is at least slightly interested in developing a critical and substantive understanding of what libraries do in the much broader context of why libraries matter.

This project also records our belief that the members of the library profession are on the brink of a new era that will witness the emergence of the "librarian–researcher" in the context of the post-industrial era, similar to a parallel emergence of the "teacher–researcher" in education (Carr and Kemis, 1986). This era in our history finds librarians entwined in an environment of intense intellectual and social ferment, and ever larger numbers of practicing librarians appear willing, indeed driven, to engage in critical and systematic investigation of library service in the face of the dramatic change and challenge so characteristic of the post-industrial era. The librarian–researcher movement first became visible among academic librarians, with attention initially focused on questions related to bibliographic instruction. It has become quite common to encounter criticisms of the movement voiced by the research establishment with the principal theme being the mistaken conclusion that the movement's motives do not go beyond the desire of academic librarians to meet the more rigorous publication requirements concomitant with faculty status in academic libraries. A more friendly conclusion would be that practicing librarians have deeper, more critical, motives for joining the "librarian–researcher movement."

Now, admittedly, at this early stage, the "librarian–researcher" movement is decidedly pragmatic and unsophisticated. But clearly, the participants in the movement are capable of overcoming the methodological shortcomings of their work. More problematical is the lack of theory that might provide direction and critical insight to the movement. What follows constitutes our reflections on the most fruitful theoretical framework for the "librarian–researcher" to consider in his or her attempt to see beyond the surface characteristics of library work and discover the structural and functional dynamics of library service in the United States. Such knowledge, once acquired, will facilitate collective and dialectical conversation among library professionals about the role of the library within the broad cultural, political, and social contexts of library service in America. Only then will librarians be capable of collectively writing their own job descriptions in the context of a critical understanding of the role of the library in American life.

The task of discovering an interdisciplinary, and critical, theoretical framework for the investigation of library problems is not easy. Since the late 1950s we have witnessed a concerted attack on dominant paradigms in the human sciences, then a rejection of earlier theoretical formulations, and finally a flowering of "Grand Theory" designed to articulate more fruitful, elegant, and explanatory social theory (Skinner, 1985). This ferment in the human sciences has created a paradigm chaos that has opened the door for an intense interdisciplinary reexamination of the theoretical foundations of the human sciences and the results, while exciting, are also incredibly complex (Bernstein, 1983; Harris, 1986a, 1986c; Skinner, 1985).

This development is further complicated by the genuinely interdisciplinary nature of the search for grand theory. As Geertz (1983, pp. 7-8, 24) notes, we are currently witnessing an era of "blurred genres" that is leading to a considerable realignment "in scholarly affinities" and that the lines "grouping scholars together into intellectual communities . . . are these days running at some highly eccentric angles." This reorientation, combined with a dramatic increase in empirical research, has led some of the world's most distinguished social theorists to publish massive overviews designed to map the new theoretical foundations of the human sciences (for example, see Coleman, 1990; Giddens, 1984; Habermas, 1984, 1989; Runciman, 1989; and Unger, 1987a, 1987b).

It is vital that librarians discover ways to break out of their own provincial straightjacket and make optimum use of these new theoretical breakthroughs in the social sciences. What must be avoided are quick salutes to faddish developments; the focus must be on the intelligent use of paradigm candidates that will support librarians in their pursuit of a critical understanding of the structural and functional characteristics of libraries, while at the same time allowing librarians to contribute to the corpus of knowledge about cultural institutions in general. In this endeavor librarians can find some guidance in the late-arriving, but useful, attempts at translating promising theoretical developments in the human sciences for the library profession (see, for example, Beagle, 1988; Benediktsson, 1989; Grover and Glazier, 1986; Harris, 1986b; and Olaisen, 1985).

But such work is uneven, and many promising developments have yet to garner even the slightest amount of attention. As a result, it might be best for librarians to attempt to focus their attempts at intelligent borrowing from the human sciences by utilizing current knowledge of library service in the United States toward directing the search for useful paradigm candidates. Such an approach seems both appropriate and possible. But to do so librarians must abandon the ingenuous idea that somehow libraries operate in a vacuum, free from the influence of political, economic, and social considerations (Carrigan and Harris,

1990). What is called for is attention to the political economy of library service in the United States; that is, the dynamic interdependence among the state, the economy, and the society at large.

The librarian–researcher can find significant clues to the political economy of libraries in the results of countless empirical studies of libraries. What becomes apparent as one searches for the way in which librarians fit into this nexus among state, economy, and society, is that libraries have always been viewed as public investments in civic virtue (Garrison, 1979; Harris, 1976). Study after study confirms the fact that libraries were founded, and have enjoyed continued support in America, as a result of the conviction that there was a connection between knowledge and virtue. Huge amounts of public treasure have been expended in an attempt to establish libraries that would contribute to the enlightenment of the American people and to the preparation of individual Americans for enlightened citizenship. From the initial phases of library development to the present, the idea of civic virtue has constituted an intensely contested concept, and it is in the nature of the contest to define and thus create the idea of civic virtue that one must look for clues about the most productive theoretical paths to follow in our current search for an interdisciplinary theoretical foundation for a critical librarianship.

Indeed, any explanation of the nature of library service must attend to the constantly evolving debate about the proper deployment of libraries and their resources in the service of civic virtue. We must attend to the changing definitions of civic virtue, especially as articulated by the State, and we must measure the impact of those changing conceptions upon the definition of the role of libraries in a democratic and capitalist society (for the 18th-century debate on civic virtue, see Pocock, 1971, 1985; and Hanson, 1985; for the contemporary debate on this matter, see Barber, 1984; Elkin, 1987; Janowitz, 1983; and Sullivan, 1986). In doing so we can discover that the American system of libraries was deliberately designed with a broadly cultural purpose of producing and reproducing the dominant social ideology in printed form, and that the library's current structural and functional characteristics are determined by its definition as an institution contrived to consume, preserve, transmit, and reproduce this dominant ideology in printed form (Harris, 1986c).

If this understanding is correct, and it is partially supported by the empirical research in the field, then we can most fruitfully direct our attention at that body of interdisciplinary research which deals productively with the subject of the production and distribution of cultural capital for ideological purposes. In what follows, we will attempt to concisely map the most promising of that research as one way of encouraging librarian researchers to break out of the narrow theoretical confines of our own research perspective.

In an earlier paper Harris (1986c) attempted to describe and assess a broadly interdisciplinary project that appeared to hold great promise for creating a paradigm of considerable usefulness in the construction and prosecution of a wide range of empirical investigations designed to further our project of constructing a knowledge base that will "explain" the library system in the United States.

That interdisciplinary project continues apace, and its value as a paradigm model for librarians is even more apparent at this point in time. Focusing as it does on the cultural reproduction of the dominant ideology in the United States, this interdisciplinary project has produced important findings which can be summarized concisely as follows. First, a wide range of studies have demonstrated the extent to which the State is engaged in the production and reproduction of the relations of production in modern capitalistic society (for this literature, see Alford and Friedland, 1985; Carnoy, 1984; Evans, Rueschemeyer, and Skocpol, 1985; Friedman, 1987; Jessop, 1982; and for a critique, Van den Berg, 1988).

We can also see how this process of production and reproduction is affected primarily through ideological means, and we now have a detailed map of the institutional sites responsible for creating, refining, disseminating, and preserving the hegemonic ideology. This work, which has great relevance for librarians, is founded on the insights of the Italian theorist Antonio Gramsci who undertook a thorough theoretical investigation of the capitalist state, which he defined as "the entire complex of practical activities with which the ruling class not only justifies and maintains its dominance, but manages to win the active consent of those over whom it rules" (Gramsci, 1971, p. 224). Gramsci concluded that the genius of the capitalist system rested in its ability to impose upon society its "ideological hegemony," which is the "intellectual and moral leadership of the ruling class objectified and exercised through institutions of 'civil society';" that is, the ensemble of educational, religious, mass media, and cultural institutions (on Gramsci, see Adamson, 1980; Boggs, 1984; Femia, 1981; Hall, 1982; Lears, 1985).

A vast array of scholars, working in many disciplines, have utilized Gramsci's insight in a project designed to illustrate the ways in which ideological hegemony is created and reproduced. Much of this work begins with Raymond Williams' (1980, pp. 38–39) insight that "we can only understand an effective and dominant culture if we understand the real social process on which it depends: I mean the process of incorporation." For Williams, this "process of incorporation" is founded upon an institutional practice he refers to as the "selective tradition," which is the way "in which from a whole possible area of past and present, certain meanings and practices are chosen for emphasis, certain other meanings and practices are neglected and excluded" (Ibid., p. 39). This selective tradition has proven to be a topic of considerable interest to students of ideological hegemony, and has proven of special interest to those interested in the creation of the literary canon and the way in which the literary canon empowers certain groups in society and systematically denies power to others (Booth, 1988; Smith, 1988; Graff, 1987; Merod, 1987; Scholes, 1989; Siebers, 1988). Increasingly, this research tradition has focused on the linkages between political and economic power and the kinds of knowledge made available, or withheld, from the people by the very agents who ostensibly are dedicated to ensuring the free and unobstructed flow of information in a democratic society.

This research trajectory has also revealed the extent to which the ideological apparatus of the United States is splintered into a number of ideological regions, and that within each of these regions one can distinguish between ideological sites by identifying the taste cultures they privilege (Kellner, 1989; Gans, 1974). Further, this research reveals the extent to which power among the various components of the ideological apparatus is asymmetrically distributed, with certain institutional sites charged with the responsibility of "creating" the dominant culture, while others are limited to playing a more marginal role of simply transmitting or preserving the dominant effective culture (Angus and Jhally, 1989; Lazere, 1987).

We have also gained considerable insight into the way in which the information professionals who staff these ideological institutions can maintain a sense of strict neutrality while participating in this ideological project. We can now see the ways in which organizing frames, subsidized information, and dependence on ideology-producing institutions allow information professionals to blink critical professional issues and focus instead on the daily routine of selecting the news, or the curriculum content, or the books (for recent views of information professionals and their asymmetrical powers, see Abbott, 1988; Freidson, 1986; Derber, Schwartz, and Magrass, 1990; and Murkerji, 1989).

Finally, thanks to the theoretical and empirical work of Bourdieu (1977a, 1977b, 1984; and Bourdieu and Passeron, 1977) we have a much clearer picture of the structure and function of the high culture realm of ideological production, a realm in which libraries appear to be embedded (Harris, 1986c). From this work we can gain a precise picture of the way in which this cultural realm is stratified. We see the extent to which these institutions are asymmetrically empowered, with certain culture-producing institutions literally dictating, albeit subtly through reviews, anthologies, and reading lists, the cultural content of those institutions that are responsible for the simple transmission and preservation of the canon in printed form. We also understand a great deal more about how this process not only produces and reproduces the dominant ideology, but also produces and reproduces its audience (for an overview of this work, see Zolberg, 1990). We can also see how our dedication to high culture in printed form actually denies access to library resources to certain classes in the society.

The conclusion that is relentlessly pressing forward is the fact that the library is an institution embedded in a stratified ensemble of institutions functioning in the high cultural region, an ensemble of institutions dedicated to the creation, transmission, and reproduction of the hegemonic ideology. Such a conclusion challenges the "apolitical" conception of the library so commonly held by library professionals, and strips the library of the ethical and political innocence attributed to it by library apologists. (For examples of the emerging study of ideology, see Agger, 1989; Boudon, 1989; Castoriadis, 1987; Johnson, 1987; McLellan, 1986; Ricoeur, 1986; Thompson, 1984.)

At this point it would seem appropriate to comment on the question of pluralism in paradigm selection. Many scholars in the social sciences generally, and a few in library and information science (Bergen, 1987; Olaisen, 1985), would insist that the adoption of a single promising paradigm from the social sciences is unwise, and what is required is a freewheeling and pluralistic attention to the wide range of contemporary candidates for paradigm status in the social sciences. However, it is our contention that such an approach would only contribute to a proliferation of superficial forays into the paradigm wars in the social sciences, and would not, given the limited resources of library and information science, contribute much to the resolution of the problem of a lack of theory to guide our empirical work. Instead, we would argue that the profession would be well advised to seek paradigm candidates that initially seem to allow for the assimilation of the characteristics, as currently understood, of library service in the United States. It is our contention that the "cultural reproduction" theory is the only one of those theories currently emergent in the social sciences that promises such possibilities. Now, if deductive tests of the theory, as imaginatively applied to problems specific to library service, fail to generate persuasive explanations, then, of course, we should call for the introduction of alternative paradigms (Dervin and Nilan, 1986).

Our charge in this chapter was to attend explicitly to paradigm or theory building. But we hasten to point out that we are advocates of methodological pluralism. That is, once appropriate theoretical models have been selected to deductively generate research hypotheses, we would endorse the imaginative and pluralistic use of the widest possible range of methods to test those deductive hypotheses. Thus, while we are convinced that we should privilege the "cultural production" paradigm as a theoretical frame for our work, we are far less adamant about the choice of methods to implement tests of the theory. All we would insist upon is the need for methods selection that would provide us with critical explanations and tests of the theory, and not just simple nonevaluative descriptions of unrelated phenomenon (for support for methodological pluralism, see for instance, Bredo and Feinberg, 1982; Fay, 1987; Feinberg, 1983; Light, Singer, and Willett, 1990; McCumber, 1989; Roth, 1987).

In an earlier essay, Harris provided a list of postulates that might guide empirical research within this emerging paradigm of cultural reproduction, postulates pointing from the broader theory to specific questions in library and information service (Harris, 1986c; see also Itoga, 1985). But we want to conclude this chapter by reemphasizing the point that what is needed is theory that will foster the objective of becoming critical. We do not require "scientific" theories designed to foster the instrumental manipulation of the natural world, but rather critical theories designed to emancipate and enlighten; critical theories that will alert librarians to the ideological frame surrounding library service (on critical theory, see, Fay, 1987; Forester, 1985; Geuss, 1981; Held, 1980; and Wolfe, 1989). Once such a theoretical knowledge is in place, the librarian-researcher will be able to undertake emancipatory work that is conscious of the contradictions inherent in the delivery of "free library service" in a capitalist society. Such theory will help unmask the naive idea that books in libraries simply reflect the best that has been thought and written in Western society, and will instead demonstrate the way in which libraries and their contents have always been linked "to the power and privilege of certain classes to represent the world through books in ways that serve their interests" (Carey, 1984, p. 108; and Harris, 1988). And finally, such theory will allow librarians to constructively and critically direct their attention to the essential foundations of professional authority in library and information science.

REFERENCES

Abbott, A. *The System of Professions: An Essay on the Division of Labor.* Chicago, IL: University of Chicago Press, 1988.

Adamson, W. L. *Hegemony and Revolution: Antonio Gramsci's Political and Cultural Theory.* Berkeley, CA: University of California Press, 1980.

Agger, B. *Fast Capitalism: A Critical Theory of Significance.* Urbana, IL: University of Illinois Press, 1989.

Alford, R.R. and R. Friedland. *Powers of Theory: Capitalism, the State, and Democracy.* Cambridge, England: Cambridge University Press, 1985.

Angus, I. and S. Jhally, Eds. *Cultural Politics in Contemporary America.* New York: Routledge, 1989.

Barber, B. *Stong Democracy: Participatory Politics for a New Age.* Berkeley, CA: University of California, 1984.

Barnes, B. *T.S. Kuhn and Social Science.* New York: Columbia University Press, 1982.

Beagle, D. "Libraries and the 'Implicate Order': A Contextual Approach to Theory," *Libri,* 38 (1988): 26–44.

Benediktsson, D. "Hermenuetics: Dimensions toward LIS Thinking," *Library & Information Science Research,* 11 (1989): 201–34.

Bergen, D. "Bergen on Harris," *Library & Information Science Research,* 9 (1987): 71–75.

Bernstein, R. J. *Beyond Objectivism and Relativism: Science, Hermenuetics, and Praxis.* Philidelphia, PA: University of Pennsylvania Press, 1983.

Boggs, C. *The Two Revolutions: Gramsci and the Dilemmas of Western Marxism.* Boston, MA: South End Press, 1984.

Booth, C. W. *The Company We Keep: An Ethics of Fiction.* Berkeley, CA: University of California Press, 1988.

Boudon, R. *The Analysis of Ideology* (M. Slater, Trans.). Chicago, IL: University of Chicago Press, 1989.

Bourdieu, P. "Cultural Reproduction and Social Reproduction," in *Power and Ideology in Education,* edited by J. Karabel and A. Halsey. New York: Oxford University Press, 1977a, pp. 487–510.

———. *Outline of a Theory of Practice.* Cambridge, England: Cambridge University Press, 1977b.

———. *Distinction: A Social Critique of the Judgement of Taste.* Cambridge, MA: Harvard University Press, 1984.

——— and J.C. Passeron. *Reproduction in Education, Society, and Culture.* London, England: Sage, 1977.

Bredo, E. and W. Feinberg, Eds. *Knowledge and Values in Social and Educational Research.* Philadelphia, PA: Temple University Press, 1982.

Carey, J.W. "The Paradox of the Book," *Library Trends,* 33 (1984): 103–113.

Carnoy, M. *The State and Political Theory.* Princeton, NJ: Princeton University Press, 1984.

Carr, W. and S. Kemmis. *Becoming Critical: Education, Knowledge and Action Research.* London, England: Falmer Press, 1986.

Carrigan, D. and M.H. Harris. "The President and Library Policy," in *Politics and the Support of Libraries,* edited by E.J. Josey and K. Shearer. New York: Neal-Schuman, 1990, in press.

Castoriadis, C. *The Imaginary Institution of Society* (K. Blamey, Trans.). Cambridge, MA: MIT Press, 1987.

Coleman, J. S. *Foundations of Social Theory.* Cambridge. MA: Harvard University Press, 1990.

Derber, C., W.A. Schwartz, and Y. Magrass. *Power in the Highest Degree: Professionals and the Rise of a New Manderin Order.* New York: Oxford University Press, 1990.

Dervin, B. and M. Nilan. "Information Needs and Uses," in *Annual Review of Information Science and Technology,* vol. 21. White Plains, NY: Knowledge Industry Publications, Inc., 1986, pp. 3–33.

Elkin, S.L. *City and Regime in the American Republic.* Chicago, IL: University of Chicago Press, 1987.

Evans, Peter R., D. Rueschemeyer, and T. Skocpol, Ed. *Bringing the State Back In.* Cambridge, England: Cambridge University Press, 1985.

Fay, B. *Critical Social Science.* Cornell, NY: Cornell University Press, 1987.

Feinberg, W. *Understanding Education: Toward a Reconstruction of Educational Inquiry.* Cambridge, England: Cambridge University Press, 1983.

Femia, J.V. *Gramsci's Political Thought: Hegemony, Consciousness and the Revolutionary Process.* New York: Oxford University Press, 1981.

Forester, T., Ed. *Critical Theory and Public Life.* Cambridge, MA: MIT Press, 1985.

Freidson, E. *Professional Powers: A Study of the Institutionalization of Formal Knowledge.* Chicago, IL: University of Chicago Press, 1986.

Friedman, J. *Planning in the Public Domain: From Knowledge to Action.* Princeton, NJ: Princeton University Press, 1987.

Gans, H. *Popular Culture and High Culture: An Analysis and Evaluation of Taste.* New York: Basic Books, 1974.

Garrison, D. *Apostles of Culture.* New York: Free Press, 1979.

Geertz, C. *Local Knowledge: Further Essays in Interpretive Anthropology.* New York: Basic Books, 1983.

Geuss, R. *The Idea of a Critical Theory: Habermas and the Frankfurt School.* Cambridge, England: Cambridge University Press, 1981.

Giddens, A. *The Constitution of Society.* Berkeley, CA: University of California Press, 1984.

Graff, G. *Professing Literature: An Institutional History.* Chicago, IL: University of Chicago Press, 1987.
Gramsci, A. *Prison Notebooks* (trans.). New York: International Publications Co., 1971.
Grover, R. and J. Glazier. "A Proposed Taxonomy of Theory: A Conceptual Framework for Theory Building in Library and Information Science," *Library & Information Science Research,* 8 (1986): 227–242.
Habermas, J. *The Theory of Communicative Action: Reason and the Rationalization of Society* (T. McCarthy, Trans.). Boston, MA: Beacon Press, 1984.
———. *The Theory of Communicative Action: Lifeworld and System.* Boston, MA: Beacon Press, 1989.
Hall, S. "The Rediscovery of 'Ideology': Return of the Repressed in Media Studies," in *Culture, Society and the Media,* edited by M. Gurevitch. London, England: Methuen, 1982, pp. 56–190.
Hanson, R.L. *The Democratic Imagination in America.* Princeton, NJ: Princeton University Press, 1988.
Harris, M.H. "Portrait in Paradox: Commitment and Ambivalence in American Librarianship," *Libri,* 26 (1976): 281–301.
———. "The Dialectic of Defeat: Antinomies in Research in Library and Information Science," *Library Trends,* 34 (1986a): 515–531.
———. "Review of Research in Librarianship," *Library & Information Science Research,* 8 (1986b): 108–112.
———. "State, Class and Cultural Reproduction: Toward a Theory of Library Service in the United States," in *Advances in Librarianship.* Vol. 14. New York: Academic Press, 1986c, pp. 211–252.
———. "Books and Power: New Directions in the History of the Book." A paper presented at the ALISE annual meeting, 1988 (unpublished).
Held, D. *Introduction to Critical Theory.* Berkeley, CA: University of California Press, 1980.
Itoga, M. "The Relation between Public Library Use and Cultural Activities," *Library and Information Science* (Tokyo), 23 (1985): 41–61.
Janowitz, M. *The Reconstruction of Patriotism: Education for Civic Consciousness.* Chicago: University of Chicago Press, 1983.
Jessop, B. *The Capitalist State: Marxist Theories and Methods.* New York: New York University Press, 1982.
Johnson, Richard. "What Is Cultural Studies Anyway?," *Social Text,* 6 (1987): 38–80.
Kellner, D. *Critical Theory, Marxism, and Modernity.* Baltimore, MD: Johns Hopkins, 1989.
Lazere, D., Ed. *American Media and Mass Culture: Left Perspectives.* Berkeley, CA: University of California Press, 1987.
Lears, T.J. "The Concept of Cultural Hegemony: Problems and Possibilities," *American Historical Review,* 90 (1985): 567–593.
Light, R. J., J.D. Singer, and J.B. Willett. *By Design: Planning Research on Higher Education.* Cambridge, MA: Harvard University Press, 1990.
McCumber, J. *Poetic Interaction: Language, Freedom and Reason.* Chicago, IL: University of Chicago Press, 1989.
McLellan, David. *Ideology.* Minneapolis, MN: University of Minnesota Press, 1986.

Merod, J. *The Political Responsibility of the Critic.* Ithaca, NY: Cornell University Press, 1987.
Murkerji, C. *A Fragile Power: Scientists and the State.* Princeton, NJ: Princeton University Press, 1989.
Olaisen, J.L. "Alternative Paradigms in Library Science," *Libri*, 35 (1985): 129–150.
Pocock, J.G.A. *Politics, Language, and Time: Essays on Political Thought and History.* New York: Atheneum, 1971.
──────. *Virtue, Commerce and History.* Cambridge, England: Cambridge University Press, 1985.
Ricoeur, P. *Lectures on Ideology and Utopia.* New York: Columbia University Press, 1986.
Roth, P.A. *Meaning and Method in the Social Sciences: A Case for Methodological Pluralism.* Ithaca, NY: Cornell University Press, 1987.
Runciman, W.G. *A Treatise on Social Theory: Substantive Social Theory.* Cambridge, England: Cambridge University Press, 1989.
Scholes, R. *Protocols of Reading.* New Haven, CT: Yale University Press, 1989.
Siebers, T. *The Ethics of Reading.* Ithaca, NY: Cornell University Press, 1988.
Skinner, Q. Ed. *The Return of Grand Theory in the Human Sciences.* Cambridge, England: Cambridge University Press, 1985.
Smith, B.H. *Contingencies of Value: Alternative Perspectives for Critical Theory.* Cambridge, MA: Harvard University Press, 1988.
Sullivan, W.M. *Reconstructing Public Philosophy.* Berkeley, CA: University of California Press, 1986.
Thompson, J. B. *Studies in the Theory of Ideology.* Berkeley, CA: University of California Press, 1984.
Unger, R.M. *False Necessity: Anti-necessitarian Social Theory in the Service of Radical Democracy.* Cambridge, England: Cambridge University Press, 1987a.
──────. *Social Theory: Its Situation and Its Task.* Cambridge, England: Cambridge University Press, 1987b.
Van den Berg, A. *Immanent Utopia: From Marxism of the State to the State of Marxism.* Princeton, NJ: Princeton University Press, 1988.
Williams, Raymond. *Problems in Materialism and Culture: Selected Essays.* London, England: Routledge, Chapman and Hall, 1980.
Wolfe, A. *Whose Keeper? Social Science and Moral Obligation.* Berkeley, CA: University of California Press, 1989.
Zolberg, V.L. *Constructing a Sociology of the Arts.* Cambridge, England: Cambridge University Press, 1990.

chapter twenty-eight

Research, Theory, and the Practice of LIS

Beverly P. Lynch

Research in library and information science has its roots in library practice. The development of theory and the design of research came only after the profession was well established. Library and information science continues to have its base in practice, although some of the authors in this book would wish otherwise. The ongoing development of theory and the design of research cannot be divorced from the profession as it is practiced.

Pierce Butler (1951) outlined three separate phases in the development of the field of librarianship. The first phase, beginning in the 1850s, found librarians becoming increasingly aware of the scholarly responsibilities associated with their work. In Butler's terms, the librarian became a bookman, thinking less of janitorial and custodial duties and more of the intellectual and literary challenges and responsibilities. The second phase, beginning roughly in the 1870s, emerged when American librarians identified the technical systems important to the development of the library. Librarians began to recognize that a book stock becomes a library only when that stock is systematically arranged, conveniently stored, and completely inventoried. The librarian consequently became a technician as well as a bookman. In the last phase, according to Butler, by the early 1920s, librarians became aware of their cultural environment. Only after these three phases of development in library practice were completed did theory and philosophy emerge. Theory followed practice; it did not lead practice.

Butler outlined his view of the development of librarianship in the early 1950s, before the new computer technologies began to emerge and to influence the practice of librarianship. The current information and technological age would add several new phases to Butler's list.

The directors of major academic and public libraries have their base in practice and have always been interested in economical ways of organizing the enterprise and the operations. They have looked to the management literature for their ideas and inspirations. The management literature continues to influence the organization and design of libraries. When the new technical developments based in computing emerged, library managers were quick to see the possibilities. Ever interested in efficient and economical operations, library managers incorporated computer technologies into their technical services operations; some managers were more successful in the beginning than were others.

There were many early efforts to incorporate the computer into libraries (Schultheiss, Culbertson, and Heiliger, 1962). The practitioners who designed the early systems taught themselves how to do so. They reflected about the resulting efficiencies in the technical processing operations that would be forthcoming. As computing operations in libraries became more sophisticated and more extensive, libraries sought to hire people with knowledge, skills, and abilities to extend their early efforts. Because the traditional source of supply, the Graduate Schools of Library and Information Science, could not provide the people with the background libraries needed, the major libraries looked elsewhere. Actually, until well into the 1970s, few people were educated or trained in the technologies the libraries needed. As a result, many people learned by doing. The professional societies, state and regional associations, vendors, and the emerging library networks offered workshops and short training courses that enabled many librarians to acquire new computing skills.

As the practitioners continued to incorporate new technologies, the Graduate Schools of Library and Information Science followed their lead and began to incorporate those aspects of the technology which seemed appropriate into their curriculum. Computer programming became an entrance requirement in some schools. Other schools acknowledged the importance of the emerging information science, changed their names, appointed faculty members from other disciplines, and adapted their curricula to incorporate the new issues and challenges. The point here is that library practice led the way in terms of incorporating new technologies into the field. Theory and research in information systems followed; they did not lead.

Many of the previous chapters in this book synthesize the response of library researchers to the inclusion of information science under the purview of librarianship. Some see (Hale, Chapter 26) a shift in paradigm. While it is too early to describe what is occurring as a paradigm shift, it certainly is true that the field now is thinking in new ways. It also is true that the incorporation of new technologies into library operations has brought about a need for a new understanding of how people use libraries and the systems maintained by libraries. This need emanates from the practitioner's concern, shaped as it has been in the past by the quest for efficient and economical designs of library operations. How people seek information is the most fundamental theoretical and overarching issue. This issue drives much of the ongoing research in the field today (Wiberley and Jones, 1989; Sievert and Sievert, 1989).

RESEARCH AGENDAS

During the past several years the profession has produced a number of research agendas, each hammered out in meetings of experts seeking to forge a consensus on what the profession needs to know (e.g., "ACRL Research Agenda," 1990; *Rethinking the Library in the Information Age,*, 1988–1989; *Research Questions of Interest to ARL*, 1987; Council on Library Resources, 1985). While there always is some dissatisfaction in the way these lists are generated (Curran, Chapter 3) agendas serve a useful purpose. They assist funding agencies in their decision making and provide the profession with an opportunity to examine current research and assess whether it is meaningful or useful (*Academic Libraries: Research Perspectives*, 1990).

Altman (Chapter 9) evaluates the three major sources of funding available to library and information science researchers. She concludes that researchers who have their base in other fields have been more successful in tapping these funds than have been the researchers working directly in library and information science. Despite the development of major research agendas, she argues that there is no consensus within the field about what problems to study and what methods to use. It is this lack of consensus, in Altman's view, that has led to the decline in support for research generated by library and information science.

Lack of consensus is a serious matter, for it does affect directly the kinds of proposals which are supported by outside funding agencies. Lack of consensus is to be expected, however, in a field undergoing extraordinary change in deciding (1) how it looks at what it does, and (2) what it wants to know about how to do its work better—more effectively and efficiently.

Using Hernon's categories of research (Chapter 1) most research agendas forged in the field emphasize the interest of the profession in action research, that is in investigations designed to assist in local decision making. What is needed in order to make the action research designs meaningful is a consideration of the profession's agendas, a review of those agendas in the context of theory construction and previous research, and the articulation of a research agenda in terms of Hernon's other research categories—basic research and applied research.

Action research is fine, as far as it goes, for the profession must investigate problems in order to make informed decisions. For the profession to be sustained and enhanced, however, basic research leading to the discovery of knowledge and to the construction of theory is essential. Applied research, that is, those investigations designed to validate theory and to test and confirm theory, also is important. In addition to undertaking basic and applied research, we must communicate the results of that research to the field. Much of the research in library and information science remains buried in dissertations or formal research reports. The practitioner seldom goes into such literature. What we have often is not a failure to translate research results adequately into the terms of practice.

Rather, there is a failure to translate them at all. McClure (Chapter 20) assesses the problem well and poses some strategies which will be useful.

Hewitt (Chapter 12) offers excellent strategies to improve the value of action research. He comments on the 175 questionnaires and surveys received in one year by the Library of the University of North Carolina at Chapel Hill. One questionnaire or survey arrives every other day in most libraries which are members of the Association of Research Libraries. While some libraries are more generous than others in their response to this onslaught—and North Carolina at Chapel Hill is one of these—the burden suggests that action research needs some review.

Hewitt offers good advice to the many practitioners, students, and faculty working in the library and information science (LIS): The first requirement when confronting any research question is to undertake a literature review. Somehow, most people engaged in action research assume they are among the first people to confront the particular problem. It rarely occurs to them that the problem may have already been addressed by someone else *and* written about. The professional conducting a survey suspects that another agency may have already confronted the problem and found a solution. That the literature already may provide an answer often is not considered.

The lack of interest in or respect for the literature of the field is a phenomenon that few understand. The disdain some members of the profession have for action research carried out by able practitioners is apparent in various chapters in this book (Van House, Chapter 7; Zweizig, Chapter 16). Action research will continue as an integral component of the research in the field. Rather than rail against it, the field must seek to enhance and improve it. Hewitt (Chapter 12), Daniel (Chapter 10), and McClure (Chapter 20) offer good advice on just how we might do that.

Library and information science, like all professions, depends upon, in ways the practitioners often do not acknowledge or are not aware of, the many researchers who are engaged in the more *basic* research questions. In a provocative quotation, Hewitt (Chapter 12, p. 165) offers legitimate claim for research:

> There must be one final caveat regarding the intrusion of research into the world of practice in a prominent way. No less a figure than Alfred North Whitehead has observed:
>
> It is a profoundly erroneous truism, repeated by all copy books and by eminent people when they are making speeches, that we should cultivate the habit of thinking about what we are doing. The precise opposite is the case. Civilization advances by extending the number of important operations which we can perform without thinking about them.

Librarianship has developed into an extraordinary field because practitioners have worked to answer questions systematically, through methods that enable action research to be designed and executed. Once there is consensus on the answer to a question, the matter is routinized and absorbed into practice, and the important operations carried out without thinking about them.

RESEARCH QUESTIONS

Beyond the several research agendas which pose questions generally emanating from practice, the field has not agreed upon the significant questions guiding the development of theory or the design of basic research. There are some positive developments in this area, however. For example, research in the patterns of information-seeking behaviors and the questions related to the man/machine interface are guiding the field into new ways of thinking about what it does. While much remains to be done and there is much to learn, the research questions being asked, in the minds of many researchers and practitioners, are the right ones.

While the profession has, as an objective, service to patrons and clientele, only recently, for example, has the profession begun to absorb the implications of some of the early work on patterns of information-seeking behavior. How the profession will respond to results that contradict current practice or professional wisdom remains to be seen.

The results of investigations can be disquieting. Those studies which contradict professional values or political realities often are ignored until further work reinforces the findings, or the results are repackaged and synthesized in the popular literature. Getz's (1980) work on the economics of the public library has virtually been ignored. A good piece of research, it projected in economic terms the benefits of closing branches in a large public library system. The work of Kent et al. (1979) on the circulation of materials in a major research library was criticized severely on all sorts of grounds, because it attacked directly the value of the materials in the collections of a major research library that were rarely used. The questions guiding such research are essential to furthering the development of theory and to influencing practice. Similar questions, difficult to identify and disconcerting to the practitioner, must guide research in the field.

RESEARCH METHODOLOGY

The continuing improvements in the methodologies employed in investigations conducted in LIS are gratifying. While there is always room for further improvements, the quality of the research designs and methodologies, and their implementation, is better now than it was a decade or two ago. Most researchers and practitioners alike believe that the improvements will continue.

Of course, there are major disagreements over what is the appropriate method to use. Social science methodologies, emphasizing surveys and basic descriptive statistical analyses, currently are the most fashionable (see Chapters 2 and 7). They are certainly appropriate to use in addressing many of the questions practitioners ask. The critical question in any investigation is, of course, what method or methods will enable me to address the research question posed.

There are fashions in methodology, however, and the field should not lose sight of that. The *Quals* versus *Quants* debate is rampant in many of the social sciences. LIS is engaged in that debate as well (Altman, Chapter 9). Historical investigations, case studies, and bibliographical investigations, have served LIS very well in the past; it is likely that some emerging research questions can best be answered by these, "unfashionable," methods. Investigations using these methodologies may lead us to important research questions that have been ignored or have not been readily apparent.

LIS research will not be immune from the fashion of the day in terms of methodology, particularly if basic research is influenced by work done in other fields. That is as it should be. Review of research by other researchers as well as by practitioners, however, should force a researcher to confront directly the appropriateness of a method. Moreover, peer review should support a researcher who is resisting fashion, when that researcher has *sound methodological reasons* for doing what he or she is doing. Peer review can be a detriment if the review processes force an inappropriate method on the investigation of a research problem.

THEORY

At present, there appears to be no agreement on the theoretical base of the field (Van House, Chapter 7). Some observers go so far as to say there is no real profession in the practice of librarianship because there is no theoretical base. Biggs (Chapter 6) views librarianship as an occupation grounded in techniques. She acknowledges that cataloging and classification may have been a base in earlier, less-complicated times. Now, Biggs is hard-pressed to identify any theoretical underpinnings.

Others are more optimistic. Brooks (1989, pp. 243–244) begins to identify characteristics of a paradigm that might be developed in library and information science. He does acknowledge that no one paradigm dominates the field at the moment. The characteristics that he identified are: (1) the origin of information, (2) the perception of information, and (3) the manifestation of information. Within each of these he identifies some theoretical questions that will provoke discussion.

Young (Chapter 17) discusses the insufficient resource allocation to basic research in library and information science, and encourages the formulation of a new knowledge service paradigm. He views a combination of basic and applied research as critical to the advancement of library and information science. Buckland and Gathegi (Chapter 5) outline the domain of library and information science as consisting of scholarly studies of library services, librarianship, related retrieval-based information services, information use, and information policy.

Grover and Greer (Chapter 8, p. 110) offer a conceptual framework of library and information science in which they identify four characteristics as common to the work of the field:

- Responsibility for the design and management of an information base, whether packaged (books, serials, software, etc.) or unpackaged (electronically stored, locally produced database in a variety of formats);
- Responsibility for the design and management of an information organization, consisting of staff, an information system, equipment, space, and financial resources which enables delivery of information from the information base to clientele;
- Responsibility for identifying and accommodating the information needs and unique cognitive and behavioral styles of individuals among the information system's clientele; and
- Responsibility for identifying the information needs of client groups and facilitating the information transfer process to those groups.

The efforts required to build or redesign theory are difficult and demanding. Yet, they are essential to the continuing growth and development of library and information science. Library researchers have the responsibility for theory construction. Practitioners might help, but they do not have the mind set to fully contemplate the issues leading to theory construction.

Every now and then a sensitive practitioner can produce a breakthrough in the thinking of the field and point toward new theory construction. Chester Barnard (1938) is an outstanding example of such a practitioner. Whether a practitioner in library and information science is poised today to make such a contribution remains to be seen.

CONCERNS

Any adversarial relationship between practitioners and educators must be reduced (McClure, Chapter 20). Several authors in this volume (Van House, Chapter 7; Zweizig, Chapter 16) wish that many academic librarians conducting research, regardless of the kind, would just do their jobs and leave *researching* to the "research professionals." As Van House (Chapter 7, p. 96) states

> applying publish-or-perish to academic librarians devalues their role as librarians. The implication is that it is better to be pseudo-faculty than genuine librarians with their own distinct expertise and unique contribution to the university community.

This attitude will not take the field very far. Watson (1985) has indicated that academic librarians publish (and will continue to do so) whether or not they are faculty members. When library school faculty members and library faculty members work more closely together on joint research projects, each profit from the interaction. The Council on Library Resources, with its joint research grant program, acknowledged the fruitfulness of the collaboration early on. It would be helpful if more researchers and practitioners would recognize the advantages of collaboration and end the artificial labeling of researchers as being either educators or practitioners. It is not an either/or proposition. *Good* researchers can be part of either community. We must work to unite the two communities and thereby improve the qualify of research—be it basic, applied, or action.

Balbach (1989) and Lynch (1989) describe the benefits of the faculty status model in one university library. The essential point they make is that the faculty status model provides a long-term view of successful library development. Many people in the field who have responsibility for recruitment and appointment carry only a short-term view; that is, they seek to hire the person who is the instant producer and do not seek the person who will influence the future directions of the library. For the field of practice to advance, the long-term view must be acknowledged and advanced.

The development of a cadre of new researchers continues to be a high agenda item. Those new Ph.D.s coming out of programs in library and information science have at least three career paths before them:

- Industry and the for-profit sector;
- The traditional library track leading to administration; and
- The education track.

The education track must compete successfully for the new researchers if the field is to continue its development and to prepare new researchers successfully. While the career opportunities are good, the costs of education are high, and the amount of student support available is slim. Without greater financial support for doctoral students to pursue their Ph.D. degrees, many prospective students will forego the opportunity for further education.

FINAL COMMENT

The field of library and information science continues to grow, develop, and be strengthened. That it is a profession is acknowledged, despite the questioning of some observers. That it is a discipline is less clear. This question about LIS as a discipline drives some of the considerations of a "paradigm shift." The research base is expanding and becoming stronger—of higher quality. We are thinking in new ways; this is brought about by the assimilation of new technologies into practice and the expansion of information science into instruction and research.

Whether there indeed is a new paradigm remains to be seen, because the definition of the theoretical base remains unclear. As questions continue to be posed, and answers provided through systematic investigations and basic, applied, and action research, the theoretical definitions should emerge. Then the question of whether there is a new paradigm can be better addressed.

REFERENCES

Academic Libraries; Research Perspectives, edited by Mary Jo Lynch and Arthur Young. Chicago, IL: American Library Association, 1990.

"ACRL Research Agenda," *College & Research Libraries News*, 51 (April 1990): 317–319.

Balbach, Edith D. "Personnel," in *The Academic Library in Transition*, edited by Beverly P. Lynch. New York: Neal Schuman, 1989, pp. 309–357.

Barnard, Chester I. *The Functions of the Executive.* Cambridge, MA: Harvard University Press, 1938.

Brooks, Terrence A. "The Model of Science and Scientific Models in Librarianship," *Library Trends*, 38 (1989): 237–349.

Butler, Pierce. "Librarianship as a Profession," *The Library Quarterly*, 21 (1951): 235–247.

Council on Library Resources. *Twenty-ninth Annual Report.* Washington, D.C.: Council on Library Resources, 1985, pp. 10–13.

Getz, Malcolm. *Public Libraries: An Economic View.* Baltimore, MD: The Johns Hopkins University Press, 1980.

Kent, Allen, Jacob Cohen, K.L. Montgomery, James A. Williams, Stephen Bulick, Roger R. Flynn, William N. Sabor, and Una Mansfield. *Use of Library Materials: The University of Pittsburgh Study.* New York: Marcel Dekker, 1979.

Lynch, Beverly P. "Commentary [on "Personnel"]," in *The Academic Library in Transition,* Edited by Beverly P. Lynch. New York: Neal-Schuman, 1989, pp. 358–362.

Research Questions of Interest to ARL. Washington, D.C.: Association of Research Libraries, 1987.

Rethinking the Library in the Information Age. 3 volumes. Prepared by the U.S. Department of Education, Office of Educational Research and Improvement, Office of Library Programs. Washington D.C.: GPO, 1988–1989.

Schultheiss, Louis A, Don S. Culbertson, and Edward M. Heiliger. *Advanced Data Processing in the University Library.* New York: Scarecrow Press, 1962.

Sievert, Donald and MaryEllen Sievert. "Philosophical Research: Report from the Field," in *Humanists at Work; Papers presented at a symposium held at the University of Illinois at Chicago, 1989.* Chicago, IL: University Library, University of Illinois at Chicago, 1989, pp. 95–101.

Watson, Paula D. "Production of Scholarly Articles by Academic Librarians and Library School Faculty," *College & Research Libraries*, 46 (July 1985): 334–342.

Wiberley, Stephen E. Jr., and William G. Jones. "Patterns of Information Seeking in the Humanities," *College & Research Libraries*, 50 (November 1989): 638–645.

Contributors

Ellen Altman is Professor and former Director of the Graduate Library School, University of Arizona, 1515 E. First Street, Tucson, AZ 85719. She received her Ph.D. from Rutgers University and has written extensively on topics related to library management and evaluation. She is best known for her work with Ernest R. De Prospo on performance measures for public libraries.

Mary Biggs is Director of Libraries at Mercy College, 555 Broadway, Dobbs Ferry, NY 10522. Mercy College is a multicampus institution in Westchester County and the Bronx, New York. She was formerly on the faculties of the University of Chicago Graduate Library School and the Columbia University School of Library Service. She has published widely on public services, academic librarianship, library education, and the publishing industry.

Michael K. Buckland is Professor of Library and Information Studies, University of California at Berkeley, Berkeley, CA 94720. He was born and educated in England, and has degrees in history (Oxford) and librarianship (Sheffield). He has experience in academic libraries at Oxford, Lancaster, and Purdue Universities; in academic administration at the University of California; and as a visiting professor in Australia and Austria. His publications include *Library Services in Theory and Context* (2nd edition, Pergamon Press, 1988).

Daniel Callison is Associate Professor and Associate Dean, School of Library and Information Science, Indiana University, Bloomington, IN 47405. His research areas include evaluation of microcomputer software for public schools, collection policy development in school library media centers, and applications of free inquiry learning in media centers and museums. He currently serves on the Board of Editors for *School Library Media Quarterly*.

Charles Curran is Associate Professor, College of Library and Information Science, University of South Carolina, Columbia, SC 29208. He holds bachelor's and master's degrees from Duquesne University and master's and Ph.D. degrees from Rutgers. He has chaired the American Library Association's Library Research Round Table and several of its standing committees, including the Research Forums Committee and the Research Development Committee. Most recently, his observations about the conduct of inquiry in library and information science have appeared in *Library & Information Science Research*.

Ablex Publishing Corp. published a book of essays, *Library Performance, Accountability, and Responsiveness*, which he co-edited.

Evelyn H. Daniel is Professor, School of Information and Library Science, University of North Carolina–Chapel Hill, 100 Manning Hall, CB#3360, Chapel Hill, NC 27599–3360. She was Dean, School of Information and Library Science, from 1985–1990. From 1976–1985, she served as Associate Professor and Assistant Dean, then Dean and Professor, of the School of Information Studies, Syracuse University. She holds an A.B. in History from the University of North Carolina–Wilmington, and a M.L.S. and Ph.D. in Library and Information Science from the University of Maryland. Her interests include school and special librarianship, information resources management, and issues pertaining to the organizational information flow and change. She has written three monographs and numerous articles in research and professional journals.

Robert E. Dugan has worked on the local, state, and Federal levels in library services, management, and research since the mid-1970s. When the chapter was written, he was State Librarian in Delaware. Currently, he is Associate University Librarian for Administration and Planning, Lavinger Library, Georgetown University, Washington, D.C. 20057. His articles pertain to library automation, statistics, and services to the disabled. He has recently co-authored a monograph describing print and electronic reference sources in public administration for students and practitioners.

Cheryl Duran is an Assistant Dean at the Graduate School of Library and Information Science, University of California, 405 Hilgard Avenue, Los Angeles, CA 90024. She received her Ph.D. from Indiana University and has acted as a consultant to the National Commission on Libraries and Information Science, the U.S. Office of Education, and the U.S. Department of Interior. She serves on the Executive Board of the Southwest Museum in Los Angeles and the Newberry Library Center for the History of the American Indian. Her research interests include: (1) demographic forecast modeling in relation to information services' delivery and utilization; (2) access patterns in the retrieval of nonbook primary source materials; and (3) ethnolinguistic factors related to cogn'..ve learning. She is currently engaged in research concerning information-seekir: behavior in ethnolinguistic communities.

Joan C. Durrance is Associate Professor, School of Information and Library Studies, The University of Michigan, 580 Union Drive, Ann Arbor, MI 48109–1346. She is a regular contributor to library literature, writing on topics such as reference success, information needs, and the provision of local government information by public libraries. Her current research projects include a W. K. Kellogg funded study of job and career information centers and a study of policy decisions of local elected officials. She is a former chair of the Public Library Association's Research Committee.

Shirley Fitzgibbons is Associate Professor, School of Library and Information Science, Indiana University, Bloomington, IN 47405. Her areas of specialization include youth library services in both school and public libraries, and library services for persons with disabilities. Her current research projects include: evaluation and measurement of youth library services, assessment of services for youth with disabilities, and investigation of successful motivators of reading by youth.

John N. Gathegi is Assistant Professor, School of Library and Information Studies, Florida State University, Tallahassee, FL 32304. He was born in Kenya and was educated in both Kenya and the United States, with degrees in psychology (USIU), political science, and library and information studies (Berkeley). He has experience in academic libraries at the University of Nairobi and Berkeley, as well as school and newspaper libraries in Kenya.

Roger Greer is Professor, School of Library and Information Management, Emporia State University, 120 Commercial Street, Emporia, KS 66801. He has been dean at the University of Southern California and Syracuse University, and Professor at the University of Denver.

Robert Grover is Professor, School of Library and Information Management, Emporia State University, 120 Commercial Street, Emporia, KS 66801. He was formerly dean at the same school and also served as Director of the School of Library and Information Science, University of South Florida.

Martha L. Hale serves as Dean, School of Library and Information Management, Emporia State University, 1200 Commercial, Emporia, KS 66801-5087. After earning her Ph.D. in Public Administration, she wrote about community analysis, needs assessment, and city management. The chapter in this book extends her current investigation into the paradigmatic shifts occurring in library and information studies.

Michael H. Harris is Professor, College of Library and Information Science, University of Kentucky, 502 King Library Building S., Lexington, KT 40506-0391. He earned his Ph.D. degree at Indiana University in 1971, and was a U.S.O.E. Fellow there. He is the author of several dozen papers and books on the social and theoretical foundations of library service in America. Professor Harris has served as the chair of the Research Round Table of the American Library Association, as President of the Border-States American Studies Association, and as President of the Kentucky Library Association. In 1972, Professor Harris was awarded the Herbert Putnam Honor Fund Award by the American Library Association, and he was Editor of *Advances in Librarianship* from 1968-1974.

Peter Hernon is Professor, Graduate School of Library and Information Science, Simmons College, 300 The Fenway, Boston, MA 02115. He received his Ph.D. from Indiana University in 1978. He teaches courses related to government information, information policy, research methods, statistics, and the evaluation of library services. He is the founding editor of *Government Information Quarterly* and the author (or co-author) of 26 books and more than 60 articles. Together with Charles R. McClure, he received the Best Book award from ASIS in 1987. He is also past chair of the Library Research Round Table and has conducted numerous research studies at the national level.

Joe A. Hewitt is Associate University Librarian for Technical Services (CB#3906, Davis Library) and Adjunct Professor, School of Information and Library Science, University of North Carolina at Chapel Hill, Chapel Hill, NC 27599–3906. He has chaired the Library Research Round Table Steering Committee and is currently Chair of the ALCTS Committee on Research and Statistics. He has published on library networks, collection development, and technical services. He won the Blackwell's North American Scholarship Award for the best paper in acquisitions and collection development in 1988 (with J. Shipman) and in 1990. Dr. Hewitt edits the series *Advances in Library Automation and Networking: A Research Annual*.

Irene B. Hoadley is Director, Evans Library, Texas A&M University, College Station, TX 77843–5000. She received her B.A. degree from the University of Texas, Austin; an A.M.L.S. and Ph.D. from the University of Michigan; and a M.A. from Kansas State University. She has served in a variety of positions at Sam Houston State Teacher College Library, Kansas State University Library, and The Ohio State University Libraries. She has been active in professional organizations, including the Ohio Library Association, the Texas Library Association, the American Library Association, Amigos Bibliographic Council, and OCLC, Inc. She presently serves on the Editorial Board of *College & Research Libraries*. She has authored numerous monographs and journal articles. Her book, the *Undergraduate Library*, received the Scarecrow Press Award for *Library Literature*.

Masaru Itoga is an Associate Professor, School of Library and Information Science, Keio University, 15–45 Mita 2-chome Minato-ku, Toyoko, Japan 108. He has published widely in Japanese on research methodologies, and is a graduate of the Library School at the University of Tokyo. He is currently a Visiting Research Professor at the College of Library and Information Science, University of Kentucky (502 King Library Building S., Lexington, KT 40506–0391), where he is collaborating with Professor Harris in a series of theoretical projects. At the same time, he is pursuing his own work on alternative approaches to research methodology.

Michael E.D. Koenig is Dean, Graduate School of Library and Information Science, Rosary College, 7900 West Division St., River Forest, IL 60305. He has a B.A. in psychology (Yale University), a M.A. in library science, a M.B.A. in quantitative methods (University of Chicago), and a Ph.D. in information science (Drexel University). His work experience includes positions as manager of information services for Pfizer Inc.; Director of Operations, Institute for Scientific Information; Vice President, Operations, Swet North America; Associate Professor, School of Library Science, and Adjunct Professor, Graduate School of Business, Columbia University; and Vice President, Data Management, Tradenet Inc. His research and professional interests include the effect of libraries and information services on productivity, bibliometrics, and the management of information functions.

Beverly P. Lynch is Dean and Professor, Graduate School of Library and Information Science, University of California at Los Angeles, 120 Powell Library, 405 Hilgard Ave., Los Angeles, CA 90024. She received her Ph.D. from the University of Wisconsin, Madison. From 1977-1988, she was University Librarian and Professor, University of Illinois at Chicago. She is the author of *The Academic Library in Transition*, *Management Strategies for Libraries*, and *Priorities for Academic Libraries* (with Thomas J. Galvin).

James M. Matarazzo is Professor, Graduate School of Library and Information Science, Simmons College, 300 The Fenway, Boston, MA 02115. From 1974 to 1988, he served as Associate Dean at Simmons College. Prior to joining the Simmons faculty, he served in various capacities at the Libraries of the Massachusetts Institute of Technology. Dr. Matarazzo is a Fellow of the Special Libraries Association and received the SLA Professional Award (1983) and the SLA President's Award (1988). He has also served as a member of the SLA Board of Directors. Professsor Matarazzo is the author of *Closing the Corporate Library* and *Library Problems in Science and Technology*. He served as Chairman and Editor of the SLA Task Force on the Value of the Information Professional and was co-editor of three editions of *Scientific Engineering and Medical Societies: Publications in Print*.

Anne J. Mathews is Director, Office of Library Programs, Office of Educational Research and Improvement, U.S. Department of Education, 555 New Jersey Ave., N.W., Washington, D.C. 20208-5571. Prior to her appointment in the Office of Library Programs in 1986, she was Professor, Graduate School of Librarianship and Information Management, University of Denver (Colorado). She has also served as consultant to the U.S. Information Agency and the U.S. Agency for International Development; and has been a reference librarian at Oregon State University, Program Director of the Central Colorado Library System, consultant to the Colorado State Library, and trainer and interviewer for several market research services. She is a graduate of Wheaton College and holds the M.A. degree in library science and Ph.D. in speech communication from the University of Denver.

Charles R. McClure is Professor, School of Information Studies, Syracuse University, Syracuse, NY 13244. He earned his Ph.D. from Rutgers University in Library and Information Services. He has served as principal investigator for a number of studies funded by the American Library Association, the National Technical Information Service, the National Science Foundation, and others. His co-authored study, funded by the U.S. Congress's Office of Technology Assessment on the National Research and Education Network (NREN), was the recipient of the American Library Association's 1990 Jesse H. Shera award for the best research paper in library/information science. He has written extensively on topics related to U.S. government information management and policies, as well as the planning, evaluation, and management of library and information centers.

Jane Ouderkirk is Director of Patron Services Division at the Connecticut

State Library, 231 Capitol Ave., Hartford, CT 06106. In addition to state experience, she has also been a public library director. Prior to assuming her current position, she worked as a Federal programs consultant and a cooperative library specialist at another state library development agency. She is a resource person to the Steering Committee for the Federal State Cooperative System project of NCES and NCLIS.

Ronald R. Powell is an Associate Professor and chair of the Department of Library Science, School of Library and Information Science, University of Missouri-Columbia, Columbia, MO 65211. He is the author of a number of articles and books, including *Basic Research Methods for Librarians*. He is the co-editor of *Qualitative Research in Information Management*, which is scheduled for publication in 1991. He has taught a variety of research methods courses over the past several years.

Jane B. Robbins is Professor and Director, School of Library and Information Studies, University of Wisconsin-Madison, Helen C. White Hall, 600 North Park Street, Madison, WI 53706. She is the editor of *Library & Information Science Research*. Her research interests focus on the research process in library and information studies.

Candy Schwartz is Associate Professor, Graduate School of Library and Information Science, Simmons College, 300 The Fenway, Boston, MA 02115. She teaches courses related to online searching, database design, indexing, and records management. She holds a B.A. and M.L.S. from McGill University, and Ph.D. in Information Science from Syracuse University. She serves on the ASIS Board of Directors, and is Vice-President of the Board of Directors of Documentation Abstracts, Inc. Her current research interests include electronic gateways to library services, and subject access to nontraditional materials.

Dorothy L. Steffens is a doctoral candidate, School of Library and Information Studies, University of Wisconsin-Madison, Helen C. White Hall, 600 North Park Street, Madison, WI 53706. She is the editorial assistant for *Library & Information Science Research*. Her areas of research interest are women studies, library education and research, and library history.

Charles T. Townley, Ph.D., is Dean, New Mexico State University Library, P.O. Box 3475, Las Cruces, NM 88003-3475. Previously, he was Head, Division of Library and Instructional Services, Pennsylvania State University at Harrisburg, Middletown, PA. He participates in professional organizations, currently chairing the ACRL Research Committees and serving as Secretary of the IFLA Section on Library Services to Multicultural Populations. A regular contributor to library research, his latest book is *Human Relations in Library Network Development*. Dr. Townley is currently engaged in research on predicting academic library performance and on compact disk union catalogs.

Information Studies, University of California at Berkeley, Berkeley, CA 94720. She has published widely in the literature of library and information science. Her research interests include measurement and evaluation of library services and the library labor market. Her recent publications include: *Measuring Academic Library Performance: A Practical Approach* (American Library Association, 1990), *Output Measures for Public Libraries: A Manual of Standardized Procedures* (2nd edition, American Library Association), and several articles on the Public Library Effectiveness Study.

Julie A.C. Virgo is the Executive Vice President of The Carroll Group, Inc. (875 N. Michigan Ave., Suite 3311, Chicago, IL 60611), a general management consulting firm. She received her Ph.D. in librarianship from the University of Chicago, where she taught for 20 years. She has served on the staff of the Medical Library Association (MLA) and as the Executive Director of the Association of College and Research Libraries (ACRL). A past Board member of MLA, ACRL, and CLENE, she was also the President of the American Society for Information Science. Dr. Virgo currently serves on the Board of the National Association for Neuro Linguistic Programming and recently chaired the U.S. Department of Education Task Force on "The Role of Professional Library Associations in Creating an Infrastructure for Research in Library and Information Science."

Peter R. Young is Executive Director, National Commission on Libraries and Information Science, 1111 18th St., Suite 300, N.W., Washington, D.C. 20036. At the time of the writing of his chapter, he was Executive Director, Faxon Institute for Advanced Studies in Scholarly and Scientific Communication, Westwood, MA. He previously served the Faxon Company as Director of Academic Information Services. Prior to joining Faxon, he was at the Library of Congress where he was Chief, Cataloging Division, Copyright Office, Assistant Chief, MARC Editorial Division, and Customer Services Officer, Cataloging Distribution Service. Mr. Young holds a M.S.L.I.S. degree from Columbia University and has worked at two university libraries, a college library, one public library, and CL Systems, Inc. He is the author of several articles on library statistics, periodicals pricing, and the relationship among libraries, information technology, and publishing.

University of Wisconsin–Madison, Helen C. White Hall, 600 North Park Street, Madison, WI 53706. From 1980 to 1982, he was Senior Research Associate at King Research, Inc. Recently, he has been the principal investigator for U.S. Department of Education research projects funded under contract (Libraries and Literacy Education Project) and as a result of a grants application (Evaluation of Adult Library Literacy Programs).

Author Index

A

Aaron, S.L., 297, 299, 300, 301, 302, 304, *314*
Abbott, A., 73, 76, *83*, 352, *354*
Aburdene, P., 101, *113*
Achleitner, H., 103, *112*
Adamson, M.C., 180, *187*
Adamson, W.L., 351, *354*
Adeyemi, N.M., 21, *26*
Agger, B., 352, *354*
Akey, S., 281, *292*
Alford, R.R., 351, *354*
Allen, B.L., 91, *99*
Allen, G.G., 271, 272, *275*
Altbach, P.G., 67, *70*
Altman, E., 22, *26*, 35, 36, 37, *43*, 211, 212, *213*
Andrews, F.M., 24, *26*
Angus, I., 352, *354*
Antieau, K., 35, 36, 37, *43*, 211, 212, *213*
Argyris, C., 261, *265*
Armstrong, J.S., 236, *237*
Ary, D., 4, *13*
Asheim, L., 7, *13*, 72, *83*

B

Babbie, E., 16, *26*, 86, *98*
Backstrom, C.H., 18, *26*
Balbach, E.D., 365, *366*
Barber, B., 350, *354*
Barg, J., 241, *249*
Barnard, C.I., 364, *366*
Barnes, A., 24, *26*
Barnes, B., 348, *354*
Barron, D., 300, 301, 302, 303, *315*
Beagle, D., 349, *354*
Beasley, K., 22, *26*
Belkin, N.J., 244, *249*

Bellassai, M.C., 286, *294*
Ben-David, J., 137, *144*
Bender, C.C., 262, *265*
Benediktsson, D., 349, *354*
Benge, R.C., 64, *70*
Bennett, W.J., 82, *83*
Bensman, S.J., 20, *26*
Benson, D.K., 18, *26*
Benson, J.L., 18, *26*
Berelson, B., 341, *345*
Bergen, D., 353, *354*
Bernstein, R.J., 349, *354*
Bierbaum, E.G., 9, *13*
Biggs, M., 80, *83*, 129, 139, *144*, 158, *158*, 268, *275*
Bishop, A., 6, 7, *14*, 39, *44*, 85, 89, 90, 91, *99*, 108, *113*, 128, *145*, 152, *159*, 180, *187*, 214, 226, 235, *238*, 248, *249*, 254, *265*, 267, 268, 269, *276*, 284, *294*
Blalock, H.M., 23, 24, *26*
Bledstein, B.J., 73, 80, *83*
Boggs, C., 351, *354*
Bolton, W.T., 281, *292*
Bookstein, A., 18, *26*, 139, *144*, 158, *158*
Booth, C.W., 351, *354*
Borko, H., 151, *158*
Bourdieu, P., 352, *354*, *355*
Boudon, R., 352, *354*
Bowen, H.R., 130, *144*
Boyer, E.L., 82, *83*
Bracy, P., 299, 301, *314*
Bradley, J., 262, *265*
Bradley, L., 262, *265*
Bredo, E., 353, *355*
Brinberg, H.R., 342, *345*
Broadbent, M., 229, *237*
Brookes, T.A., 92, 94, *98*, 363, *366*
Brownstein, C.N., 120, *126*

375

Bryant, P.K., 4, *13*, 24, 27, 91, *99*
Buckland, M.K., 64, 65, 69, *70*, 94, *98*, 283, *292*
Buckley, B.J., 67, *70*
Budd, R.W., 23, *26*, 96, *98*, 123, *126*, 129, 132, 133, *144*
Bulick, S., 362, *366*
Bunge, C.A., 298, *292*
Bunge, M.A., 68, *71*
Burek, D.M., 241, *249*
Burgess, R.G., 23, *26*
Busha, C.H., 17, 19, *26*, 28, 136, *144*
Butler, P., 109, *112*, 280, *292*, 358, *366*

C

Cameron, K.S., 287, *292*
Campbell, D.J., 19, *26*
Capra, F., 102, 103, *112*
Carey, J.W., 354, *355*
Carnoy, M., 351, *355*
Carpenter, R.L., 24, *26*
Carr, W., 348, *355*
Carrigan, D., 349, *355*
Castoriadis, C., 352, *355*
Chatman, E.A., 284, *292*
Chen, C.-C., 284, *293*
Cheney, L.V., 82, *83*
Childers, T., 88, *98*, 107, *112*, 136, *144*, 267, *276*, 287, 288, *292*
Clark, K., 288, 291, *293*
Cleary, R.E., 98, *99*
Cleveland, H., 340, *345*
Clow, D., 65, 66, *71*
Cohn, J., 362, *366*
Coleman, J.S., 349, *355*
Collings, D.G., 20, *26*
Conant, R.W., 152, 154, *158*
Cook, M.K., 19, *26*, 269, 273, *276*
Coughlin, C., 269, *275*
Craver, K.W., 312, *314*
Creth, S.D., 148, *159*
Crismon, D.L., 282, *293*
Cronin, B., 156, *158*, 340, *345*
Cronin, M.J., 22, *26*
Crowder, M., 67, *71*
Crowley, T., 288, *293*
Culbertson, D.S., 359, *366*
Culkin, P.B., 228, *239*
Curran, C.C., 33, 42, *43*

D

Daft, R.L., 92, 96, *98*
Dalrymple, P., 122, 123, *127*
Daniel, E.H., 129, 133, *145*
Danton, J.P., 70, *71*
Davidson, T.N., 24, *26*
Davis, C.H., 123, *127*
De, M., 4, *13*, 24, 27, 91, *99*
D'Elia, G., 286, *293*
DeProspo, E.R., 22, *26*, 253, 264, 265, 286, *293*
Derber, C., 352, *355*
Dervin, B., 284, 288, 289, 291, *293*, 295, 343, *345*, 353, *355*
DeWath, N.V., 286, *294*
Dewdney, P., 289, *293*
Dickson, A.J., 66, *71*
Didier, E.K., 299, 301, *315*
Doty, P., 228, 235, *238*
Dougherty, R.M., 21, *26*
Downes, R., 342, *345*
Drake, M.A., 190, 195, *196*, 317, 318, 321, *325*
Drott, M.C., 18, *26*
Durbin, R., 86, 87, 88, *98*
Durrance, J.C., 282, 283, 284, 285, 286, 288, 289, 292, *293*
Dyer, E.R., 20, *27*

E

Eaton, J., 19, *27*
Ehrenreich, B., 77, *83*
Eisenbeis, K., 139, *145*
Eliot, C.W., 129, *145*
Elkin, S.L., 350, *355*
Elman, S.E., 76, 82, *83*
Elwell, C., 241, *249*
Emard, J.-P., 241, *249*
Enger, K.B., 91, *98*, 241, *249*
Engle, M., 180, *187*
Ennis, P.H., 6, *13*, 73, *83*
Etzioni, A., 7, *13*
Evans, G.T., 228, *237*
Evans, P.R., 351, *355*

F

Fang, J.R., 71, *69*
Farah, B.D., 4, *13*, 24, 27, 91, *99*
Fay, B., 353, *355*
Fedder, A.N., 299, *315*

Feehan, P.E., 89, 90, 92, *98*, 107, *113*, 180, *187*
Feinberg, W., 353, *355*
Femia, J.V., 351, *355*
Ferguson, M., 103, *113*
Fidel, R., 23, *27*
Fischer, R.G., 20, *27*
Fitzgibbons, S.G., 51, *55*, 140, 141, *145*, 219, *226*
Fleming, M., 241, *249*
Flynn, R.R., 362, *366*
Forester, T., 353, *355*
Fox, M.A., 269, 273, *276*
Fraley, R., 123, *127*
Freeman, H.E., 22, *29*
Freeman, M.S., 267, *276*
Freidson, E., 73, *83*, 352, 353, *355*
Freidland, R., 351, *354*
Friedman, J., 351, *355*

G
Gans, H., 352, *355*
Garrison, D., 350, *355*
Garrison, G., 18, *27*, 280, *293*
Garrison, L.P., 200, *203*
Gathegi, J.N., 65, 67, *71*
Gaver, M.V., 296, 300, 301, 302, 303, 304, 314, *315*
Gay, L.R., 16, *27*
Geertz, C., 349, *355*
Geiger, R.L., 137, 138, 139, 140, *145*
Gers, R., 288, *293*
Gerzog, A., 282, *294*
Getz, M., 362, *366*
Geuss, R., 353, *355*
Gibson, C.F., 229, *237*
Giddens, A., 349, *355*
Glass, G.V., 163, 164, *177*
Glazier, J., 18, 23, *27*, 105, 107, *113*, 349, *356*
Glesecke, J., 342, *345*
Glogoff, S., 200, *203*
Golden, G., 18, *27*
Goldhor, H., 3, *13*, 17, *27*, 136, *145*
Golub, A.J., 4, *13*, 24, *27*, 91, *99*
Gorman, M., 82, *83*
Graff, G., 351, *356*
Gragg, W.L., II., 89, 90, 92, *98*, 107, *113*, 180, *187*
Gramsci, A., 351, *356*

Greco, C.M., 19, *26*
Greer, R.C., 109, 110, *113*, 340, *345*
Griffin, R.W., 92, 96, *98*
Griffiths, J.M., 150, *158*
Grotzinger, L., 306, *315*
Grover, R., 23, *27*, 105, 107, *113*, 340, *345*, 349, *356*
Guba, E.G., 103, *113*, 343, *345*
Gudim, M., 340, *345*

H
Habermas, J., 349, *356*
Hafner, A.W., 24, *27*
Hale, M.L., 103, 105, *112*, *113*, 340, *345*
Hall, S., 351, *356*
Hanks, G., 73, *83*
Hanson, R.L., 350, *356*
Harris, M.H., 19, *27*, 69, *71*, 87, 99, 108, *113*, 115, 116, *127*, 261, *265*, 348, 349, 350, 352, 353, 354, *355*, *356*
Harter, S.P., 17, *26*, 136, *144*, 202, *203*
Havener, W.M., 89, 90, 92, *98*, 107, *113*, 180, *187*
Hawkins, H., 129, 130, 131, 134, *145*
Hayes, R.M., 20, *27*, 42, *43*, 107, *113*, 122, *127*, 134, *145*, 148, 150, 151, 153, *158*, 192, *196*
Healey, J.S., 269, *276*
Heaps, W.A., 302, *315*
Heiliger, E.M., 359, *366*
Heilprin, L., 268, *276*
Heim, K.M., 7, *13*, 134, 139, *144*, *145*, 281, *294*
Heinritz, F.J., 21, *26*
Held, D., 353, *356*
Hendrick, C., 342, *345*
Hennessy, J.A., 69, *71*
Hernon, P., 4, 6, 8, *13*, 22, 24, 25, *27*, 91, 99, 153, *158*, 262, *265*, 270, *276*, 284, 288, *293*, *294*
Heron, D.W., 170, *178*
Hildreth, C.R., 228, 234, *237*
Hoadley, I.B., 234, *238*
Hoover, A.J., 65, *71*
Houser, L., 46, *55*, 94, *99*, 116, *127*
Hurley, R.J., 299, 302, *315*
Hursh-Cesar, G., 18, *26*
Hurt, C.D., 318, *325*
Hwang, H.R., 4, *13*, 25, *27*, 91, *99*

Author Index

I
Isaac, S., 17, 27
Itoga, M., 353, *356*

J
Jackson, B.B., 229, *237*
Jacobs, L.C., 4, *13*
Jaeger, R.M., 24, *27*
Jaffe, A.J., 24, *27*
James, W., 133, *145*
Janaske, P.C., 31, *43*
Janowitz, M., 350, *356*
Jencks, C., 73, 76, 77, *83*
Jenkins, D.L., 269, 273, *276*
Jessop, B., 351, *356*
Jhally, S., 352, *354*
Johnson, D.W., 49, *56*, 285, *295*
Johnson, R.D., 6, *13*, 352, *356*
Jones, W.G., 359, *366*
Judd, C.M., 16, *28*
Juliussen, E., 244, *249*
Juliussen, K., 244, *249*

K
Kantor, P.B., 22, *27*, 93, *99*
Kaplan, A., 5, *13*
Karande, A.G., 339, *345*
Kaser, D., 19, *27*, 152, *159*
Katzer, J., 6, 9, 10, *13*, 85, 90, 92, *99*, 122, *127*, 190, 195, *196*, 241, 244, *249*
Kaufman, P.T., 174, *178*
Kellner, D., 352, *356*
Kemmis, S., 348, *355*
Kent, A., 362, *366*
Kerlinger, F.N., 16, *27*
Kester, D.D., 89, 90, 92, *98*, 107, *113*, 180, *187*
Kidder, L.H., 16, *28*
Kidston, J.S., 18, *28*
King, D., 150, 152, *158*
Kinnucan, M.T., 91, *99*
Klem, L., 24, *26*
Kochen, M., 247, *249*
Koek, K.E., 241, *249*
Koenig, M.E.D., 229, *237, 238*
Kohl, D.F., 123, *127*
Koos, F.H., 305, *315*
Kraemer, H.C., 19, *28*
Kraft, D., 201, 202, *203*
Krathwohl, D.R., 4, *13*, 261, *265*
Krueger, R.A., 261, *265*

Kulthau, C.C., 284, *294*, 304, *315*
Kuhn, T.S., 116, *127*, 336, *345*
Kuo, L.-L., 4, *13*, 24, 27, 91, *99*

L
Lancaster, F.W., 10, *13*, 17, 18, 22, *28*, 202, *203*
Larson, M.S., 109, *113*
Lawler, E.E., III., 254, 300, 301, *362*
Lazere, D., 352, *356*
Lears, T.J., 351, *356*
Lee, F.R., 142, *145*
Lee, S., 139, *145*
Leedy, P.D., 17, *28*
Leimkuhler, F.F., 21, *28*
Leisner, A.B., 282, *293*
Lesser, B., 280, *295*
Lewis, D., 23, *26*
Light, R.J., 353, *356*
Lincoln, Y.S., 103, 105, *113*, 337, 338, 343, *345*
Lofland, J., 23, *28*
Lofland, L.H., 23, *28*
Lowrie, J.E., 300, 301, 302, 304, *315*
Lynch, B.P., 154, 155, *159*, 364, *366*
Lynch, M.J., 3, 7, *13*, 18, 22, *28*, 29, 33, 36, 37, 40, *44*, 85, 90, 93, 95, *99*, 190, 195, *196*, 268, 276, 281, 286, *294, 295*
Lynton, E.A., 76, 82, *83*

M
Machlup, F., 69, *71*, 170, 171, *178*
MacKee, M., 20, *28*
MacMullin, S.E., 284, *294*
Madden, M., 281, *294*
Magrass, Y., 352, *355*
Mansfield, U., 69, *71*, 362, *366*
Marchand, D.A., 229, *238*
Marcum, D., 139, *144*
Markuson, B., 139, *145*
Marshal, C., 261, *265*
Marshall, J.D., 19, *28*
Martell, C., 4, *13*
Martin, S.K., 228, 231, 232, 234, *238*
Martyn, J., 17, 20, *28*
Mason, M.G., 153, *159*
Matarazzo, J.M., 5, *13*, 320, 321, 324, *325*
Mathews, A.J., 34, 41, 42, *44*, 141,*145*
McCabe, B.P., Jr., 262, *265*
McClure, C.R., 6, 7, *13*, 14, 22, *27*, 29, 37, 39, *44*, 85, 89, 90, 91, 92, 93, *99, 100*,

108, *113*, 128, 137, *145*, *146*, 152, *159*, 180, *187*, 214, *226*, 228, 235, *238*, 248, *249*, 254, 262, 263, *265*, 267, 268, 269, *276*, 281, 284, 286, 288, *294*, *295*, 328, 333, 334, *335*
McCombs, C., 19, *28*
McCumber, J., 353, *356*
McCurdy, H.E., 98, *99*
McLellan, D., 352, *356*
Mellon, C.A., 126, *127*, 261, *265*
Merod, J., 351, *357*
Metz, P., 270, *276*
Michael, W.B., 17, *27*
Miller, M.L., 304, *315*
Mills, C.W., 74, *84*
Minor, B., 302, *315*
Mintzberg, H., 130, *145*, 165, *178*
Mitroff, I.I., 258, 259, *266*
Moffatt, M., 6, *14*
Moffett, W.A., 281, *294*
Mohr, L.B., 86, 87, 88, 98, *99*
Molhot, P., 228, *238*
Momenee, K., 134, *146*
Montanelli, D.S., 268, 269, 271, *276*
Montgomery, K.L., 362, *366*
Monypenny, P., 329, *335*
Moore, N., 17, *28*
Moran, B.B., 273, *276*, 304, *315*
Morgan, G., 338, *345*
Mouly, G.J., 5, *14*, 16, 17, *28*
Murkerji, C., 352, *357*
Murray, A.D., 284, *295*

N
Nachmias, C., 16, 17, *28*
Nachmias, D., 16, 17, *28*
Naisbitt, J., 101, *113*
Nelson, J., 284, *293*
Nelson, M.J., 91, *99*
Newby, G.B., 244, *249*
Newhouse, R.C., 18, *28*
Nielsen, B., 288, *294*
Nilan, M., 353, *355*
Novallo, A., 241, *249*

O
Odi, A., 85, 94, *99*, 267, *276*
Ogilvy, J., 103, *113*, 336, 337, 338, 339, 343, *346*
Olaisen, J.L., 349, 353, *357*
Olsgaard, J.K., 180, *188*

Olsgaard, J.N., 180, *188*
O'Malley, P.M., 24, *26*
O'Neill, E., 21, *28*
Owen, A., 37, *44*, 286, *294*

P
Palmour, V.E., 284, 286, *294*, *295*
Pao, M.L., 20, *28*
Paris, M., 151, *159*
Passeron, J.C., 352, *355*
Patton, M.Q., 23, *28*, 261, *265*
Peritz, B.C., 107, *113*
Person, R., 139, *145*
Peters, T., 342, *345*
Pocock, J.G.A., 350, *357*
Powell, R.R., 3, 5, *14*, 17, 21, 23, *27*, *28*, 137, *145*, 148, 156, *159*
Prentice, A., 190, 195, *196*
Prusak, L., 5, *13*, 321, 324, *325*
Ptacek, W., 291, *294*
Pungitore, V.L., 286, 289, 292, *294*
Putnam, R., 261, *265*

Q
Quarterman, J., 262, *265*
Quirk, G., 91, *98*, 241, *249*

R
Ravichandra Rao, I.K., 24, *28*
Rayward, W.B., 78, *84*
Razavieh, A., 4, *13*
Reeves, W.J., 73, 74, *84*
Reilly, K.D., 20, *28*
Relyea, H.C., 153, *158*
Richardson, J.V., 25, *27*
Ricoceur, P., 352, *357*
Riesman, D., 73, 76, 77, *83*
Robbins, J., 7, *14*, 35, 36, *44*, 49, *56*, 139, *144*, 147, *159*, 199, *203*, 270, *276*, 285, *295*, 318, *325*
Robinson, B., 288, *294*
Rochester, M., 68, *71*
Rockart, J.F., 229, *238*
Rodger, E.J., 22, *29*, 37, *44*, 93, *99*, *100*, 281, 286, *293*, *295*
Rodgers, W.L., 24, *26*
Rosenbaum, M., 241, *249*
Rossi, P.H., 22, *29*
Rossman, G.B., 261, *265*
Roth, P.A., 353, *357*
Rothman, J., 254, *266*

Rowley, J.E., 21. *29*
Rowley, P.J., 21, *29*
Rowntree, D., 24, *29*
Rueschemeyer, D., 351, *355*
Runciman, W.G., 349, *357*

S

Sable, M.H., 66, *71*
Sabor, W.N., 362, *366*
Saracevic, T., 340, *345*
Schaefer, W.D., 82, *83*
Schlachter, G.A., 6, *14*, 306, *315*
Schmidt, C.J., 73, *83*
Schmidt, K.A., 339, *345*
Scholes, R., 351, *357*
Schön, D.A., 74, 78, 79, 82, *84*, 92, *99*, 165, 166, *178*, 257, 261, *266*
Schrader, A.M., 46, *55*, 94, *99*
Schultheiss, L.A., 359, *366*
Schuster, J.H., 130, *144*
Schwartz, P., 103, *113*, 336, 337, 338, 339, 343, *346*
Schwartz, W.A., 352, *355*
Scott, M.M., 229, *238*
Segal, J.A.S., 228, 234, *238, 239*
Serebnick, J., 202, *203*
Seward, L.J., 288, *293*
Sewell, R.G., 268, *276*
Shafer, R.J., 19, *29*
Shaw, W., 228, *239*
Shera, J.H., 109, *113*, 115, 126, *127*, 151, *159*, 267, *276*
Sherman, D., 69, *71*
Shiflett, D.L., 19, *29*
Shils, E.A., 74, *84*, 129, *145*
Shontz, M.L., 304, *315*
Shrivastava, P., 258, 259, *266*
Siebers, T., 351, *357*
Sievert, D., 359, *366*
Sievert, M.E., 359, *366*
Silverstein, J., 241, *249*
Simon, H.A., 88, 89, 94, 95, *99*
Simpson, I.S., 24, *29*
Simsova, S., 20, *29*
Singer, J.D., 353, *356*
Skinner, Z., 349, *357*
Skocpol, T., 351, *355*
Smit, P.H., 247, *249*
Smith, B.H., 351, *357*
Smith, D.M., 261, *265*
Smith, I.A., 69, *71*

Smith, L.C., 20, *29*
Smith, P., 82, *84*
Snelson, P., 269, *275*
Spirer, H.F., 24, *27*
Spring, M.B., 7, 8, 9, *14*
Sproull, N.S., 17, *29*
Stanley, J.C., 19, *26*
Starr, P., 75, 78, *84*
Stenstrom, P.F., 268, 269, 271, *276*
Stevens, N., 199, *203*
Stevens, N.D., 199, *203*
Stevens, R.E., 19, *29*
Stewart, A.J., 241, *249*
Stewart, J.A., 91, *98*
Strauss, A.L., 25, *29*
Stroud, J., 300, 301, 305, 306, 307, *315*
Stueart, R.D., 148, *159*
Suchman, E.A., 22, *29*
Sugnet, C., 228, *239*
Sullivan, L., 268, 269, *276*
Sullivan, W.M., 350, *357*
Swank, R.C., 64, *71*
Swisher, R., 4, *14*, 21, *29*, 92, *99*, 137, *146*
Sykes, C.J., 82, *84*

T

Tague, J., 136, 137, *146*
Taylor, R.S., 284, *294*
Tees, M.H., 317, 318, *325*
Thiemann, S., 19, *28*
Thomas, K.W., 93, *99*
Thomison, D., 306, *315*
Thompson, J.B., 352, *357*
Thorp, R.K., 23, *26*
Townley, C.T., 268, 269, *276*
Tsai, M., 107, *113*
Turock, B.J., 284, 285, 286, 287, *295*
Tyman, W.G., Jr., 93, *99*

U

Unger, R.M., 349, *357*

V

Vagianos, L., 280, *295*
Van den Berg, A., 351, *357*
Van de Ven, A.H., 5, *14*, 88, *99*
Van Fleet, C., 282, 283, 284, 286, 288, 289, 291, 292, *293, 294*
Van Gorder, B.E., 240, *249*
Van House, N., 22, *29*, 37, *44*, 93, 94, *99*,

Author Index

100, 267, *276*, 281, 286, 287, *293*, *294*, *295*
Van Rijsbergen, C.J., 244, *249*
Varlejs, J., 122, 123, *127*, 272, *276*
Veaner, A., 320, *325*
Via, B., 123, *127*
Vining, A.R., 261, *266*
Virgo, J.A.C., 190, 195, *196*
Von Bertalanffy, L., 105, *113*

W

Wallace, D.P., 20, *29*
Warner, E.S., 284, *295*
Watson, P.D., 125, *127*, 365, *366*
Webster, D., 139, *145*
Wedgeworth, R., 190, *196*
Weil, B., 22, *29*, 93, *100*
Weimer, D.L., 162, *166*
Weiss, C.H., 23, *29*
Weiss, M.J., 283, *295*
Werrell, E., 268, 269, *276*
Whetten, D., 84, 86, 89, 93, 94, *100*
White, E.C., 20, *29*
White, H.S., 134, *146*
Whitlatch, J.B., 289, *295*
Wiberley, S.E., Jr., 359, *366*
Willett, J.B., 353, *356*
Williams, J.A., 362, *366*
Williams, M.E., 116, *127*
Williams, R., 351, *357*
Wilson, P., 96, *100*, 281, *295*
Winger, H.W., 73, *83*
Winter, M.F., 73, *84*
Wolfe, A., 353, *357*
Woolls, B., 298, *315*
Wurman, R.S., 340, *346*
Wurzburger, M., 18, *29*
Wynar, B.S., 136, *146*

Y

Yates, V., 92, 96, *98*

Z

Zamora, G.J., 180, *187*
Zipf, G., 9, *14*
Zolberg, V.L., 353, *357*
Zweizig, D.L., 22, *29*, 37, *44*, 49, *56*, 93, *99*, *100*, 281, 284, 285, 286, *294*, *295*

Subject Index

A

Academic departments
  advantages and disadvantages of, 137
  investment in, 11
Academic discipline, *see* Discipline
Academic freedom, 268
Academic libraries, *see* Libraries
Academic research community, and practitioner community, 166
Academic scholarship programs, IIA support of, 245
"Access-based services," 231
Accountability, 216
  of the library, 183–84
  of state libraries, 328, 333
Accreditation; *see also* Committee on Accreditation (COA), ALA
  and productive scholarship, 122–25
  and research, 193
ACRL, *see* Association of College and Research Libraries (ACRL)
ACRL Research Agenda (app.), 277–78
Action-oriented research, funding for, 154
Action plan, to fund research, 222–24
Action research, 92–93, 360
  def. of, 5
  limitations of, 93
Ad Hoc Committee on Future Online Library Information Systems, 174f
Administration, *see* Library administrator
Administration, allocated time for (table), 132
Administrative problems, as focus of research, 116
Agencies, public, *see* Public agencies
Agenda; *see also* Research agendas
  construction of, 32–36
  def. of, 32

national
  alternatives to, 36–37
  def. of, 32–33
  in the 1980s, 32–35
  in the 1990s, 35–36
Agenda setting, 49–51
  examples for, 37–38
  mandated by the Federal government, 41
  political nature of, 36
ALA, *see* American Library Association (ALA)
ALANET (ALAs electronic network), 262
ALISE, *see* Association for Library and Information Science Education (ALISE)
Alliance for Excellence: Librarians Respond to a Nation at Risk (1984), 45, 48; *see also A Nation at Risk*
  on benefits of LIS research, 46
Alumni community, funding from, 140–41
AMA, *see* American Medical Association (AMA)
American Association of School Librarians (AASL), 298
American Libraries, 201
American Library Association (ALA), 187; *see also* Associations, professional; Public Library Association (PLA); Special Libraries Association (SLA)
  accreditation role of, 122–25
  ALANET, 262
  membership interests of, 190
  and research leadership, 282
  research support by, 36
  role in agenda setting, 37
American Medical Association (AMA), agenda setting by, 37–38
American National Standards Institute (ANSI) report guide, 264

Subject Index   383

American Society for Information Science (ASIS)
   award presentation by, 245
   research support by, 36
Annual industrial investment, for LIS research, 219
Annual research investment estimate, 218–19
ANSI report guide, 264
Applied LIS research, *see* LIS research
Applied LIS research, funding support for, 220
Applied research, 92–93, 217, 360
   def. of, 5
   expenditures for (table), 220
Applied research methods, resources for, 21–22
Articles, research, *see* Research articles
Articulation, degree of (in FOR), 258–59
ASIS, *see* American Society for Information Science (ASIS)
Assessments topics, 181
Assistantships, 135
Association, def. of, 189
Association for Library and Information Science Education (ALISE), 186–87; *see also* Association of Research Libraries (ARL)
   1990 conference of, 72
   report on faculty holding Ph.D., 134
   research support by, 36
   statistics on scholarship aid, 135
Association of College and Research Libraries (ACRL); *see also* Association for Library and Information Science Education (ALISE)
   CE courses offered by, 185
   research agenda of (app.), 277–78
   support for academic LIS research, 274
Association of Research Libraries (ARL), *see* Association for Library and Information Science Education (ALISE); Associations, professional
Association of Research Libraries (ARL), influence of library administrators on, 173
Associations, professional; *see also* American Library Association (ALA); American Society for Information Science (ASIS)
   authority of, 192
   characteristics of, 189–90
   focal point for outsiders, 195
   IIA support of, 246

   limiting leadership role, 190–92
   and research politics, 191–92
   research role for, 193–95
   sponsorship of research, 36–37, 274
Assumptions
   about public libraries, 281–82
Assumptions, identified in research, 205
Authors' Guide to Journals in Library and Information Science (1982), 199
Automated data sources, for library decision-making, 170–71
Autonomy of researcher, 191
Awards, i, 185, 318; *see also* Funding; Grants
   from IIA, 245

B

Baber award, 185
Backlogs, publication, 202
Basic LIS research, 360
   funding strategies for, 222–24
   funding support for, 220
Basic research, 217
   def. of, 5
   expenditures for (table), 220
Basic research questions, 361
Behavioral sciences, *see* Social science research
Beliefs, associated with dominant paradigm, fig. of, 104
Bibliographic control, as a factor in international research, 67
Bibliographical research, 19–20
Bibliography
   as disciplinary center, 72
   research in, 115
Bibliometrics, 20
BMDP (Biomedical Computer Programs), 25
Borko's research agenda, 151–54
Bottom-up approach; *see also* Agenda setting
   versus top-down approach, 180
British council, two perceptions of, 65
Building an Infrastructure for Library Research (1989), 35, 42, 122
Bureaucracies, characteristics of, 130
Burlesque schtick, 31, 31f

C

CAI projects, *see* Computer-Assisted Instruction projects
Carnegie Foundation for the Advancement of Teaching, support for scholarly activities, 142

384 Subject Index

Case studies, 6
Causality, disciplinary perspective of, 337–38
CD-ROM (Compact Disc-Read Only Memory) databases
  impact on networks, 231–32
  number of, 241
"Centers of excellence," 248
Centrality of academic department, 11
Change, accommodation of, 342
Chemical Abstracts Service, at Stage II, 229
Chief Officers of State Library Agencies (COSLA)
  research leadership role of, 332–33
  role in collaborative research, 291
Chronological History of Library Research and Demonstration Grants (HEA II-B, 1977–1989), 50–51 (app. B), 57–62
Citation patterns, as impact measure, 37
Clearinghouse functions, 194
Client, in research vs. consulting, 207–8
Client perspective, 261–62
Client satisfaction measures, SLA research agenda on, 319
CLR (Council on Library Resources), see Council on Library Resources (CLR)
COA, see Committee on Accreditation (COA), ALA
Coalition building, to bridge researcher/practitioner gap, 291
Cognitive elements (in FOR), 258–59
Collaborative research, see Research
"Collection-based services," 231
Collection development, education for, 77
Collections, of state libraries, 328
Collections focus, to user needs focus, 344
College and Research Libraries, scope of, 201
College Library Technology and Cooperation Grants Program (HEA II-D), 51–53
Collegial support, for academic librarian researchers, 273
Commercial services, threat to networking, 232
Commission, national
  composition of, 40
  and research policy setting, 42–43
  role of, 39–41
Committee on Accreditation (COA), ALA
  as a bridge, 155
  LIS research supported by, 63–64
Committee on Research, 186
Committees, research, 274, 291, 317–18
Communication, *def. of,* 253
Communication strategies, for researchers, 260–64
Communication technology, 233–34
Compact Disc-Read Only Memory (CD-ROM), impact on networks, 231–32
Compact Disc-Read Only Memory (CD-ROM) databases, number of, 241
Comparative librarianship, 20, 68
Comparative studies, in international LIS research, 68–69
Comparison, *def. of,* 68
Competence in research, 174–75, 183, 192
Computer-Assisted Instruction projects, 52
Computers in libraries, 359
Concepts and terms, defined in research, 205
Conferences and preconferences
  focused on research, 185, 194
  IIA support of, 246
  review of papers submitted, 269–70
Confidentiality issues, 213
"Conflict, Interdependence, Mediocrity: Librarians and Library Educators" (1983), 78
Conflicts, between researchers and decision makers, 253–57
Congress, and the NREN, 228
Consensus building, 236, 360
Consortia, research
  role of, 228–35
  to support state library research, 333
Constituencies approach, 287
Consulting, 206–7
  contrasted with research, 207–11
  versus LIS research, 209
  recommendations for, 212–13
Consulting firms
  and confidentiality issues, 213
  grants to, 118–21
  research by, 204
  role in research, 206–7
  silence of, 210–11
Consumer of research, resources for, 16–17
Continuing education, in research, 185
Control over research agenda, *see* Political context
Cooperation, international, in research, 237
Cooperative Research Grants, awarded to practitioner-educator pairs, 80

Cooperative Research Grants program, of the Council on Library Resources (CLR), 184–85
Corporate libraries, value of, 321–22
Cosmetic boards, role of, 197
Council for Scientific Affairs (of AMA), agenda setting by, 37–38
Council on Library Resources (CLR)
   and Cooperative Research Grants program, 80, 184–85
   fellows grant award by, 171f
   funding by, 222
   influence of library administrators on, 173
   and networking economics, 232
   research agenda of, 152–54
   and research agendas, 360
   research support by, 36, 141, 219
   support for LIS research centers, 139
   support of collaborative research, 365
Courses, see Curriculum
"Critical mass" of researchers, 156, 270, 273
   associational support for, 193–94
   in school librarianship, 304
Cross-disciplinary research, see Interdisciplinary research
Cuadra Associates *Summary Report* (1982), 32–33, 48–50, 117
Cultural context for research, 111
Culture
   as a factor in international research, 66
   research, in public libraries, barriers to, 280–282
"Culture of professionalism," 80
Cumulation concerns, in research vs. consulting, 210
Cumulation of research, IIA role in, 247
Curriculum; see also LIS curriculum
   growth and differentiation of, 136–37
   research component of, 144, 187

D

Data analysis, 171
   guides to, 23–25
Data and research, concerning library services, 329
Data collection and storage issues, 327, 330, 334
Decision makers
   frames of reference of (*fig. of*), 259
   research communication to (*fig. of*), 263
Decision making
   in library, 170–71
   research support for, 11

Deductive approach, 115
Degree orientation, in departmental differentiation, 137
Delphi study, 20
Demonstration, 302
   def. of, 205
Dept. of Education, *see* U.S. Dept. of Education
Descriptive research, 87–88
Descriptive statistics, 91
Descriptive studies, and operational decision making, 170
Development, expenditures for (table), 220
Developmental stage hypotheses, for information management (*fig. of*), 230
DIALOG search, state library research, 331–32
Diffusion of Innovations in Library and Information Science (1986), 48–49
Diffusion of Library Innovation, 34
Diffusion of research, *see* Research dissemination
Direct support, kinds of, from IIA, 243–45
Disciplinary-based research, 9
Discipline, 365; *see also* Knowledge base; Profession; Theory
   attributes of, 7–9
   of information science, 110–11
   key questions for, 337–38
   of library and information science, 72–73, 79, 347–48
   research potential of, 10
   research role in, 74–75, 148
Dissemination of research, *see* Research dissemination
Dissertations, inclusion of foreign references in, 70
Dissertations concerning school libraries, 305–10
   level of programs focused on (table), 310
   sorted by research method, 306–7
   sorted by subject, 310–11
Distance, as a factor in international research, 66
Distance education techniques, for research training, 270, 273
Division of Information Science and Technology (of NSF), 117
Doctoral degree programs; *see also* Professional degree programs
   advantages to LIS schools, 133–34

examination of, 125
re-design of, 81
Doctoral degrees
  for dissertations related to school libraries (table), 307
  school-library related
    granted by ALA accredited schools (table), 309
  as terminal degree, 136
Doctoral students, 133–36; *see also* Students
  foreign, 67–68
Domain, accommodating changes in, 342
Domain issues, for a discipline, 337–38
Domain of inquiry (in FOR), 258–59

E
Economic context of research, 111
Editorial board
  criteria for member selection, 199
  and improving research, 201–2
  purpose/duties of, 198–99
Editors
  and improving research, 201–2
  role in research production, 198
  on role of consulting, 211
Editors of LIS journals, composition of, 91
Education, Department of, *see* U.S. Dept. of Education
Education and training
  recommendations for, 95, 174–75, 183, 270, 272–73, 333
Education Consolidation and Improvement Act, Ch. I and II, 46–47
Educational Resources Information Center (ERIC), 48
Effect
  def. of, 31
  of 1980s agenda setting, 34–35
Elementary and Secondary Education Act, 297
Elements of FOR (*fig. of*), 259
Embarras de richesses, 241
Empirical research methods, 73–74, 82–83
Encyclopedia of Library and Information Science, 65
Engineers (quants), 116–17
Environment
  cultural, impacting on libraries, 358
  economic, affecting state library research, 327–29
Environment factors, affecting LIS practitioner research, 163–64

Environmental context
  affecting faculty productivity, 130–32
  for LIS research, 111, 152
Epistemologies, research, 214–15, 261; *see also* Quals (qualitative researchers)
Epistemology, social, 109–10
Equipment and Dataset support, 243
ERIC, *see* Educational Resources Information Center (ERIC)
Estimate of national research investment, 218–19
Evaluation research, 88
  resources for, 22
Evaluation training programs, 333–34
Ex post facto analysis, 170
Experimental research, 19
External relations, ACRL agenda for (app), 278
External validity, 4, 256
  handled in research vs. consulting, 209

F
Facilitating Information through Cognitive Models of the Search Process (1989), 50
Facsimile transmission, at Stage III, 229
Falsification of findings, 211–12
  in research vs. consulting, 208–9
Farmington Plan, 70
Fax, 229
Faxon Institute for Advanced Studies in Scholarly and Scientific Communication, funding by, 222
Federal funding
  for basic research (table), 220
  competition for, 120
  for LIS research, 219
    shrinking of, 117–21
  to LIS researchers, decline of, 120
Federal funding for libraries, 46–47
Federal funding for LIS research; *see also* Funding; HEA II-B, Higher Education Act, Title II-B
Federal State Cooperative System (FSCS), 329
Fellowships, 134–36
  through IIA, 243, 245
Field, characteristics of, 364
Field experiments, using operational decisions, 169–70
Field-initiated projects, 206
  publication output from, 50–51
  RFPs for, 50

Subject Index 387

Field-initiated research, review of, 55
Financial aid, as a research investment tool, 143
Financial support, as constraint on research, 182
Fire/criticism, of LIS research agenda for the 1980s, 33–34
FOR, *see* Frames of reference (FOR)
Forces, driving, associations' support of research, 192–93
Forecasting, 88
Foundation Center, 219–20
Foundations
   funding research, 219–20
Frames of reference (FOR)
   assessment of, 260
   6 factors involved, 258
   conflicting, 254–57
   of decision makers (*fig. of*), 259
   def. of, 257
   of researchers (*fig. of*), 259
Frontiers, national, 64
"Functions and Responsibilities of State Library Agencies," 331
Funding
   acknowledgement of, 243–44
   campus, *see also* Federal funding; Institutional support
      for research, 181
   competition for, 191
   external, 184
   of externally conducted research, 243
   federal, *see* Federal funding
   for LIS research
      differentiation of, 139–41
   opportunities for, 185
   for research, 215–16
   for research in school librarianship, 298
   strategies for, 221–24
Futures, research agenda on, 319

G

Gatekeepers, role of, 77
Gaver, Mary
   on implementing research, 304
   influence on school library research, 299
   on research in school library media centers, 296–97
Generalization, differing perspectives on, 256
Geographical context for research, 111

Gibson & Jackson domains (1987) (*fig. of*), 230
Global economy, 223
Goal model, to measure impact, 287
Goal-setting process, in public libraries, 286
Goals, Guidelines, and Standards Committee (PLA), 286
Goals, institutional; *see also* Mission
   research influence on, 180–81
Government-University-Industry Research Roundtable, 54
Grades, and professional success, 76–77
Gramsci, Antonio, on ideological hegemony, 351
"Grand Theory," 349
Grants; *see also* Awards; Fellowships; Funding
   awarded by NLM (table), 117–19
   awarded by NSF (table), 117–21
   awarded by OLLRP, USDE, 117–18, 120
   awarded by SLA, 318, 324
   awarded through HEA II-D, 51–53
   date, institution, title, cost (app. B), 57–62
   history of HEA II-B awards (app. A), 56
   need for, 82
   through IIA, 243
Griffiths, Jose-Marie, at Tennessee's LIS school, 138–39
Gross National Product, used to estimate funding needs, 218–19

H

Hawkins-Stafford Elementary and Secondary School Improvement Amendments of 1988 (P.L. 100-297), 330f
"He learned much that other men . . . ," 130
HEA II-B, Higher Education Act, Title II-B; *see also* Library Research and Demonstration Program (HEA II-B)
   annual research funding through, 219
   funding for research, 42
   funding history of, app. A, 56
   history of research grants under (1977–1989), app. B, 57–62, 50–51
   RFPs for field-initiated research, 50
   RFPs for field-initiated research, publication output from, 50–51
   support for library career training, 135
   support for LIS research, 46
   trends in grant awards, 141f
HEA II-C, Higher Education Act, Title II-C, 46–47

388 Subject Index

HEA II-D, Higher Education Act, Title II-D, 46–47, 51–53
Health Sciences Library, U North Carolina at Chapel Hill
  mission statement of, 172
Hegemonic ideology, 351
  preservation of, 351–52
Heisenberg's Indeterminacy Principle, 338, 338f
Hierarchial concept, paradigm shift impact on, 338–39
High culture realm, 352
Higher Education Act, see HEA II-B, Higher Education Act, Title II-B
Higher Education Amendments of 1986, 51–53
Historical research, 19–20
"Hot topics" for research, 37–38
House of Representatives (U.S.), 228
H.R. 3131, see National High Performance Computer Technology Act of 1989
Human behavior, focus of LIS research, 106
Hypermedia, 342
Hypertext, 235
Hypothesis testing, see Research—scientific

I

Ideological differences, regarding the conduct of LIS research, 115–17
Ideological hegemony, creation and reproduction of, 351–52
Ideology; see also Theory
  preservation of, 351–52
IIA, see Information Industry Association (IIA)
Illinois LIS Research Institute, 138
Impact, 32
  def. of, 31, 36
  of LIS research, 92–94
  of 1990s agenda setting, 35–36
  of 1980s research agenda, 33–35
  technological, 52
Impact measures, a convergence of approaches to, 287–88
In-house research, IIA support for, 244
Indirect support, provided by IIA, 245–46
Inductive approach, 115
Industry-sponsored research, 140–41; see also Vested interests
Industry-supported research, 217–18; see also Consulting

Inertia, organizational and personal, a challenge to academic library research, 270–71
Inferential statistics, 91, 171
Information, def. of, 340
"Information Age," 101
Information engineering, def. of, 111
Information explosion, 342
Information gathering, see Data collection and storage
Information industries (fig. of), 242
Information Industry Association (IIA)
  LIS research support by, 241–48
  LIS research support by (fig. of), 243
  membership of, 240–41
Information industry companies, LIS research expenditures by, 218–19
Information needs research, 287
  key to understanding social needs, 283–85
Information needs researchers, and public librarians, 288
Information organization, and digitalization, 235
Information organization management, def. of, 111
Information policy, def. of, 153
Information policy environment, of research, 111
Information professional, SLA task force on value of, 320–21
Information professionals; see also Librarians
  4 responsibilities of, 110
  role to preserve ideology, 352
Information psychology, def. of, 111
Information science
  def. of, 116
  as disciplinary core, 73
  disciplinary status of, 110–11
Information science research, NSF preference for, 120
Information seeking behavior, 359
Information systems, components of, 229–30
Information technology, and networks, 228–35
Information technology and communications, ACRL agenda for (app), 278
Information technology capabilities, ratios of (fig. of), 233
Information transfer approach, 340
Information use patterns, 340; see also User needs research
Information utilities, see Information Industry Association (IIA)

Inquiry process, 214–15
  activities of, 4
  domain of (in FOR), 258–59
  in social sciences, 207
Institute for Scientific Information (ISI),
    awards of, 245
Institutional goals, *see* Goals, institutional
Institutional support, constraint on research,
    182–83
Institutions granting doctorates
  in school librarianship, 308
  in school librarianship (table), 307
"Instructions to authors," 202
Interaction research, between librarians and
    faculty, 184–85
Interdisciplinary research, 349–51
  centers of, 80–81
  departmental constraints on, 137–38
  need for, 98, 102, 112
  to protect LIS education, 151
  for theory building, 95
Interest, arousal of, 88
Internal research, 243
Internal validity, 4; *see also* Validity
International access, 342
International LIS research
  characteristics of, 64
  comparative studies in, 68–69
  difficulties in, 65–68
  improvement of, 69–70
  inappropriateness for dissertations, 70
  interest in, 66–67
International research, networks facilitating,
    237
International Standards Organization (ISO),
    234–35
INTERNET (electronic network), 262
Introduction to Scientific Research in Librarianship (1972), 136
Investments; *see also* Funding
  in LIS research, 218–19
  value and research, 216–17
ISI Information Science Doctoral Dissertation
    Award, 245
Issues; *see also* Policy issues; Political context
  in 1986 Research Agenda Project, 49–50
  affecting research, 45–46, 114, 154, 180–84, 205
  book's highlighted, 364–65
  concerning public librarians, 283
  concerning special libraries, 322–25
  concerning state libraries, 329–32
  of confidentiality, 213
  consulting vs. research, 207–11
  for a discipline, 337–38
  in LIS research, 150
  ownership, 32
  LIS research program, 53–55
  local public policy, 285
  and new technologies, 227–28
  related to private funding agencies, 214–19
Issues in Library Research—An Agenda for the 1990s (1986), 49
Issues in Library Research: Proposals for the 1990s (1986), 54
"Ivory tower," 339

J

JASIS, *see Journal of the American Society for Information Science* (JASIS)
JELIS, *see Journal of Education for Library and Information Science* (JELIS)
Jesse H. Shera Award for Research, i
"Joint Statement on Faculty Status of College and University Librarians" (1988), 179
Journal of Education for Library and Information Science (JELIS), scope statement for, 201
Journal of the American Society for Information Science (JASIS), scope statement for, 201
Journals; *see also* Publications; Research articles
  funding acknowledged in, 243–44
  impact on research, 36, 274
  increasing pages and issues, 202
  LIS, 197
    deans' ranking of (table), 124
    editorial boards of, 91
    popular, research in, 201
    in public librarianship, 283
    refereed, 199–200
    research, criteria for, 89–90
    and research distinctions, 96
    in school librarianship, 298, 301–2

K

King Research, 48
Knowledge base; *see also* Discipline; Theory
  for LIS discipline, 72–73
  for professional practice, 76–77
  for students, 150–51

Knowledge demands, versus producing capabilities, 138
Koenig stage hypothesis, 229, 230 (table)

L

Laboratory opportunities, in the library, 183
Language, effect on international research, 66
Leadership, intellectual, role for library administrator, 175–77, 282–83
Leadership to encourage research, 175–77, 271–72
  in public libraries, 282–83
  in state libraries, 332–33
Learning opportunities, from questionnaires, 167–68
Legislative and regulatory context, of research, 111
Lexikon des Bibliothekswesens, 65
Librarian-researcher, 348, 350; *see also* LIS researchers
Librarians; *see also* Discipline; Information professionals; Librarianship; LIS faculty; Profession
  constraints on, 182–84
  and LIS educators, 78
  and research, i
  research dollars for, 118, 120
  self-image of, 74
  state, training for, 333
Librarianship; *see also* Discipline; Librarians; LIS researchers; Profession
  academic
    research challenges in, 269–71
    research role in, 267
  American, social science research model for, 348
  developmental phases of, 358
  disciplinary status of, 79, 347
  paradigm shift influence on, 344
  public
    journals in, 283
    research context of, 279–80
  research role in, iv, 77–78, 115, 155, 179–80
  research styles for, 79–83
  school
    dissertations related to, 305–10
    doctorates related to, institutions granting, 307–9
    journals in, 298
    research agenda for, 298
    research background for, 297–98
  status of, 9, 79, 365
Libraries
  academic
    LIS research in
      reasons for, 267–69
      strengthening of, 271–74
    research opportunities in, 268–69
  American, cultural purpose of, 350–54
  corporate, value of, 321–24
  and networks, 231–32
  public
    assumptions regarding, 281–82
    barriers in, 280–82
    goal-setting process in, 286
    infrastructure in, 289–92
    planning/evaluation in, 285–88
    research leadership in, 282–83
    survey of leaders in, 282f
  research in, 169
  school
    and dissertation methodologies (table), 306
    research about, analysis of, 298–99, 307–9
    research review analysis, 303–4
  state, *see* State libraries
Libraries and Literacy Education, 50
Library
  concept of, 179
  social role of, 109
Library administration, ACRL agenda for (app), 277
Library administrator; *see also* Library decision makers
  agenda setting role of, 173–74
  federal agency reviewer, 173
  influence on library organization, 172–73
  and library organization, 358–59
  mediating role of, 166
  policy making role of, 164
  and research needs articulation, 173–74
  research support role of, 163
Library and information science services, *see* LIS services
Library and information science (LIS); *see also* Discipline; LIS research
  disciplinary status of, 72–73, 80, 347–48

Subject Index 391

professional status of, 73–74
status of, 11–12
Library and information science professionals, *see* LIS professionals
Library and information science research, *see* LIS research
A *Library and Information Science Research Agenda for the 1980s* (1982), 32–33, 48, 50, 117
Library and Literacy Education (1988), 49
Library and Research Demonstration Program (HEA II-B), funding for research, 141
Library collections and organization, ACRL agenda for (app), 278
Library committee reports, references in, 166–67
Library decision makers; *see also* Library administrator
and messes, 257
perspectives of, 254–57
as research audience, 254
Library educators, *see* LIS educators
Library Journal, 301
Library Literacy Program (Title VI, LSCA), 46
Library Networks Study, 34
Library organizations, library administrators influence on, 172–73
Library planning documents, references in, 166–67
Library research, *see* LIS research
Library Research and Demonstration Program, projects review, 211
Library Research and Demonstration Program (HEA II-B), 48, 206; *see also* HEA II-B, Higher Education Act, Title II-B
Library Research Center, 291
Library research committees, *see* Research committees
Library Research Round Table (LRRT) ALA, 186
composition of, 190
and research program, 1
research support by, 36
and state library research, 333
Old library saying, 31f
Library Services and Construction Act (LSCA)
and LIS research, 46
and public library programs, 284–85

Library Services for Indian Tribes and Hawaiian Natives Programs (Title IV), 46
Library Services in Theory and Context (1988), 69
Linked systems, 234
LIS consulting, *see* Consulting; LIS research
LIS curriculum; *see also* LIS education; Professional degree programs
introducing research into, 148–49, 156–58
relevance of, 76–77
research component of, 149
LIS education, 149–50; *see also* Dissertations; Doctoral degrees; LIS schools; Professional degree programs; Students
ACRL agenda for (app), 277
future of, 155–56
inadequacy of, 280
and information industries, 246
paradigm shift effects on, 344–45
purpose of, 147
research on, 150
research role in, 136–37, 142, 149, 187
role in universities, 151
separated from librarianship, 155
LIS educators
as gatekeepers, 77
and librarians, 78
survey of three, 152–54
LIS faculty
allocation of time by (table), 132
compared to COA members, 123–25
competition for, 247
differentiation of, 130–32, 143
expectations of, 131
grants to, 118–21
incentives for, 96–97
and information industries, 246
involvement with SLA, 318–20, 322
percentage with Ph.D., 134, 281
productivity of, 107–8, 122–25
compared to IS faculty, 134
publication records of (table), 124
ranking of, 122–23
role identification, 129
shortage of, 82–83, 97
status of, 179, 365
support for, 143
LIS "Farmington Plan," 70

392 Subject Index

LIS professionals; *see also* Discipline; Librarians; Profession; Professional practice
    constraints on, 182–84
    initiatives for, 186–87
LIS R&D, 220
LIS research, 12, 106, 112; *see also* International LIS research; Issues; Research; Research agenda
    in academic libraries, 217, 270
    ACRL agenda for (app), 278
    agenda for, 151–54
    analysis of, 107–8
    assessment of, 55, 106–9
    causality issues for, 341
    characterization of, 152
    clarification of, 204–6
    committees on, 186, 274, 291, 317–18
    communication of, 253, 260–64
    courses on (*fig. of*), 157
    cumulation of, 97
    def. of, 114
    domain issues of, 339–41
    editors' role in, 201–2
    foundation support for, 221
    funding for, 120, 139–40, 154, 219–24
    guides to, 17–18
    IIA support for, 241–46
    and related issues, 246–48
    IIA support for (*fig. of*), 243
    impact of, 92–94
    implications for, 105–6
    improvement of, 89–92, 108–9, 125–26, 246–48
    incentives for, 215–16
    international context of, 64–65
    LIS writing on, 85
    versus membership demands, 190–92
    needs for, 109–12
    paradigm for, 9–10, 111–12
    problems in, 97–98
    programmatic issues, 53–55
    purpose of, 209
    research centers involved in (*fig. of*), 245
    in the 1990s, 42
    stakeholders in, 254
    status of, 128
    and Supercomputer Centers (*fig. of*), 245
    support for, 46–53, 218–19, 224–25
    that is "good enough," 255

LIS research agenda, 93–94, 108–9; *see also* Agenda; Research agenda
    ownership of, 32
    proposed by Borko, 151–54
    redefinition of, 223–24
    for the 1990s, 35–36
    for the 1980s, reaction to, 33–35
    set by associations, 36
LIS research institutes, *see* Research institutes
LIS research production, *see* Publication output
LIS researchers, 85, 154
    accommodations by, 264
    classification of, 115
    as communicators, 253f, 260–64
    competition for, 97
    frames of reference of (*fig. of*), 259
    grants to, 117–21
    and information industries, 246
    perspectives of, 254–57
    problems from messes, 257
    and public librarians, 283
    resources for, 15–16
    and state libraries, 291
LIS schools; *see also* Doctoral degrees; LIS education; LIS faculty; Professional degree programs; Students
    closing of, 142, 151
    led by practitioners, 359–60
    research environment in, 128–29
    research in curriculum, 149
LIS services, 288–89
    ACRL agenda for (app), 277–78
    international context of, 64–65
    nature of, 350
LIS students, *see* Students
"Listaphobia," 34–35
Literature, focus of LIS research, 116
Literature review, of research methods, 15–30
Local public policy issues, 285
Local systems, threat to networking, 232
Local systems development, as a Stage II event, 234
Location-specific research, by foreign doctoral students, 67–68

M

Manuals
    community-centered, 286f
    for evaluating Federal library programs, 287

Subject Index 393

planning and evaluation, from the PLA, 285–87
Marchand stages (1983) (*fig. of*), 230
Market research, 247
Mathematics in research, 115
"Mature professions," 109
Measures of productivity, SLA research agenda on, 319
Measures of user satisfaction, SLA research agenda on, 319
Mechanisms for research promotion, 280–81
Messes, versus problems, 257
Metaphors
  affected by paradigm shifts, 338
  in FOR, 258–59
Methodologies, *see* Research methodologies
Microcomputers, role in research production, 202
Mission
  of state libraries, 329
  statements of, commitment to research, 171–72
Model and demonstration programs, 302
Model projects (1950–1970), in school libraries, 304
Models
  for LIS research, 111–12
  of operations research, 21
  for research roundtable, 54
Moores' Law, 229, 231
Motivation, versus association objectives, 191–92
Multidisciplinary approach, to ordering domain, 341
Multidisciplinary fields, status of, 148
Multiple constituencies approach, 287

N
A *Nation at Risk* (1982), 45, 297; *see also* Alliance for Excellence . . .
National Center for Education Statistics (NCES), 329
National Defense Student Act, 297
National Federation of Abstracting and Information Services (NFAIS), 241
National Football League (NFL), agenda setting by, 38
National Goals for Education (1990), 297
National High Performance Computer Technology Act of 1989, 228

National Institute of Mental Health (NIMH), agenda setting by, 38
National Library of Medicine (NLM), 117
  and collaborative research, 196
  research budget of, 118
  research investment by, 219
  research support by, 141
  at Stage II, 229
National Research and Education Network (NREN), 228
National Research Council (NRC), education and improvement review, 55
National Research Council's Government-University-Industry Research Roundtable, 54
National Science Foundation (NSF), 117
  funding barriers, 141f
  research expenditures by, 118
NCES (National Center for Education Statistics), 329
Network Management Institute (1989: Rosary College), 232
Networking, economics of, 231–32
Networks
  membership in, 232
  research role of, 227–36
Neutral questioning, 289
"The New American Scholar," 142
New Directions in Library and Information Science Education (1985), 48
NFAIS, 241
1980s agenda, *see* Agenda
1986 Research Agenda Project (OLP), 49
1990s Agenda, *see* Agenda
NLM, *see* National Library of Medicine (NLM)
Nonprofit institutions, expenditures by (table), 220
Nonresearch articles, 90
Nontraditional library programs, 287
Northwestern University, investment criteria, 11
NRC (National Research Council), 55
NREN (National Research and Education Network), 228
NSF, *see* National Science Foundation (NSF)

O
Objectives, of this book, iv–v
Office of Educational Research and Improvement (OERI)

394 Subject Index

history of R&D grant awards (app. B), 57–62
role of, 47, 55
Office of Libraries and Learning Resources (Dept. of Ed.), 117
Office of Library Programs (Dept. of Ed.)
agenda for the 1990s, 49
agenda project recommendations of, 50
agenda setting by, 108–9
and collaborative research, 290
evaluation of Committee on Accreditation (COA), ALA, 122
financial problems of, 120
and library research, 185
programmatic issues raised, 45–46
and research dissemination, 53
and research roundtables, 54
role in research review, 55
role of, 47
support for LIS research centers, 139
Office of Technology Assessment (OTA) report, 227–28
Online Computer Library Center (OCLC), 234
and collaborative research, 196, 290
a HEA II-B product, 48
research projects of, 235–36
role in IIA research support, 248
Online databases, number of, 241
Operational decisions, treated as field experiments, 169–70
Operations research (OR), 21
Ordering a domain, 337–38
Organization of information, and digitalization, 235
Organizational change process, study of, 171f
Organizational realities
inertia, 270–71
the three P's of, 255
Organizational research, 88
Organizational structures, differentiation of, 137–39
OSIRIS (Organized Set of Integrated Routines for Investigation of Social Science Data), 25
Output measures, 22
limitations of, 286–87
Output Measures for Public Libraries (1987), 37, 286
"Outstanding Information Science Teacher Award," 245
Ownership, private, move to shared access, 342

P
Paradigm
dominant, and associated beliefs (*fig. of*), 104
emergence of, 343
for LIS research, 9–10
new
characteristics of, 102–5
influence on LIS professions, 103–5
new, candidates for, 349–50
selection of, 353, 363–64
of the "whole" of state libraries, 334
Paradigm shift, 103–4, 336–39, 359, 365–66
consequences of, 343–45
Paradigm wars, 166, 353
Parent organization, *see* Universities
Partnerships with practitioners, *see* Practitioner-educator pairs
Perception studies, 311
Perceptions and values, in LIS services/research, 65
Performance Measures for Public Libraries, 22
"Peril of sub-optimization," 231–32
Personal inertia, 271
Personality, power, and politics, 255
Perspectives, *see* Frames of reference (FOR)
PLA, *see* Public Library Association (PLA)
Planning, and research, 184
Planning and evaluation manuals, 285–87
PLA dissemination of, 289
Planning and Role Setting for Public Libraries (1987), 286
Planning process, impact on research agendas, 37
Policy issues, 285
in HEA II-B funded studies, 48
Political context
of agenda setting, 36
of international research, 66
of LIS research, 38–43
of research, 111, 191–92
Political economy of library service, framework for LIS research, 350
Politics, power, and personality, 255
Positivism, *see* Research epistemologies
Positivism, 108–9, 165; *see also* Research—scientific
failure of, 261
in LIS research, 116
Post hoc analysis, 170
Potential of academic department, 11

Subject Index 395

Power
  as context for library services, 351–52
  politics and personality, 255
  sharing of, 342
Practice and research, recommendations for, 95–96
Practitioner community; *see also* Librarians; LIS faculty; LIS professionals; Profession
  and academic research community, 166
  criticism of LIS research, 92–93
  research needs articulation for, 173–74
  research role of, 96
  surveys by, requirements for, 168
Practitioner-educator pairs, 81–82
  cooperative research grants to, 80
Practitioner-oriented guide, to historical research, 19
Preconferences and conferences
  IIA support of, 246
  on research, 185, 194
  review of papers submitted, 269–70
"Preparation of Scientific Papers for Written or Oral Presentation" (1990), 264
Prescriptions to advance research in LIS schools, 143–44
Presentation guide, 264
Presentations, 262–64
President's Task Force on the Value of the Information Professional, 321–24
Principle of Least Effort (Zipf, 1949), 9–10
Private agencies
  funding by, 216
    strategies for obtaining, 221–24
  funding by (table), 220
Problem conceptualization, 257
  in research vs. consulting, 208
Problem-oriented research, 284–85
Problems, versus messes, 257
Product communication, in research vs. consulting, 210–11
Product evaluation, in research vs. consulting, 210
Product-oriented research, versus problem-oriented research, 248
The *Production and Distribution of Knowledge in the United States* (1962), 171
Profession, 365; *see also* Discipline; Librarians; LIS faculty; Practitioner community
  advancing to a discipline, 156
  assumptions of, 165

characteristics of, 7–9, 73, 73f, 267
  def. of, 109, 193
  of library and information science, 73–74, 79, 109–10
  paradigm influence on, 103–5
  research role in, 75–77, 88–89, 109, 148, 180
Professional; *see also* LIS professionals
  beginning, 176–77
  information, SLA task force on value of, 320–21
  versus technician, 104–5
Professional associations, *see* Associations, professional
Professional bureaucracies, characteristics of, 130
Professional degree programs, *see also* Doctoral degree programs; LIS education; LIS schools
  functions of, 75–77
  relevance of, 75–77
  research role in, 82, 89
Professional practice
  models of, 78–79
  separated from LIS education, 155
  theories in, 88
Professional schools, *see* Professional degree programs
Professional success, and grades, 76–77
Professionalism, culture of, 80
Professionals, information, role to preserve ideology, 352
Professions, survey across, 194–95
Profit-making, with LIS research, 248
Projects, joint, 194–95
Proposals for the 1990s, 35
Propositions for research communication (*fig. of*), 263
Public agencies, funding from, 215–16
Public good, networks as, 232
Public Library Association (PLA), role in agenda setting, 37
Public librarianship, *see* Librarianship
Public libraries, *see* Libraries
Public Library Association (PLA)
  leadership role of, 282, 291–92
  research support by, 281
Public Library Data Service (PLDS), 329
Public Library Data Service Statistical Report '88, 286
Public Library Development Program (PLDP), 285–86

The *Public Library Effectiveness Study* (1989), 50
Public services, ACRL agenda for (app), 277-78
Publication output
    from 1987 field-initiated proposals, 50-51
    of COA members, 122-25
        compared to journal ranking (table), 124
    editors' role in, 198
    from HEA sponsored projects, 48
    of LIS faculty, 107-8
    quality of, 200
Publication type, in research reviews, 300-302
Publications, 195; *see also* Journals; Research articles
    increase in, 91-92, 202
    research, included in research reviews (table), 301
Pure research, *see* Basic research

Q

Qualitative research methods, 22-23, 261
Quality improvement of research
    editors' role in, 201-2
    IIA role in, 246-48
Quality of papers, submitted to ACRL conferences, 269-70
Quals (qualitative researchers); *see also* Research designs; Research epistemologies
Quals (qualitative researchers), 115-17
Quals-Quants partnership, 126
Quants (quantitative researchers), 115-17
Questionnaires, 167-68
Questions, *see* Research questions

R

Ratios, technology capabilities growth (*fig. of*), 233
R&D expenditures (table), 220
Reading processes, disciplinary center, 72
Realities
    of organizations, 255
    of professional associations, 190-92
Reality tests (in FOR), 258-59
Recognition
    from IIA, 245
    as reward, 181
Refereeing process, 199-201
    def. of, 199
    double-blind, 200

Referees, options for, 200
Reference effectiveness, research in, 288-89
Reference librarianship, education for, 77
Reflection-in-action, 83
    versus technical rationality, 78-79
Released time, 131-32, 269
Relevance; *see also* Librarians; LIS research; Profession
    criteria for, 93
    of degree programs, 75-77
    of research, 5-6
Reliability, 205-6
    def. of, 4
Report writing, 263-64
Research; *see also* Agenda; Inquiry process; Issues; LIS research; Theory
    about networks, 227-35
    agency funding for, 117-21
    allocated time for (table), 132
    collaborative
        association support for, 194-95
        facilitated by networks, 236
        IIA role in, 247
        kinds of, 195-96
        by public librarians, 290-92
        ways to perform, 80-83
    constraints on, 329
    versus consulting, 207-12
    curriculum support for, 136-37
    and decision making, 11
    def. of, 3-6, 32, 205
    funding for, 215-16
    increase of, 96-97
    industry support for, 217-18; *see also* Consulting
    versus membership demands, 190-92
    perceptions of, 165
    and practice, 95-96, 177, 360-61
    professional responsibility, 180
    in public libraries, 290
    purpose of, 64
    in reference effectiveness, 288
    role in disciplines, 74-75
    role in librarianship, 155
    role in professions, 75-77, 109
    role in state libraries, 327-29, 331-32
    role of networks in, 235-36
    in school librarianship, 311-14
    scientific, 204, 336; *see also* Positivism
        characteristics of, 205-6
        def. of, 4-5

emphasis on, 175
emulation of, 115
social science, *see* Social science research
in special libraries, 324-25
steps in, 205
support for, 224-25
versus teaching, 129-30
topics for, 362
Research administration, 38-39
Research agenda, 360-62
proposed by SLA, 318-20
questions in, 362
for school librarianship, 298, 313-14
Research Agenda (1986) project, 49
Research and demonstration grants
through HEA, products of, 48
through HEA II-D, categories of, 52
Research and Information Resources, Director of (SLA), 318
Research articles; *see also* Publications
classification of, 89-90
in *Special Libraries*, 318
study of, 107-8
Research base, 6-7; *see also* Knowledge base; Theory
Research categories (Hernon's), 5-6
reviewed, 360
Research centers; *see also* Research institutes
IIA support for, 244-45
support for, 144
and vested interests, 138
Research Committee (ACRL), 274
Research Committee (PLA), survey of state library research, 291
Research Committee (SLA), 317-18
Research competence, 174-75, 183
of association members, 192
Research consumption, 16-17
in public libraries, 290-92
Research continuum, 138
Research designs; *see also* Positivism; Quants (quantitative researchers); Research methods
objectives for, 261
types of, 6
Research dissemination, 165-66
by public librarian researchers, 289-90
by researchers vs. consulting firms, 210-11
through presentations, 262-64
Research epistemologies, 214-15
alternatives to positivism, 261

Research institutes; *see also* Research centers
examples of, 138-39
and vested interests, 138
Research interaction, between librarians and faculty, 184-85
Research investigation, steps in, 205-6, 274-75
Research Issues project, 53-54
Research Library Group (RLG), research projects of, 235-36
Research Library Information Network (RLIN), 234
Research methodologies
quals versus quants debate, 362-63
redesigning of, 260-61
in school library research reviews, 302
shifts in, 337, 343
use of multiple, 344
Research methods
applied, 21-22
selection of, 353
shifting of, 343
for studies of school librarianship, 299
and techniques, 18-22
types of, 6
used in dissertations (school library), 306-7
comparing Ed.D and Ph.D (table), 307
Research priorities, *see* Research agenda
Research production
influences in, 297-98
result of 1980s agenda, 34-35
Research questions, 362; *see also* Inquiry process; Issues
Research recognition, 245
Research record (SLA), 324-25
Research roundtable, 37
recommendations for, 50, 54, 290-91
Research skills
distance education for, 270
limitations of, 183
training for, 174-75, 272-73
for state librarians, 333
Research strategy
how to's, 205-6, 274-75
Research study, development of, 16-18
Resource allocation
research support for, 172
role of state libraries, 327
Resource/evidence availability, in international research, 67-68

398 Subject Index

Rethinking the Library in the Information Age (1988–1989), 10–11, 12f, 37, 50, 108–9, 122, 268–69
   and collaborative research, 290
   on information needs, 292
   ingredients for commission infrastructure, 40
   2nd research agenda, 35–36
   and public library LIS research, 279–80, 283
   and research agendas, 360
   research center proposal in, 139
   and research role in policy making, 93–94
   on role of consulting firms, 206–7
   support for national commission, 42
Revenue, of IIA companies, 241
Review, introductory, of this book, ii–iii
Reviews, research
   of school library research, 299–304
   discussion of, 303–4
   of school library research (table), 300
Reward structures
   in academic libraries, 269
   clarification of, 272
   for LIS research communication, 256–57
   university, for teaching and service, 82
Rockart eras (1984) (*fig. of*), 230
Rutgers University, and workload concept, 132

S

S. 1067, *see* National High Performance Computer Technology Act of 1989
Sabbaticals, 131–32
Sampling, 18–19
SAS (Statistical Analysis System), 24
Satanic Verses, differing perceptions of, 65
Scholarly output, *see* Publication output
Scholarship, prerequisite for COA service, 123
School librarianship; *see also* Librarianship
   research in
     funding for, 313
     recommendations for, 312–14
     research agenda for, 313–14
     in the 1980s, 311
School library media centers, research role in, 296
School library media programs, and student achievement, 304
School library media specialists, *see* Librarianship
School library media specialists (*fig. of*), 133
Science, characterization of, 210

"Scientific progress . . . ," 128
Scientific research, *see* Research—scientific
Scientists (quants), 116
Scope statements, 200–201
Self-image of librarians, 74
Self-interest, 80
"Semi-professions," 7f
Senate (U.S.), 228
Skepticism, 205, 208–9
SLA, *see* Special Libraries Association (SLA)
Social epistemology, 109–10, 115–16
Social science research, 86–89, 207
   functions of, 87–88
   guides to, 16–17
   product evaluation in, 210
Social science theory, *def. of*, 86
Social theorists (quals), 115–16
Societal needs, 283–85
Sociology of information, *def. of*, 110
"Spaghetti code," 235
Special Committee on Research (SLA), 316–17
Special Libraries Association (SLA), 316–17
   research agenda of, 323–24
   research agenda of (*fig. of*), 319
Special Programs Grants and Research Awards (SLA), 318
Special Programs Grants Awards (SLA), for *Valuing Corporate Libraries*, 324
Speech recognition by computers, 231
Sponsorship, 217
SPSSx User's Guide (1986), 24
Staff development program, 164
Staffing, SLA research agenda on, 319
Stage hypotheses comparison, for information managers (*fig. of*), 230
Stage I (pre-1971) of information systems, 229
Stage II (1971–1989?) of information systems, 229, 232–34
Stage II capability growth (*fig. of*), 233
Stage III of information systems, 229, 232–34
Stakeholders, in LIS research, 254
Standards, 234–35
Standards for Library Functions at the State Level (ASCLA, 1985), 327
State libraries
   collections of, 328
   research in, 331–32
   research roles of, 326
State library agencies
   increasing research use in, 291

reference skills training by, 288
research role of, 185–86
The *State Library Agencies, A Survey Project Report* (ASCLA, 1989), 331
State library-funded white paper series, 291
State organizations, 185–86, 288, 291
Statistical methods, 115; *see also* Empirical research methods
  review of, 91
Statistical Package for the Social Sciences, 24
Statistical reports, on school libraries, 304
Statistics
  consumer guides to, 23–24
  descriptive, 91
  inferential, 91, 171
  library, collected by NCES, 330
  need for, 181
  for scholarship aid, 135
  state libraries collect, 327
Status of academic department, 11; *see also* Discipline; LIS faculty; Profession
The *Status of Research in Library/Information Science* (1989), 39
Stipulations, value-laden, 216–17
Strategies
  how to's, 274–75
  to improve research in state libraries, 332–34
  to increase research, 184–86
  for research communication, 260–64
Stroud's baseline report (*DAI*), 305
Students; *see also* Doctoral students; LIS students
  differentiation of, 132–36
  knowledge base of, 150–51
  learning objectives for, 147
  research education for, 126
Study, research, *see* Research study
Subject categories
  of dissertations concerning school libraries, 310–11
  in school library research reviews, 302–3
Subject degrees with MLS, 176
A *Summary of Issues in Library Research*, 35
Summary Report by Cuadra Associates (1982), 32–33, 48–50
Supercomputer Centers, 244–45
Survey, of three LIS educators, 152–54
Survey research, 18–19
Surveys
  conducted about state libraries, 332
  conducted by state libraries, lack of access to, 330
  quality of, 168
  response to, 167–68
Syllabus and objectives (*fig. of*), 157
Systems design, 52
  technological ramifications of, 232–34

T

Taste cultures, 352
Teaching
  allocated time for (table), 132
  versus research, 129–30
Teaching load, management strategies for, 131
Technical rationality, versus reflection-in-action, 78–79
Technician, versus professional, 104–5
Techniques, communication, 260–64
Technology, focus for LIS research, 117
Technology impact studies, 52
Technology infrastructure, 111
Tenure, 143
Terminal degree, 133
Textbooks, research methods, 136–37
The *Status of Research in Library/Information Science* (1989)
  optimism in, 128
Themes, underlying this book, 10–12
Theoretical framework, for LIS research, 349
Theory; *see also* Discipline; Knowledge base; Positivism; Research base
  building of, 86–87, 94–95
  follows practice, 359–60
  international context of, 64–65
  for LIS discipline, 72–73
  need for, 353–54
  role in practice, 88
  testing of, 87
Theory building
  need for consensus, 363–64
  for research in school librarianship, 313–14
Think tank, 292
Thinking, short-term, 190
Thinking (from A.N. Whitehead), 165, 361
Time, constraint on research, 182
Timeliness, differing perspective son, 256
Title HEA II-B, *see* HEA II-B, Higher Education Act, Title II-B
Title I, II, III LSCA, *see* Library Services and Construction Act (LSCA)
Title II-B studies, post-agenda, 34–35
Title IV (LSCA), support for LIS research, 46

Top-down approach; *see also* Agenda setting versus bottom-up approach, 180
Tradeoffs, between research and teaching, 129–32
Training in research, 174–75, 183, 270, 272–73, 333
Triangulation, 343

U

Undergraduate LIS education, 133
Understanding events/institutions, 88
United States Dept. of Education, *see* U.S. Dept. of Education
Universities; *see also* Institutions granting doctorates; LIS education; LIS schools
  expectations of, 129–30
  expenditures by (table), 220
  role of LIS education in, 151
University, Pierce's *def. of*, 129
University-based center, *see* Research centers
University of North Carolina at Chapel Hill
  mission statement, 172
  questionnaires study at, 167, 167f
  released time program, 131–32
University reward structures, *see* Reward structures
Unobtrusive testing of reference effectiveness, 288
U.S. Dept. of Education; *see also* HEA II-B, Higher Education Act, Title II-B; Office of Library Programs (Dept. of Ed.)
  and client definition problems, 208
  funding of school library research, 304
  HEA grants for research, 141
  history of R&D grant awards (app. B), 57–62
  and the "peril of sub-optimization," 232
  research funding by, 204–5
  research investment by, 219, 274
  research role of, 290
User issues, SLA research agenda on, 319
User needs research, 270, 283–85
  role of state library in, 327
User satisfaction measures, SLA research agenda on, 319

V

Validity, 205–6
  testing of, 208–9
  types of, 4
Value-laden stipulations, 216–17
Value of information professional, SLA task force on value of, 320–21
Values and perceptions, 65
Vested interests, 138; *see also* Industry-sponsored research
Visibility of academic department, 11
"visiting researcher" positions, 333

W

Warehousing books, to disseminating information, 340
"We-them" adversarial relationships, 254–55, 257, 364–65
White-paper series, state library-funded, 291
Whitehead, Alfred North, on thinking, 165, 361
Word processors, in research production, 202
Workload, faculty, at Rutgers University, 96–97, 132
Workload concept, 132, 143
"Workshop of Building a Library Research Infrastructure" (1988), 185
World knowledge economy, 223

Y

"Yo-yo posture," 187

www.ingramcontent.com/pod-product-compliance
Lightning Source LLC
Chambersburg PA
CBHW071228290426
44108CB00013B/1335